W9-CSK-915

RANK AND FILE

Also edited by T. H. McGuffie

PENINSULAR CAVALRY GENERAL
(*Harrap*)

A trumpeter *c.* 1800 by Henry Fuller

. . . dead or living, drunk or dry,
Soldier, I wish you well.

A. E. Housman

ACKNOWLEDGEMENTS

The books and papers from which the extracts in this volume have been drawn come from a wide range of sources. Particular thanks are due to the Librarian at the War Office, Mr. D. W. King, and his staff; the Librarian of the Royal United Service Institution, Brigadier John Stephenson, and his staff; His Grace the Duke of Northumberland; Mrs. M. B. M. Fraser of Barry and Mr. Jack Corbett of Harborne, Birmingham; and the Council of the Society for Army Historical Research, who gave kind permission for extracts from their quarterly Journal.

Permission to include the poem *Epitaph on an Army of Mercenaries* has been granted by The Society of Authors as the literary representative of the Estate of the late A. E. Housman, and Messrs. Jonathan Cape Ltd., publishers of A. E. Housman's *Collected Poems*. The extract from *Progress of a Ploughboy to a Seat in Parliament* edited by William Reitzel has been reproduced by kind permission of Faber & Faber Ltd. Also extracts from *The Chronicle of Henry Metcalfe* edited by Sir Francis Tuker have been reproduced by kind permission of Cassell & Company Ltd. Lines used from the *Prelude* to *Departmental Ditties*, *Tommy* and *Songs from Books* by Rudyard Kipling have been reproduced by permission of Mrs. George Bambridge, Messrs. Methuen & Messrs. Macmillan.

The extract from Field Marshal Sir William Robertson's *From Private To Field Marshal* is reproduced by kind permission of Messrs. Constable & Co. Publishers and the Trustees of the late Field Marshal Sir William Robertson, G.C.B., G.C.M.G., G.C.V.O., D.S.O.

Special thanks are also due to Captain R. G. Hollies-Smith of the Parker Gallery, Albemarle Street, London, who gave all his knowledgeable enthusiasm and help. All illustrations are by courtesy of the Parker Gallery.

T. H. McGuffie

CONTENTS

TWO

TOWARDS BATTLE

Chapter Four: Discipline in Peace and War

Chapter Five: After Duty

Chapter Six: Non-commissioned Officers: Officers

Chapter Seven: Billets in Peace and War

Chapter Eight: On the Move in Peace and War

Chapter Nine: Soldiers at Sea

THREE

IN ACTION

Chapter Ten: Life on Campaign

Chapter Eleven: First Time in Action

Chapter Twelve: Skirmishes and Savage Warfare

Chapter Thirteen: Siege

Chapter Fourteen: Victory

Chapter Eighteen: Prisoner of War

FOUR

FAREWELL TO ARMS

Chapter Nineteen: After-Life

Chapter Twenty: L'envoi

ILLUSTRATIONS

INTRODUCTION

THE passages which follow are all taken from books or documents written by men who served in the ranks of regular armies, save for those taken from 'Mrs. Christian Davies', who by enlisting as a man followed a fugitive husband into the field. Most of them served in the British Army, but soldiers from other armies also appear: in the French forces which retreated from Moscow in 1812; in the Foreign Legion; a few in the War between the States. The earliest are those who fought in the Civil War between King and Parliament; all of them finished their service before 1914. Chronologically there are gaps. Very little material of this sort is available for such periods as the reign of Charles II or the years between 1713 and 1756. On the whole, however, the chief difficulty has been one of selection, both between books and between extracts. Not more than a third of what was originally chosen has survived in this collection, and many excellent sources have had to be omitted. It is true that here one can find Cobbett, whose eight formative years as a regular soldier are too often ignored when his later activities are considered; the inimitable Rifleman Harris; John Shipp, who against all the odds achieved promotion from the ranks not once but twice; and 'Wully' Robertson, who died a field marshal. But Sergeant Deane of the 1st Foot Guards and his Journal of Marlborough's War, the solid memoirs of James Anton of the 42nd, the mercurial William Lawrence's breathtaking description of his own flogging, the kind of record rarely found, Private Wheeler's remarkable journal (first printed at Corfu in 1824, and more recently reissued in a most welcome new edition by B. H. Liddell Hart) and many other writings by rankers soldiering, not only in the British but in other armies, have had to be omitted from this volume.

An attempt has been made to give extracts long enough to be intrinsically valuable as connected narrative or description, and which may give the reader some notion as to what sort of individuals these soldiers were. There is the ebullient Wharton, a London apprentice marching away to Worcester in 1642 and regaling his master with vivacious and charmingly phrased accounts of his entry into a military life; the melancholy Alexander Alexander, an artilleryman in Ceylon whose two volumes (1830) tell the story of his soldiering against a most equivocal background of strife with his family; the articulate 'G.B.', to whom his religious experiences (like those of two other unused sources, Bugler William Green of the Rifle Brigade and Sergeant Stevenson of the 3rd Foot Guards) were the most important part of his army career. Here is the terrific figure of Sergeant Bourgogne. One American infantryman, Theodore Gerrish, served as a private in the 20th Maine and then became a clergyman. Bancroft spent his military life in India, being present at the four great actions of the Sutlej campaign as a Bengal Horse Artilleryman. The melancholy but meticulous Gunner Marjouram kept records in great detail of the Maori War of 1860. One sentimental legionnaire, Erwin Rosen, who served for only a few months before deserting, possessed a quick eye for detail and quickly cashed in on his brief experience. Some, like Rifleman Harris and Mole, the King's Hussar, had their work edited for them by friends. And who can separate Defoe from 'Mother Ross', any more than from Robinson Crusoe and Alexander Selkirk? One or two are laconic, like Clarke, with his diary-like notes. Others are loquacious, like Ryder; one or two eager to improve the lot of serving soldiers, like MacMullen. None of them, it must be remembered, is on oath. Farquharson published his account of the Light Brigade at Balaclava nearly thirty years after the event, Metcalfe's records were printed for the first time almost a century late, Foster's 'true and exact relation' of 1642 appeared over 180 years afterwards. Some were undoubtedly deliberately written for effect, like François's reminiscences of Valmy and Wavre. But, in one way or another, a great deal of the truth about the life of an ordinary soldier in peace and war becomes apparent from these pages. The scenery of their stories shifts from Scotland to the Antipodes, from Quebec to Montevideo, from African jungles and the veldt to the North-west Frontier or Algeria.

Extracts have been arranged in four parts, each dealing mainly with one aspect of army life. Some sides of military service tend to be very fully treated, others are somewhat empty; there is naturally more about victories than about defeats, less on the practical details of weapons (nearly always taken for granted in any contemporary account) than on discipline. Nor is it possible to compartmentalize very thoroughly: recruiting and training, battle and religious thought, skirmishes and campaigning, tend very often to merge. On the whole, spelling and punctuation have been modernized, save where too much of the original flavour might be lost, as in the simple records of the anonymous Royal Dragoon in Spain during the War of the Spanish Succession. Details of each book or source are given in the bibliography at the end of the volume, and a short index enables any reader who wishes to do so to follow the fortunes of one particular soldier through his own 'moving accidents by flood and field'.

T. H. McGuffie

ONE

FIRST STEPS

I have eaten your bread and salt.
I have drunk your water and wine.
The deaths ye died I have watched beside,
And the lives ye led were mine.

Rudyard Kipling

I

RECRUITS AND RECRUITING

Enlistment (1693) in search of a vanished husband

IN THE morning I thought of going in search of my dear Richard, and this gave some ease to my tortured mind. I began to flatter myself that I should meet no great difficulty in finding him out, and resolved in one of his suits, for we were both of a size, to conceal my sex, and go directly for Flanders, in search of him whom I preferred to everything else the world could afford me, which, indeed, had nothing alluring, in comparison with my dear Richard, and whom the hopes of seeing had lessened every danger to which I was going to expose myself. The pleasure I found in the thoughts of once more regaining him, recalled my strength, and I was grown much gayer than I had been at any time in my supposed widowhood. I was not long deliberating, after this thought had possessed me, but immediately set about preparing what was necessary for my ramble; and disposing of my children, my eldest with my mother, and that which was born after my husband's departure, with a nurse (my second son was dead), I told my friends, that I would go to England in search of my husband, and return with all possible expedition after I had found him. My goods I left in the hands of such friends as had spare house room, and my house I let to a cooper. Having thus ordered my affairs, I cut off my hair, and dressed me in a suit of my husband's, having had the precaution to quilt the waistcoat, to preserve my breasts from hurt, which were not large enough to betray my sex, and putting on the wig and hat I had prepared, I went out and bought me a silver-hilted sword, and some Holland shirts: but was at a loss how I should carry my money with me, as it was contrary to law to export above £5 out of the kingdom; I thought at last of quilting it in the waistband of my breeches, and by this method I carried with me fifty guineas without suspicion.

I had nothing upon my hands to prevent my setting out; wherefore, that I might get as soon as possible to Holland, I went to the sign of the Golden Last, where Ensign Herbert Laurence, who was beating up for recruits, kept his rendezvous. He was in the house at the time I got there, and I offered him my service to go against the French, being desirous to show my zeal for his majesty King William, and my country. The hopes of soon meeting with my husband, added a sprightliness to my looks, which made the officer say, I was a clever brisk young fellow; and having recommended my zeal, he gave me a guinea enlisting money, and a crown to drink the king's health, and ordered me to be enrolled, having told him my name was Christopher Welsh, in Captain Tichbourn's company of foot, in the regiment commanded by the Marquis de Pisare. The lieutenant of our company was Mr. Gardiner, our ensign, Mr. Welsh.

We stayed but a short time in Dublin after this, but, with the rest of the recruits, were shipped for Holland, weighed anchor, and soon arrived at Williamstadt, where we landed and marched to Gorcum. Here our regimentals and first mountings were given us. The next day we set out for Gertrudenburg, and proceeded forward to Landen, where we were incorporated in our respective regiments, and then joined the grand army, which was in expectation of a general battle, the enemy being very near within cannon-shot. Having been accustomed to soldiers, when a girl, and delighted with seeing them exercise, I very soon was perfect, and applauded by my officers for my dexterity in going through it.

MOTHER ROSS

Attempted enlistment (1694) by a schoolboy

BEFORE I enter upon the Particulars of the Ensueing Journall I think it not amiss to give my Reader an Account of my first Entering into the Army, and Regiment aforesaid, then commanded by Sir James Lessley; I entered as a Soldier with Ensigne William Haliday to serve in the Regiment aforesaid.

Upon the 25th day of March, 1694, and came to the Regiment then Quartered in the Cannongate Edenburgh the day following, and the next day was Shewn to Sir James with severall other Recruits.

Upon Sir James's takeing a view of me, he was pleased to Say to Ensigne Haliday, 'What my friend Haliday, do you bring me Children for Soldiers? I did not Expect this from You, for You know Wee want men,' Ensigne Haliday answered in an Humble Manner, that he must Confess I was too Young, but that it was Intirely my own Desire and that my Parents could not diswade me from it, therefore they Desirous I should be under His Honour's Care, whereupon Sir James asked Whose Childe I was and if he had any knowledge of my parents, the Ensigne told Sir James my father's name, whom Sir James knew, and said he knew my Grandfather also, whereupon Sir James turned to me with a frown, and Said, 'You young Rogue, how came you to Run away from your Parents?' I answered him I did not run away, but came with their Consent to be a Soldier. 'A Soldier!' says Sir James with a Smileing Contenance, 'go home, Young rogue, and go to School,' to which Ensigne Haliday made answer and said, 'Sir, if you turn him back he will certainly go with some other Recruiting Officer, and that would very much vex his parents.' Then Sir James said, I should go home upon ffurloe, and let him have three months pay advance, and his ffurloe for a full year, both of which I had next morning, and comitted to the Charge of Ensigne Haliday's Brother to See me safe home, which the Gentleman performed, and I went again to School, and continued till such time as I broke up for Christmass, at which time Ensigne Haliday came from Flanders to Scottland in order to raise Recruits. I being informed of his arrival at his Brother's in the Evening, went the next morning like a Dutifull Soldier to wait upon my Officer, desired one of his Brother's Servants to acquaint him I was come to wait his Commands, and he ordered the Servant to bidd me come up to him, and I immediately went up to his Chamber. He asked me very kindly how I did, and Whether I continued my Resolution of going abroad. I answered, 'Yes, Sir, indeed I do and will continue it.' Then said the Ensigne, 'it's Sir James's orders that I shall give You the remainder of your pay what you are behind,' and he paid me accordingly, and ordered me to go home and keep close to School until such time as he wanted me, which was not till the 27th of April following. At which time he sent a Serjeant for me to meet him the next day at Kircaldie, which I accordingly did, and then he asked me again in the presence of the Provost of the Town Sir Robert Douglass and his Brother, if I continued Stedfast in my Resolution to go abroad. I answered them I did, and was come there for that purpose. Whereupon he gave me my Pay to the 30th day of April inclusive, and the day following being the 29th we went on board of a Transport, and on May Day weighed Anchor and Sett Sail. The Fleet was Designed for Ostend, but the vessel Wee were in made Campheer and from thence went in Billinders to Sluice in Flanders, and from thence to Bridges by Land, and the next day being the 27th of May, 1695 Wee arrived at the Regiment's head quarters about two in the afternoon at Lafine in the Camberland of Ambought, where Sir James reviewed the recruits. And when he came to me, he asked Ensigne Haliday if I was the Furloe Boy, the Ensigne answered I was. 'Very well,' says Sir James Hallady, 'take care and have an Eye over him.' The Ensigne answered Sir James obliged so to do, and then Wee were dismissed and sent to our Quarters. The Regiment continued in their Quarters about a Fortnight afterwards before the Campaigne opened.

SERJEANT JOHN WILSON

A quick intrododuction to active service, 1702

ON FRYDAY February the 26, 1702 (O.S.), I entertained myself a soldier in Her Majesties Royal Regiment of Dragoons commanded by the Right Honourable Thomas, Lord Raby, the troop commanded by Lefttennant Coll. Killigrew, then lyeing at Gurcum in Holland. On the 5 of March I took shiping at Harwich in the county of Essex and on Fryday the 10 of the same month I landed at Williamstot in Holland, a very pritty towne, situated on a large fine river, but we did not lye in the towne but quartered upon the boors for the convenience of furrage for our horsses, so we keept on, marching downe towards our regment. On Sunday the 14 of March we marched throw Breedah, a very fine city, but did not lye in it but went into a little village, and on Tuesday the 23 of the same month we came to Gurcum, where the regment's quarters ware. We soone received our accutrements, so I lay thare in quarters until the first of May (new stile) 1703, then we marched into camp.

A ROYAL DRAGOON IN THE SPANISH SUCCESSION WAR

Enlistment and early drill, 1773

I HAD now arrived at a remarkable epoch in my life; since it was that which in a great measure gave a cast to its future operations. It was on the 10th of August, 1773, then in my 17th year, when being seduced to gambling by some evil companions, with whom I thoughtlessly associated, I lost my little all. This juvenile stage of existence is truly critical to both sexes. Forgetful of all the moral lessons so anxiously inculcated in my mind by my father, I was blind to my danger, and united with those who became my corrupters, and worst enemies. Afraid to return and tell my father of my indiscretions, who would have rebuked and forgiven me, I shrank from my best hope, parental admonition, and formed the resolution of entering for a soldier. Accordingly I went to one serjeant Jenkins, who kept a public house opposite the lower barrack gate, and enlisted with him for the 9th regiment of foot, which was then stationed in Waterford. On the 24th I joined the regiment, and was put into the hands of a drill serjeant, and taught to walk and step out like a soldier. This at first was a disagreeable task to me. During twenty-one days I was thus drilled four hours each day. However, having at last rectified the most prominent appearance of my awkwardness, I received a set of accoutrements, and a firelock, and was marched every morning from the barrack to the bowling green, near the water-side, to be instructed in the manual exercise.

The most disagreeable days of a soldier, are these in which he begins to learn his exercise. And it is seldom that he entertains much regard for those who teach it him. Hence the office of a drill serjeant, although one of the most important, is not one of the most thankful. However, without disparaging the soldier's character (an offence of which, I hope, I shall not be thought guilty), I must own that some of the old drill-serjeants were unnecessarily, if not wantonly severe.

SERJEANT LAMB

Diversions of a recruit, 1789

IN ONE of these walks I happened to cast my eye on an advertisement, inviting all loyal young men, who had a mind to gain riches and glory, to repair to a certain rendezvous, where they might enter into His Majesty's Marine Service, and have the peculiar happiness and honour of being enrolled in the Chatham division. I was not ignorant enough to be the dupe of this morsel of military bombast; but a change was what I wanted; besides, I knew that marines went to sea, and my desire to be on that element had rather increased than diminished by my being penned up in London. In short, I resolved to join this glorious corps; and, to avoid all possibility of being discovered by my friends, I went down to Chatham, and enlisted into the marines as I thought, but the next morning I found myself before a Captain of a marching regiment. There was no retreating; I had taken a shilling to drink His Majesty's health, and his further bounty was ready for my reception.

When I told the Captain that I thought myself engaged in the marines, 'By Jasus, my lad,' said he, 'and you have had a narrow escape'. He told me, that the regiment into which I had been so happy as to enlist was one of the oldest and boldest in the whole army, and that it was at that time serving in that fine, flourishing and plentiful country, Nova Scotia. He dwelt long on the beauties and riches of this terrestrial paradise, and dismissed me, perfectly enchanted with the prospect of a voyage thither.

I enlisted in 1784, and, as peace had then taken place, no great haste was made to send recruits off to their regiments. I remember well what sixpence a day was, recollecting the pangs of hunger felt by me, during the thirteen months that I was a private soldier at Chatham, previous to my embarkation for Nova Scotia. Of my sixpence, nothing like fivepence was left to purchase food for the day. Indeed, not fourpence. For there was washing, mending, soap, flour for hair-powder, shoes, stockings, shirts, stocks and gaiters, pipe-clay and several other things to come out of the miserable sixpence! Judge then of the quantity of food to sustain life in a lad of sixteen, and to enable him to exercise with a musket (weighing fourteen pounds) six to eight hours every day. The best battalion I ever saw in my life was composed of men, the far greater part of whom were enlisted before they were sixteen, and who, when they were first brought up to the regiment, were clothed in coats made much too long and too large, in order to leave room for growing.

We had several recruits from Norfolk (our regiment was the West Norfolk); and many of them deserted from sheer hunger. They were lads from the plough-tail. All of them tall, for no short men were then taken. I remember two that went into a decline and died during the year, though when they joined us, they were fine hearty young men.

I have seen them lay in their berths, many and many a time, actually crying on account of hunger. The whole week's food was not a bit too much for one day.

My leisure time was spent, not in the dissipations common to such a way of life, but in reading and study. In the course of this year I learnt more than I had ever done before. I subscribed to a circulating library at Brompton, the greatest part of the books in which I read more than once over. The library was not very considerable, it is true, nor in my reading was I directed by any degree of taste or choice. Novels, plays, history, poetry, all were read, and nearly with equal avidity.

Such a course of reading could be attended with but little profit: it was skimming over the surface of everything. One branch of learning, however, I went to the bottom with, and that the most essential too: the grammar of my mother tongue. I had experienced the want of knowledge of grammar during my stay with Mr. Holland; but it is very probable that I never should have thought of encountering the study of it, had not accident placed me under a man whose friendship extended beyond his interest. Writing a fair hand procured me the honour of being copyist to Colonel Debieg, the commandant of the garrison. I transcribed the famous correspondence between him and the Duke of Richmond. The Colonel saw my deficiency, and strongly recommended study. He enforced his advice with a sort of injunction, and with a promise of reward in case of success. I procured me a Lowth's grammar, and applied myself to the study of it with unceasing assiduity.

The edge of my berth, or that of the guard-bed, was my seat to study in; my knapsack was my bookcase; a bit of board lying on my lap was my writing desk; and the task did not demand anything like a year of my life. I had no money to purchase candle or oil; in winter time it was rarely that I could get any evening light but that of the fire, and only my turn even of that. To buy a pen or a sheet of paper I was compelled to forgo some portion of food, though in a state of half-starvation; I had no moment of time that I could call my own; and I had to read and to write amidst the talking, laughing, singing, whistling and brawling of at least half a score of the most thoughtless of men, and that, too, in the hours of their freedom from all control. Think not lightly of the farthing that I had to give, now and then, for ink, pen, or paper. That farthing was, alas! a great sum to me! I was as tall as I am now, I had great health and great exercise. I remember, and well I may! that, upon one occasion, I, after all absolutely necessary expenses, had, on a Friday, made shift to have a halfpenny in reserve, which I had destined for the purchase of a red herring in the morning; but, when I pulled off my clothes at night, so hungry then as to be hardly able to endure life, I found that I had lost my halfpenny! I buried my head under the miserable sheet and rag, and cried like a child.

Though it was a considerable time before I fully comprehended all that I read, still I read and studied with such unremitted attention, that, at last, I could write without falling into any very gross errors. The pains I took cannot be described: I wrote the whole grammar out two or three times; I got it by heart. I repeated it every morning and every evening, and, when on guard, I imposed on myself the task of saying it all over once every time I was posted sentinel. To this exercise of my memory I ascribe the retentiveness of which I have since found it capable, and to the success with which it was attended, I ascribe the perseverance that has led to the acquirement of the little learning of which I am master.

I was soon raised to the rank of Corporal, a rank, which, however contemptible it may appear in some people's eyes, brought me in a clear twopence per diem, and put a very clever worsted knot upon my shoulder, too. As promotion began to dawn, I grew impatient to get to my regiment, where I expected soon to bask under the rays of royal favour. The happy days of departure at last came: we set sail from Gravesend, and, after a short and pleasant passage, arrived at Halifax in Nova Scotia.

COBBETT

A boy of ten joins the Army, 1795

I WAS, one morning in that year, about the month of January or February, busily employed in a field close by my master's house, when, who should I see but one of the parish officers making towards me, with a large paper in his hand. I began to muster and parade my crimes, but found, on a fair review, that I had done nothing that merited the interference of an officer; so I stood up boldly till he approached me, and smilingly said, 'Shipp, I have frequently heard of, and observed your great wish to go for a soldier.' He then read the paragraph, and asked me if I was willing to go; for that, if I was, the parish would rig me out decently, and that he would take me to Colchester. My little heart was in my mouth; I repeated his words, 'Willing to go!' and eagerly assured him of the rapture with which I accepted his offer. The affair was soon concluded so down went my shovel, and off I marched, whistling, 'See, the conquering hero comes.' By four o'clock of the same day, to the honour and praise of the parish be it spoken, I was rigged out in my new leather tights, new coat, new hat, new shoes, new everything—of which I was not a little proud. I begged, as a particular favour, that I might sport colours in my hat; and even this was permitted to my vanity, as long as I remained in the town. I took an affectionate leave of all my old playfellows and my good mistress; and even my cruel master was not neglected by me, for I never had malice or unforgiveness in my disposition. The next day, by seven o'clock in the morning, I was on my way to Colchester, and, when I was seated on the front seat of the coach I would not have exchanged situations with the grand pasha of Egypt, or the king upon the throne of that land of which I was a native. Scarcely had I seated myself, and adjusted my feet in a safe situation, than I indulged my coach companions by whistling several martial airs; but, coming to a well-known turn of the road, from which you take the farewell peep at Saxmundham, as much as I loved my king, I stopped short in the middle of the national anthem, and my eye bent its way instinctively towards my native village, where I first saw the light of heaven, and rested on the little village spire, which reared its Gothic head over the remains of my poor mother. Towards this painfully interesting object I looked and looked, till the place of my nativity was buried from my sight by the surrounding trees. When bereft of this view, I felt pensive and sad, and could only console myself by reflecting, that I did not fly from my parental roof; nor was I deserting aged parents, or unprotected sisters, for I had no one to bewail my departure. Yet I could not help feeling that I left something behind me that hung like a magnet to my heart; with all my misfortunes, all my cares and troubles, still I could not quit, without a pang, the place of my birth, and the tomb of my beloved mother. At last, three gentlemen on the coach, having heard my history from the person who accompanied me, cheered me up by saying, that they knew the corps I was going to, and that they were all lads like myself. This notice from strangers so enlivened me, that I began to regard myself as no small personage, and I talked as much as any of them, until we arrived at an inn in Colchester, where we dined. Here I was marched off to the colonel of the corps in which I was to serve; from the colonel to the adjutant; from the adjutant to the sergeant-major; from the sergeant-major to the drum-major; and thence to his wife, an old drunken Irish woman, but as good a creature as ever drank whisky. In the custody of this lady, the friend who came with me left me, first giving me a hearty shake of the hand, and wishing me every happiness.

JOHN SHIPP

A runaway son enlists in the Royal Artillery, 1801

ANOTHER feeling, not the least powerful, urged me on: I longed to show my father I could rise in the world without his aid, and that all his prophecies of me would be falsified; for, in his anger, he had repeatedly said, I would end in being a soldier, then get flogged and desert, and finish my career at the gallows. I could not bring myself to think he had ever thrown me off, but still indulged the hope, that when he found I did behave well as a soldier, and was not that weathercock he called me, I might yet be aided by him in obtaining that commission on which I had set my heart.

As I sauntered about the streets of Glasgow, I saw the new guard marching to relieve the old, their band playing a cheerful air. This being the first military band I had ever heard, I was quite charmed with it, and followed, unconsciously taking the step and holding up my head. A military enthusiasm instantly seized me, and I felt as if a soldier's life was the only station for which nature had designed me.

When they halted, I addressed a recruiting sergeant, belonging to a highland regiment, who was looking on, with, 'That is a fine band, sergeant,' he answered me with a grunt. I looked at him alike amazed and offended; I meant it as an introduction to my offering myself to him as a recruit. Again I said, 'This is a fine day,' Donald would not take the hint, and only gave a second grunt. I left him in disgust, wondering how a soldier could be so very stupid. I am now aware that I was far too well dressed.

Soon after I met a sergeant belonging to the Royal Artillery, and accosted him with a 'Good morning, sergeant.' He was a man of quite another stamp than the highlander; we were soon as intimate as if we had been acquainted for years. He requested me to go to a public house, and have something to drink, which I refused; but I begged to have a walk on Glasgow Green with him; and away we went.

While we walked, so frank and friendly did he appear that I laid open my whole heart to him, and felt grateful for the interest he appeared to take in my welfare. When he had heard me out he said, 'As a recruiting sergeant you may think I have an interest in what I say, but I assure you, I have none. As your friend, I give my advice, which I have weighed thoroughly and impartially; and I say enlist at once, my brave fellow; it is the only thing for a young lad of spirit in any situation, but more so in yours. You have lost too much of your time already; if you enlist now you will receive this day's pay, and you may think yourself very fortunate to get into so fine a corps. It is the best and most honourable under the crown, and has many advantages no other soldiers enjoy. We have superior pay, superior clothing, little marching, always riding with the guns when on expedition, &c. Then you have your marching money, no musket or kit to carry, just a sword such as you see the party wear. Besides, there is no flogging in the Royal Artillery, but every encouragement is held out for young men of every description, and much more so to such fine-spirited, well-educated, young fellows as you.'

Thus he harangued, holding out a thousand false promises, with which I shall not trouble the reader, and concluded with his solemn assurance, that I would be a sergeant in six months, and an officer in a year or two at the very farthest. All this I firmly believed; and I only stipulated that I was not to march up and down the town with the party, nor be seen much in his company. To this he readily agreed, under the proviso that I must appear before him at least once every day; and if I wished to leave the town for any time, I must get his leave, and then I might go where I pleased.

Everything being thus arranged, I congratulated myself upon my good fortune, and requested to be sent off to the regiment immediately, but was much disappointed when he told me I could not join for three months, as he had sent of his last recruits only a day or two before. I then walked with him to the rendezvous, where he at once laid down a shilling which I took up, as an earnest that I was willing to serve my king and country in his Majesty's 6th Battalion of Royal Artillery.

After drinking his Majesty's health, and success to his arms, the sergeant asked me to go to a surgeon, who, lived in the High Street, to be examined. So deep was the impression the taunts and mockeries which I suffered in Dundonald had made, that I was afraid I would not pass, and felt a gleam of satisfaction when the surgeon pronounced me a fine, active, healthy young man, able for service. In truth, I was both surprised and delighted to find myself pronounced like the rest of mankind by a competent judge.

Next forenoon, I went cheerfully to David Dale, Esq., Charlotte Street and was attested, on Saturday the 25th April, 1801. This ceremony was to me a very serious thing, as it was done with due solemnity; I looked upon it as a very binding obligation. I was sworn in as born in Glasgow. The sergeant entered me as a day-labourer. At this I remonstrated, but he silenced me by saying that it was his instructions, for all those who had no trade, to be entered as labourers. I was forced to submit, but felt, for the first time, that I had suffered a severe degradation.

As it may be curious to many, I will give a detail of the price I received for this disposal of myself. The bounty was eight guineas, and a crown to drink his Majesty's health. Now I, being an ignorant lad, was open to every imposition. I was to receive five guineas at present, and the other three, intended for regimental necessaries, as soon as I joined the regiment. This I objected to, for I was better furnished in everything, except regimentals, than many an officer: But it was of no avail; the sergeant said, he must abide by his regimental orders.

My five guineas, therefore, I received under the following deductions, viz:—

Bounty			£5. 5. 0.
	King's health ..	0. 5. 0.	
	Surgical inspection,	0. 1. 0.	
	Justice of peace attestation ..	0. 1. 0.	
	Enlistment money	0. 1. 0.	
			8. 0.
			£4. 17. 0.

This was the exact sum I received at this time. Whenever I objected to any thing, the sergeant's answer was, it was the rule in the service; and by this same rule he excused all his impositions, such as half-a-crown I had to pay the drummer, for beating the points of war, this was a constant rule, and could not be dispensed with. I must also buy a cockade from him, and a suit of ribbons for his wife; this was also a constant rule. In short, everything was the rule that tended to fleece the poor recruit. These same ribbons for the wife, for instance, were sold regularly to every recruit, as the sergeant always laid them aside for the next occasion. Perhaps they had been bought and sold a hundred times, for any thing I know.

ALEXANDER ALEXANDER

A shepherd-boy joins the Army, 1803

MY FATHER was a shepherd, and I was a sheep-boy from my earliest youth. Indeed, as soon almost as I could run, I began helping my father to look after the sheep on the downs of Blandford, in Dorsetshire, where I was born. Whilst I continued to tend the flocks and herds under my charge, and occasionally (in the long winter nights) to learn the art of making shoes, I grew a hardy little chap, and was one fine day in the year 1803 drawn as a soldier for the Army of Reserve. Thus, without troubling myself much about the change which was to take place in the hitherto quiet routine of my days, I was drafted into the 66th Regiment of Foot, bid good-bye to my shepherd companions, and was obliged to leave my father without an assistant to collect his flocks, just as he was beginning more than ever to require one; nay, indeed, I may say to want tending and looking after himself, for old age and infirmity were coming on him; his hair was growing as white as the sleet of our downs, and his countenance becoming as furrowed as the ploughed fields around. However, as I had no choice in the matter, it was quite as well that I did not grieve over my fate.

My father tried hard to buy me off, and would have persuaded the sergeant of the 66th that I was of no use as a soldier, from having maimed my right hand (breaking the fore-finger when a child). The sergeant, however, said I was just the sort of little chap he wanted, and off he went, carrying me (amongst a batch of recruits he had collected) away with him.

RIFLEMAN HARRIS

First steps into the Army, 1804

I HAVE the advantage of being an Irishman. . . .

My parents, I regret to say, were Roman Catholics. . . .

Meantime I had arrived at the fourteenth year of my age; a period, generally speaking, of no small vanity and self-complacency and in which many men think themselves qualified, by the dignity of their teens, to shake off the trammels of parental guidance. Among others, I determined to walk alone; but unfortunately I cannot on reflection boast of my first step. Among the youths with whom I contracted some acquaintance was a dissolute lad, about my own age; by whose enticement, when only just turned fifteen, I enlisted in the Queen's County Militia. Not that my conduct, like his, had been openly immoral; yet he had gained over me an

SANTA CLARA PUBLIC LIBRARY
SANTA CLARA. CALIF.

ascendancy I could not resist. Evil communications corrupt good manners; and perhaps the apparent freedom, the frankness and gaiety of an open-hearted soldier's holiday life had an influence which, though not acknowledged was really felt. But O my mother! for when I became a soldier she was still living. I had in this deed of hardyhood well nigh forgotten her. . . . I was taken before Captain Fitzmaurice, the Officer in command at the recruiting station and was kindly received. He expressed himself pleased with my look and healthy appearance; made several minute enquiries relative to my family, and at once engaged me as his servant. After serving in the Corps about twelve months, I received, principally I believe on account of my youth, an honourable discharge, while the regiment was stationed at the Castle Barracks in Limerick, and returned to the quietude of home.

A SERGEANT OF THE 43RD LIGHT INFANTRY

Troubles of a raw recruit, 1806

ON THE 6th April, 1806, I enlisted in the 43rd regiment of the line, and in company with several other recruits proceeded to Bristol, at which place, after a rough passage, we safely landed; and in a few days reached the town of Ashford in Kent, where the regiment was quartered.

The sleeping room of which I was an inmate was an oblong building of unusually large dimensions, and was occupied by three companies, of an hundred men each. They were chiefly volunteers, and, of course, young soldiers, many were Irish, many more were English, several Welshmen were intermingled, and a few scotch men came in to complete the whole. Most of these, and that was the only point of general resemblance, had indulged in excessive drinking. Some were uproariously merry; on others the effect was directly the reverse; and nothing less than a fight, it matter not with whom, would satisfy. Meantime, as they were unable to abuse each other in language mutually intelligable, exclamations profoundly jocular or absurdly rancorous ran through the building. Never will the occurrence of that night be effaced from my mind. Surely, I thought, hell from beneath is moved to engulf us all. . . . In a few weeks we marched to more convenient quarters, a few miles distance. The solutary restraints of discreetly managed discipline spoke chaos with order, and my situation became comparatively comfortable.

A SERGEANT OF THE 43RD LIGHT INFANTRY

A recruiting party's adventures, 1805

WHILST in Winchester, we got a route for Ireland, and embarking at Portsmouth crossed over and landed at Cork. There we remained nine weeks; and being a smart figure and very active I was put into the light company of the 66th, and, together with the light corps of other regiments, we were formed into light battalions and sent off to Dublin. Whilst in Dublin. I one day saw a corps of the 95th Rifles, and fell so in love with their smart, dashing, and devil-may-care appearance, that nothing would serve me till I was a Rifleman myself; so, on arriving at Cashmel one day, and falling in with a recruiting-party of that regiment, I volunteered into the second battalion. This recruiting-party were all Irishmen, and had been sent over from England to collect (amongst others) men from the Irish Militia, and were just about to return to England. I think they were as reckless and devil-may-care a set of men as ever I beheld, either before or since.

Being joined by a sergeant of the 92nd Highlanders, and a Highland piper of the same regiment (also a pair of real rollicking blades), I thought we should have all gone mad together. We started on our journey, one beautiful morning, in tip-top spirits from the Royal Oak at Cashmel; the whole lot of us (early as it was) being three sheets in the wind.

When we paraded before the door of the Royal Oak, the landlord and landlady of the inn, who were quite as lively, came reeling forth, with two decanters of whiskey, which they thrust into the fists of the sergeants, making them a present of decanters and all to carry along with them, and refresh themselves on the march. The piper then struck up, the sergeants flourished their decanters, and the whole route commenced a terrific yell. We then all began to dance, and danced through the town, every now and then stopping for another pull at the whiskey decanters. Thus we kept it up till we had danced, drank and shouted and piped thirteen Irish miles, from Cashmel to Clonmel. Such a day I think I never spent, as I enjoyed with these fellows; and on arriving at Clonmel we were as glorious as any soldiers in all Christendom need wish to be. In about ten days after this, our sergeants had collected together a good batch of recruits, and we started for England. Some few days before we had embarked (as if we had not been bothered enough already with the unruly Irish Paddies), we were nearly pestered to death with a detachment of old Irish women, who came from different parts (on hearing of their sons enlisting), in order to endeavour to get them away from us. Following us down to the water's edge they hung to their offspring, and, dragging them away, sent forth such dismal howls and moans that it was quite distracting to hear them. The lieutenant commanding the party ordered me (being the only Englishman present) to endeavour to keep them back. It was however as much as I could do to preserve myself from being torn to pieces by them, and I was glad to escape out of their hands.

At length we got our lads safe on board, and set sail for England.

RIFLEMAN HARRIS

A fugitive play-actor enlists, 1806

I WAS now sixteen years of age, tall and well made, of a genteel appearance and address. Amongst my new acquaintances, were a few who had formed themselves into a spouting club, where plays were acted to small parties of friends, who were liberal in their encomiums. I was quite bewildered with their praise, and thought nothing but becoming another Roscius, making a fortune, and acquiring a deathless name. I forsook my classical authors for Shakespeare, and the study of the stage. Thus, notwithstanding the many tears of my mother, and entreaties of my father, I hurried to ruin. I was seldom at home, as my parents constantly remonstrated with me on the folly of my proceedings. This I could not endure: I had been encouraged and assisted by them in all my former whims. All my undertakings were looked upon, by them, as the doings of a superior genius. To be crossed now, I thought the most unjust and cruel treatment.

I had, through the interference of my new acquaintances, got introduced to the Manager of the Theatre at Edinburgh, who was pleased with my manner and appearance. The day was fixed on which I was to make my trial. I had now attained the summit of my first ambition. I had not the most distant doubt of my success. Universal applause, crowded houses, and wealth, all danced before my imagination. Intoxicated with joy, I went home to my parents. Never shall the agony of their looks be effaced from my memory. My mother's grief was loud and heart-rendering, but my father's harrowed up my very soul. It was the look of despair—the expression of his blasted prospects—prospects he had so long looked forward to, with hope and joy—hopes, that had supported him in his toil and privations, crushed in the dust. It was too much; his eyes at length filled with tears, and raising them to heaven, he only said, or rather groaned. 'God, thy ways are just and wise; thou hast seen it necessary to punish my foolish partiality and pride: but, O God! forgive the instrument of my punishment.' Must I confess, I turned upon my heel, and said with the most cool indifference, (so much had the indulgence of my former life blunted my feelings towards my parents) 'When I am courted and praised by all, and have made you independent, you will think otherwise of my choice.' 'Never, never;' he replied, 'you bring my grey hairs with sorrow to the grave.'—'Thomas, Thomas, you will have our deaths to answer for,' was all my mother could say, tears and sobs choked her utterance.

I went to the Theatre, and prepared for my appearance. The house was crowded to excess. I came upon the stage with a fluttering heart, amidst universal silence. I bowed, and attempted to speak; my lips obeyed the impulse, but my voice had fled. In that moment of bitter agony and shame, my punishment commenced. I trembled; a cold sweat oozed through every pore; my father and mother's words rung in my ears; my senses became confused; hisses began from the audience; I utterly failed. From the confusion of my mind, I could not even comprehend the place in which I stood. To conclude, I shrunk unseen from the Theatre, bewildered, and in a state of despair.

I wandered the whole night. In the morning early, meeting a party of recruits about to embark, I rashly offered to go with them; my offer was accepted, and I embarked at Leith, with seventeen others, for the Isle of Wight, in July, 1806.

The morning was beautiful, and refreshing. A fine breeze wafted us from the roads. The darkness of the preceding night only tended to deepen the gloomy agitation of my mind; but the beauties of the morning scene stole over my soul, and stilled the perturbation of my mind. The violent beat of the pulse at my temples subsided, and I, as it were, awoke from a dream. I turned my eyes, from the beauties of the Forth, to the deck of the vessel on which I stood: I had not yet exchanged words with any of my fellow-recruits; I now enquired of the serjeant, to what regiment I had engaged myself? His answer was, 'To the gallant 71st; you are a noble lad, and shall be an officer.'

"71ST"

Re-enlistment of a former officer, 1807

THE routine of dissipation which was kept up at Wakefield, was not to be sustained by me without expense; and to meet these expenses I spent more than my income. This extravagance—with the loss of fifty pounds, of which I was robbed by my servant, and the assistance of a designing sergeant, who took advantage of my youth and inexperience—soon involved me in debts, to liquidate which I was obliged to apply for permission to sell my commission. This, in consideration of my services, was readily granted; and, having effected a sale, I paid every shilling of my debts, and with the residue of the money repaired to London, where, in about six months, I found myself without a shilling, without a home, and without a friend. Thus circumstances, my fondness of the profession induced me to turn my thoughts to the army again. I could see no earthly difficulty why I should not rise in the same way I had before; and accordingly I enlisted at Westminster, in his majesty's 24th Dragoons, and in two or three days after went with the recruiting-sergeant to the cavalry depot at Maidstone, then under the command of Major-General George Hay. I had not been there long before an officer, who had served with me in campaigns in India, arrived at the depot, and, immediately recognizing me, my history was made known to the commanding officer, and I was promoted to the rank of sergeant. I remained at the depot for about three months, at the expiration of which we were ordered to India, and I embarked as acting quarter-master on board the *New Warren Hastings*, Captain Larkins, and sailed from Spithead on the 8th day of January 1808.

JOHN SHIPP

Why men entered the Army in the 1840's

1.	Indigent.—Embracing labourers and mechanics out of employ, who merely seek for support	80 in 120.
2.	Indigent.—Respectable persons induced by misfortune or imprudence	2 ,, 120.
3.	Idle.—Who consider a soldier's life an easy one	16 ,, 120.
4.	Bad characters.—Who fall back upon the army as a last resource	8 ,, 120.
5.	Criminals.—Who seek to escape from the consequence of their offences	1 ,, 120.
6.	Perverse sons.—Who seek to grieve their parents	2 ,, 120.
7.	Discontented and restless	8 ,, 120.
8.	Ambitious	1 ,, 120.
9.	Others	2 ,, 120.

MACMULLEN

A soldier's son joins the Bengal Horse Artillery, 1841

YEARS rolled on, until at length on the 7th of December, in the year of Grace one thousand eight hundred and forty-one, when leather breeches and long boots, brass helmets with red horse-hair manes, and jackets with ninety buttons, or, 'by our Lady' a hundred, were the favourite dress of the Bengal horse artillery, who vaunted themselves, and with justice and reverence be it spoken, the finest specimens of that arm in the world; when shaven chins and upper lips, and mutton-chop whiskers (according to regulation) were the order of the day—the readers' very humble servant attained the mature age of 18 years, and his service began to count towards a pension or, what was called, in those days, his 'man service' began to run. He was then stationed in Dum-Dum, which was still the head-quarters of the artillery arm of the Honourable East India Company. The height of his ambition was then, and had long been, to become a horse-artillery-man. He had spent the whole nine long years of his boy service in the foot artillery (better known by the classical appellation of 'Old Fogs'—an expression which stank in his nostrils, and was fraught with all sorts of ridiculous and disagreeable associations). Had spent these years, too, almost entirely under canvas; and if marching from one end of India to the other and back, could be said to be good training for a professional pedestrian, he was certainly entitled to set up business as one on his own account, and make a good thing of it. For example, the writer's first march from Dum-Dum to Agra, which lasted three months; the next was from Agra to Jodhpore, and back to Agra again, which lasted three months more. Then he marched from Agra to Cawnpore, then back to Dum-Dum, and, of course, had to walk every inch of the way. But he had made up his mind that, if possible, he would cut the dismounted branch of the service, and if there was marching to be done, it should be either on a horse's back or on a gun-carriage. He had a soul above 'gutter-slapping', and set about having his desire gratified.

BANCROFT

At Cawnpore: An N.C.O. and raw recruits' money, 1841

THEY had not been permitted to enjoy the barracks many days, when the horse and foot artillery recruits were ordered to march and join their respective troops and companies higher up; and here the pay-sergeant of the troop to which the horse artillery recruits had been attached, was ordered to pay them up and close their accounts. The night prior to that on which they were to resume their march to Meerut, they were summoned to attend the pay-sergeant at his quarters; when there, each recruit was called on to sign his accounts, after having done which, he received Rs. 2, with which he appeared to be satisfied. When the writer was called in and asked to sign, he took the liberty of asking how much money he was to receive after his signature? and was told that, as a special case, and out of compliment to his good looks and general appearance, he would receive five rupees. To the amazement of the pay-sergeant, the writer declined to sign, for neither his comrade nor himself had received any pay for three months, and had drawn no rum the whole march, while the others had drawn two drams of rum daily. His comrade was then called upon to sign, which he sturdily refused to do, and they were coolly then informed that if they persisted in their refusal, they should be sent to the guard-room—to which abode of bliss they were despatched, after much wrangling, but were released, and again called to the presence, when the writer received Rs. 30, and his comrade Rs. 20, and then they signed their accounts as having been made up correctly. This was not the case; the accounts were all wrong, and they were deliberately swindled out of what would have been to them a large sum. The writer got the largest sum because he made the most noise, and showed the most determined front of resistance to the desire that the accounts should be signed; he was perfectly aware that there was a much larger sum due to him, for the sake of of peace and quietness however, and knowing full well how hard a matter it would be to obtain a redress, he accepted the sum offered him and advised his chum to do the same. When the remaining recruits ascertained how liberally the writer and his comrade had been treated, they fell upon the pay-sergeant en masse, and created a great disturbance. They were pacified, however, by the receipt of Rs. 3 each in addition to the Rs. 2. they had already received on their first signing. They (most of them) spent their money in the canteen that night, and went drunk to their beds in the open air, from which they were roused from their uneasy slumbers in the morning to march to their destination with aching heads and pockets void of coin.

BANCROFT

Enlistment of a lad from a military family, 1844

I AM a native of Twyford, in the county of Leicester, and from childhood have had a strong inclination for the army; although my father (who is an old soldier, and was at Waterloo) always tried to set me against it, by telling me that for the least offence the cat-o'-nine-tails would be made use of. He would also describe to me the horrors of the battle of Waterloo, thinking in that way to turn my mind from a soldier's life; but instead of turning me, this only made me the more anxious to become a soldier; and I never was so happy as when I was listening to him talking about it; till at last he would say, 'Boy, don't ask me any more foolish questions, for you will not understand me if I talk for a month, until you have been to see.' He had served ten years in the 1st. Dragoon Guards; also, his brother and cousin. They were at the battle of Waterloo, and were all wounded. My father received three wounds, and his brother eleven.

Time passed on, and in the year 1843 I was in service at Nottingham. I had a good place, and a good master: he was a remarkably clean man, and we agreed very well; but at the same time, I had been watching the soldiers as they went to church from the barracks, and I thought it was the finest sight that I had ever seen. Their very looks made me wish I was among them. I wondered how they did to step so regularly, and was so foolish as to think their legs were all tied together. It was altogether a mystery to me, for I had never before seen soldiers, with the exception of one on furlough. After seeing all this I was not likely to content myself long; so one night I went up to the barracks, and tried to enlist; but I was not high enough for them, as they were heavy dragoons —the 6th Enniskillens.

At the beginning of 1844, I made myself known to sergeant Dyer, of the 32nd. regt., who was then recruiting at Nottingham. He was a fine-looking man, and dressed very smartly. He was trimmed all over with silver lace, and wore an officer's cap; he did not lose an inch of his height, for he was very proud. One night he took me to his house (for he was a married man) to measure me, as I would not go to a public-house with him. The sergeant measured me and said, 'Barely 5 ft. 6 in., my lad; but you're young, and I shall try to get you passed.' I had not quite made up my mind, so I did not enlist that night; but a few nights after I was going down the Long Row on some business for my master, when I met the sergeant, and I said to him, 'Well, I want a place.' 'That's right, my lad; thrust your body into the army, and make a man of yourself,' said the sergeant. At the same time he held out a shilling, but I told him I should not take it there; so we went to his house, and I thus enlisted in the 32nd regiment, being then in my twentieth year. I went straight away home, and told no one; although I saw my uncle and my sister: but the next day I told my uncle, and he told my master. They were both very sorry, and tried to persuade me to pay the 'smart', and not go; but I would not consent. My master asked me if I had anything against his place; or what induced me to go. I told him that I had nothing against him, but I had made up my mind to enlist. The next day I told my sister, and she was almost ready to go beside herself.

On an afternoon a few days later, my sister's husband and I started from Nottingham to Twyford, a distance of about thirty miles; though I had agreed that he should not tell my father or mother that I had enlisted. We got as far as Melton that night, but it snowed so fast that we did not go any further. The next morning we arrived at home.

My father was surprised to see us there so early; but I said we had just come to see them, and that we must go back that night. My mother (poor old creature!) thought that all was not right, or I should not be going back so soon. Our secret was very near being found out, for my coat was hanging up, and my mother went to it, and was feeling in the pockets, and had got my duplicate in her hand before I saw her. I snatched hold of it before she had got it open, and told her that paper was not for her or any one to look at, and that she must not see it; so I got it away again. My mother was very uneasy all day. At four o'clock we started back. My father came about two miles on the road, and I told him that I had enlisted. The old man made a great trouble of it, and I felt very sorry for him; but before he left us, he bade me be a good soldier, and never desert my colours. He then bid me 'good-bye', and we arrived at Nottingham, by train from Syston, that night.

Early in the morning, shortly after, the sergeant came to say that I must be up at his house in an hour's time, for we were to march that morning at ten o'clock; and I was glad that the order had come. At nine o'clock, the whole of the recruits had met at the Bull's Head: and when I saw them altogether a pretty sight there was! I was ashamed of being among them; for they were a dirty, ragged lot of blackguards—some of them then nearly drunk.

We started in charge of a corps of the Rifles; for we were not all for one regiment. We were marching for Manchester, where my regiment was then stationed. On arriving there, we went to Tibb-street, where six companies were lying. The first soldier I saw belonging to the regiment was a man as sentry on the outside of the barracks. It was raining a little, so the sentinel was cloaked, and I thought I never saw such an object in my life before. He had on his knapsack, and shouldered his long musket with his bayonet fixed. I was now sick of my job, and I began to repent of my bargain.

We did not stop here; we went to Salford barracks, where our head quarters were. On the way we met another soldier of the 32nd. I never saw such a poor-looking thing in my life; he was a thick, short man, and hump-backed. His dress was too large for him, and looked dirty. I had now seen quite enough of the foot-soldiers, and began to think I should not be a soldier long; but on meeting some more of the men, I saw they were smart and clean-looking, which put me in better spirits, and I afterwards learned that the other man we met was a pioneer.

On arriving at the barracks we went before the colonel, who was a keen, sharp man. He soon took a survey of us: he asked me many questions. He told me to take care of myself, and I should go on to make a soldier. We then went to the hospital, and passed the doctor. We were ordered to remain in there until we had got our regimentals. We had been there about an hour, when a corporal came to take us to the tailor's shop to be measured for our clothes. I could not help looking at this corporal, for he stood 6 ft. 7 in. in height. After being measured we were brought back to the hospital, and now we were to commence soldiering.

The first thing that happened was—in came a man and said, 'Where are those "cruiteys"?' and then commenced and cut our hair off so short that I could not get hold of it. This hurt me more than anything. I could not help weeping to see my hair cut off as bare as though it had been shaved.

We were kept in the hospital two days. The second day we fitted on our clothes, which they had not taken much pains with; and on my remarking that mine were a deal too large, I was told they were just right for my drill. We were then taken to the barracks, to the company to which we belonged—No. 4 company, then on detachment at Tibb-street. I was attached to the Grenadiers. On going to the barrack-rooms, we passed some officers, when I heard one of them say, 'He has got a watch now, but he will not have it long'. I thought, 'You will be wrong'. It appeared he knew the tricks the old soldiers would play to get it out of me.

RYDER

Volunteer soldiers at the beginning of a war: Federal Army, 1861

ONE of our fixed ideas was that a single Yankee could whip five rebels with the utmost ease. Some placed the number as high as twelve; but I think that any man in my company venturing incredulity as to our ability easily to vanquish the rebels in the ratio of five of them to one of ourselves, would have been summarily ejected from the company. Like Gideon of old, we wanted no faint hearts in our band.

As part of the same delusion, men used to suggest, not wholly in fun, that our regiment, or at any rate the troops from Connecticut, should take the contract of thrashing the rebels for so many thousand dollars, the job to be completed, inspected and passed upon by competent European commissioners, not later than the end of July, or no charge at all to be made.

Quite as laughable were the pictures we drew to ourselves of the manner in which we were to make the campaign. When I enlisted, and for some days thereafter, I fully expected to carry a trunk with me, and a commodious number of changes of raiment; on finding which impossible, I felt as downcast as did the hundred days' man whom I met at Bermuda Hundred in '64, who, being just out from Ohio, hadn't had any pie or any butter for his bread since leaving Fortress Monroe. How, too, we loaded ourselves with pistols, bowie-knives, and a whole lot of other furniture that was, we thought, going to be handy when we got down South. One might be called upon to clinch with a rebel. The rebel would, of course, be the underdog, but might not let you up, you know. How convenient to reach round behind you, draw your bowie-knife and coax him to relax his grip! One very devout soldier carried his family bible. The knapsack that tugged at my wretched shoulders when we left Hartford for the front on June 10th of '61, would have made a camel pant, containing wares enough to have stocked a country store. This lugging about of Egyptian pyramids upon our backs we soon abandoned, as we did with the bowie-knives and pistols. One man in our company, however, never marched with less than sixty or seventy pounds in his knapsack, to the end of the war. His calling before had been that of a pack-pedlar, and he said he experienced a certain difficulty in not falling forward on his face, unless he had about the old load strapped behind.

Alas, the knapsack was but one among our burdens that dreadful day on which we set forth for the war. Such uniforms as we writhed under! I perspire at the thought of them now, after the lapse of a quarter of a century. As the United States

Government was unable to provide us in this respect, the excellent Governor Buckingham, of Connecticut, had assumed to do it. He, good man, had rigged us out with suits of the thickest sort of gray woollen, made, one would have thought, especially for midwinter wear in Greenland. There were heavy gray felt hats to match. We had no blouses. The coats were short, without skirts; the pants of so generous girth that if any hero, beating perchance a hasty retreat, should have the misfortune to lose his knapsack, he might not be destitute of a good place to bestow his blanket. Some of the trousers were three inches too long; some nearly as much too short. The average coat, too, had a considerable surplus of circumference. Vests there were none; for which lack, coarse, heavy, gray flannel shirts, with the redundant longitude of the trousers, were expected to make amends.

We had a cartridge-box, haversacks, canteens and old-fashioned Springfield muskets. Not being graduates of a Turvey drop Academy, we had little taste in arranging this gear when we came to don it. Here would be a tall man with the straps for those utensils so short as to bring his canteen, haversack and cartridge-box well up under his arms; yonder a little five-footer would go 'hepp,' 'hepp,' 'hepp,' along, with those same indispensable appurtenances flopping half way to his heels. Some had their overcoats strapped neatly and compactly plumb on the top of their knapsacks; others fastened them on in so dowdy a way as to suggest that they meant the very frightfulness of their appearance to drive back the foe, on the principle which Sidney Smith must refer to when he mentions a man the mere look of whose face was a breach of the peace, he was so homely.

And then what inimitable marching! My company was about equally divided at first between men who could keep no time at all, those who could keep some time but not much, and those who could keep a good deal of time if each were permitted to do it in his own way. In a word, it took a long while for us to become strong in rhythm.

ANDREWS

Old soldier and recruit: Confederate Army

THE recruit—our latest acquisition—was so interesting. His nice clean clothes, new hat, new shoes, trimming on his shirt front, letters and cross-guns on his hat, new knife, for all the fellows to borrow, nice comb for general use, nice little glass to shave by, good smoking tobacco, money in his pocket to lend out, oh, what a great convenience he was! How many things he had that a fellow could borrow, and how willing he was to go on guard, and get wet, and give away his rations, and bring water, and cut wood, and ride horses to water! And he was so clean, and sweet, and his cheeks so rosy, all the fellows wanted to bunk with him under his nice new blanket, and impart to him some of their numerous and energetic 'tormentors'.

And then it was so interesting to hear him talk. He knew so much about war, arms, tents, knapsacks, ammunition, marching, fighting, camping, cooking, shooting, and everything a soldier is and does. It is remarkable how much a recruit and how little an old soldier knows about such things. After a while the recruit forgets all, and is as ignorant as any veteran. How good the fellows were to a really gentlemanly boy! How they loved him!

MCCARTHY

Enlistment: early days of a young Lancer, 1877

I WAS seventeen and three-quarters years old when, having decided to seek my fortune in the army, I took the 'Queen's Shilling' from a recruiting sergeant in the City of Worcester on the 13th November, 1877. The minimum age for enlistment was eighteen, but as I was tall for my years the sergeant said the the deficient three months would involve no difficulty, and he promptly wrote me down as eighteen years and two months—so as to be on the safe side—and that has been the basis of my official age ever since. For some reason that has now escaped my memory I was detained at Worcester for four days, receiving in the meantime two shillings and a halfpenny per diem for board and lodgings. The odd halfpenny strikes one as being a queer item, but it had no doubt been arrived at by Her Majesty's Treasury after careful calculation of the cost actually incurred. The recruiting sergeant, a kindly disposed individual, took possession of the whole sum, giving me in return excellent, if homely, accommodation and food at his own house.

The regiment I selected to join, the 16th (Queen's) Lancers, was stationed in the West Cavalry Barracks, Aldershot, and on arrival there, on a wet and dreary November evening, the first people I met there were the 'orderly officer' and the regimental sergeant-major, both of whom showed a sympathetic interest in me. I was at once posted as No. 1514 to 'G' Troop, the officer saying to me as I went off, 'Give your watch to the sergeant-major of your troop, my lad,' and as I wrote home a few days later I did so, 'for it is unsafe to leave it lying about, and there is nowhere you can carry it with safety.'

The life of a recruit in 1877 was a very different matter from what it is now. The system introduced in 1871–72 by Mr. Cardwell—one of the greatest War Ministers the Country has ever had—under which men enlisted for twelve years' regular service, had not yet had time to get into full swing. Regiments were, therefore, still composed mainly of old soldiers who, although very admirable comrades in some respects and with a commendable code of honour of their own, were in many cases, not in all—addicted to rough behaviour, heavy drinking, and hard swearing. They could not well be blamed for this. Year in and year out they went through the same routine, were treated like machines—of an inferior kind—and having little prospect of finding decent employment on the expiration of their twenty-one years' engagement, they lived only for the present, the single bright spot in their existence being the receipt of a few shillings—perhaps not more than one—on the weekly pay-day. These rugged veterans exacted full deference from the recruit, who was assigned the worst bed in the room, given the smallest amount of food and the least palatable, had to 'lend' them articles of kit which they had lost or sold, 'fag' for them in a variety of ways, and, finally, was expected to share with them at the regimental canteen such cash as he might have in the purchase of beer sold at 3d a quart.

It so happened that I joined the regiment on pay-day, and accordingly the greater number of my newly-found companions spent the evening at the canteen—then a mere drinking saloon—or at public-houses in the town. On return to quarters, if not before, old quarrels were revived or new ones were started, and some of them had to be settled by an appeal to fists. One of these encounters took place on and near the bed in which I was vainly trying to sleep, and which was itself of an unattractive and uncomfortable nature. Argument and turmoil continued far into the night, and I began to wonder whether I had made a wise decision after all. I continued to wonder for several nights afterwards, and would lie awake for hours meditating whether to see the matter through, or get out of bed, put on my plain clothes (which I still had) and 'desert'. Fortunately for me another occupant of the room removed the temptation these clothes afforded, for, having none of his own, he one night appropriated mine, went off in them, and never came back.

Shortly before the period of which I write it had been the custom for a married soldier and his wife, with such children as they possessed, to live in one corner of the barrack-room, screened off with blankets, and in return for this accommodation and a share of the rations the wife kept the room clean, washed and mended the men's under-clothing, and attended to the preparation of their meals. This custom was not without its good points, as the women exercised a steadying influence over the men, while the latter seldom if ever forgot that a woman was in the room, and any one who did forget was promptly brought to order by the others. Still, it could not be wholly without its undesirable side, and the transfer of all women to 'married quarters' was a distinct change for the better.

The barrack-room arrangements for sleeping and eating could not be classed as luxurious. The brown bed-blankets were seldom or ever washed; clean sheets were issued once a month; and clean straw for the mattresses once every three months. Besides the beds, the only other furniture consisted of four benches and two deal tables. The men polished their boots on the former, and the latter were used for cleaning the remaining articles of kit as well as for dining tables. Table-cloths there were none, and plates and basins (paid for by the men) were the only crockery, the basin being used in turn as a coffee-cup, tea-cup, beer-mug, soup-plate, shaving-mug, and receptacle for pipe-clay with which to clean gloves and belts.

The food provided free consisted of one pound of bread and three-quarters of a pound of meat, and nothing more of any kind. Groceries, vegetables, and all other requirements were paid for by the men, who had a daily deduction of 3½d made from their pay of 1s. 2d. for that purpose. The regulation meals were coffee and bread for breakfast; meat and potatoes for dinner, with soup or pudding once or twice a week; tea and bread for tea. If a man wished to have supper or something besides dry bread for breakfast and tea he had to purchase it from the barrack hawkers or canteen. Putting the cost of this at 4½d a day, he thus had to expend a total of eightpence a day on his food, besides which he was subjected to a further daily charge of a penny for washing. This left him fivepence a day or about three-shillings a week, and even this was not all clear pocket-money, for after the first free issue he had to keep up the whole of his underclothing as well as many articles of uniform, and also supply himself with cleaning materials, such as polishing paste for brasses, oil for steel equipment, and soft soap for saddlery.

A beneficent regulation, recognizing these drains on the unfortunate man's pay, laid down that in no case should he receive less than a penny a day! In my regiment the custom was never to give less than a shilling a week, but even this sum did not go far to supplement the allowance of food, to say nothing of beer and tobacco.

ROBERTSON

Enlistment in the Foreign Legion: 1890

THE door of the Commandant's office opened suddenly and a non-commissioned officer appeared, and, to my consternation, shouted out my name. Instinctively I rose and answered 'Present,' just as if I were answering to a callover at school, all the other occupants of the room eyeing me curiously as I did so.

In response to a gesture from the sergeant I stepped across, entered the office, and found myself in the presence of a gentleman in the uniform of a major of the line, who was seated at a big table covered with papers and text-books. He was a red-faced man of about forty, with short-cropped grey hair and a heavy moustache of the same tint. The eyes that looked into mine had a kindly light in them, which belied the somewhat brusque manner of their owner.

I uncovered as I entered the room, and saluted him with the stereotyped 'Bonjour, Monsieur!' to which he nodded a response, and, without further preamble, said:

'So you are desirous of enlisting in one of the Regiments Etrangers?'

'Yes, sir,' I replied.

'Since when have you come to that decision?'

This unexpected question rather nonplussed me, but regaining my composure I answered with apparent coolness:

'Oh! since yesterday.'

He smiled, and then said, to my astonishment and anger:

'Eh bien! you are a fool, my friend. Ah! that hurts you, doesn't it?' (I had flushed at his observation). 'Sure proof that stern discipline would not suit you,' he continued. Then in a softened and more kindly tone he rattled along so quickly that there was no chance of putting in a word:

'Sacre bleu! The Legion—why, you don't know what it is. Well, I will tell you—hard work—hard knocks—hard discipline, and no thanks. And how does it end? Your throat cut by some thieving Arab if you have luck; if not, wounded, and then his women make sausage meat of you. In Tonquin the same sort of thing—only worse, with fever and sunstroke into the bargain. A bad business! yes, a bad business!' he continued: 'You look like a gentleman—you are one, I'm sure. Mind you I don't mean to say there are not others over there —there are many—poor fellows! Your family, too!—think of them—such a sudden decision. Sapristi! and all for some trifling bêtise, sans doute. A petticoat, I'll swear—don't deny it—I have been young also—a faithless sweetheart—Pish! There are a thousand others who would be delighted to console you. No! No! a good dinner, the Moulin Rouge, and tomorrow you will be cured, Sacre bleu!' He laughed, and added: 'Try that; and if tomorrow you still feel the cravings for a military career, well, come and see me.'

Disappointed and somewhat resentful, for at the time I did not appreciate the kindly attention which underlay the advice he had given me, and imagined that I had been treated with undue contempt and familiarity, I replied:

'Tomorrow I shall return, sir!'

He laughed again good-naturedly, and said:

'Well, well, we shall see;' at which I bowed and left the room.

The outer office was silent and deserted, for it was the luncheon hour. I was annoyed at this, having counted on obtaining more information from the other men who had come to join. However, recognizing the inutility of waiting there, I proceeded to my usual restaurant in a very disappointed state of mind, though in no way turned from my determination.

At an early hour the next morning I returned to the Rue St. Dominique. The major, my friend of the day before, received me with many deprecatory remarks concerning my persistence; but seeing that they were evidently lost on me, he carefully perused my passport, which I had been particular to bring with me, and I was passed on to the doctor for examination. 'Bon pour le service,' ran the verdict given, and I was then signed on for a period of five years.

After much waiting a feuille de route, a railway requisition for Marseilles, and the sum of three francs for expenses, were given to me. The sergeant-major who handed them to me was kind enough to mention that should I fail to put in an appearance at my destination within the next forty-eight hours, I would be considered a deserter, and treated as such. I left Paris that evening from 'Gare de Lyons', and arrived at Marseilles about twenty four hours afterwards.

MANINGTON

A Birmingham boy enlists in a Highland regiment, 1891

In September, 1891, a very ordinary family of twelve were sitting round the dinner table—Father, Mother and ten children, when I casually mentioned to one of my brothers that my friend intended joining the Seaforth Highlanders and that I should like to go with him.

At this announcement there was silence for a few moments, then one of my sisters said, 'Huh! You would be too afraid to go for a soldier.'

Although only sixteen years of age I said to myself, 'I'll show them whether I am afraid or not.' So I went with my young friend the next day and saw the Recruiting Sergeant. After looking me over, he said, 'Don't forget to say you are eighteen, or you won't pass through.'

I passed the test for height, chest measurements and weight, etc., and was duly presented with the Queen's shilling with which I went home, very proud to think I was going to do something worth while.

At this time I was earning 10s. per week, and one of my jobs was to carry ingots of gold on my shoulders, size about 14 to 16 in. long by 6 in. wide and 2 in. thick, to the rolling mills, and sit and wait while they rolled it into a coil of sheet metal, for making gold brooches, etc., for me to bring back. Imagine boys going through the streets in the jewellery quarter of Birmingham, unprotected, carrying ingots of gold as I had to in those days. Gangsters and smash-and-grabs were unheard of then.

It was a sad leaving, as I had never left home before, although one of the family of twelve. But I soon brightened up, as the next day we were sent to Fort George, our Regimental Depot in the north of Scotland, about seven miles from Inverness, and fitted out with our gorgeous Highland uniform, with kilt, sporran, feather hat and red tunic, etc., which I really think was the attraction to boys of our age at the time. How proud we were the first time we were allowed out 'on pass'.

In a few days we were drafted to our regiment, and then

stationed in Fermoy in Southern Ireland, where we settled down to the serious business of soldiering, right turn and left turn by numbers on the barrack square, commencing at 6 o'clock in the morning.

CORBETT

2

TRAINING AND UNIFORMS

First days in the Army, 1795

ON THE following morning I was taken to a barber's, and deprived of my curly brown locks. My hair curled beautifully, but in a minute my poor little head was nearly bald, except a small patch behind, which was reserved for a future operation. I was then paraded to the tailor's shop, and deprived of my new clothes—coat, leathers, and hat—for which I received, in exchange, red jacket, red waistcoat, red pantaloons, and red foraging-cap. The change, or metamorphosis, was so complete, that I could hardly imagine it to be the same dapper little fellow. I was exceedingly tall for a boy of ten years of age; but, notwithstanding this, my clothes were much too large, my sleeves were two or three inches over my hands, or rather longer than my fingers; and the whole hung on me, to use a well-known expression, like a purser's shirt on a handspike. My pride was humbled, my spirits drooped, and I followed the drum-major, hanging my head like a felon going to the place of execution. I cut such a queer figure, that all who met me turned round and stared at me. At last, I mustered up courage enough to ask one little chap what he was staring at, when he replied, 'Ask my eye, Johnny Raw;' at the same time adding his extended fingers and thumb to the length of his nose. Passing some drummers on their way to practice, I got finely roasted. 'Twig the raw-skin!'—'Smoke his pantaloons!'—'Them there trousers is what I calls a knowing cut!'—'Look at the sign of the Red Man!' &c., &c. Under this kind of file-firing I reached my barrack, where I was doomed to undergo the same routine of quizzing, till at length I got nettled, and told one of the boys, if he did not let me alone, I should take the liberty of giving him a good threshing. This 'pluck', as they termed it, silenced my tormentors, and I was permitted, for a time, to remain unmolested. In this interval the drum-major went out, having first put my leathers &c., into his box, of which he took the key. I sat myself down on a stool, which might not inaptly have been styled the stool of repentance; for here I began first to think that soldiering did not possess quite so much delight as I had pictured to myself. Still I resolved to put a good face on the matter, and so mixed with my comrades, and in an hour was as free and as much at home with them all as if I had known them for years. The drift of my new acquaintances, in being thus easily familiar with me, was soon apparent; for one of the knowing ones among them called me aside, and asked me if I knew where to sell my coloured clothes; as, if not, he would go with me, and show me. I told him that the drum-major had them. 'Yes,' replied he, 'I know he has; but you see as how he has no business with them. Them there traps should be sold, and you get the money they brings; and if you don't keep your eye on the fugleman, he will do you out of half of them.' He further said, that, when he enlisted, he got more than five shillings for his things. I replied, that of course the drum-major would either sell them for my benefit, or permit me to do it; and, if the latter, that I should be thankful for his kindness. At this moment he entered, when the boy, who had just spoken to me, approached him, and said, pointing to me, 'That there chap says as how he wants to sell them things of his in your box, and that I am to go with him, to show him the place where I sold my things.' To this false-hood I could not submit, and I therefore went up to the drum-major, and said, 'Sir, I said nothing of the kind; all I said was, that I supposed you would either dispose of the things for my benefit, or allow me to do so,'—'Yes, yes,' said the drum-major, 'that's all right; I will sell them for you, and you shall have the money.' The boy here turned upon his heel, muttering something like fudge! and the things were put into a handkerchief and carried off into the town. When the drum-major had left us, the same boy came up to me, and called me a liar, stating that he had a great mind to thresh me; and, as a proof of his inclination, he attempted to seize my nose between his finger and thumb. I got in a rage, and told him, if he ventured to touch me, I would fell him to the ground; when all the boys gathered round us, and said, 'Well done, Johnny Raw!'—'Well done, old leather-breeches!'—'That's right, Johnny Wapstraw!' Finding that I did not venture to strike the first blow, my antagonist called me a coward. This I knew I was not; so, as I could submit to his insolence no longer, I struck him, and to it we went in right earnest. After half a dozen rounds my opponent gave in. This, my first victory, established that I was neither a coward nor to be hoaxed with impunity. Eulogiums were showered down upon me, and the shouting and uproar were beyond description. I understood afterwards that he was a great bully, and always fighting. Our boxing-match had just concluded, when the drum-major entered, and produced the proceeds of my clothes; viz., £1. 1s. 6d. for a new hat, coat, waistcoat, and leathers: a fair price, some said; while others thought they ought to have fetched thirty shillings; but I was very well satisfied, and stood hot rolls and butter to all around, not forgetting my antagonist, who shook hands, and said it was the first time he had ever been beaten, and that he would some day, in friendship, have another trial. I assured him that I should be at any time at his service, and thus this matter ended.

First acquaintance with a queue

After this I went into town, to purchase a few requisites, such as a powder-bag, puff, soap, candles, grease &c.; and, having procured what I stood in need of, I returned to my barrack, where I underwent the operation of having my hair tied for the first time, to the no small amusement of all the boys assembled. A large piece of candle-grease was applied, first to the sides of my head, then to the hind long hair; after this, the same kind of operation was performed with nasty stinking soap—sometimes the man who was dressing me applying his knuckles, instead of the soap, to the delight of the surrounding boys, who were bursting their sides with laughter, to see the tears roll down my cheeks. When this operation was over, I had to go through one of a more serious nature. A large pad, or bag filled with sand, was poked into the back of my head, round which the hair was gathered tight, and the whole tied round with a leather thong. When I was dressed for parade, I could scarcely get my eyelids to perform their office; the skin of my eyes and face was drawn so tight by the plug that was stuck in the back of my head, that I could not possibly shut my eyes; and to this, an enormous high stock was poked under my chin; so that, altogether, I felt as stiff as if I had swallowed a ramrod, or a sergeant's halberd. Shortly after I was thus equipped, dinner was served; but my poor jaws refused to act on the offensive, and when I made an attempt to eat, my pad behind went up and down like a sledge-hammer.

JOHN SHIPP

A soldier's load and equipment on the march, 1808

THE weight I myself toiled under was tremendous, and I often wonder at the strength I possessed at this period, which enabled me to endure it; for, indeed, I am convinced that many of our infantry sank and died under the weight of their knapsacks alone. For my own part, being a handicraft, I marched under a weight sufficient to impede the free motions of a donkey; for besides my well-filled kit, there was the great-coat rolled on its top, my blanket and camp kettle, my haversack, stuffed full of leather for reparing the men's shoes, together with a hammer and other tools (the lapstone I took the liberty of flinging to the devil), ship-biscuit and beef for three days. I also carried my canteen filled with water, my hatchet and rifle, and eighty rounds of ball cartridge in my pouch; this last, except the beef and biscuit, being the best thing I owned, and which I always gave the enemy the benefit of, when opportunity offered.

Altogether the quantity of things I had on my shoulders was enough and more than enough for my wants, sufficient, indeed, to sink a little fellow of five feet seven inches into the earth. Nay, so awkwardly was the load our men bore in those days placed upon their backs, that the free motion of the body was impeded, the head held down from the pile at the back of the neck, and the soldier half beaten before he came to the scratch.

RIFLEMAN HARRIS

Gun accident, 1811

ONE occurrence I witnessed here almost incredible: a Portuguese governor touched at Colombo, early in the year 1811; on the firing of the salute, Gunner Richard Clark was blown from the mouth of his gun right into the air, and alighted upon a rock at a considerable distance in the harbour, yet escaped without a bone being broken, almost unhurt. It was the most miraculous escape I ever witnessed; he was but an awkward soldier at the best; the gun of which he was No. 1, went off by accident, but not just at the time of loading, otherwise the left arm, or perhaps both arms, of No. 2. had been blown off, as No. 2 loads and rams home, along with No. 1. The gun was just loaded when she went off, through the negligence of Clark, in not spunging properly. He was not at his proper distance, like the other man, nor yet near enough to receive the whole flash. To the astonishment of everyone, he was seen in the air, the spunge-staff grasped in his right hand, the rammerhead downwards, which first struck the rock as he alighted on his breech. The rock was very thickly covered with sea weed. A party was sent down to bring up the body, as all concluded him killed upon the spot; he was brought up only stunned and slightly singed, and was at his duty again in a few days; while No. 5, who served the vent, had his thumb, with which the motion-hole is stopped during the loading, so severely burned, it was feared he must have lost it, and it was only saved by the skill of the surgeon.

To make the circumstance more plain to unmilitary

readers, I shall state the duties of gunners in firing:—At all garrison guns, No. 1. sponges. No. 2. loads and rams home with No. 1. the odd numbers being always on the right of the gun, and the even on the left; No. 5 serves the vent, and No. 6. fires. In field pieces No. 7 spunges, No. 8 loads and rams home with No. 7. No. 9. serves the vent and No. 10 fires. No. 1. does not begin to spunge intil he sees the vent served; if he sees any remissness, he is allowed to strike or daub No. 5. with the spunge, which he dare not resent, No. 1. receiving credit for his activity. If the gun goes off in loading, the thumb is witness whether he did his duty or not, if it is burned he receives praise, if it is not he is punished. The thumb is sometimes so severely injured, that amputation is necessary.

ALEXANDER ALEXANDER

Domestic details of a soldier in the 1840's (India)

Pay and Stoppages

BEFORE I conclude my narrative I will give you in detail how the soldiers of the Old Bengal Horse Artillery were paid, fed, and clothed, just to shew the vast difference between them and the soldiers of the present day; the condition of the latter is better known to the reader, perhaps, than to the writer.

The pay of the gunner was..		Rs. 14. 6. 8.
Monthly stoppages		
Extra messing and servants	Rs. 7. 3. 0.	
2 drams of rum per day ..	3. 3. 8.	
		10. 6. 8.
Balance, all told		Rs. 4. 0. 0.

Rations per Day

Bread 1 lb; beef 1 lb; in the summer and 1½ lb. in the winter, a pinch of dirty salt, and 3 lbs all told of fire-wood.

Clothing and stoppages for same

1 Dress jacket, biennially, of the very worst description of

blue cloth, trimmed with yellow braid, with 99 brass buttons, scarlet cuffs and collar; 1 pair of coarse Oxford mixture overalls, with a single yellow stripe down the sides, biennially.
1 pair of buck-skin breeches, or pantaloons, of good quality biennially.
1 pair long boots (or Rs. 5 instead) annually.
1 pair jack spurs (steel) once for all.
1 pair white leather gloves, annually.
1 cloak (more like an overcoat) of coarse blue cloth, triennially.
1 brass helmet, triennially, with a leopard skin turban and a long red horse-hair mane flowing down the back: all but the helmet to be paid for!
1 silk girdle (yellow and red stripes) by paying for the same.
1 stable jacket, cap, a pair of Wellington boots and a pair of brass spurs, all to be paid for.

Half mountings for alteration of clothing Annually	Rs. 1. 0 0
Placed under stoppages for fitting the clothing	Rs. 10. 0. 0.
Stable jacket, cap, boots and spurs ..	Rs. 15. 0. 0.
A summer kit	Rs. 25. 0. 0.
Total ..	Rs. 50. 0. 0.

Besides the above stoppages a recruit on joining his troop was made to pay his share toward mess tables, forms, mess utensils, copper boilers, and provide himself with a cot and box: I leave you to guess how long a recruit was under stoppages, having only Rs. 4 of a monthly balance to pay off his debts.

The luxury of a punkah in barracks was not known in those days.

Bedding
A coarse chintz quilt, with about 3 lbs of cotton stuffed into it, was issued annually, and before the quilt was in use a month the cotton got lodged all at one end of it.

I will further inform my readers, that on the line of march all soldiers were placed under stoppages for the carriage of their bedding, at the rate of one camel to every eight men, which amounted to Rs. 8., per month between the eight men, and the marching and campaigning in those days generally lasted for a lengthened period, there being no railways in India; and still, on the whole, the 'Old Bengals' were a happy and contented race of beings. After all their shortcomings, they were full of life and spirit, and were always ready when required.

BANCROFT

Early days in the Army, 1843

THAT afternoon we commenced drill for the first time, which we got on pretty well with. Many were the schemes laid to get me off, to spend my money and pawn my watch; but I resisted them all. I was not liked among that sort of men because I would not join in with them. Being in the colour-sergeant's room, he had marked me, and saw that I resisted all. He took me under his own care, and very kind he was. He took my clothes which I had come up in, and put them away; and if I did not wish to sell them, he said, I might send them home. So as I could not get one half their value, I sent them home to my brothers.

I found our rations very scant. I could have done with as much more very well; but in a short time I could do very comfortably with them, and with what little I could buy, and I never was without a pound in my pocket. I soon got on with my drill, and had my clothes altered to fit me. I now began to be altogether very content, and even proud when I walked out. I bought an extra kit, so as to always have one clean and neat to show at kit inspection.

One day, while standing on parade, the colonel was inspecting all the recruits; he was finding great fault as he came along the ranks, but when he came to me he took my cap off my head, and said he wanted to see them all like *that*, and that all should take a pattern by me for all my things. Another day at kit inspection, some time after, the officer was finding fault with some of the kits; but when he came to mine, he told them he wanted to see them all like it. One old soldier, who felt rather nettled about it, spoke up and said, 'it was always likely to look well; for everything was nearly new.' The officer said, 'But they are clean, and laid out in good order.' I would have rather the officer had not said anything, for it made some of the old soldiers very surly with me; though others would give me good advice, and would show me how to do anything. I gave them a bit of tobacco, or a pint of ale now and then. Altogether I got on very well; for if I had enemies I had friends. I was dismissed from drill in three months, and was sent from Salford barracks to join my company at Tibb-street, and a good character was sent from Captain Baines to my captain (Robyns) by the corporal who took me to my company. I now commenced my duty as a soldier, and I was very contented.

At this time Ireland was in a very disturbed state. On the 6th of June, 1844, we had the route for Ireland. We went by train to Liverpool. There were six companies of us. On the morning of the 8th, we went on board the *Rhadamanthus* steamship and set sail for Dublin. We did not land till about 10 o'clock on the 9th, at Kingstown. We then went by railway to Dublin, and then marched to Richmond barracks, where we were quartered.

I liked Ireland very well; but our duty was hard. We had many field-days in Phoenix Park. While lying at these barracks, one day in March, two men asked the captain to let them go on furlough; but to one he said, 'I cannot recommend you, for you have not been long out of gaol;' and to the other, 'you have not been back from desertion long, so I cannot recommend you'. We were on parade, and he came to me, and said,' Ryder, fall out; you have never been on furlough, have you?' I said, 'No.' The captain then told me to get my recommendation made out, and he would sign it; but he did not wait for me to get it made out, as he did it himself.

Now, if any one had told me that I should have gone on furlough, an hour before, I could not have believed it; for I had never thought of such a thing, as I had only been twelve months a soldier, and only the day before I had sent a letter home to say that I should ask next year for a furlough, not having been long enough yet to get one. I had my furlough signed by the Colonel by 4 o'clock, for six weeks; in fact from the 14th of February to the third of April, 1845.

I set sail that night at ten o'clock from Dublin to Liverpool, and the day but one after I was at home at Twyford. It was dark when I got home; I opened the door, and went in, to the no small surprise of my father and mother. My poor old mother (as soon as she saw me) fell down on the floor as if she had been shot; and I thought the poor old creature would have died, for she was a long time before she came round. I passed the first part of my time very well, but during the latter I was very unsettled; I was tired of being about, doing nothing. So I was glad when the time came for me to return, and I bade my friends farewell.

RYDER

Enlistment, 1853: destination, 1854, Balaclava

I FIRST joined the army in June, 1853, enlisting into the 17th foot regiment, at Taunton, in Somersetshire, from there being sent to the Royal Barracks, Dublin, where the first efforts to make a soldier of me were undertaken. After learning my drill at Dublin, I was drafted to Templemore, and afterwards from there to Cork, again leaving Cork in May, 1854, and sailing for Gibraltar, our regiment having to relieve the 55th foot, this regiment then proceeding to the 'front'. After a few months stay at Gibraltar, our orders also came to leave for the 'front' and we arrived at Balaclava in November, 1854, where we pitched our tents, having to camp there for some time. And then began our experience of the soldier's life whilst on campaign, the weeding out of the weaklings commencing in real earnest—in our tent alone we were reduced from 19 down to eight in the first three months—and this, not by the hand of the enemy, but by those fell companions of active service—exhaustion and disease—for it was no unusual sight in the morning to see the dead bodies of two or three men taken out from the tents, the men having passed away during the night, owing to the ravages of exhaustion or dysentry, and no wonder at this, when the food we had to live upon is taken into consideration, for raw beef and pork were delicacies at this time, occasionally washed down with coffee—the coffee being previously prepared by us by being put into a piece of old biscuit bag and pounded. Chocolate also used to be sent out to us, this reaching us made up in shape something like a big flat cheese; this chocolate we found would burn, so breaking it into pieces and piling stones around, we then would set fire to it, place our canteen on the top and then wait for something warm; this being the only way we succeeded in doing so for the first few months.

PARSONS

Mr. Russell of The Times *and Private Wickins: Indian Mutiny*

MR. HENRY [*sic*] RUSSELL has been pleased to write declamatory letters from the inactivity of the troops at Nawabgunge. He hinted that the Brigadier was unfit to command the brigade, but the Commander-in-Chief gave the lie to this by appointing him Brigadier of the 2nd class at Byram Ghat in December. It so happens that there are men in India who are well acquainted with this newspaper writer and I myself prove to the falseness of his letters on more than one occasion. Russell is a man who is easily brought [*sic*] over, but such men as Brigadier Purnell care not for his declamatory letters. Neither does he wish to purchase his favour at the expense of dinners to this detested correspondent, for detested he is by every honest English soldier. If a colonel or a general wishes to figure in prominence in the home papers, let him make friends with Russell by entertaining him at dinners where there is plenty of wine and spirituous liquors and furnish him with camp equipage and carriage for the same when in the march, and he may soon expect to see his name in the Gazette with a C.B. attached.

Still what he calls inactivity I call harassing duty. Suppose that Russell had been a common soldier instead of a correspondent. I fancy that I see him fully accoutred, falling in on parade with sixty rounds of ammunition, his rifle and bayonet weighing 11 pounds and a half, his haversack with two days' provisions in it and lastly a water bottle slung by his side. Having imagined him to have fallen in on parade with his regt, he now marches off with it. The regt halts after having gone over 11 mile of ground knee-deep in dust and almost dying for a drop of water. He is next put on piquet, where he remains till the next morning, when he is permitted to take his belts off, while he washes his hands and face. And before he has been able to get a drop of coffee, the regt is again on the move. Fresh ground is taken up either to the right or left or maybe we go a mile farther, where there is a bridge and we are there to intercept them. Three or four days at a time are passed in this way. Yet all this marching out and in in all weather and at all hours of the night or day was, in Mr. Russell's opinion, three months' ease—we were lying inactive at Nawabgunge. Would he not have sung a different song if he was there to have gone through the above? I think he would.

WICKINS

The impact of active service on a soldier's outfit (Confederate Army)

THE men soon learned the inconvenience and danger of so much luggage, and, as they became more experienced, they vied with each other in reducing themselves to light-marching trim.

Experience soon demonstrated that boots were not agreeable on a long march. They were heavy and irksome, and when the heels were worn a little one-sided, the wearer would find his ankle twisted nearly out of joint by every unevenness of the road. When thoroughly wet, it was a laborious undertaking to get them off, and worse to get them on in time to answer the morning roll-call. And so, good, strong brogues, or brogans, with broad bottoms and big, flat heels, succeed the boots, and were found much more comfortable and agreeable, easier put on and off, and altogether the more sensible.

A short-waisted and single breasted jacket usurped the place of the long-tailed coat, and became universal. The enemy noticed this peculiarity, and called the Confederates 'gray jackets', which name was immediately transferred to those lively creatures which were the constant admirers and inseparable companions of the Boys in Gray and in Blue.

Caps were destined to hold out longer than some other uncomfortable things, but they finally yielded to the demands of comfort and common sense, and a good soft felt hat was worn instead. A man who has never been a soldier does not know, nor indeed can know, the amount of comfort there is in a good soft hat in camp, and how utterly useless is a 'soldier hat' as they are generally made. Why the Prussians, with all their experience, wear their heavy, unyielding helmets, and the French their little caps, is a mystery to a Confederate who has enjoyed the comfort of an old slouch.

Overcoats an inexperienced man would think an absolute necessity for men exposed to the rigors of a northern Virginia winter, but they grew scarcer and scarcer; they were found to be a great inconvenience. The men came to the conclusion that the trouble of carrying them on hot days outweighed the comfort of having them when the cold day arrived. Besides they found that life in the open air hardened them to such an extent that changes in the temperature were not felt to any degree. Some clung to their overcoats to the last, but the majority got tired lugging them around, and either discarded them altogether, or trusted to capturing one about the time it would be needed. Nearly every overcoat in the army in the latter years was one of Uncle Sam's captured from his boys.

The knapsack vanished early in the struggle. It was inconvenient to 'change' the underwear too often, and the disposition not to change grew, as the knapsack was found to gall the back and shoulders, and weary the man before half the march was accomplished. The better way was to dress out and out, and wear that outfit until the enemy's knapsacks, or the folks at home supplied a change. Certainly it did not pay to carry around clean clothes while waiting for the time to use them.

Very little washing was done, as a matter of course. Clothes once given up were parted with forever. There were good reasons for this: cold water would not cleanse them or destroy the vermin, and hot water was not always to be had. One blanket to each man was found to be as much as could be carried, and amply sufficient for the severest weather. This was carried generally by rolling it lengthwise, with the rubber cloth outside, tying the ends of the roll together and throwing the loop thus made over the left shoulder with the ends fastened together hanging under the right arm.

The haversack held its own, and was found practical and useful. It very seldom, however, contained rations, but was used to carry all the articles generally carried in the knapsack; of course the stock was small. Somehow or other, many men managed to do without the haversack, and carried absolutely nothing but what they wore and had in their pockets.

The infantry threw away their heavy cap boxes, and cartridge boxes, and carried their caps and cartridges in their pockets. Canteens were very useful at times, but they were as a general thing discarded. They were not much used to carry water, but were found useful when the men were driven to the necessity of foraging, for conveying buttermilk, cider, sorghum, etc., to camp. A good strong tin cup was found better than a canteen, as it was easier to fill at a well or spring, and was serviceable as a boiler for making coffee when the column halted for the night.

Revolvers were found to be about as useless and heavy lumber as a private soldier could carry, and early in the war were sent home to be used by the women and children in protecting themselves from insult and violence at the hands of the ruffians who prowled about the country shirking duty.

Strong cotton was adopted in place of flannel and merino, for two reasons; first, because easier to wash; and second, because the vermin did not propagate so rapidly in cotton as in wool. Common white cotton shirts and drawers proved the best that could be used by the private soldier.

Gloves to any but a mounted man were found useless, worse than useless. With the gloves on, it was impossible to handle an axe, buckle harness, load a musket, or handle a rammer at the piece. Wearing them was found to be simply a habit, and so, on the principle that the less luggage the less labor, they were discarded.

The camp-chest soon vanished. The brigadiers and major-generals, even, found them too troublesome, and soon they were left entirely to the quartermasters and commissaries.

One skillet and a couple of frying pans, a bag for flour or meal, another bag for salt, sugar and coffee, divided by a knot tied between, served the purpose well. The skillet passed from mess to mess. Each mess generally owned a frying pan, but often one served a company. The oil-cloth was found to be as good as the wooden tray for making up the dough. The water bucket held its own to the last!

Reduced to the minimum, the private soldier consisted of one man, one hat, one jacket, one shirt, one pair of pants, one pair of drawers, one pair of shoes, and one pair of socks. His baggage was one blanket, one rubber blanket, and one haversack. The haversack generally contained smoking tobacco and a pipe, and a small piece of soap, with temporary additions of apples, persimmons, blackberries, and such other commodities as he could pick up on the march.

The company property consisted of two or three skillets and frying pans, which were sometimes carried in the wagon, but oftener in the hands of the soldiers. The infantry-men generally preferred to stick the handle of the frying pan in the barrel of a musket, and so carry it.

The wagon trains were devoted entirely to the transportation of ammunition and commissary and quartermaster's stores which had not been issued. Rations which had become company property, and the baggage of the men, when they had any, was carried by the men themselves. If, as was sometimes the case, three days' rations were issued at one time and the troops ordered to cook them, and be prepared to march, they did cook them, and eat them if possible, so as to avoid the labor of carrying them. It was not such an undertaking either, to eat three days' rations in one, as frequently none had been issued for more than a day, and when issued were cut down one half.

The infantry found out that bayonets were not of much use, and did not hesitate to throw them, with the scabbard, away.

The artillerymen, who started out with heavy sabres hanging to their belts, stuck them up in the mud as they marched, and left them for the ordnance officers to pick up and turn over to the cavalry.

The cavalrymen found sabres very tiresome when swung to the belt, and adopted the plan of fastening them to the saddle on the left side, with the hilt in front and in reach of the hand. Finally sabres got very scarce, even among the cavalrymen, who relied more and more on their short rifles.

MCCARTHY

Two different attitudes towards military appearance: Victory march: Washington, D.C. 22 & 23 May, 1865

THERE was, evidently, a determination on the part of our officers that the army of the Potomac, which was to be reviewed on the first day, should make as fine an appearance as the army of General Sherman, which was to be reviewed on the following day. Many articles of new clothing were dealt out to the men; white gloves were provided for a large portion of them; we took great pains to have our uniforms, guns and equipments all in excellent order; and when we fell into line that morning, we were a fine a looking body of troops as were ever mustered upon the continent. It is impossible for me to describe that royal scene; the buildings were all draped in national colors; flags were flying in every direction; the sidewalks were packed with spectators; every square and yard was thronged with the vast multitude; the windows, balconies and roofs of buildings were filled and covered with human beings; the great stands erected were occupied by officers of high rank in both civil and military life; the tiers of seats were filled with thousands of school children, all dressed in white, who hurled hundreds of beautiful bouquets of flowers upon us as we passed; we marched with columns closed to half distance, with thirty men abreast; the artillery posted around Washington thundered forth a grand welcome: the bands all played the national airs; the people cheered until they were hoarse; banners waved and handkerchiefs fluttered. When a regimental color made its appearance in the procession, that was torn and tattered it was a signal for the most uproarious applause; and thus, through the day, the nation welcomed its defenders.

We marched through Pennsylvania avenue, and up to the edge of Georgetown, recrossed the Potomac river, and reached our camping ground early in the evening. It had been a very severe day's march, but I imagine it will always be remembered with much pleasure by every soldier who participated in it.

On the following day we had the pleasure of seeing Sherman's veterans as they marched along the same route. The contrast in the two armies was a most ludicrous one. As I have already stated, our officers had shown much anxiety to have us present a very soldierly appearance as we marched in review, and, much to our disgust, had insisted upon our drawing new caps and wearing white gloves: but Sherman's men went to the other extreme. One would have supposed, as he observed them, that they were making their renowned march through Georgia, instead of marching in review through the streets of Washington. Such an appearance as they made! There were evidently no attempts to keep their lines closed up and well-dressed as they advanced, but each man marched to suit his own convenience. Their uniforms were a cross between the regulation blue and the Southern gray. The men were sunburned, while their hair and beards were uncut and uncombed; they were clad in blue, gray, black and brown; huge slouched hats, black and gray, adorned their heads; their boots were covered with the mud they had brought up from Georgia; their guns were of all designs, from the Springfield rifle to a cavalry carbine, which each man carried as he pleased, whether it was at 'a shoulder,' or 'a trail,' or a 'right shoulder shift'; and thus ragged, dirty, and independently demoralized, that great army, whose wonderful campaigns had astonished the world, swept along the streets of the capital, whose chief honor they had so bravely defended. The great chieftain, Sherman, rode at its head, tall, spare, bronzed; grimly he rode, in plain uniform, as if utterly indifferent to all the honors a grateful country was pouring upon its honored son. The men chatted, laughed and cheered, just as they pleased, all along the route of their march. Our men enjoyed this all very much, and many of them muttered, 'Sherman is the man after all.' The two armies encamped near each other for several days, and soon a quite bitter rivalry sprang up between them. Sherman's men regarded the army of the Potomac with considerable contempt, and thought that, although we understood all about 'reviews' and 'dress parades' we knew nothing of great campaigns and desperate battles. On the other hand the army of the Potomac stoutly contended that if Sherman had encountered the army of General Lee, in Georgia, instead of a small force of 'bush-whackers,' his army would never have 'marched down to the sea.' These discussions soon became warm, and resulted in frequent skirmishes between the two armies.

GERRISH

A field-day mishap, c. *1870*

WE HAD many fine field days on the Curragh, and one of them I shall never forget. There were five regiments of cavalry engaged, double that number of infantry, and about forty field-guns. At the further end of the Curragh, towards Rath-bride, ran an isolated ridge, occupied by a skeleton enemy, and the plan of attack included the forcing of this position, by the infantry, which was carried out in gallant style, whilst the cavalry in two bodies, hovered on either flank, the left being composed of Lancers, and the right of Hussars and Dragoons.

Beyond the ridge the country fell into the level again, across which the beaten foe would have to retreat, and to make a nice finish to the day's operations it was arranged that a couple of squadrons from each body of cavalry should charge in pursuit. In order to accomplish this, they had to skirt the ends of the ridge, and then incline to right and left, until they met in the centre of the plain beyond, when they were to form in one line and charge.

My troop was amongst those selected for the right cavalry division and as the signal to go was given away we dashed, slashing and cutting the pursuing practice in fine style; and after rounding the end of the ridge made for the point of juncture in the plain beyond. But now ensued an altogether unexpected development for, as the two small bodies of cavalry approached each other, either through the excitement of the men, and their horses, or through the empetus of their gallop, instead of wheeling so as to come into line they followed a diagonal direction, until they rode 'bash' into one another, almost front to front at the point of contact. The Lancers lowered the points of their lances to avoid spitting our men, and some catching in the ground jerked the riders out of their saddles, whilst all of us came into violent collision. For a moment it seemed like a regular battle-field, many of the horses being bowled over, and others, with empty saddles, dashing madly about. As far as I myself was concerned the feeling I had when I saw a smash inevitable was 'Look out for Phil Garlie' (a well known military 'mind yourself' expression) and warding off a thrust from a gallant Lancer, he received the benefit of a whack from my sword, and the next moment I came full tilt against one of his comrades, and we both rolled on the turf.

This untoward business occurred through the men being allowed to go too fast, and getting out of hand, and was the fault of the officers. Such a finale to a field day in time of peace has, I fancy, been rarely seen. The general and all the infantry, who had crested the ridge, were looking at us, as well as thousands of spectators, and the former came galloping down with his staff, and when he arrived within shouting distance of our officers, it was about the only time in my life that I felt no ambition to be a captain. On taking note of the casualties it was found that about half-a-dozen of our men were injured by lance-thrusts and about the same number of Lancers from sword digs, whilst several of the horses had their shoulders put out from the effects of concussion. I am glad to be able to add that no ill-blood resulted from this nasty incident, which was just the sort of thing to start an inter-regimental feud; but the gallant Lancers and ourselves would not permit it to disturb our good fellowship, and we remained the best of friends.

MOLE

Cavalry dress, 1877

THE 'kit' with which I was issued free of cost consisted of a valise, stable-bag, hold-all (containing knife, fork, spoon, razor and comb, shaving, hair, lace, button, clothes and boot brushes), three baggage straps, tin of oil, tin of blacking, tin of brass paste, cloak cape, lance-cap and plume, two forage caps, tunic, jacket, overalls (trousers), pantaloons, canvas ducks, jack-boots and spurs. Wellington boots and spurs, ankle-boots, braces, three shirts, three pairs of socks, two pairs of pants, two towels, and a piece of soap. Finally, I was given a lance, sword, pistol, cartridge-case, cap-case, and numerous belts—an amount of armament that completely staggered me.

Uniform was of a very unpracticable kind, especially the undress part of it. This comprised skin-tight overalls, an equally tight 'shell jacket' cut off short above the hips, and a forage cap of about the size of a breakfast saucer, and kept in its place immediately above the right ear by a narrow chin-strap worn under the lower lip (never under the chin in the cavalry, except on mounted parades). There were no 'British-warms' or woollen 'jumpers' as to-day, and cloaks were not allowed to be worn when off duty without a regimental order to that effect. This order was never given except when the weather was very inclement. Later on the forage cap became a 'free issue', and was thoroughly disliked by everybody because of its ugly shape and abnormally large size as compared with the regimental pattern.

The first occasion on which it was worn by the regiment was at an inspection by the Duke of Cambridge at York in 1881, when an official hint was sent round the barrackrooms beforehand that it was to be put well on the top of the head, and generally made to appear as hideous as possible. Every one did his best, or rather his worst, to comply with the hint, and when the Duke—never in too good a temper early in the day—came on parade, the sight of the disfigured regiment nearly gave him a fit. It was alleged that he went back to the Horse Guards and wrote a furious letter to the War Office condemning the cap, but it remained the regulation article for some years afterwards, although the original pattern was still allowed to be worn off parade, and at the expense of the owner.

ROBERTSON

Cavalry horses and their temperaments

Before closing my last chapter I must say a word or two about horses, for most of my service was spent in looking after their welfare. They varied as much in disposition as the men did. Some were always gentle and docile; others, when they first joined, wild and nervous; but all, with very few exceptions, were amenable to kindness and eager to learn. Their colours gave a very fair idea of their constitutions or characteristics. Bright chestnuts and light bays were invariably high-spirited animals, but of nervous unsettled temperament and delicate constitution. Dark chestnuts and glossy blacks were hardy, and, as a rule, good tempered. Rich bays possessed great spirit, but, were at the same time, docile. Dark greys and iron greys were hardy and of good constitution, whilst light greys were just the reverse. The hardest and best working horses of all were roans, either strawberry or blue, which were always even-tempered, the easiest to train, and took kindly to everything. They were, in fact, just the opposite to a rusty black, which gains the palm for pigheadedness. Another curious indication of a horse's character could be gleaned from its white stockings. A horse with one white leg is a bad one; with two white legs, you may 'sell it to a friend;' with four white legs, you may trust it for a spell; but with three white legs, you may safely lay your life on it.

MOLE

Training programme: French Foreign Legion

I will give you, naturally translated, my company's weekly programme as it was hung up on the blackboard every Saturday:

Monday	6–7	Boxing
	7.30–10	Company drill
	12.	Military march.
Tuesday	6–7	Gymnastics.
	7.30–10	Skirmishing.

	11–12	Instruction in hygienic rules in the field
	1.	Work under the quartermaster's direction.
Wednesday	5.30–6.30	Boxing
	7	Company musters for bathing
	8–11.	Mending uniforms, preparation for inspection by the colonel.
Thursday	5.30	March to the shooting-range
	12–1	Instruction in first-aid to wounded
	1.15.	Work under the quartermaster's orders.
Friday	5	Military march
	1–2	Instruction in taking cover in flat ground
	2–3.	Work under the quartermaster's orders.
Saturday	5.30	Run over six kilometres
	8–11	Company drill
	12	Cleaning of barracks and quarters
	4.	Inspection of the barracks by the colonel. The men stand beside their beds in duck suit.

N.B. At the 11 o'clock muster each morning a part of the uniform to be named each day by the adjutant, has to be presented for inspection.

ROSEN

Uniform issue: French Foreign Legion

FROM there we were marched to the stores to draw our kits, and very good kits they were, too. First of all we were fitted with a pair of red trousers each. They were hardly a Pimlico fit even, for they contained enough material to make a pair and a half as trousers are worn in the British army, but there was a lot of chopping and changing before every one was satisfied. Then came a double-breasted black tunic with red facings and green epaulettes with red fringe; a blue greatcoat or capote, which is made so that the skirts can be buttoned back to leave the thighs free, and is always worn when on the march, usually directly over the shirt; a blue undress blouse or frock; a red kepi with the Legion's badge, a seven flamed grenade, in brass; two white canvas fatigue suits; two pairs of shoes, with the exact fitting of which great care was taken; a pair of black leather gaiters; two pairs of linen spats, such as are worn by our Highland regiments; shirts, towels, drawers; a knapsack very much like the pattern discarded in the British army forty years ago; a bag containing cleaning materials; and, lastly, a blue woollen cumberbund to wind round the waist. This last is a most sensible article to provide for men who have to soldier in hot climates, for it does away with the necessity of wearing a cholera belt, and the support it gives to the back is a great comfort when marching. British soldiers serving in India and in Egypt often wear something of the sort, but the Government does not provide it.

Now what articles of an English soldier's kit are missing from the above list? Why, socks. They don't wear socks in the Legion. Some wear pieces of linen—called chausettes Russes, or Russian socks—wrapped round their feet, but the majority wear nothing at all between the bare feet and the leather.

When the kits had been issued we were told that there was an allowance of seventeen centimes a day, about a penny three-farthings, for the upkeep of underclothing and white suits, and that anything left of this allowance at the end of a quarter would be paid in cash after a reserve of thirty francs had been accumulated. There were very few legionaries who got any cash income from this source, but a few very careful men did manage to draw four or five shillings a quarter.

We were now allotted to our barrack-rooms and told to change into our drill suits at once and bring our civilian clothes to the company office when we had done so.

The barrack-room we were sent to was a large one containing thirty beds, but there was nobody in it when we entered, the inhabitants being out at drill.

All the occupied beds had a card above them bearing the owner's rank, name and regimental number, with his kit neatly folded on the shelf, and the corporal who accompanied us told us to make ourselves at home on any of the beds not having these signs of being already bespoken.

When we had got into our white suits we took our plain clothes in our arms and went over to the company office together.

'Would you like me to sell your clothes for you?' asked the sergeant-major. 'I shall get a better price than you would, perhaps.'

I replied that I would be glad to give the clothes to any one who would take them off my hands, and Petrovski echoed me. We were not sacrificing much, for civilian clothes fetch next to nothing at Sidi-bel-Abbes, and ours, though of the best, would probably not have fetched more than five shillings.

After orders we recruits were taken over to the company stores again to receive our rifles, bayonets and accoutrements. We were told to spend the afternoon in getting those in good order, in readiness for a start at drill next morning; and the afternoon was not too long for the job, for my things, at any rate, appeared to have been in stores for some time and were sadly out of order.

There is no pipeclay in the Legion. All the belts and straps are of black leather, like those worn by our rifle regiments, and the getting them up is a slow and painful process, every part having to be heel-balled until it is as evenly polished as the heel of a new boot. Mine gave me a great deal of trouble, as I had never done anything of the sort before, and had declined Swartz's offer to do it for me. I am afraid that when I laid the task aside as having been done satisfactorily my belts compared very unfavourably with those of the old soldiers, but the officers and non-commissioned officers are not hypercritical with recruits, and I soon got into the way of shining them so that they looked as well as anybody's. The Gras rifle, though it was very dirty and neglected, gave me no trouble at all, as I already knew pretty nearly all there was to know about firearms, and the way I set about cleaning it elicited commendation from the corporal.

MARTYN

Regimental pride: a Highland bandsman and bayonet fighter

In 1893 we moved to Tipperary and in '95 we came to Aldershot, where we were to undergo strict training for foreign service. During this time I joined the band and was given a bassoon to learn to play, which I may say I picked up fairly quickly. When Queen Victoria visited Aldershot on her periodical inspections, she always liked the Highland Regimental Bands to play to her during the evenings while staying there. I remember one evening when we were playing, I was so very close to her that I could have put my hand through the open window and touched her as we were formed in a half-circle, and I was at the end of the half-circle and very close to the window. Prince Henry of Battenberg was very solicitous of our comfort and repeatedly came out to us to enquire of the Bandmaster if we were all right for refreshments.

During our training for Active Service we formed teams in order to learn proper bayonet fighting. My team was so successful that eight of us were struck off all duties for three months of intensive training under the pick of the Aldershot Gymnastic Staff.

Without boasting I am proud to say we beat all comers in the Aldershot Division, I myself winning second prize in individual bayonet fighting. Then we were sent to London to take part in the Annual Grand Military Tournament held in the Agricultural Hall, Islington.

Our training diet during this period was bread, meat, and one pint of beer per day; no pudding, potatoes, or soft stuff, and plenty of exercises in lunging, thrusting, backing, etc. I think we were also as quick as cats on our feet! When fighting cavalry we always tried to make the horses shy so that it would take the rider's attention from our bayonet for a moment during which we could thrust it home before he had time to recover.

On arriving in London we went to the Tournament and when we marched into the arena to fight in the semi-final for the army, there was Queen Victoria in the Royal Box with the Prince of Wales (later King Edward VII), Prince George and other Royal children standing around their grandmother, the Queen. We had the good fortune to beat the Grenadier Guards' team in the semi-final, and the next day we again marched into the arena to meet the Scots Guards for the Championship. The Royal Family were again present as on the day before and seemed keenly interested in this sport, which ended in a draw, being an equal number of winners and losers on each side, and the two Commanders had to fight for the winning points, the Scots Commander winning two points to our one. On returning to Aldershot we were made quite a fuss of for upholding our regiment (the Seaforths) and returning as second team in the British Army.

CORBETT

3

BARRACK LIFE

First steps in the Army, 1800

Now I began to drink the cup of bitterness. How different was my situation from what it had been! Forced from bed at five o'clock each morning, to get all things ready for drill; then drilled for three hours with the most unfeeling rigour, and often beat by the sergeant for the faults of others. I, who had never been crossed at home—I, who never knew fatigue, was now fainting under it. This I bore without a murmur, as I had looked to it in my engagement. My greatest sufferings were where I had not expected them.

I could not associate with the common soldiers; their habits made me shudder. I feared an oath—they never spoke without one: I could not drink—they loved liquor: They gamed—I knew nothing of play. Thus was I a solitary individual among hundreds. They lost no opportunity of teasing me; 'Saucy Tom' or 'The distressed Methodist' were the names they distinguished me by. I had no way of redress, until an event occurred, that gave me, against my will, an opportunity to prove that my spirit was above insult.

A recruit who had joined at the same time with myself, was particularly active in his endeavours to turn me into ridicule. One evening, when I was sitting in a side-window reading. Of an old newspaper he made a fool's cap, and unperceived by me, placed it upon my head. Fired at the insult,

I started up and knocked him down.—'Clear the room; a ring, a ring,—the Methodist is going to fight,' was vociferated from all sides. Repenting my haste, yet determined not to affront myself, I stood firm, and determined to do my utmost. My antagonist, stunned by the violence of the blow, and surprised at the spirit I displayed, rose slowly, and stood irresolute. I demanded an apology. He began to bluster and threaten, but I saw at once that he was afraid; and turning from him said, in a cool decided manner, 'If you dare again insult me I will chastise you as you deserve; you are beneath my anger.' I again sat down and resumed my reading, as if nothing had happened.

From this time I was no longer insulted; and I became much esteemed among my fellow-soldiers, who before despised me. Still, I could not associate with them. Their pleasures were repugnant to my feelings.

'71ST'

Barracks and training before the Crimean War

ARRIVED at Rochester, I remained at a public-house, agreeably to the instructions of the old staff-sergeant, until he came up with the other recruits, when we proceeded together to the barracks, and being there duly handed over by him to the proper authorities, were marched to the Receiving house. The number of recruits already there was upwards of two hundred, the larger part of whom were in no way distinguished for orderly conduct, while many of them had vice and ruffianism stamped indelibly on their faces.

It was, however, only natural to expect that characters of this description should be met with in a place where the very offscourings of several of the principal cities of the United Kingdom were congregated. Rogues and scoundrels were jumbled together en masse; and these, despite their relationship, agreed in no one respect, save in fleecing their more simple companions, by means of cards, pitch and toss etc., to the utmost extent of their knavish abilities, and in utter contempt of Her Majesty's regulations touching gambling. They likewise indulged without restraint in the use of the most foul and abominable language, and I certainly felt considerable pain of mind as I asked myself, are these to be my future companions? Hard fare I little cared for, and it matters not to me how rough my bed might be; privations of this nature are inseparable from a soldier's lot; but the prospect of mingling for any lengthened period with some of the individuals I saw in the Receiving house, was, I must acknowledge, excessively disheartening. I was not then aware what a surprising alteration for the better in many respects, subjection to a strict and uniform discipline would effect in them in a little time.

All recruits on their first arrival at Chatham, are sent to the Receiving house; hence its name; and are obliged to remain there until they pass the garrison doctor, and are finally approved of by the lieutenant-colonel of the provisional battalion; when they receive their uniforms, and are sent to their several depots. The sleeping accommodations in this place were any thing but of the best; no one being allowed sheets, because they are said to be retentive of a certain contagious disease, of a most disagreeable though not very dangerous character; and as to the beds, they were, as one of my companions facetiously expressed it, like the continent of Asia, thickly peopled with black, brown and white inhabitants. The origin and perpetuation of this nuisance, may in part be ascribed to the uncleanly habits of some prior to enlistment.

Into this den of living abominations was I thrust with my companions, and half an hour might have subsequently elapsed, when a huge Yorkshire fellow made his appearance, who had been installed as hair-cutter or rather hair-shearer to the establishment; and who, ex officio, was armed with an enormous pair of scissors, which reminded me of the implement used by farmers for clipping hedges. As I chanced at the time to be best at hand this worthy of the staff at once commenced operations on my head; constructing his parallels and approaches towards its vertex with such accuracy and expedition, that in a few moments I was in a similar situation to one most coveted in the halcyon days of boyhood, when I might be pommeled by my school-fellows, without mercy, and be in no danger of having my hair pulled by an antagonist, a punishment, by the by, I dreaded as much as ever blacky did a kick in the skin. This close hair-cutting system, it is said, has been adopted in order that recruits may, like barber's shops, be known by their bare poles, should they desert, or attempt to quit the barracks before being clothed in uniform.

As night approached, I began, in Yankee parlance, to calculate when I should stow myself away during the hours sacred to repose; for, fatigued as I was after a first voyage, to lie in any of the beds was a thing out of the question altogether. After due consideration of the matter, I was fain to betake me to the boards by way of a resting place; and even thus would soon have been wrapt in the arms of the god of dreams, but for the other denizens of the attic, among whom a row extraordinary arose, owing to there not being a sufficiency of bed clothes for the whole, and a system of monopoly having been adopted in consequence, by the stronger recruits.

This conduct was not quietly submitted to by the others, and blankets and quilts were pulled about in a way highly detrimental to government property; the crises meantime approaching when black eyes and bloody noses might in due course be expected. But while the fray was still in embryo, the entrance of the superintending corporal, the sole monarch of the place, put an end to all further squabbling: and as we chanced to have got into a wrong room, he ordered us all to decamp forthwith. Fortunately for me, a sergeant of my corps now appeared and directed us of the 13th to follow him to the quarters of our depot. The Receiving house being, it seemed, too full to admit of our stay. My new quarters I found to be very heaven, compared with the place I had left. Clean sheets were given to me, and a soldier of the room in which I was located, good-naturedly making down my bed, I trundled into it; and being heartily tired, was soon wrapt in sleep.

The sun streamed broad and bright through a window at the head of my cot when I awoke on the ensuing morning, greatly refreshed by a night of unbroken slumber; and after I had breakfasted upon tommy (soldier's term for brown bread) and insipid coffee, the latter being served up in tin dishes, I fell in with a number of other recruits, and was marched to the hospital, to be inspected by the principal surgeon. This is a most trying ordeal to such as may have symptoms of a cutaneous disease. As a necessary measure, they are at once incarcerated in a ward specially appropriated for persons having disorders of this description; and where a residence, for any period, however short, is by no means agreeable. But it was not my bad fortune to be consigned to this ward, or to make the acquaintance of its guardian angel, generally known by the sobriquet of Jack Skilly, a title given in consequence of his being the dispenser of skilly (the military name for gruel) to patients affected with diseases of the skin. What his original appellation was, I cannot say; and I am confident it would be necessary to refer to the muster-roll of his depot, for accurate information on this head.

I returned to my barrack-room in undress uniform; so that I was now to all intents and purposes a soldier. On the ensuing morning I was sent to drill, with the club or awkward squad; our instructor being a corporal lately returned from India, who was as cross as possible at having been ordered to teach us; considering that more forward recruits should have been placed under his care. Owing to this circumstance nothing we did pleased him; and apart from having no taste for club winding, I was glad to make my escape in a few days out of his squad, and to get into one more advanced. As I was attentive, I soon became a sort of favourite with my instructor, who placed me on the right flank of his division, which was the post of honour, and indeed, owing to the kindness of this man, and his never using abusive language like others, my time during drill passed tolerably pleasant, and I became somewhat reconciled to my new mode of life.

Probably some reader may wish to know the daily routine of my duties and amusements at this period. I rose at five o'clock in the morning, and made up my bed; which occupied at the least a quarter of an hour, and was rather a troublesome job. I then made my toilet, and at six turned out for drill, from which we were dismissed at a quarter to eight, when we breakfasted. From ten till twelve we were again at drill; had dinner at one, in the shape of potatoes and meat, both usually of the most wretched quality; and at two fell in for another drill, which terminated at four; after which hour my time was at my own disposal until tattoo, provided I was not order on piquet. During this period of leisure, I generally amused myself by strolling in the vicinity of the garrison (no soldier being permitted to go to a greater distance than one mile) or by reading; the owner of a circulating library in Rochester having consented to trust me with his volumes on my depositing a small sum in his hands. There was no garrison library then, which must be a matter of surprise to every one who knows of what benefit such institutions are to the soldier, who, having thus the means of amusement and instruction within his reach, is in many instances altogether prevented from going to the beer-shop to pass his leisure time.

MACMULLEN

Gibraltar during the Crimean War

Manuscript by Gunner William Whitehead, R.A. (see *Journal of the Society for Army Historical Research*, Vol. XL, pp. 214–17.)

THE Rock rises perpendicularly to the height of 1400 feet, at the bottom of which, and on the western side, a rough road is formed, protected by strong barrier gates, which forms the only means of entrance to Gibraltar from the Spanish lines. The road itself is hewn out of the solid rock, and defended by strong guards, who would immediately close the gates in the event of an alarm from the outlying guards and sentries. All along the face of this perpendicular acclivity looking towards the neutral ground, and reaching even to the very summit subterraneous passages are hewn out of the solid rock, and holes capable of allowing the mussle of a gun to protrude, are cut out distances of six or seven yards apart. These, together with the extensive works, built in solid masonry, at the base, and fortified with guns of vast calibre, render this part of the rock the most formidable place in Gibraltar, to which the Spaniards give the name 'la bocoa fuego' or the mouth of fire. The caverns, which are hewn out of the rock, are very damp and consequently, very disagreeable, the more so when the guns are fired, as they are then filled with smoke, so that it is rather difficult to breathe. On the very summit of this position of the rock, is erected a mortar battery. On this part of the rock alone, viz. the north front, not less than about three hundred guns are mounted, which you will, I dare say, guess must be tier over tier, as the whole extent is only about a mile.

About a quarter of a mile from this entrance, the market place of Gibraltar is situated. It is the form of a square, and surrounded with batteries, the mussels of the guns frowning over the peaceable and animated mass of human beings, transacting their respective business underneath, while reared on the summit of a lofty flag-staff, placed on an elevated position of the battery, the flaunting flag of Britain is gaily seen waving gloriously in the breeze, from sunrise to sun-set.

In the market the scene is indeed most busy, and animated, during the hours in which it is open. Each commodity has its own portion of the square assigned to it. On one side is arranged, in a row line, poultry of all descriptions, confined in huge cages, while in front of the noisy bipeds large creels of eggs patiently await a purchaser. These commodities are exported from Barbary in Africa, and are sold by the Moors, dressed in the pictureesque garb of that country. A good size hen fetching about five reals and half (or one shilling and sixpence). Eggs 6d per dozen. In another side meat of all descriptions may be seen exposed for sale at about the same prices which are realized at home. A third side is devoted solely to the disposal of vegetables, which are very abundant and in general, of a different description to what are sold at home. Pumpkins, jams, olives, tomatoes etc., form the most common articles of food, while potatoes, cabbage, and other homely vegetables are rare, and of course, sold at high prices. Potatoes are now selling at 8d per stone, which may be reckoned the lowest rates, as they are in the greatest plenty at present. They are, in general, brought from Spain along with the vegetables.

On the fourth side, nothing but fruit is exhibited, and in such profusion, and variety, that it perfectly dazzles the eye of a stranger. Fruits of which we have only read hitherto are displayed here in the greatest abundance. Heaps of oranges, lemons, prickly pears, (a most delicious and cheap fruit), grapes, pomigranites, figs, apricots, almonds, dates, quinces are sold at remarkably cheap rates, while raisons, figs, almonds, currants and dates, and all other dried fruits are sold at merely nominal prices. All the fruit are the productions of Spain, and are therefore sold by the tawny complexioned natives of that sickly Country.

Close by the market but without the line wall and approached by a drawbridge of considerable width, a spacious wharf is built in the shape of a semi-circle, which is the only place at which passengers, goods etc., can be landed for Gibraltar. All round this wharf which goes by the name of Waterport, sentries are posted, who in conjunction with the Police scrutinize every person who passes the barrier of this great fortress.

All along the sea line a lofty wall of solid masonry, in some places upward of 100 feet thick, provided with, where necessary, drawbridges and port cullises, affords ingress and egress, but immediately on the firing of the first evening gun, all gates, drawbridges and barriers, are closed until morning gun arouses the lethargic inhabitants from their slumber. This wall extends all around the face of the rock, or western side, fronting the bay.

On its top, at intervals of a few yards, ordinance of a heavy nature may be seen frowning menacingly along its entire extent, which irrespective of the batteries erected in the background, effectively protect the town, from any assault of an enemy. Exactly underneath, or more correctly speaking, within these masonry walls appartments or hollows, in the structure, are formed which constitute the magazines, storehouses, and barracks of the soldiery stationed here. They are consequently bomb-proof, and would afford very secure shelter in the event of a bombardment, but in time of peace, during the rainy season, are very damp and uncomfortable, and unprovided with windows or any place in which we could make a fire, except portions which are appropriated as cookhouses. In fact, they have to all appearances, the resemblance of huge vaults, dark lofty echoing chambers, communicating by means of arches with one another, and provided with little or no ventilation, and very insufficient light. You may judge therefore, how dismally we are situated when I inform you that each of these chambers contains from 30 to 40 men, and there being no light to speak of afforded, but by means of the door, together with the fact of incessant rain for weeks at a time, and the supply of oil, wherewith to give artificial light being very scanty, is it to be wondered at that drunkeness prevails so much among the troops in Gibraltar, or that we are glad to escape from the filthy atmosphere of our barrack rooms, should congreet [*sic*] in masses around the tables of the numerous wine houses, and there seek amid the joyous songs and hearty jests of our own countrymen, to pass the time until the trumpet summons us back to our dismal abode.

So much for the winter season of the year. But in the summer, when even the very air is painfully oppressive how much more nauseous and sickening must the sensation be when the accumulated exhalations of about 40 individuals, some of whom, perhaps overcome with liquor, pollute the already tainted air they breathe, thus explaining the reason that the British Army requires to be recruited so frequently and accounting for the fact that out of the numerous re-inforcements added from time to time to its ranks very few indeed survive 21 years of such a polluted existence as the British Soldier is doomed from these causes to undergo.

Ah! would in our youth we had been aware of the flattery and deceit so conspicuous in our enlistment, contrasting as it does so finely with the hardships and sorrows of a soldier's life. The red and blue coat would have lost its charms and failed to beguile the heart of those who had now sworn with their lives to keep up the pomp, parades and circumstance of war.

These barracks take their name from the battery overhead, the artillery occupying only a few rooms here and there so as to divide the men to the guns and render the place as effectually and promptly manned as possible: Junpez Bastion Barracks, Orange Bastion Barracks, etc., those being the names of the batteries forming the roofs of our houses or barracks.

Between the line wall which I have thus attempted to describe and the top of the rock, the town of Gibraltar rises gradually row upon row, upon the face of the acclivity to the height of 600 feet. And the houses being all whitewashed in accordance with the sanitary arrangements of the Governor, and for the most part are built in the oriental style having a flat roof, their situation and aspect enables a spectator to obtain view of the harbour. The streets are very irregular in formation and badly paved, many of them inclining to a gutter in the centre, which during the rainy season swells to a stream and carries every particle of filth along with it to the ocean. Others of them are no more nor less than a succession of steps of a yard or two in width. It is to be considered in my opinion, a great cause of blessing that the rain descends in such torrents as it does, as from the great population and truly characteristic filthyness of the Spaniards much cause of plague and pestilence is removed for to such an extent does this physical indolence prevail that it is not an uncommon occurence on a warm day to see numbers of the filthy people basking in the sun and removing the venom [*sic*: 'vermin'?] from each others persons, it being considered an agreeable pastime. But how can their condition be otherwise when their abodes are literally swarming with creeping things of all descriptions, from the huge tarantula to the diminutive louse?

The shops are in some degree worthy of notice. The most flourishing of these establishments are situated in the main street, which is in point of fact the only thoroughfare in Gibraltar which can at all lay claim to respectability. Some of the mercantile houses therein situated assume the appearance of the respectable and thriving shops of any small town at home, but they are few, while the greater portions are but miserable attempts to dispose of worthless goods at exhorbitant prices, no taste whatever being displayed in the decoration of their windows or professional neatness and activity in serving a customer which we justly admire in merry England. Not even a signboard above their doors, some of these merchants if they wish to intimate to the passers-by that sugar, soap, tobacco, pipes, blacking, etc, is on sale at their establishments attach a parcel of sugar, a bit of soap, a pipe and a cake of bleaching each to a piece of string and hang these articles above and outside the door where they remain dangling in the air throughout the day to the annoyance of customers entering the shops and the infinite amusements of those to whom such sights are not familiar. Or if the landlord of a wine house wishes to attract people to his cellars to taste his wines and spirits he causes to be daubed over his door a scrawl which if a spider had fallen into a bottle of ink and then crawled over the stone, would have left a track almost as legible.

There has however of late been a considerable improvement in civilization among the community of this city which may be attributed to the growing advancement of the age, the rapidity of intercourse by the aid of steam with more enlightened countries such as England and France and by the indefatigable exhertions of their Governor, Sir James Ferguson, in promoting the advancement of civilization and cultivating the progress of improvement both in a useful and ornamental point of view, the latest of which, and most beneficial to the community at large, has been the introduction of gas throughout Gibraltar and the erection of public baths and washhouses, in order to mitigate the scanty supply of fresh water which has hitherto been so difficult of access and at the same time productive of so salutory an effect on the condition of the poorer classes of the inhabitants.

[After describing the rain-water-filled tanks, each guarded by a sentry, and accessible only from morning gunfire to 12 o'clock noon, and the selling for three half-pence a barrel of this rain water, Whitehead goes on:] The troops are supplied with the same description of fluid, there not being a drop of spring water on the rock, the only difference being that a certain individual, called the contractor, agrees to bring in carts a regulated quantity daily to the barracks for a stated sum of money paid him by government. Each man is allowed about two gallons per day, to serve all purposes such as cooking, washing, etc. You may therefore perceive how utterly dependent we are upon the clouds for the great and universal boon of fresh water, so providently accorded to the whole of creation by the divine giver of all good, and although it is said of Gibraltar in speaking of its likelihood to resist the ravages of a siege that it is supplied with water and provisions to sustain a garrison for seven years and powder and shot to last for ever: yet I apprehend that in the event of the clouds retaining their moisture, the horrors of thirst would attack the defenders of this devoted fortress long ere seven years revolution of the sun had proclaimed the existence of the siege for such a lengthened period.

WHITEHEAD

Drill and housing at Aldershot in the 1870's

THE cavalry recruit was kept hard at work, riding-drill, stables, foot-drill, gymnastics, and school following each other in bewildering fashion from six in the morning till six in the evening, without any appreciable interval for rest. Riding-school was the terror of most recruits, few of whom had ever been across a horse. For some weeks no saddle was allowed, no stirrups, for some months, and the chief aim of the instructor, or 'rough-rider,' was not to give his pupil confidence but as many falls as possible. The 'rough-rider' deserved his name, for he was as rough with a young horse as with a young recruit. He seldom possessed a decent pair of hands, and his system of training a horse was of the break-down rather than the break-in type. These unintelligent methods have long since passed into oblivion.

Gymnastics, or physical exercises, were conducted on much the same lines. Every recruit was expected to do the same thing in an equally proficient way, no allowances being made for differences in ages, build, or general physical capacity.

A robust constitution was required in winter to withstand the cold and draughty stables and the biting winds which swept across the barrack square during foot-drill, where the shivering recruit would struggle to grasp the explanations of drill gabbled out by his instructor, and painfully endeavour to master the mysteries of the 'goose-step' and the art of drawing swords 'by numbers'. I succumbed twice during my first winter, once being in hospital for two months with rheumatic fever brought on by exposure.

When a man 'reported sick' he was marched at about nine o'clock in the morning to the medical inspection room of his regiment, and after waiting about in all weathers for an indefinite time was seen by a medical officer. If considered a case for admission he was given an aperient, whether he wanted it or not, in the shape of half-a-pint of vile-tasting liquid known as 'black-strap'. He was next marched off to hospital, which might be anything up to a mile or more away, and there he was interviewed by another doctor before being 'admitted' to hospital. Next he was told off to a ward, where he might hope to arrive about mid-day, after having been on the move for some three or four hours. In the afternoon he would put on his hospital clothing, give his own into store, and lie down to await the visit of the medical officer in charge of the ward on the following morning. He was then again examined, treatment was prescribed, and if all went well he received it during the afternoon, or some thirty hours after the first set out from his barrack-room.

Accidents and other special cases would be dealt with more or less immediately, but ordinary medical cases dawdled on in the manner I have described, greatly to the discomfort of the patient and sometimes at the risk of his life. There was no nursing service, at any rate in the hospitals I had the misfortune to visit. Nursing and dressing were the duty of the 'orderly' of the ward, and this individual was apt to regulate the amount of attention he gave to his patients by the amount of tips they gave to him.

Permission to be out of barracks after 'watch-setting'—half-past nine at night—was sparingly granted, and allnight passes were practically never given. The 'roll' was called at watch-setting, when every man not on leave had to answer his name, and to make sure that none went out afterwards one and sometimes two 'check' roll-calls were made by the orderly sergeant-major at uncertain hours during the night. Each orderly-sergeant handed in at watch-setting a statement showing the number of men sleeping in each of his troop rooms, and equipped with this the orderly sergeant-major, accompanied by the corporal of the guard, visited the rooms and counted the sleeping occupants. It was a favourite devise of absentees, before going out, to fold up their bed as in daytime, so that the visiting sergeant-major might perhaps not notice their absence; while others would try to deceive him by leaving a made-up dummy in their beds. 'Breaking-out of barracks' was the crime, and twenty-eight days confinement to barracks was usually the punishment, for this form of absence.

To 'break-out' of barracks was a simple matter at Aldershot, for although the gates at the end of them were kept locked after watch-setting, and had a high wall on either side, an unenclosed public road ran along the front which was accessible to everybody. This was not the case with all barracks, most of them being surrounded by high walls, topped with broken glass. When we were at Brighton, where the walls were of this kind, an amusing incident occurred in connection with a man who was trying to get back again after successfully breaking out. Not being able to scale the walls, he hit on the idea of returning in an officer's brougham, which was being brought back to barracks by a friendly coachman after depositing the officer and his wife at their house in the town. Unfortunately the military police sergeant looked inside the brougham before allowing it to leave the barrack gate, and the offender accordingly found himself in a worse predicament at orderly room next morning than if he had walked into barracks and surrendered.

Of all days of the week Sunday was the most hated—a sad confession to make, but none the less true. After morning stables there was a general rush, often with little or no time for breakfast, to turn out in 'full dress' for 'divine service'—attendance at which was compulsory. On return to barracks there was another scramble preparatory to the commanding officer's inspection of stables, horses, saddlery, and barrack-rooms. From early morning till half-past one in the afternoon there was more work to be done, more grumbling and swearing, and more fault-finding than on any other day, all of which could have been avoided had the inspection been carried out on a week-day. The reason they were made on Sunday was certainly not because there was no time for them on other days. The real reason probably was that Sunday was the most convenient day for the officers, as it left them greater leisure to follow their social and sporting pursuits during the week. It was only natural that the men should resent being hustled about and made to do unnecessary work on the one day of the week observed by everybody else in the country as a day of rest.

Divine service was not held for all denominations at the same time, but at hours suitable to local facilities. It might be at any time between eight o'clock and noon, and therefore it was not uncommon for men, on moving to a new station, to ask to change their religion if by so doing they would attend church or chapel at such an hour as would enable them to escape from the detested inspections. Many amusing stories are told about these changes, one being of a man who asked his sergeant-major to enter him in the books as belonging to the 'Plymouth Brethren'. He was promptly told that no such religion was officially recognized, and that he would be put down as a Roman Catholic!

On Christmas Day 1877, I was detailed for my first military 'duty' that of stable-guard or looking after the troop-horses out of stable-hours. The custom was to employ the most recently joined recruits on this particular day, so that the old soldiers might be free to make the most of their Christmas dinner, which was provided by the officer commanding the troop, and included a variety of eatables never seen on any other day, as well as a liberal supply of beer. The casks containing the beer were brought some time before to the barrack-room where the dinner was to be held, and were placed under charge of a man who could be depended upon to see that they were not broached before the appointed hour. Had this happened—as it sometimes did—rather awkward incidents might have occurred when the officers visited the room just previous to the dinner to wish the men a merry Christmas and to receive similar wishes in return. If any individual did, by some means or other contrive to start his festivities too early, efforts were made to keep him in the background until the officers had left.

It was the practice to see that all members of the troop who were absent on duty should be specially well cared for, and in my case the dinner brought to the stable consisted of a huge plateful of miscellaneous food—beef, goose, ham, vegetables, plum-pudding, blancmange—plus a basin of beer, a packet of tobacco, and a new clay pipe!

At night the horses were looked after by a 'night guard' which paraded about five or six o'clock in the evening and came off duty at reveille on the following morning. It was mainly composed of recruits and other men who were required to attend training or do other work during the day-time. The chief duties of a 'sentry' of the night guard were to perambulate outside the stables, tie up any horse that might get loose (some of the old troop-horses were extraordinarily clever at slipping their heads collars and finding their way to the corn-bin), see that the doors were kept closed, and, in the phraseology of the 'orders', 'call the corporal of the guard in the event of fire or other unusual occurrence.' The sentry was armed with either a sword or carbine (no ammunition) though what assistance he was supposed to derive therefrom in the performance of his duties no one ever understood.

The nights were sometimes intensely cold and always interminably long, although the two hours 'on' sentry were followed by four hours 'off', and to the tired recruit the bales of forage offered tempting resting-places. That way lay danger if not disaster, for once he succumbed to the temptation to sit down it was a hundred to one that he would fall asleep, and if he did he might wake up to find himself confronted by an officer or non-commissioned officer going the 'rounds', with the result that he would be made prisoner and tried by court-martial. The punishment for this crime was invariably two months' imprisonment, and although young soldiers must be made to realize their responsibilities when on sentry, a little more consideration in dealing with tired lads not yet out of their teens would not have been misplaced. I have known more than one lad ruined for life because of undue severity of punishment for a first offence.

Military training lagged far behind, notwithstanding the many lessons furnished by the Franco-German War of 1870, and was still mainly based on the system inherited from the Peninsula and Crimean campaigns. Pipe-clay, antiquated and useless forms of drill, blind obedience to orders, ramrod-like rigidity on parade, and similar time-honoured practices were the chief qualifications by which a regiment was judged. Very few officers had any ambition beyond regimental promotion. 'Squadron leader' was a name and not a reality, for beyond commanding it on parade this officer had no responsibility or duty of any kind connected with the squadron as such. In all other respects each of the two troops which then formed a squadron was a separate and independent unit, the troop commander being subordinate only to the regimental commanding officer. Once a week or so the latter held his 'field-day', when the regiment as a whole attended parade and spent the greater part of two or three hours in carrying out a series of complicated drill-book movements: equally good result could have been secured in half the time, and with half the expenditure of horse-flesh and strong language. For the remainder of the week training, as understood in those days, was the preserve of the adjutant, whose parades were attended only by those officers who were junior to him in rank, and by a comparatively small proportion of the men. For the drill of recruits on foot the adjutant was also responsible, and in riding drill the riding master was supreme. Troop officers had no responsibility for either one or the other.

As already mentioned, Lancer regiments carried sword, lance, and a muzzle-loading horse pistol, and about half-a-dozen men in each troop known as scouts or skirmishers, had a carbine as well. They had a very sketchy knowledge of the use of this weapon, and, like every one else, but a hazy idea of either scouting or skirmishing. Later, carbines were issued to all men, and the horse-pistols were withdrawn; but for some years musketry, was universally hated and deemed to be a degradation and a bore. In no case could it have been made of such value, since the annual allowance of ammunition was fixed at forty rounds a man, and thirty rounds of these were fired at distances between 500 and 800 yards.

Manœuvres as practised in more recent years were practically unknown, though there was a legend amongst the old soldiers that they had taken place at Cannock Chase some years before I joined. The nearest approach to them was the 'field-day' held, perhaps half-a-dozen times during the year, by the

Generals in command of the larger stations, or by the Commander-in-Chief, the Duke of Cambridge. The first one I attended was held on the ground at the back of the Staff College, the whole of the Aldershot garrison—about a division—taking part in it. I remember that towards the end of the battle—a field day always entailed a 'battle'—my squadron was ordered to charge a battalion of the opposing infantry. Down came our lances to the 'engage', the 'charge' was sounded, and off we went at full speed, regardless of everything except the desire to make a brave show worthy of our regimental predecessors who had delivered the immortal charge at Aliwal some thirty odd years before. The enemy received us in square, with fixed bayonets, front rank kneeling and rear rank standing, the orthodox method of dealing with a cavalry charge. Finding our opponents too strong—or for some other reason—the order was given, 'troops right-about-wheel', and so near were we that, in wheeling the outer flank was carried on to the infantry and one of the horses received a bayonet in his chest. Being too seriously wounded to live he was shot but in other respects we were congratulated on having accomplished a fine performance. No doubt it was magnificent, but it was not the way to fight against men armed with rifles.

These defective methods of training in general were due in a large measure to the system of voluntary enlistment, under which recruits were received in driblets throughout the year, and more especially perhaps to the fact that the four different arms were kept severely apart from each other. The cavalry training was the business of the Inspector-General of Cavalry at the Horse Guards, the local General having little or no say in the matter. Artillery were mainly stationed at Woolwich, and engineer units at Chatham, each having, like the cavalry, its own special General and staffs and its special representatives at the Horse Guards. Combined training of the different arms, without which it is nonsense to expect intelligent co-operation in war, was therefore impossible. There may have been, and probably were other obstacles in the way of improvement, but one would think that most of them could have been surmounted, given more impetus from the top. It was not forthcoming, and for this the Duke of Cambridge, Commander-in-Chief from 1856–1895 (thirty-nine years) must be held accountable. He was a good friend of the soldier and extremely popular with all ranks in the army, but he was extraordinarily conservative in his ideas on the training and education of brother officers and men. He seems to have believed, quite honestly, that the army as he had found it, created by such a master of war as the Duke of Wellington, must be the best for all time, and he had not realized the changes which had since taken place in the armies of Europe. I have been told that he once took the chair at a lecture given to officers of the Aldershot garrison on the subject of foreign cavalry, when he proved to be a veritable Balaam in commending the lecturer to the audience. 'Why should we want to know anything about foreign cavalry?' he asked. 'We have better cavalry of our own. I fear, gentlemen, that the army is in danger of becoming a mere debating society.'

Many of the younger generation of officers were fully alive to the fact that better organization, education, and training were necessary, the most notable amongst them being Lord Wolseley, the best-read soldier of his time. From 1882 onwards he was the moving spirit in the path of progress, and thanks to his energy and initiative, and to the support he received from Sir Evelyn Wood and other keen-sighted soldiers, apathy and idleness began to go out of fashion, and hard work became the rule; study was no longer considered to be 'bad form', but a duty and an essential step to advancement; hunting on six days of the week was no longer admitted to be the only training required by a cavalry leader; and in general the professional qualifications of our regimental officers began to reach a much higher standard. I shall refer to this matter again when describing my experiences at Aldershot some thirty years later.

Before leaving the subject of training, I may mention that once a year the non-commissioned officers and men of each troop had to compete between themselves for classification in the use of the sword and lance, the troop-winners then fighting off for the regimental prize. When first introduced, rather crude notions prevailed as to how the competition should be carried out, and it was the custom to place the two adversaries at opposite ends of the riding-school, give the order to attack, and then leave them to charge down on each other at full speed much in the same way as the picture-books represent the tournaments of centuries ago. With the single-stick used as a sword not much damage could be done; but with a stout ash pole nine feet in length representing the lance the case was different. For the rider and his horse to be ridden down or rolled over was a common occurrence, and it was seldom that one or more of the competitors was not carried off to hospital, especially if the competition happened to follow pay-day. This rough business had its value as it taught the men how to defend themselves; and incidentally it afforded a certain class of individual an opportunity for paying off old scores against non-commissioned officers against whom he had a grudge. To him it was a matter of indifference what the umpire's decision might be, provided he 'got one in' against the object of his resentment. When I became sergeant, and subsequently troop sergeant-major, I had occasionally to deal with attacks of this kind, but being careful at all times to keep fit in wind and limb by constant practice with foils and single-sticks, and by taking regular running exercise, I was capable of giving back quite as good as I received. My most successful year was, I think, 1886, when I was lucky enough to secure all the first prizes in the troop—sword, lance, and shooting—but pride had its usual fall (literally) when, as troop-winner, I fought for the regimental prize and, with my horse, was bundled head over heels by a better man.

ROBERTSON

Mortuary scare, Bangalore

THIS 'dead-house', as our men called it, was situated about a hundred yards from the hospital, being the last building on that side of the cantonments. It was a very lonely spot, hidden from view by a belt of dark trees, and further isolated by a wide nullah, or dry ravine, in which many cobras lurked. Whenever a body lay in the mortuary it was the custom to post a sentry there, with orders to knock against the door now and again with the butt end of his carbine in order to scare away the rats, bandicoots, and other vermin which infested the place. The post, both from its solitude and the nature of the duty, was shunned by everyone, and particularly by young soldiers, whose imaginations were worked upon by ghastly stories told them by older hands of what they had seen and heard when on sentry there.

One evening, when mounting guard, I found a sentry had to be furnished for the mortuary, and I accordingly told off one for the post. After watch-setting I went the rounds, and then returned to the main guard and sat down for an 'easy'. About mid-night I was suddenly startled by the cry of 'Sergeant of the guard,' and going out was told something was wrong up at the hospital, and the call had been passed for me. I made my way there as quickly as possible and found that the sentry stationed over the dead-house had deserted his post, and neither the threats of the corporal, nor the advice of his comrades, could induce him to return to it.

I asked the man, who was deadly pale, and trembling with nervous excitement, what was up; but all I could get from him was that there was 'something' in the dead-house, and it 'called to him like a voice from the tombs.' Ignoring his fears I pointed out to him that there were serious consequences for deserting his post, and the additional shame he would have to endure of being laughed at by the regiment. But he would not budge an inch. 'I can stand their laughing,' he observed, 'but I can't stand that,' jerking his thumb towards the direction of the dead-house. Then as I spoke sternly to him not to trifle over a serious matter, but return at once to his duty, or take the consequences, he took off his belt and throwing it on the floor, exclaimed, 'There! put me in the clink, Sergeant. I'll do two years sooner than go to that post again.'

There was nothing to do but to post another sentry, and I called for a volunteer. This put the men on their mettle, and a soldier of some years' standing responded, and accompanied by the corporal we set out for the dead-house. We walked along without speaking, for there was something uncanny and awe-inspiring in the task on which we were bent, and in the dark night and black shadows of the trees that surrounded the dreaded house where the dead man lay, and an involuntary shudder ran through me as I saw by the light of the waning moon, which was just rising, a large cobra glide across the path leading to the mortuary door. Around us reigned a silence still as death, broken once only by the weird howling of a pack of jackals on the plain beyond.

On reaching the dead-house we all halted, and I bent my head down to the keyhole to try and catch any sound within. But I heard nothing. I then made a circuit of the building, without finding anything to account for the sentry's scare. As I returned, the new man was popping a ball cartridge into his carbine. 'Man, ghost, or devil,' said he, in a grim voice, 'they'll have the benefit of this if they come any of their hanky-panky tricks on me,' and with that he came to attention at his post.

I was just turning to go back, when my eye caught sight of a grated window, probably intended for ventilation, in the side of the dead-house, and about eight feet from the ground, and the thought occurred to me to have a look into the place as the moon was shining full on to it. So calling to the corporal, I asked him to give me a lift up, the grating being a little beyond my reach, and with his assistance I got hold of the bars, and pulled myself up.

As my eyes reached the level of the aperture a sight met them which paralysed me. For there, within a few inches of me, and with the moon shining full upon it, was the white, scared face of the dead man, and his eyes staring into mine with a lack-lustre look. Then a low voice proceeded from his lips and I heard him ask, 'Chum, what's the time?'

I gave a yell and dropped to the ground and the next moment was panicking away, followed by the corporal and sentry, after the latter, either by accident or in his excitement, had fired off his carbine. But they never caught me and I was well ahead of them at the hospital guard-room, into which I dashed, to the consternation of the men, and throwing myself down upon a bench, panted to regain my breath.

In a few seconds the corporal and sentry had arrived, and everyone was crowding round us asking what was up. My first words were, 'My God, no wonder that poor fellow deserted his post.' Then turning to the corporal I said, 'Send for the key of the dead-house at once.'

It was soon brought, and everyone left the guard-room to accompany the hospital sergeant to the mortuary. The door was opened, and then it was all explained, for there lay the poor inmate in his shroud, doubled up on the stone just under the ventilator at which he had appeared to me.

It seems that the doctor had given him up that morning, and told the orderlies he had only a few hours to live. After midday the poor fellow had gone off in a faint, and this had been mistaken for death, and as it was too late then to hold the usual postmortem, the body was removed to the dead-house. There at midnight he had come to his senses with the result I have recorded.

The doctor was sent for and everything done to try and revive the poor fellow; but he was dead indeed now, and the next day filled the grave that had been dug for him whilst he was yet alive.

MOLE

Barracks: French Foreign Legion, 1890

I ARRIVED in Marseilles about nine o'clock in the evening, and having addressed myself to a non-commissioned officer who was on the platform, I was conducted by him to the depot, known as the 'Incurables,' and lodged for the night. This was my first experience of a military bed, and barracks, and it must be confessed that I was not favourably impressed by their cleanliness, or rather their want of it. Here I met again my friend of the recruiting office, and six other volunteers for the Foreign Regiments, and learnt from him that his name was Balden, and that, like myself, he had been placed in the first of these two corps. He had arrived the day before, and told me that we should leave for Oran on the morrow by the steamer *Abd-el-Kader*.

The next morning, 1st March, 1890, we awoke for the first

time to the note of the bugle sounding the reveil; and after a wash and brush up in the lavatory, came back to the barrack-room, where I had slept, to partake of the usual morning meal of the French soldier—a mug of sweetened black coffee and a slice of bread.

The room in which we had passed the night was, together with the furniture it contained, of the regulation type, to be met with in the barracks of most Continental armies. It was about 75 feet long, and 20 broad; there was a door in the middle of each of the longest sides, and three windows at either end. It contained twenty-four cots, six on either side of the doors. These beds consist of two iron trestles, with three pine planks laid over them. A straw mattress, a bolster, a brown blanket, and two coarse sheets complete the outfit. Along both sides of the room is a shelf upon which each French soldier arranges his neatly-folded kit, which must be placed just above the bed he is occupying. From several hooks fixed underneath the shelf, are suspended the water-bottles, belts, cartridge cases, bayonets, and canvas wallets of the men. These, must, of course, be arranged in a similar and regulation manner by each one. In the middle of the room, between the two doors, is the gunrack in which all the rifles of the occupants are placed. Between the rack and the window, at either end of the room, is a plain wooden table with benches; it is at this that the meals are taken. Just over every cot is suspended, from a nail in the edge of the shelf, a card bearing the name, number and grade of the man who occupies it. The room lodges two squads, each of which is under the orders of a corporal; the 'non-coms' being responsible for the maintenance of order and cleanliness. Generally the rooms in French barracks present a very clean and smart appearance. Such was not the case with the one we slept in at Marseilles; but this can easily be accounted for by the fact that it was used by a succession of passing recruits, who possessed no kit and no knowledge of their duties, and who occupied it for two or three days at a time, or for a night only.

At nine that morning I was detailed off by a sergeant to go with another man and fetch the meal for the room. We brought it back from the cook-house in a sort of big wooden tray with a handle at each end. The repast consisted of a load weighing about one pound and a half—the day's ration of bread—and a tin pannikin full to the brim with stewed white beans, a piece of boiled beef and two boiled potatoes, for each recruit. I must say that the food did not appeal to me at the time, but it was good and clean, and exercise and a healthy appetite soon made it palatable.

Food in the French army varies somewhat in its composition—that is to say, lentils or rice are sometimes substituted for beans, pork or mutton for beef; but the mode of cooking was the same at each meal, and it was only on such grand occasions as the 14th July or New Year's Day that roast meat was given.

The Corporal conducted me to the tent in which I was to lodge, pointed out my place, and went with me to the stores to draw a straw mattress, sleeping-sack bolster and blanket. This done, he showed me how to fold them up and to dispose my kit.

This tent, like the others, in the camp, was of the ordinary bell-shaped pattern. Round it a small trench is dug to prevent the rain from coming in. The floor is of beaten earth, and is about six inches higher than the ground outside of it. It usually gives shelter to eight men. During the day the mattresses are doubled up and placed round the interior close to the flies, which are then lifted so as to secure ventilation.

The blankets and sleeping-sacks are folded neatly and placed on the top of the bedding. About 6 feet from the ground is a circular board, and through the centre of this the pole of the tent passes, thus serving as a shelf on which the pannikins, tin cups, spoons, forks and knives of the men are kept. Underneath this shelf are hooks on which the rifles, belts and waterbottles are hung. Each man's knapsack is placed flat on the ground to the right of his bed, and his kit, which must be well folded, is placed upon it. The inside of the tents are kept very clean and tidy, and presents quite a smart appearance. This particular one contained seven occupants, including the corporal. The camp, which sheltered from five to six hundred men, was situated in a grove of laurel and eucalyptus trees; and during the spring and summer it presented a very picturesque and sylvan appearance. The weather was still very cold, and my first experience of out-door life was rather a trying one. The winter of 1890 was exceptionally severe, as may be judged by the fact that on the morning of the 9th March I awoke to find the tent I was in covered with snow—an almost unprecedented occurrence in Algeria.

During the first few days of my service, I, together with the last batch of recruits, was drilled in camp each day. When we had sufficiently mastered the art of forming fours, marching and halting at the word of command, we were allowed to go out with the other companies to morning exercise on the parade ground outside the main gate of the town.

At 9 a.m. we would march through the town back to camp, with the drum and fife band at our head. At 9.30 the first meal was served out. At 10 the companies assembled to hear the daily 'report' read; and from 10.30 to 4 p.m. the time was taken up by gymnasium classes, fencing lessons, and the lectures and explanations given by the sergeants on duty, of the different text-books.

The whole day of Wednesday in each week was occupied by route-marching, and the afternoon of Friday by shooting on the range. The evening meal was at 4.30, and afterwards all men not on duty or the defaulters' book could go out till the retraite, which was at 8.45. Roll call was sounded at 9, and 'lights out' at 10 p.m.

The life, though somewhat hard for a recruit, is not so bad as one might imagine. Discipline is always somewhat irksome at first, but one gets used to it. Some of the 'non-coms' were objectionable, and seemed to delight in getting the men into trouble; but they were exceptions, and I managed to keep clear of them, thanks to my efforts to do my best, and a certain amount of goodwill. The corps maintained a great reputation for smartness, and a very searching kit inspection took place every Saturday afternoon. It was then that the private whose accoutrements were dirty, or whose linen was unwashed, got into serious trouble.

In the barracks there were lavatories, a wash-house, bath-room and an abundant supply of water; in the camp a stream which ran through it served in the same purposes. With a little trouble a man could keep himself and his outfit in a state of cleanliness, and it was his own fault if he did not.

Much has been said concerning the iron discipline which reigns supreme in the Legion, but whilst serving with the corps I never suffered any real inconvenience from it: unless a punishment of 'two days to barracks' can be considered of much account. It was well merited, for, through sheer carelessness, or perhaps because I wanted to get out a little sooner, I forgot that I was orderly man for the day, and left all the tin platters in the room after the evening meal was finished, instead of taking them down to the cook-house.

MANINGTON

British Army barracks in the 1890's

'REVEILLE' was sounded at 5.30 a.m. but there were no cups of tea brought to us. My barrack room accommodated about sixteen beds with a sergeant in the far corner, who, at the last sound of the bugle, would sit up in his bed and look around the room to see if everyone was dressing. Should there be one unfortunate soldier asleep the sergeant would feel under the bed for an Indian club, kept there for the purpose, and aim it at any sleeping figure. If he should be hurt, he would be sent to hospital, saying it was an accident, as no one dared to say anything to the contrary.

The Government only allowed us a salary of 1s. per day, less 3½d for buying potatoes, salt, tea, sugar, butter, tobacco, cigarettes, beer etc., the ½d. per day being deducted for washing shirts, towel, socks, this work being done by the married women of the regiment. Also 1 lb. of bread and ¾ lb. meat including bone, fat, etc., but we still enjoyed ourselves on the 8½d per day left us, especially on occasions when we were not required to replace any article of kit or clothing out of this amount. But sometimes I was so hungry at night. Fortunately, the heavy drinkers were lighter eaters, and many times I have felt along the barrack shelves and found a dry crust for my supper. To be poor and independent is nearly an impossibility.

CORBETT

TWO

TOWARDS BATTLE

The troopship's on the tide, my boys, the troopship's
on the tide,
O it's 'Special train for Atkins' when the trooper's on
the tide.

Rudyard Kipling

4

DISCIPLINE IN PEACE AND WAR

Penalty of desertion in the 1770's

ILL usage actually proved so oppressive and nearly intolerable to a party of our men, who were driven almost to abandon the service, that several of them, from continued extortion, and the hardship owing to it, actually conspired together to desert. Happily, however, for them, after proceeding some short way in pursuance of their plot, they were induced, from apprehension of the danger attending such rashness, or probably from the reviving energy of loyal motives, to return in time, before their intention of quitting the regiment could be known. This salutary determination perhaps was suggested by the confinement of a deserter at that time who had to undergo the sentence of a court-martial. The party alluded to, no doubt dreaded, that if they acted rashly as they at first intended, a similar punishment might soon await themselves. However, on the day subsequent to their returning to the barrack, after resolving to resume their military duties, the unfortunate man who deserted was taken out for punishment, attended by the entire regiment.

This was the first man I saw flogged. Being at that time (as I have already observed) only seventeen years of age, with all the warm youthful emotions operating within me, the spectacle made a lasting impression on my mind. I well remember, during the infliction of his punishment, I cried like a child.

SERJEANT LAMB

Flogging, 1801

ALMOST every morning there were some absent without leave, and the flogging was of course threatened in a more terrific manner.

This threat of flogging was no idle matter in our eyes; there being scarce a day in which we did not see one or more of the soldiers get from three to seven hundred lashes. We never could see any crime these poor fellows had committed to merit such cruelty. We heard their crimes read to us indeed, as we were all forced to be present, such as unsoldierlike conduct, (this was a common crime, laid to our charge at drill every day a hundred times,) or insolence to bombardier 'A' or lance-corporal 'B' on duty. For petty misdemeanors, such as these, I saw the men every day punished with a severity I had never beheld exercised on the slaves in Carriacou. At this time, and indeed for years after, I have actually trembled at the threat of a lance-bombardier; and not myself only, but the stoutest and oldest soldier did the same; for so severe was the discipline, that if he had only malice enough to make the charge, a flogging was certain to follow.

The first man I saw punished my heart was like to burst. It was with difficulty I could restrain my tears, as the thought broke upon me of what I had brought myself to. Indeed, my spirits sunk from that day, and all hopes of bettering my condition in life fled forever. I had hitherto only seen the pomp of war—the gloss and glitter of the army; now I was introduced into the arcana of its origination, and under the direct influence of its stern economy. I felt how much I had been deceived.

Another circumstance I must not omit before I leave Chatham; it made a great impression on me and all the troops. A poor fellow of the 9th regiment, said to be a farmer's son in Suffolk, had the misfortune to be found asleep on his post. General Sir J. Moore had the command of the Chatham division at the time; he was a severe disciplinarian. The soldier was tried by a court-martial, and sentenced to be flogged; all the troops were paraded to witness the punishment. It was a very stormy morning; the frost, which had continued for some days, gave way during the night, and the wind and sleet drove most pitiously: it was a severe punishment to stand clothed looking on, how much more so to be stripped to the waist, and tied up to the halberts. The soldier was a fine-looking lad, and bore an excellent character in his regiment; his officers were much interested in his behalf, and made great intercession for him to the General. But all their pleading was in vain, the General remained inflexible and made a very long speech after the punishment, in which he reflected in very severe terms on the conduct of the officers and non-commissioned officers present, observing, that if they did their duty as strictly as they had any regard for their men, they ought never to report them to him, for he would pardon no man when found guilty. The poor fellow got two hundred and twenty-nine lashes, but they were uncommonly severe. I saw the drum-major strike a drummer to the ground for not using his strength sufficiently. General Sir John Moore was present all the time. At length, the surgeon interfered, the poor fellow's back was black as the darkest mahogany, and dreadfully swelled. The cats being too thick, they did not cut, which made the punishment more severe. He was instantly taken down and carried to the hospital, where he died in eight days afterwards, his back having mortified. It was the cold I think that killed him; for I have often seen seven hundred lashes inflicted, but I never saw a man's back so horrible to look upon.

ALEXANDER ALEXANDER

Discipline: Craufurd on the road to Vigo, 1808

THE Rifles liked him, but they also feared him; for he could be terrible when insubordination showed itself in the ranks. 'You think, because you are Riflemen, you may do whatever you think proper,' said he one day to the miserable and savage-looking crew around him in the retreat to Coruna; 'but I'll teach you the difference before I have done with you.' I remember one evening, during the retreat, he detected two men straying away from the main body; it was in the early stage of that disastrous flight, and Craufurd knew well that he must do his utmost to keep the division together. He halted the brigade with a voice of thunder, ordered a drum-head court-martial on the instant, and they were sentenced to a hundred a-piece. Whilst this hasty trial was taking place, Craufurd, dismounting from his horse, stood in the midst, looking stern and angry as a worried bulldog. He did not like retreating at all that man.

The three men nearest him, as he stood, were Jagger, Dan Howans, and myself. All were worn, dejected, and savage, though nothing to what we were after a few days more of the retreat. The whole brigade were in a grumbling and discontented mood; and Craufurd, doubtless, felt ill-pleased with the aspect of affairs altogether.

'D—n his eyes!' muttered Howans, 'he had much better try to get us something to eat and drink than harass us in this way.'

No sooner had Howans disburdened his conscience of this grown, than Craufurd, who had overheard it, turning sharply round, seized the rifle out of Jagger's hand, and felled him to the earth with the butt-end.

'It was not I who spoke,' said Jagger, getting up, and shaking his head. 'You shouldn't knock me about.'

'I heard you, sir,' said Craufurd; 'and I will bring you also to a court-martial.'

'I am the man who spoke,' said Howans. 'Ben Jagger never said a word.'

'Very well,' returned Craufurd, 'then I'll try you, sir.'

And, accordingly, when the other affair was disposed of, Howan's case came on. By the time the three men were tried, it was too dark to inflict the punishment. Howans, however, had got the complement of three hundred promised to him; so Craufurd gave the word to the brigade to move on. He marched all that night on foot; and when the morning dawned, I remember that, like the rest of us, his hair, beard and eyebrows were covered with the frost as if he had grown white with age. We were, indeed, all of us in the same condition. Scarcely had I time to notice the appearance of morning before the general once more called a halt—we were then on the hills. Ordering a square to be formed, he spoke to the brigade, as well as I can remember, in these words, after having ordered the three before-named men of the 95th to be brought into the square:

'Although,' said he, 'I should obtain the goodwill neither of the officers nor the men of the brigade here by so doing, I am resolved to punish these three men, according to the sentence awarded, even though the French are at our heels. Begin with Daniel Howans.'

This was indeed no time to be lax in discipline, and the general knew it. The men, as I said, were, some of them, becoming careless and ruffianly in their demeanour; whilst others again I saw with the tears falling down their cheeks from the agony of their bleeding feet, and many were ill with dysentery from the effects of the bad food they had got hold of and devoured on the road. Our knapsacks, too, were a bitter enemy on this prolonged march. Many a man died, I am convinced, who would have borne up well to the end of the retreat but for the infernal load we carried on our backs. My own knapsack was my bitterest enemy; I felt it press me to the earth almost at times, and more than once felt as if I should die under its deadly embrace. The knapsacks, in my opinion, should have been abandoned at the very commencement of the retrograde movement, as it would have been better to have lost them altogether, if, by such loss, we could have saved the poor fellows who, as it was, died strapped to them on the road.

There was some difficulty in finding a place to tie Howans up, as the light brigade carried no halberts. However, they led him to a slender ash tree which grew near at hand.

'Don't trouble yourselves about tying me up,' said Howans, folding his arms; 'I'll take my punishment like a man!'

He did so without a murmer, receiving the whole three hundred. His wife, who was present with us, I remember, was a strong, hardy Irish-woman. When it was over, she stepped up and covered Howans with his grey great-coat. The general then gave the word to move on. I rather think he knew the enemy was too near to punish the other two delinquents just then; so we proceeded out of the cornfields in which we had been halted, and toiled away upon the hills once more, Howan's wife carrying the jacket, knapsack, and pouch, which the lacerated state of the man's back would not permit him to bear.

RIFLEMAN HARRIS

Military murder: India, 1844

A LANCE-SERGEANT had confined a man for gambling, afterwards getting him released without punishment, by giving him a good character. The soldier nevertheless, considered himself aggrieved, and secretly resolved on a terrible requital. Loading his musket, he watched for the return of the sergeant, who had gone in the meantime to the bazaar, and shot him through the back as he was about to enter his room.

On learning what had happened, I proceeded to the barrack where the foul deed had been committed. The sergeant was still in the same place where he had fallen on being shot, with a small dark pool formed by his heart's blood beside him. No change had passed over his features, his clothes were still left unbuttoned, and his stock unclasped; and but for the crimson spot beside him, one would almost have imagined that he slept.

Next day the remains of the murdered man were borne to the grave. The road thither lay beneath the cell where the assassin was in durance, and I was told that he seemed much agitated on hearing the beat of the muffled drum, and the melancholy music of the solemn dead march, as the procession passed his prison.

He was but a very young soldier, and was said to have been instigated to the act by a worthless scoundrel with whom, unfortunately for himself, he had associated. Many a youth is ruined in the army by bad company, who might otherwise have become a good man, an honour to his corps, and a respectable supporter of national glory.

The murdered man, whose name was Slack, was represented as not being of a very tyrannous disposition, but as ignorant and illiterate, having been a sweep prior to enlistment. His melancholy end created a great sensation in the regiment; some condemned, others applauded the deed; but the men had been too accustomed to death for the circumstances to dwell long upon their minds to the exclusion of other matters, and although but a few days intervened until Patrick's day, it was by that time almost forgotten.

Four months later, the warrant for the execution of the murderer of Slack, was received from the Governor-General and Council, the only authority in India which can inflict death on a European soldier. Up to the moment he heard he must die, the unhappy man had buoyed himself up with the hope that he would escape at the most with the transportation of life.

Nothing can be more solemn or impressive than a military execution. On this occasion all the troops at the station were drawn up so as to form three sides of a square, the gallows occupying the centre of the vacant side. When every preparation was made, a guard proceeded to the criminal's cell, who was dressed in a white gown, and had his irons knocked off. He was then placed in a dooly, and borne to the left flank of the troops, where the procession was already formed. First went the band, playing the 'Dead March', with drums muffled, next a portion of the guard followed by four soldiers bearing a coffin. After these came the criminal, accompanied by a friend in lieu of a clergyman; the rear was brought up by the remainder of the guard. Thus marshalled, the procession moved slowly along side the square, till it reached the gallows, at the foot of which the coffin was placed, the band then filing to the rear of the regiment. The criminal, left alone with his guard and executioner, now mounted the platform with a firm step, the rope was adjusted round his neck. 'Mother, mother!' exclaimed the unhappy man, 'what will you say to this!' the next moment the drop fell, and he was swinging in mid-air.

After the lapse of a few minutes, the several regiments marched off the ground in column sections, getting the word 'eyes left' as they passed the gallows, a few paces beyond which the bands struck up lively quick steps. For some time afterwards the white clad corpse remained suspended from the disgraceful tree. The soldier, whose existence had thus been terminated, was but a mere youth, having scarcely attained his twentieth year. He was buried by the side of the man whom he had murdered, over whom the sergeants of the corps had already erected a handsome tomb.

MACMULLEN

Discipline and executions in India in the 1840's

ON ARRIVING at Meerut we received a number of volunteers from other regiments which were going to England, and it was remarked by many, that after these volunteers joined us a great deal of drunkenness was witnessed in the regiment. The new comers appeared to lead our men off, and through their getting connected together, drunkenness and mutinous conduct commenced to a fearful extent, forty men having been transported within a few months, and many other having been differently dealt with, as by imprisonment and flogging. This had all taken place in this station and one or two others near it; but the most of it in ours.

The Commander-in-Chief had repeatedly warned the men by General Orders, cautioning them that striking superior officers was punishable by death, and that he should be compelled to carry it into execution, if the crime was not put a stop to. The commanding officers of the regiment had done all in their power to impress it upon the men's minds that the extremity of the law would certainly be carried out, and that before long some one would die for his folly. I saw our Colonel, when he had formed us into a square, sit upon his horse, cautioning the men until the tears ran down his face on to the horse's neck. He was our second Colonel and was well liked by all. He was very severe when severity was required. His name was Hill. He had been all his time in the regiment, but left us shortly after, and went to the 21st Regiment.

Not long after this a man was tried and sentenced to death, but was recommended for mercy on account of his previous good character. He got off with transportation, the Commander-in-chief being still unwilling to put a man to death.

Before many days more had passed over, four more came before him. One was a man of the artillery, who struck the doctor while in hospital. Another was a man of the 9th Lancers, who had struck the commanding officer in the face with his cap. The third was a man of my regiment, accused of striking a sergeant whilst he was being tried by a district court-martial. The fourth was a man of the 80th Regiment; but what his crime was I do not know, as the regiment marched down the country after the first execution, and this man got off with being transported for life.

The first of these men was shot. The next case was that of a man of the 9th Lancers. I saw this. It was early in the morning, before daylight, that we paraded for the execution, and formed in three sides of a square, the open side being left for the balls to pass through when the soldiers fired. The unhappy man was then brought from his cell, under an escort of a section of men, commanded by an officer, his arms being tied behind him by a cord a little above the elbow, so that his hands were in some degree at liberty. He was taken to the left of the square, next to his own regiment, for it was not yet day-break. We all stood silent and sorrowful, waiting for the first dawn of the morning. Everything was so still that a pin might be heard to fall. I stood trembling all over, until I could not keep a limb still—my teeth chattered in my mouth; but this was greatly owing to weakness, as I had but just come from hospital. However, several fainted, and others had to fall out. Day soon broke. After the first dawn I could see the party stand with the prisoner, when they were ordered to proceed in the following manner: first the provost with his arms reversed; then the band and drummers, playing the 'Dead March', the drums being muffled with black; next the firing party, with arms reversed; then the coffin, borne by four men; next to this the prisoner, in company of the minister praying, and his comrade on the left of him, flanked by a man on either side with swords, the escort following. They started from the left; the band played the dismal and solemn march, which made my blood run cold. As he passed his own regiment he bade his officers and the men farewell, and told them he hoped it would be a warning to all to keep from drink; for it was that and bad company that had brought him to this. He saluted his colours as he passed them. When they got up to my regiment I looked at him. He was pale, though he appeared to be prepared for his fate, which I suppose he was. The minister had hold of his arm, but he walked with a firm step, keeping the step to the drum, and with the party. He was dressed in a clean white shirt, a black handkerchief, his stable jacket (with the collar turned back), white trowsers, and stable cap. As soon as he got to us, he began to weep, and was going to say something; but the minister spoke to him, and I suppose told him to continue in prayer. Poor man! I thought my heart would melt in me, when I saw him so close to me; as I was up in the front. Several men being unable to stand it, they had fallen to the rear. As he passed our Colonel and colours, he saluted them, and bade all farewell. On getting to the end of the square, they turned across to the open side, about the middle, and the coffin was put on the ground. The escort fell back; the firing party took up their distance; the man knelt upon his coffin; the provost blufted him, and then drew back; the minister read the funeral service; the man prayed; as the minister finished, he said, 'Lord, have mercy upon my soul!' and the minister putting up his hand as a signal that all was finished, the report of the muskets was heard as they poured out a volume of smoke, and the man fell dead. Two balls had passed through the heart, one through the breast, another through the head, and another through the thigh. After the whole of us had marched by the body, it was put in the coffin as it fell, and buried.

On the morning of the 28th we paraded, as on the previous day, to witness another military execution. This was a man of my regiment. His name was Jurden, and he was an Irishman and a volunteer. His offence was striking a sergeant; but what his reason was for doing so, I do not know. He said he wanted to get transported. He did this before the other men were executed. Everything was carried on at this as on the other occasions, except that this man was a Catholic, and was attended by the priest. He did not walk so firmly as the other men; he reeled several times; and I believe he would have fallen had he not been supported by the priest and his comrades. He fell pierced by seven balls through the body. When he was informed that he was to be shot he wept bitterly. His cries were enough to melt the heart of the stones of his cell, had it been possible. He had seen the other two men shot, as all the prisoners were marched up to the place in order to witness the execution.

This example had the desired effect, for we had no more striking superior officers. The punishment for striking is very severe, and some people do not hold with it; but such must be the case while the British army is composed of such a set of men as it is, of all characters and dispositions, or discipline would never be kept.

RYDER

Changes in military habits in the 1850's

BLESSED be providence, the writer saw a wonderful change for the better in the habits of the men before he left the old Bengal horse artillery. He saw the crime of drunkenness, and even the habit itself, reduced almost to a minimum in other troops and batteries, and takes credit for having himself assisted in the good work in his own. This wasn't done by punishment! but by the introduction of a reading-room, a coffee-shop, and malt liquor, but not much of the latter. For example, the writer's troop was quartered in Peshawur from 1850 to the end of 1853, and he has often seen the orderly sergeant drawing the troop's rum in a quart bottle! for, say, about four old soldiers, who imagined, foolishly, that the stimulant could not be done without! In those days there was no draught malt liquor issued to us, but the writer obtained permission from his commanding officer to purchase such quantity of bottled beer and porter as was daily required. This cost Rs. 12 a dozen, and was issued to the men at half price, say, eight annas per bottle, the difference being accounted for from the canteen fund accumulations. The men had their comfortable bottle of beer or porter, and a snug room in which to enjoy it.

The scheme was highly successful, for it harmlessly absorbed the spare money the men might be possessed of, for which they received a per contra of enjoyment, and Major Waller had a sober, steady troop for the remainder of the writer's time in it.

BANCROFT

Military execution of five deserters: Army of the Potomac, 1863

THE court-martial found the deserters guilty, and sentenced them all to be shot. The 29th of August was the day when the sentence of death was to be carried into execution, and the whole Fifth corps was to witness the spectacle. The regiments were massed in columns by divisions around a hollow square. The lines were so formed that nearly every man in the corps could obtain a view of the whole situation. The lines were all formed, and for some moments we waited for the arrival of the solemn procession. It soon made its appearance, and while the description of it may not impress my readers with much force, I can assure them that it made a deep and lasting impression upon the minds of those who witnessed it. Every detail had evidently been arranged for the special object of making a solemn impression upon the interested spectators. Let us for a moment imagine the scene. On a broad level field, the old Fifth corps with its bronzed veterans and tattered flags, closed in solid columns around the open square. The impressive silence was not broken by a single sound. Each line of soldiers looked more like the section of a vast machine than a line composed of living men. The silence was suddenly and sadly broken by the sounds of approaching music,—not the quick, inspiring strains with which we were so familiar, but a measured, slow, and solemn dirge, whose weird, sorrowful notes were poured forth like the moanings of lost spirits. Not a soldier spoke, but every eye was turned in the direction from which came the sad and mournful cadences, and then we saw the procession. First came the band of music, of which I have spoken. Each musician seemed to comprehend the solemnity of the occasion, and this knowledge inspired with ability to discharge the responsibility. Slow and measured was their step; sad and painful was their music; solemn as eternity was the impression that swept over us. Next came a detachment of the provost guard, numbering sixty men. The provost guard consisted of men who were detailed from the several regiments, and in their selection special regard was made to the soldierly qualities of the individuals. This detachment, as well as the one of the same size making up the rear of the procession, was composed of the finest looking men that could be selected from the entire provost guard. Each one was tall and erect in form; all were well drilled and neatly clad; with the precision of drilled veterans they kept step to the slow and solemn music. This is the firing party. Next followed a black coffin carried by four men, and close after that came one of the condemned men, then another coffin, and following that the second criminal; and thus in regular order they came, the rear of the procession being made up of the second detachment of the provost guard, of which I have already spoken. This detachment, like number one, was composed of sixty men. The prisoners were all clad alike, in blue pants, and white shirts, each man's hands were manacled behind him, and a guard was on either side. The five prisoners were marched to the centre of the square where the graves had already been prepared. Each prisoner was also accompanied by a priest or chaplain. It was reported at the time that there were two Protestant chaplains, two Catholic, and one Jewish priest, each prisoner, I suppose, being allowed to select one of his own religious belief.

The coffins were placed near the open graves that were to receive them.

Faithfully and well did the men of God perform their duties toward those who were about to die, and eternity, I suppose, will record the results. The last exhortation was given, the last word spoken, and the clergymen withdrew from the presence of the condemned. Each of the doomed men was then blindfolded with a thick and heavy bandage. The officers in charge then stepped back upon a line with the soldiers who were to fire. The sixty men were ready to perform their sad duty. One rifle in each twelve was loaded with a blank cartridge, so that not one of the firing party should know that he had taken the life of a fellow being. The second detachment was placed in such a position that they could complete the work if any of the condemned should survive after the first fire.

After the bandages were placed upon the eyes of the men, there was a moment of awful suspense. To the anxious spectators it seemed to be an age. Then clear and sharp the voice of the commanding officer rang out 'Ready!' and instantly each of the sixty guns obeyed the command. Once more the officer's voice was heard, 'Aim!' and sixty rifles were brought into position, twelve being aimed at the breast of each victim. Intently we watched and listened. At last we heard the fatal word, 'Fire!' There was a gleaming flash, a line of curling smoke, a sharp crash like the report of a single rifle. We looked again. The provost guard was standing at 'Shoulder arms'. Five bleeding forms were lying limp and lifeless upon the ground where they had fallen; the deserters had met their doom. Law had been enforced; the penalty inflicted; the outraged government avenged. The lines were quickly in motion, and the regiments marched to their respective camps, each soldier feeling more keenly than ever before the solemn responsibilities of his position.

GERRISH

Field punishment in Dahomey: French Foreign Legion

IT WAS here that I saw the barbarous punishment of the crapaudine applied for the only time it came under my notice. At one time this punishment used to be inflicted in barracks for even trifling offences, but General de Negrier put a stop to it, and a great many other abuses, when he was in command of the Algerian Army Corps, and it had fallen into such disuse that I had never seen it up till then. On this night at Sabovi during the search for water an Italian who belonged to the Legion got at loggerheads with a sergeant and struck him. When they returned to camp the sergeant reported the occurrence, and it was decided to punish the man with the crapaudine. It must be remembered that in most armies he would have been tried by drum-head court-martial and shot.

He was stripped naked, his hands were pinioned behind his back, and his ankles were tied together. Then his ankles were lashed to his wrists, and he was thrown on the ground looking very much like a trussed fowl. The agony incidental to this constrained position must have been almost beyond human endurance after a time; but in this poor man's case the punishment was intensified by the fact that in no long time after he was tied up his body was literally covered with a swarm of black ants—and any one who has been in tropical Africa will know what that means.

After the man had been in this position about an hour his cries were agonising. To stop them a gag was placed in his mouth, which had the effect of reducing his cries to much more distressing moans. The man was eventually released after about three hours of it, and he was then so ill that he had to be taken to the hospital and did no more duty during the campaign.

I have a very strong opinion that in almost every case of a private soldier striking a superior the superior is in some way to blame; and in this particular case there was only too much reason to suppose that the row was brought about by a tactless sergeant unnecessarily irritating a man whose nerves were on the stretch. Every man who is placed in authority over other men ought to have it impressed upon his mind that treacle is a better medium for catching flies than vinegar

MARTYN

A military prison: French Foreign Legion

THE prison in the barracks at Sidi-bel-Abbes used always to loom before me like a threatening spectre.

On both sides of the entrance to the barracks, close to the road, but separated from it by a high wall, lay the two little houses with their flat tin roofs which caught the sun's rays so pitilessly. Inside there were rows and rows of cell doors in the long narrow corridors. The single cells were a little more than three yards long and one yard broad; the general cells were perhaps five yards square. There was no light, and a little hole in the wall and an opening over the door were the sole means of ventilation. The floor was flagged or of clay. There was a wooden bench in each cell, a water-jug, and an old tin pail. The single cells and the general cells were exactly alike in their 'fittings'—whether five men or fifty were shut up in these cells made no difference! They got, according to the regulations, one water-jug and one pail! I was never (and even to-day that is a satisfaction to me) shut up in the Legion's prison. But I have seen enough, when I was on guard there, to have had quite enough of the prison without any nearer experience of it.

I repeat: five yards square, thirty, forty, or more occupants: an air-hole nine inches in diameter high up in the walls and a tiny crack over the door.

Any of these cells would at once be condemned by a veterinary as unfit even for a pigsty!

Before reveille at five o'clock in the morning all the sentries on guard were marched up to the prison, and the sergeant opened the cells, whereupon an awful stench streamed out. He read out the names from the prison register, and the prisoners came out of the cells into the passage as their names were called. Then they began to clean up. The pails were carried by two men, accompanied by a sentry, to the sewer openings in the barrack-yard. When the bigger cells were overfilled (and this was almost always the case) they looked awful. The room was like a sewer, flooded, pestilential. . . . To clean the cells there were only a couple of old brooms in the prison. A few pails of water were flooded over the floor, carelessly and hurriedly, for the sergeants did not care about wasting too much time on the 'prisonniers.' A little water and a few strokes with the broom! What is not washed away trickles through the cracks and crannies in the stone floor and forms a new basis for pestilence.

The bowl of black coffee which forms the legionnaire's breakfast is not given to the prisoners. They get no breakfast. They are allowed to wash themselves at the basin in the corridor. Then they are led out to work, on an empty stomach, frozen through by the chilly African night spent uncovered on a hard wooden bench, and faint from breathing in that pestilential atmosphere.

All those who were sentenced to short terms of imprisonment were commandeered to clean up the barrack-yard, to split wood, and to break stones.

The prisoners with longer sentences, and those in cellule, had to go out to the 'march of punishment', marching round in a small circle for two hours on end, carrying heavy bags of sand, now and then doubling for the sake of variety. When the corporal in command was in bad temper he made them go through a course of Swedish gymnastics into the bargain. This was tremendous work when burdened with the heavy sack, and it strained the muscles and nerves in a way that nothing else could.

At ten o'clock the prisoners were given soup. They never got full rations, since as long as they were in prison their mess allowance ceased as well as their pay.

The soup is thin, and the piece of meat which swims in it is as small as may be. . . . Their bread rations consist of half of what they get in the company. The prisoners in solitary confinement are placed on starvation diet. Their soup consists of hot water with little bits of potatoes and bread-crusts, and they only get this every other day. In the interval they have to live on bread—on a quarter of the Legion's bread rations. One must have seen how terribly emaciated these poor fellows become in a few days to be able to do justice to the barbarity of a system which has three main ideas: undernourishment, overwork, frightful sanitary conditions.

After they have finished 'dinner', their work begins again. The drill suits had got dirty, and bore signs of the nights they had gone through. The operation, too, of emptying the tin pails cannot be performed without the suits being considerably the worse for it.

But the drill suits were only changed when an inspection by the colonel was imminent, and clean underclothes were a luxury absolutely unknown in prison.

The sergeants on guard always considered it an important part of their duties to treat the prisoners as badly as possible. In the prison it simply rained curses. Many sergeants took an especial delight in inspecting the prisoners every three hours throughout the night. They had to come out into the yard, and the sergeant read their names and numbers by the light of the lantern, taking as long about it as he could, while the poor wretches had to stand there motionless in their thin clothes for half an hour in the cold night air. This would be repeated three or four times a night. In this way the sergeant managed to while away his dreary night on guard, and had in addition the pleasing sense of having played his little part in the regiment's system of justice. Under discipline in the Foreign Legion they understand a series of variations, improvements or otherwise, on the mediaeval systems of torture.

It is merely the petty offences against discipline that are punished in these hovels.

I was on the watch in the narrow corridor of one of these prisons, pacing to and fro on the cold flags with fixed bayonet. Eight hours before the poumpistes, Rader and the rest of them, had been brought in. Through the narrow opening between the wall and the prison a little strip of starlit sky could be seen, and down the narrow passage the cold night wind howled. But it could not drive away the pestilential stench which hung heavy over the prison and which was perpetually being increased by the vapours from the ventilation holes and the tiny openings in the cellules. This awful smell tortured my nerves and rendered sentry-go in the prison anything but pleasant.

Besides Rader and his fellow-deserters, there were forty others in the general cell. When at ten o'clock at night the sergeant inspected the prison and the cells were opened, I saw how the men lay huddled together on the wooden benches, man to man, like sardines packed in a tin. But in spite of this scarcely twenty out of the forty prisoners could find room on the bench. The others crouched in the corners, sleeping with their knees drawn up to their chins; several lay on the bare floor, filthy though it was. It was freezing cold for them in their thin drill clothes. The prison blankets they had been given were hardly worth calling blankets, ancient rags, so thin that one could see through them like a veil and so small that the men had the choice of covering their feet or their bodies; the blankets were not big enough to do both. They were stiff with dirt and most of them were alive with vermin. In the daytime they were just thrown into a corner of the cell.

It was no wonder that the men who had just been shut up in this cell could not sleep. Once I heard Rader ask gently who was doing sentry. He must have stood on the shoulders of one of his comrades to be able to reach the ventilation hole, which was high up in the wall. When I answered it was I, he said he could not stand it any more in there—hadn't I a cigarette? I spitted a packet of cigarettes on my bayonet and handed it up to him.

'Keep up your pecker, old man,' I whispered.

'Good Lord, good Lord . . .' was the reply, in a pitiful tone which hadn't even a touch of Rader's droll humour left in it.

The sound of groans and curses reached me continually from the cell; all spoke very gently for they knew that they would be severely punished if a noise was heard. It is a prison custom for the sentry in the corridor to let the butt of his rifle fall loudly on the floor when he hears the sergeant coming. This is a warning signal. When in their excitement they spoke a little louder I could now and then hear through the opening what they were saying. In eloquent French, one of the prisoners, whose accent proclaimed him to be a man of education, was complaining of life in the Legion, and all was still in the cell while the ringing voice spoke in passionate excitement.

Snatches of what I heard are still fixed in my memory:

'My God, if I could only die! My friends, I've always done my duty here.—I've marched and marched and marched for four long years.—For four years I've borne burdens, exposed to wind and weather, and have tired my strength.—Four long years! Yes, I've lost my tie, oh, la la, a thin blue rag worth a couple of centimes—and was marched off to prison! I'd stolen the tie, I'd sold it—who believes the word of a legionnaire! Mea culpa, my friends!'

'Mea maxima culpa!' repeated the speaker quietly. ''Tis true one has never been much use and has made a monstrous thing of one's life—you and I and all of us! And why not? That's all past and done with now. All the same—I'm ashamed of the country in which the Foreign Legion can exist. I'm a Frenchman. But I say: Damn the Legion, damn the land of the Legion. . . .'

And over all there hung the pestilential vapours in the tiny room with the crowded humanity within.

When I was relieved at midnight the sergeant asked: 'Anything unusual?'

'No, nothing special,' I answered.

ROSEN

5

AFTER DUTY

Saints and Malignants in Worcester, 1642

THIS day, our companies exercising in the fields at Worcester, one of the Lord General's soldiers shot at random, and, with a brace of bullets, shot one of his fellow soldiers through the head, who immediately died. Sabbath day, about the time of morning prayer, we went to the Minister, when the pipes played and the puppets sang so sweetly, that some of our soldiers could not forbear dancing in the holy choir; whereat the Baalists were sore displeased. The anthem ended, they fell to prayer, and prayed devoutly for the King, the bishops, etc; and one of our soldiers, with a loud voice, said, 'What! never a bit for the Parliament?' which offended them much more. Not satisfied with this human service, we went to divine; and, passing by, found shops open, and men at work, to whom we gave some plain exhortations; and went to hear Mr Sedgwick, who gave us two famous sermons, which much affected the poor inhabitants, who, wondering, said they never heard the like before; and I believe them.

WHARTON

Army language, 1796

THE general character of the army, for the profanation of God's holy name, is well known; and the temptations a young man has to encounter, from the very general practice of this vice, are very great. The religious instructions I had received, and the knowledge I had of the scriptures, deterred me from acquiring a habit of swearing. I frequently reproved my comrades for it; and having done so, pride of heart also operated to prevent me from swearing myself, lest my comrades should, in ridicule, retort my reproofs upon me; and this they did not fail to do, if at any time I was guilty of an oath, or any thing approaching to it.

'G.B.'

Barrack life on the Rock of Gibraltar, 1797

THERE was a Society of Methodists in Gibraltar, chiefly composed of men, belonging to the different regiments in the garrison. They had a small place, where they had started meetings for prayer and exhortation; there were a few of these Methodists in our regiment. Shortly after I joined it, the commanding officer gave out an order, for none of the regiment to attend any of their meetings. What effect this order had, in deterring any from attending at the time it was issued, I know not: it had not at least a permanent effect, for I know that several did attend afterwards, and no notice was taken of it. I went to this meeting place only once, all the time I was in Gibraltar, and I was nearly a twelve-month in the place. This shows what a careless state of mind I was in; for I may say it was the only religious exercise I was at, all that time. There were indeed prayers read to the garrison, every Sunday morning on the grand parade, when the weather was dry; but the Chaplain was always at such a distance, that I never heard a word he said. There was a Chapel at the Governor's residence, where service was performed through the day, but I never was in it.

I began to fall into company which led me frequently to get intoxicated; I did not indeed fall into a habit, nor acquire an inclination for intoxicating liquors for their own sake; but had the same circumstances continued, I have great reason to fear, that an appetite for them would have been formed, and that I might have turned out a habitual drunkard. Gibraltar has, indeed, peculiar temptations, to produce a habit of drunkardness. The wine is cheap; the place is warm; and in time of war with Spain, there is very little fresh provisions, and what is fresh, is very indifferent. There is a great deal of hard labour for the soldiers, for part of which they get extra pay; by the evening, many of them are fatigued, and actually need a refreshment beyond their ordinary provisions; but those who need the refreshments are not content to go and get what they require for themselves; they often take one or two of their comrades with them, and having once sat down in the wine house, they generally sit until either their money is exhausted, or their time; (for the moment the gun fires for the men to be in their barracks, the wine houses must be emptied and shut, until after the new guards are marched away to relieve the old ones next morning, that no soldier may have it in his power to get drunk before guard mounting.) Those who are treated one night, treat in their turn those who treated them, when they get pay for work.

Many of the barrack rooms are uncomfortable, on account of their size, containing sixty or more men. This greatly destroys social comfort: for one or two individuals can molest all the rest; so that select retired conversation cannot be enjoyed. Any thing of that kind is always ready to be interrupted by the viscious and ignorant, who do not fail to scoff and gibe, at what they do not understand or relish themselves. Among so many men, too, there will always be found some, who take a malicious pleasure in making their neighbours unhappy. This renders the barrack room quite uncomfortable during the evening, which, as the greater part are employed at work, or otherwise occupied during the day, is the principle time when they can be together. This, along with other things, induces those who have a little money, to spend the evening in the wine house with their more select companions. Different sorts of vermine are very plenty in the barracks; and it is the common excuse for drinking, that they cannot get a sound sleep unless they be half drunk. It was customary at that time to settle the men's accounts once in two months; and, as very little pay was given to the soldiers over their rations during the intervals, the greater part had a considerable sum to receive; and then drinking was so very common, that to prevent a multiplicity of punishment, it was found necessary to have no parade, except in those for guard, in order that the money might be the sooner done; and the different regiments in the garrison had to take different days to settle their men's accounts, that the garrison might not be involved in one general state of intoxication at the same time. But I hear that matters are differently managed now; the men are oftener settled with, and get a larger proportion of their pay weekly, which prevents them from having so much money to receive at once. The most comfortable time I had, was when I was upon guard. There are many very retired guard stations, some of them in elevated situations, on the very summit of the rock, 1300 feet above the level of the sea, from which the view is surely grand, and where a fine opportunity is afforded for meditation. I sometimes took my Bible to guard with me, but I never made much use of it.

'G.B.'

Food and home comforts in Ceylon, 1803

FROM the depression of mind I then lay under, but more especially from the miserable diet we got, I became extremely ill. I was never free from inveterate flux and other troubles; our food was not only bad in itself, but cooked by the black cooks belonging to the garrison, in the most dirty and careless manner and we, being strangers in the country, could not alter their slovenly fashions. When the meat was brought to the cooking place, it was thrown down upon a dirty mat, and chopped up, then cooks sat down upon their hams, placing a knife between their toes, and cut it up into small pieces, and thus daubed all about, and without being even washed, it was boiled in curry, the rice being boiled at the same time in another earthern vessel called a chattie, as all their boiling is done in earthern vessels, and then brought into the barracks at twelve o'clock when the soldiers gathered round them like as many voracious hounds, with their chatties in their hands, bawling, blaspheming, and grumbling, not so much at the quality as the quantity of their food.

At night we got what was called supper, which consisted of a small cake of rice flour and water, and a liquid called coffee, although there was not a single grain of the berry in it. What we used for sugar was called jaggery, which was made up in cakes, very insipid and dirty; it bore no resemblance to the sugar used in Europe. At eight o'clock in the morning we got breakfast brought to us in the same manner; it consisted of the same cake, fish, or bullocks' liver, and jaggery water, and this formed the daily diet of the British troops in Ceylon. Had it been of good quality, and properly cooked, it was well enough, our allowance of liquor, which was arrack, was one quart per day to five men, or about two drams to each.

The beef, of which we had a pound per day, was given out along with the rice in the morning, for which sixpence per day was kept off our pay. But it was rather carrion than beef. The cattle sometimes buffaloes, sometimes bullock, having been used in their husbandry were generally lean, old or diseased, the meat was soft, flabby, and full of membraneous skin; it had a rank, heavy, loathsome, odour, was offensive to both sight and smell, and hurt me more than the climate, and was, I am certain, the cause of much of the disease and death which thinned our numbers. The rice, too, was small, and of a bad quality, full of dust and dirt, from which our rascally cooks were at no trouble to free it.

ALEXANDER ALEXANDER

An Artillery man's native wife: Ceylon, 1805

I FELT sinking fast under the fatigue and climate, both of which were aggravated by the diet, which did not agree with me. My confirmed flux, for which I tried every remedy, both native and European, that I could obtain, brought on a weakness in my spine and thighs, so that walking was a burden to me, and I suffered great pain. In this dilemma the old soldiers of the 19th advised me to take a native wife, who would cook for me, and purchase better food in the Pettah Bazaar than was used in the barrack-mess. Let misery be to what extent it may, I felt that when there is a choice, life is still sweet.

I had been refused leave to be out of the barrackmess once

before; I applied to Captain Napier, who granted my request, as it was the custom in Colombo. The next step was for leave to erect a hut in the garrison, for which I applied to Lieutenant-Colonel John Hatton, of the 66th, commandant, who granted it at once. I then set about getting my hut put up, which, after all, was not so good as the huts of the slaves in the West Indies, over whom I had formerly borne command. I then began to look for a wife, or rather a nurse—love was out of the question. My affections were elsewhere all engrossed; but I must either take a wife or die.

My choice fell upon a Cingalese; she was of a clear bronze colour, smooth-skinned, healthy and very cleanly in her person and manner of cooking, which was her chief recommendation. Puncheh was of a good or bad temper just as she had any object to gain, for ever crying out poverty, and always in want either of money or clothes. She imagined every person better off than herself; often pretended to be under the necessity to pawn her necklace and other ornaments, and boasted how much she was reduced since she came to live with me. Then she would pretend to be sick, and lie in bed for twenty-four hours together; and neither speak, nor take food or medicine, but lie and sulk. I was completely sick of her at times, for she would not leave me, neither would she stay.

When these sullen fits came on, I in vain endeavoured to sooth or flatter her; I had not money to satisfy her extravagance, my victuals remained uncooked, and the hut in confusion. There was no alternative but to follow the example of the others. I applied the strap of my great coat, which never failed to effect a cure, and all went on well for a time. She bore me a son, a fine little boy, who died young. Often have I sat and looked with delight upon his infant gambols. As is the custom here, he smoked cigars as soon as he could walk about. It was strange to see the infant puffing the smoke into the air, and forming circles with it, until weary, then running and placing his head upon his mother's bosom, to quench his thirst from her breast, before finishing his cigar.

What alone caused me to submit to her humours was that I

now began to get stronger and better in my bowels, for my food was cleanly cooked and properly done.

Shortly afterwards, Lieutenant-Colonel Colebrooke wrote from Colombo, desiring a number of our black sheep to be sent to head-quarters, under command of a steady lance-bombadier; as a punishment, they were to be marched by land all the way, in full marching order, arms and kit. I was selected by Captain Alms, at which I was very happy, for I would then be at head-quarters, and I immediately began to prepare. My first concern was to send off Puncheh, my native wife, by sea before me, as the fatigue was too great for her. We parted with some concern, expecting to meet again, but I never saw her more; for our route was delayed from time to time, and at length it was given up altogether. I continued to send money for a considerable time to her, until I heard from Colombo, by some of our men, that she had got another husband, when I broke off all correspondence with her.

ALEXANDER ALEXANDER

The Vivandière *of a Napoleonic infantry regiment*

I FORGOT to mention that when the 161st half-brigade was incorporated with us, I arranged to get into my company, a young laundress, who belonged to that half-brigade. She was seventeen or eighteen years old, very nice, and married to an old German sergeant, who had belonged to the Swedish regiment. This young woman chose me for her friend. She was not very rich, but I had still a few sous left from the little business I carried on at Juliers, when I sent about flying columns and appropriated their pay and provisions; following the example of the war-commissaries. I procured for this little princess the means to get a small barrel of spirits, to hang across her shoulders, a funnel, and some glasses, and asked the captain of the 2nd battalion to appoint her *vivandière*. She looked as pretty as a cupid following the heroes of Mars.

I undertook to fit her out according to her rank and new title. I procured for her one of those carts called a char-a-banc in Germany, with two horses, which had been com-

Just joined the regiment, 1820

Contemporary caricature of U.S. trooper
'marching to Saratoga with plunder'
c. 1780

Dragoon uniform *c.* 1690

British troops in a Canadian winter *c.* 1840

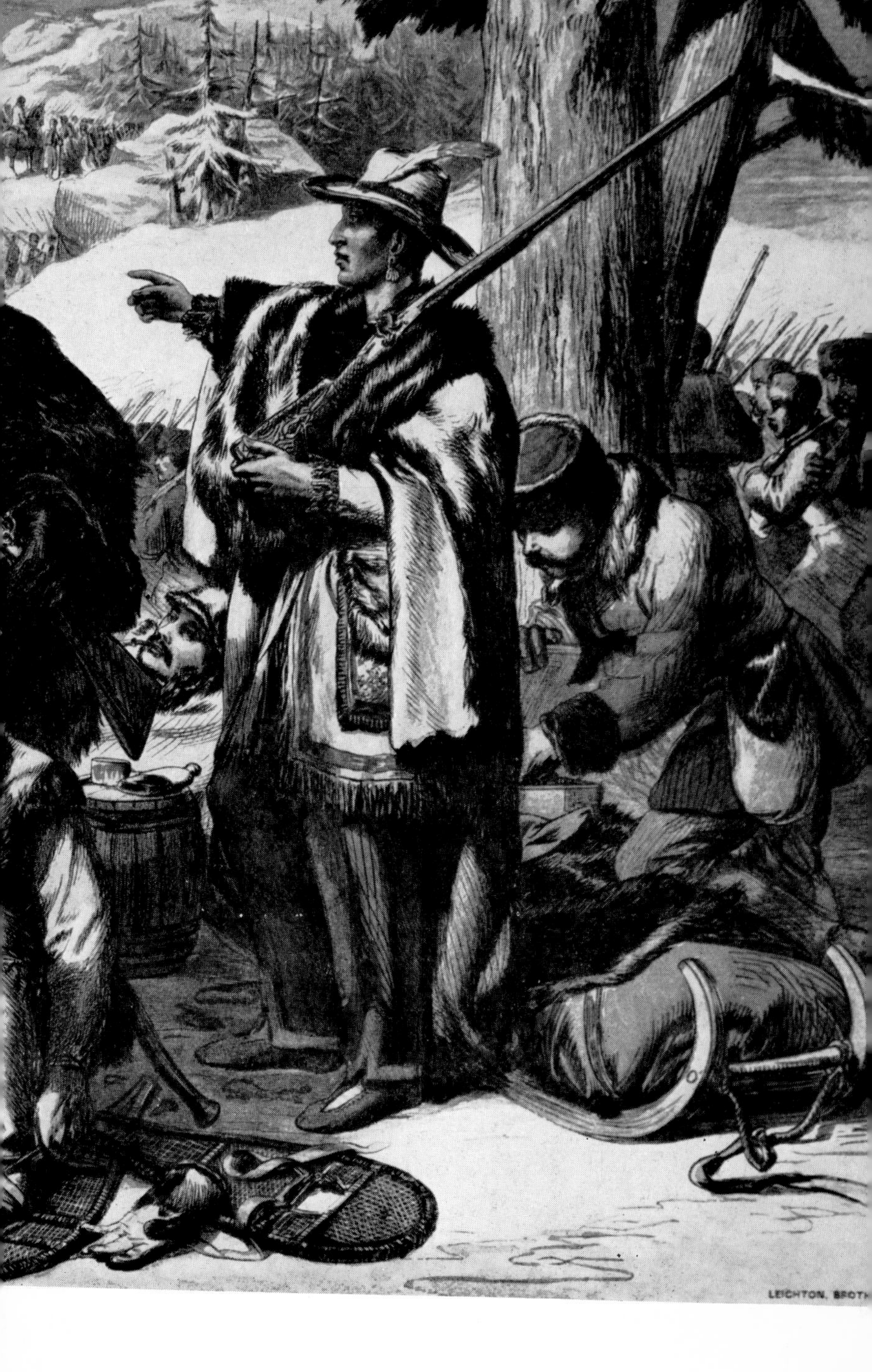
LEIGHTON, BROTH

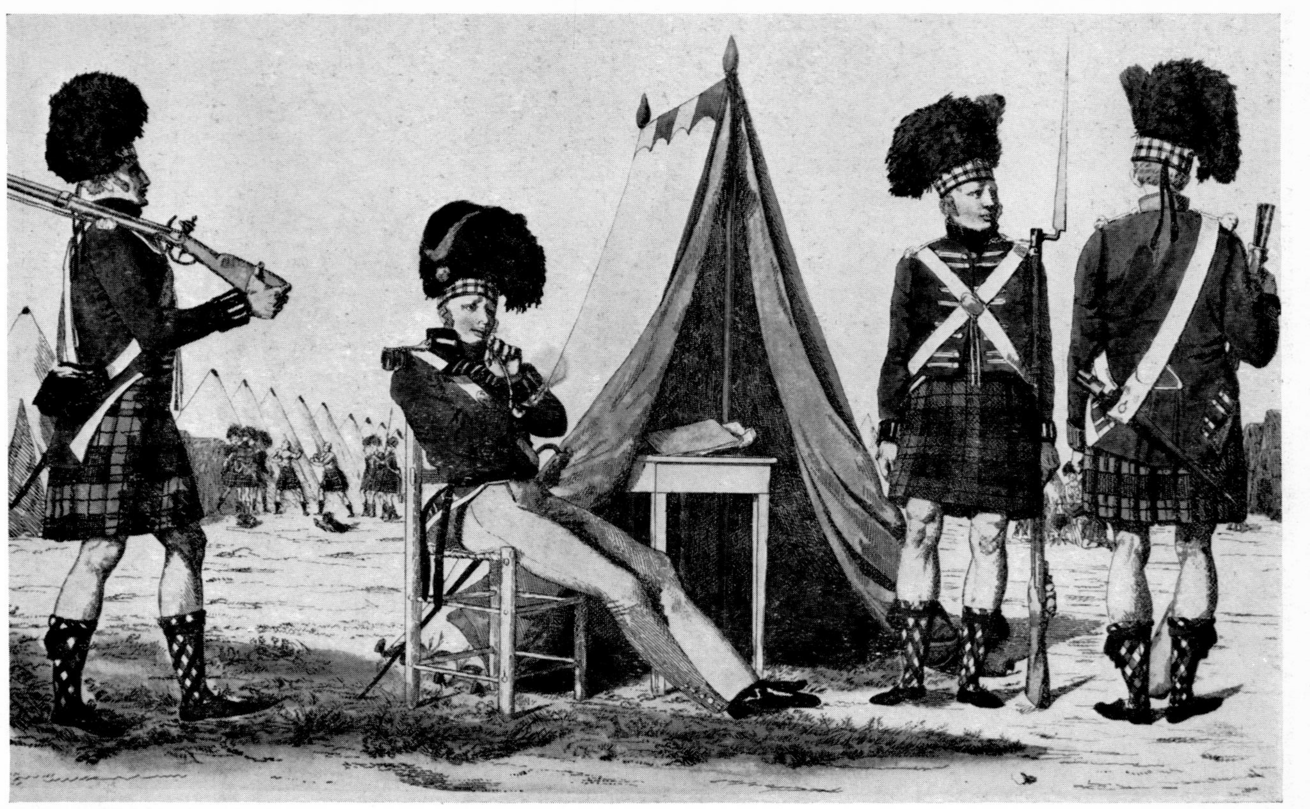

British troops (Scots) outside Paris, 1815

French troops (infantry and pioneers) probably in the Crimea

2nd Life Guards relieving guard, 1844

mandeered from a rich peasant. She could then purchase wholesale. Her husband was pleased at seeing the prosperity of his dear better-half; he liked me very much, and knowing that it was to me she owed her splendour, he often said to me, 'Quarter-master, my wife is at your service.'

Finally wishing to make my princess happier, and spare her fatigue on the marches, I went into partnership with one of the Chamborand's hussars. When he was on outpost duty at night, I went out to see him. He was watching an Austrian sentinel. He gave me his pistol, and I made a wide circuit, came on the enemy's sentinel, blew out his brains, and took his horse. The first expedition succeeded—at that time the Government paid 400 francs, in paper, for every horse captured. My hussar, who had helped me to get the horse, claimed 200 francs, which I could not give him, but I promised that I would get him a horse for himself by the same means within a fortnight, with his help; but it was not until my fourth expedition that I could secure the horse and man—one of Banko's dragoons.

I gave the first horse to the little *vivandière*. As it was marked, it was noticed that it was a captured charger, and she was ordered to say where she got it. She said I gave it her, but did not know how I had obtained it. I was sent for, and went to the headquarters of the division. I related the story of my feat, and, thanks to the bravery with which I had obtained these horses, I was allowed to keep them, and was mentioned in the orders of the day.

FRANÇOIS

At Kurnal: Station-life in the 1840's

AND now, like a young bear, the writer had all his sorrows before him; riding school, drills of all kinds, morning, noon, and afternoon; and at night—every night—to a late hour, there were dances arranged for the exercise and amusement of both sexes. For be it known to all men, that at the time the writer spoke of, the station at Kurnal was literally swarming with specimens of the gentler sex; there were widows, there were spinsters, staid and frisky, of a certain or uncertain age; there were blooming damsels, the well-grown daughters of men either of troops or batteries or other regiments, cavalry and infantry, the various depots of which were quartered in the station, their head-quarters being at Cabul viz—, H.M.'s 44th foot, and first troop, first brigade, horse artillery (both massacred on their retreat from Cabul); the third troop, first brigade, horse artillery, and 3rd light dragoons with General Pollocks force, and the 13th light infantry with General Sale at Jellalabad—and 'the nateral consiquins is', an old soldier explained to the writer, 'that thim that knows their husbands as died, want to get others; then, again, thim grass widdys isn't partiklar; thim anshint ould maids is av the wan opinyin wid thim; an as for the young craters; why, of coorse, they want to sail in the same boat! Begorra Kurnal's a grate place now for a tindir harted yuth like me'—he was as grey as a badger—had lost all his teeth and was fifty if he was a day—'to come to!'

So there was dancing and singing in Kurnal; there was marrying and giving in marriage, and the writer contrived to get through his drills, be dismissed from them all, and become a bona fide duty-soldier in about six months.

BANCROFT

Soldiers' wives: India in the 1840's

THE only European troops at Sukkur, beside our corps, was a company of horse artillery, who were as dissolute a body of men as I ever met with, and nearly an equitable mixture of English, Irish, and Scotch. A few of them had very pretty half-caste wives, whom they had got out of the Byculla orphan school at Bombay, where any soldier of good character and possessed of capital to commence house-keeping, may obtain a helpmate. These girls are tolerably well educated, and would make grateful and affectionate wives, were it not that soldiers in general make such bad husbands. For a while after marriage they may get on pretty well, but they soon become negligent, and return drunk to their berths. Half-caste women are almost invariably passionate and vindictive, readily taking offence, especially if they think that it is offered in consequence of their colour, and hence they view the indifference of their European husbands in the worst possible light—neglect their household duties as a matter of course; and will soon learn to drink, and smoke the hookah all day long if they can; becoming slatterns in every sense of the word. It must, however, be admitted that in any country a bad, dissolute husband can scarcely fail to make a bad wife; unless, indeed, the wife is a strong-minded person, who thoroughly knows the duties of her station.

In countries like Ireland, where there is such a prolific supply of the gentler sex, and where so many are destined neither to be wooed nor won, becoming in due time that half-nondescript sort of animal termed old maids, persons can form no idea of the scarcity of white women in India. There, he is fortunate a man who has two or three tolerable looking daughters on the eve of womanhood; he requires no fortunes to get them off his hands; but, on the contrary, propitiatory presents shower in upon him from a dozen individuals, all ready to pay handsomely in that way, or any other, for being permitted to marry into his family. Nor need the death of a husband be a matter of much regret to a woman, for she is besieged by admirers while the tears which decency demands are still coursing one another down her cheeks. When in Calcutta, I was told it was no uncommon thing for men in the Company's civil employment to become regularly there to inquire if there were any decent soldiers' widows to be had; and I knew one woman personally who was the wife of three husbands in six months, and another who had married her fifth husband, having children by every one of them.

MACMULLEN

A Soldier's Farewell, 1854

Poetry wrote by William Whitehead when under orders for the Crimea

Farewell to thee, Faversham, my friends and my home
Since then duty calls me away
I go in a land of wild tumult to roam
All attired in battle array.

Dear parents, farewell, a long long adieu
Now my eyes they grow dim with a tear
To leave you and the spot where my infancy grew
With all I must love and Revere.

And now dear brothers and sister a tender goodbye
Thou hast ever been loving and true,
Sharing alike my laugh and my sigh,
As with joy or misfortune they grew.

And last but not lost my sweet fair art thou
Oh doubt not my constancy dear,
T'is madness to swear else much I could vow,
But all I give or will ask is a tear.

Sweet Faversham though plain and unassuming thou be
Now my heart to thee fondly does cling
Each object in thee now seems sacred to me
And new thoughts new endearments bring.

But enough! Grim war does summons me hence
And I deem it my duty to fight
T'is an honour to stand in proud England's defence
When once she is proved in the right.

Then farewell to Faversham, my friends and my home,
Adieu I am bound for the east.
And when I am far over old ocean's white foam,
Your rememberance pray give me at least.

(signed) W. Whitehead, Gunner,
No. 5. Co., 5th Battn, R.A.

WHITEHEAD

Regimental life at home after the Crimean War

I SOON had many opportunities of forming an opinion of the regiment in which so many of my days were to be passed. It was at this time filled with seasoned and veteran soldiers, many of whom had been seventeen and eighteen years in India. Nothing delighted me more than to get one of these old soldiers 'on a line' telling tales of Kalapoosh. They were very diffident about their own deeds; but when describing what their comrades had done, their tongues were loosened, and some of the stories beat anything I ever heard or read of.

The 14th Hussars contained as fine a body of fighting men and as smart a set of soldiers as any in the British army, their only fault being a liking for pongelo, for, truth to tell, they were hard drinkers. It must also be admitted that they were not as clever with the pen as with the sword, and in the matter of 'the three R's' could not be compared with the young soldiers of the present day, who are scholars by Act of Parliament. But it is an ill wind that blows nobody any good, and my education now stood me in good stead; for of the fifteen men in my room, not one could write, and only one could read, and my ability to do both soon proved to my advantage.

It began this way. One day an old soldier beckoned me aside, and asked me in a mysterious way to have a wet with him at the canteen. I thanked him but declined; whereupon he produced a letter, and shoving it into my hand, asked me to read it to him. This I did, much to his delight, and after thanking me, he offered me sixpence (as I had declined a drink) which of course I refused.

'Well, I won't forget it, anyhow,' he said; 'and if you'll only write an answer back for me, I will boss your arms up when you come off drill, and if anyone rides rough over you, just you let me know, and I'll see to it.'

This started the ball rolling, and in a short time I was reader and secretary to the whole room. There were some queer letters indited by me at times, for I always had a bit of fun in me, and it would come out when I had to write to two different girls from the same man, who had left a brace of sweethearts behind him in Manchester. Sometimes I slipped in a bit more than was dictated, and then, to the men's joy, the answers came back with unexpected remittances of postage-stamps and which my persuasive pen had brought. There was this curious thing about it, that—although these old soldiers freely trusted me with their secrets—when it came to posting the letters, every man would put his own into the box himself.

There was one funny fellow, in particular, who often availed himself of my penmanship—a cockney of the name of Fruiterer, but always called Rootee on account of his fondness for bread. He was a very 'caius' (artful) chap, and had some well-to-do-friends in London, from whom he often received money, which went as fast as it came, in grub—for Rootee was an exception to the general rule, and liked eating better than drinking. When I began to write his letters for him I came in for a full share of his feasts, and he was always inventing new excuses to pile up the agony, and urging me to pitch his folks some extra thrilling yarn about his hardships, and especially his hunger. One day, when funds were very low, and he was desperately hard up for something to say, he asked me:

''Cruity, scratch your head, and tell us something to sling at 'em.'

I suggested, offhand, the first thing that occurred to me.

'Write home and swear you've lost a wheelbarrow while on stable-guard, and if you don't pay for it Splodgers will have you sent to cells.'

'That's the hammer!' he shouted, jumping up and slapping his knee. 'That will knock the dollars out of 'em!'

The letter was written, and posted, and a sovereign came back within twenty four hours—seventeen and sixpence being the price of the barrow, and the odd half crown to buy an extra good one to appease Splodgers. The result of this shower of gold was that old Rootee forgot his prudence, and 'chanced his arm'—as the saying goes, when a man risks losing his stripes—by a visit to the canteen, which brought him about nightfall to the guard room, and the next afternoon I had the sorrow of seeing him perspiring under pack drill. When I whispered in a friendly way he might find it easier to wheel his kit on a barrow, he glared at me, and didn't take the advice in the spirit in which it was offered.

Apart from becoming a bit of a favourite in the room, from writing the men's letters for them, I gained by it myself, for I soon earned a character for keeping my arms and accoutrements clean. I hope I accepted the commendation this brought me with befitting modesty, for, truth to tell, the men whose letters I wrote deserved it all.

Life at Hounslow, with a few ups and downs, was, on the whole, very pleasant. I had got into the swing of duty by this time, and no longer found it irksome, and when I wanted a holiday I could generally get leave by putting in a pass. Occasionally the routine of life was broken by a commanding-officers' field-day on the heath made famous by highwaymen; or better still, by a grand-field-day at Wormwood Scrubbs, when we were sometimes brigaded with the two cavalry regiments of the Guards at that time quartered in London. These were termed 'ladies' days', from the number of the fair sex who used to grace the scene. The operations always included the cutting and pursuing practice at the gallop, and as we passed the saluting point to the tune of 'Bonnie Dundee', we never failed in getting a roar of applause from the spectators, and a special waving of handkerchiefs from the ladies.

In November, we were ordered to take part in the Lord Mayor's procession. The majority of the men were told off as the advance and rear escort, but about forty including myself—were sent up with that number of horses for the use of some extra mounted police. I had at this time a rather skittish young Irish trooper, which was not considered suitable for constabulary work, so I was ordered to take up Old Will instead. We marched under the command of the riding master, who was an Irishman by birth, but considered to have a Turkish appearance, and nicknamed Omer Pasha. On reaching the Guildhall, we dismounted, and unsaddling our horses, made them over to the police. Old Will fell to the lot of a stout and particularly pompous peeler, who looked him up and down with a troubled and anxious air. 'Is he quiet?' he asked me in a whisper, slipping a shilling into my hand. 'He's a wooden sheep'—said I—'on wheels'. With that I got his saddle on Old Will's back, and told him to climb up.

Gathering the reins loosely in his left hand, the policeman mounted, but before he could get home in his seat, Old Will—who evidently thought he had a 'cruity on his back—was off like a flash of lightning, and there was a merry five minutes of riding-school play in the courtyard of the Guildhall, as he dodged in and out of the other horses as if the rough rider's whip were trailing behind him. As for the bobby, he convulsively dug in his heels, and clutched hold of the pommel of his saddle with his right hand, trying to get a purchase on the reins with his left, which was jerking about somewhere on a line with the back of his head.

'Keep your spurs out of him, you bottle-blue marine!' shouted out Omer Pasha.

'Put the skid on the wheel!' I cried as he passed me for the second time.

He did neither, for just then the saddle turned round, and he was deposited on the flags amidst the jeers of the bystanders. Of course, Old Will came to a dead halt, and stood waiting with a patient look in his face, just as he was accustomed to do at riding school when a recruit dismounted without leave.

MOLE

A comrade's opinion: Federal Army, 1861

FRISBEE had not very many faults. The only ones I can readily recall were swearing, gambling, lying, drinking, stealing and speaking evil of the orderly sergeant; but in these few, I feel constrained to testify he was an adept and did not do things by halves. In drinking, however, we had one man who was more than a match for Frisbee. It was Bill Pilkington. He avowed that he did not care for the quality of the whiskey if it would only make the drunk come, and that he never allowed an opportunity for getting drunk to pass unimproved. I could take oath that during my acquaintance with him this was strictly true.

ANDREWS

Soldiers' pets in Victorian India

MANY of the men took up some pursuit as a hobby, such as keeping pets, training birds to talk, catching cobras, collecting butterflies and the like. I think the birds at Bangalore were the first things to attract their attention, for they were so different to the English ones. There were three varieties that frequented our barracks: the sparrows, crows and kites. First in everyone's affections came the sparrow, for he was in evidence everywhere. He was very much like his English brother, only cleaner, glossier and tamer. He would fly in at the open verandah, when the men were at meals, and without the least fear, hop about on the tables and help himself to a bit of anything he fancied, often perching on the edge of a basin and tasting the milk or cold tea. The men encouraged them, and never attempted to drive them away, for all looked on the sparrow as one of the few links between us and old England, and whatever else was trapped or shot, the little brown bird never had a finger raised against him, for we loved him in India as we did Robin Redbreast at home.

Artful old Jack Crow was quite a different customer. His character was as black as his looks. Still the men never killed him in barracks, though the crows took care to give a wide berth to anyone carrying a gun outside them, for they knew the use of it as well as the armourer-sergeant. Jack Crow was a professional thief, a felon in feathers. It was the custom for the native boys to carry the soldiers' dinners across from the cook-house to the barracks in open baskets, and these the crows considered it their duty to requisition. If ever the boys' attention was diverted for a few seconds, down hopped a crow in a twinkling and whipped off a piece of hot steak or a chunk of pudding, and flew away with it to the roof of a neighbouring bungalow. And then it was a sight to see the native cook gesticulating and cursing the old crow, who between each mouthful would caw back at him in an insulting way. Our men delighted in devising traps to catch these crows, and cunning as the birds were, they could be enticed into a room and captured. And now they had to submit to a badge, or, as I think they regarded it, the decoration of captivity. A thin piece of wire was inserted between the two holes in their upper beak, and a button, or disc of metal, or little bell—attached, each troop having its distinctive token—and the birds were then let loose, none the worse for the operation. In time nearly every crow in barracks wore one of these symbols of capture, and as they attached themselves in particular buildings, we could always tell which troop they belonged to by the badge they wore. Mighty proud Jack Crow grew of his Legion of Honour, especially of the bell, and it was a comical sight to see a row of these birds perched on the roofs, shaking their heads up and down, tinkling their bells, and seeming their actions to say 'Me got medal too, same like soldier Sahib.'

Kites, the third variety of barrack birds spent most of their time soaring and circling high in the sky. But should any servants pass along with a piece of meat exposed in a basket on their heads, or even in a plate in their hands, often a kite would swoop down with incredible swiftness from a tremendous height, and sweeping it off with his claws, fly up again and devour it on the wing. It was great fun to see this trick played on a raw recruit who might be crossing from the coffee-shop with a savoury stew he was licking his lips over in anticipation, until there came a whistle of wings and a rustle of feathers, and off went the solid part of his feast, leaving him only the unsubstantial gravy. At meal times these kites would descend and circle screeching round the bungalows; and the men, when they had finished their meals, would often toss the bones and fragments in the air, which the birds never failed to catch with their claws before the morsel reached the ground. These kites served a useful purpose as general scavengers, and the men were strictly prohibited from shooting them.

The tame or domestic birds, kept in cages, were chiefly parrots, and minahs, the latter being a sort of starling. Many of these were brought round for sale, and could be purchased for a copper. Some of the men went in for teaching them to talk, and a common method of doing so was to lower a cage some distance down a wall, and then lean over the edge and shout down the expressions to the parrot or minah which he was required to learn. Many an orator has turned out in this way and sold for twenty or thirty rupees. Sometimes a man with a touch of caustic humour not uncombined with business acumen, would teach his bird the uncomplimentary nick-name of his troop-sergeant-major, and, when it was proficient, hang its cage up in a commanding position, where to the delight of the men, but chagrin of the victim, it would give public utterance to the obnoxious designation. I remember one instance in which a sergeant was so derided, that to stop the annoyance he bought the parrot for a large sum of money and then wrung the poor bird's neck.

Of course, there were many four-footed pets kept in barracks, by the men, no restrictions being placed on their doing so. Dogs were the most popular. They were generally chained up under the shade of the trees between the troop bungalows and their principal delight was a bandicoot hunt. The bandicoot is a monster rat, a regular elephant among rodents, and has lots of fighting in him. Great numbers infested every building and stable, and provided rare sport for the terriers. There was always a good market for really game dogs amongst the wealthy natives and Europeans; so that dog breeding and training was a source of profit as well as pleasure. Next to dogs came monkeys, but their dirty and michievieous habits prevented them from becoming favourites and they were not nearly as popular as the mungoose, a bright-eyed merry-mannered little creature, something like a large grey ferret, which everyone seemed fond of. The mungoose was clean, easily tamed, and affectionate, and soon evinced a great attachment for his master, these animals were generally kept in the bungalows, fastened by a chain to the men's cota, who frequently carried them out for an evening stroll, and took them to the canteen, snuggled away in the insides of their coats, from which they peeped out, all wide awake, with their little ferrety eyes purling round. The mungoose is supposed to be invulnerable to the bite of the most venomous snake, but this is not the case, for I have witnessed many of their plucky combats with cobras, and though they generally killed the snakes, it would sometimes happen that the mungoose missed his spring, and got bitten by the reptile. He would continue his attack and generally kill the cobra, but he always died himself in a few minutes. The mungoose's method of attack is singular; having come upon a cobra in the open, he begins racing round and round him at great speed, taking care however to keep out of striking distance. The cobra rears itself up, expands its hood and with its eyes tries to follow the rapid circular movement, of its enemy, turning its head quickly first to one side, then to another as its assailant disappears and reappears in the course of its circuit. This constant motion at length forces the snake to lower its head for a rest, when the mungoose seizes the opportunity, and springing forward fixes its teeth behind the cobra's head and in spite of its contortions and writhings, holds on like grim death till it is dead. If the mungoose misses its spring the snake has its chance, but whether bitten or not, the mungoose always returns to the attack. These deadly combats are, I am persuaded, the result of a natural antipathy, for the mungoose never eats the snake. It was the great bravery of these plucky little fellows in attacking so deadly a foe that endeared them to every soldier's heart.

Most of the married people kept pigeons, ducks, rabbits, and fowls. Amongst the latter were some grand specimens of the Indian game or fighting cock, and many a sporting match used to be brought off in the dry ravines around Bangalore, their sandy sides and bottoms forming the fine natural pits. The natives were very fond of cock-fighting, and the taste soon spread to the men of our regiment, and I must plead guilty to a weakness myself for what I have heard called a demoralizing sport. Many of my neighbours kept a fancy bird or two, and each man had an opinion of his own, and bragged about what his cock could do, and at last, an opportunity offering, I determined to keep one as well.

Our riding-master, old Omer Pasha, had a rare bird which I had often admired. It stood nearly three feet high, and its leg was like a young ostrich's. It was very decently behaved as long as it was let alone, but if ever a cock crew within sound, he would stalk off and kill it as a matter of duty.

MOLE

Soldiers' amusements: shadow theatre in the jungle: Foreign Legion

SINCE I had been detached on special service I had messed with these two telegraphists, and it was not long before we were the best of friends. Bougand, the marine, and Gremaire, the gunner, were Parisians of good family and education; and, thanks to their natural versatility and wit, we soon found means of introducing a certain amount of fun into our existence, which helped to relieve the terrible monotony of life in the fort.

By nailing a damp sheet over a window which gave upon the gun-platform, and with the aid of a powerful lamp, sometime used for signalling at night, we started a shadow theatre. Our troupe and scenery we cut out of thick cardboard, and we were able to present adaptations of some of the most popular dramas and comedies of the day, the text and mise-en-scene of which would have been a startling revelation to the original authors.

These performances were given twice a week, and lasted from 7.30 till 9 p.m., and our audience was composed of all the Legionaries not on duty and such of the native troops as cared to attend. There was, of course, no accommodation for the spectators, who were indeed above such details; and they contented themselves with standing, or squatting upon the hard ground to watch the show. Though some of our audiences saw fit to make rude remarks concerning the tone of voice in which the feminine roles were read, the majority were unsparing of their applause; and the appearance of the silhouettes of such famous artists as the golden-voiced Sarah or the two Coquelins brought down the house. Now and again some ready-witted interruption from one of the spectators or the actors would cause the temporary disappearance of the actors from the stage and a momentary cessation of the performance, for, unable to control our emotions or continue the dialogue, we would fall on the floor of the little mat-shed hut, where we would lie convulsed with laughter, until the noisy public threatened to pull down the house unless we continued the play.

Success ofttimes breeds foolhardiness and in an evil hour, finding that we had exhausted the repertoire our memories offered us, of plots from the Parisian stage, we decided to draw on local incidents for the construction of our plays. At first all went well, for such fares as The De-Tam's Defeat, in which that chief, after refusing the hand of the Governor-General's daughter and a big dowry, died through incautiously tasting the contents of a tin of bullybeef, supplied by the Commissariat for the use of the troops, were successful, and produced no untoward results. But, craving for still greater popularity, we were foolish enough to put upon our stage the too-transparently caricatured counterpart of one of the senior non-commissioned officers in the company of native troops, who, though an excellent soldier, was possessed of many eccentricities. This veteran resented our impudence, and we were reported and obliged to suspend our performances.

MANINGTON

Soldiers' pets in the South African War

It is a remarkable fact that dogs throughout the campaign have shown a strong fancy for troops on the march, leaving their owners in the towns and farms and joining the columns. They certainly did not join us because of any food thrown away, so numerous were they at one period that many had to be destroyed.

Many animals have been made pets of by the various regiments. The 2nd Grenadiers had a pet goat for a long time which followed them for miles over the veldt. An illustration shows one of these pets, 'Jack', a prettily marked fox terrier, with his master, Private R. Lauchlan, of P Company 2nd Scots Guards. Jack was presented to us by a trooper of the Hussars at Port Elizabeth in April, 1900; he was then only a puppy six weeks old. During his puppy days he was carried by various men of the company until he was strong enough to keep up with the battalion. He was present at the Battle of Biddulphsberg, and whilst advancing with the battalion was severely burned by the blazing veldt; his burns were carefully treated, and ultimately he recovered from his injuries. Jack knows perfectly well that the Eighth Division has been indifferently fed, for he also has shared our hardships and privations, having experienced, like ourselves, many heavy marches on light rations. He has learned also the art of taking whatever shelter offers when the troops advance in attack order, and well knows the sound of the Mauser bullet when it passes unpleasantly near. After a heavy day's march he patiently waits until his master makes down his bed on the veldt, and then he creeps into some snug place to enjoy the rest he thinks he has so well deserved.

'Mick', a black and white dog, belonging to the 26th Kent Yeomanry, has, like his comrade 'Jack' been often under fire, and was a well-known and favoured camp-follower. He returned to England, and enjoys a comfortable home with Captain Bertram Pott, who commanded the Company.

MOFFETT

Leisure time in the French Foreign Legion

THE daily walk in Sidi-bel-Abbes was part of the Legion's sacred tradition. At five o'clock the gigantic gates of the barracks were closed and only a little side door remained open. Here the sergeant of the guard posted himself and carefully inspected every body who wanted to go out, so that the Legion's reputation for chic should not suffer. The uniform to be worn in town was prescribed every day by a special regimental order; each legionnaire had to wear the same uniform, red trousers and blue jacket or white trousers and blue overcoat, and everybody took an especial pride in looking as trim and smart as possible.

Three thousand soldiers of the Legion used to stroll about the streets of Sidi-bel-Abbes every evening. For me this daily walk was a wondrous change from the Legion's routine. Above the gleam of the electric arc lamps shone the starry glory of a southern sky. Little black boys in white breeches, whose countless folds might have told endless stories of stolen trifles they had concealed, lounged at the street corners and cried the evening paper, the *Echo d'Oran*; Arabs in white burnouses, carrying in their hands the dangerous Arabian sticks, in which they find a never-failing missile, stood motionless, silently watching with looks of suspicion the 'Rumis', the white foreigners who will always remain foreigners to them and whose customs they will never be able to understand. All Sidi-bel-Abbes was promenading; citizens of the town, officers and civilians of the 'Bureau Arabe' with their womenfolk. In between came the Legion's heavy soldier-steps and the sound of gently rattling bayonets.

Four streets, which run exactly north, south, east, and west, to Oran, Daya, Maskara, and Tlemcen, divide the town at right angles. They are the main streets in which the European shops and fashionable cafés lie. For private financial reasons the legionnaire does not buy in these shops and in the fashionable cafés he is badly treated. The legionnaire has no business in the main streets—from the honest citizen's point of view.

Between the blocks of the main streets, however, a labyrinth of small courts and alleys is hidden. There the Spanish Jews and Arabs live, there trading and bargaining go on incessantly.

In this maze of dark alleys the men of the Legion were at home, in the treacherous wineshops which depended on the custom of the soldiers. 'Bar de la Legion', or 'Bar du Legionnaire', or 'Bar de Madagascar' these hovels called themselves. Good wine is ridiculously cheap in Algeria. But out of the legionnaires extra money must needs be made. They were given a brew in the wineshops made from grapes which had been pressed already two or three times and to which a little alcohol lent flavour and 'aroma'. Beside the wineshops were Mohammedan restaurants in which one could eat 'kuskus' and 'galettes', tough pancakes with honey; restaurants in which knives and forks were looked upon as accursed instruments, which doubtless the devil of the Rumis must have invented for devilish purposes unintelligible to a true believer. Poverty and filth reigned in these places, but they were good enough for the poor despised legionnaire. One café in this quarter had an individuality of its own, depending exclusively on the custom of the Legion. In a corner by the theatre a pretty little Spanish girl had put up a wooden hut and filled it with rickety old chairs, to be treated and used with great care, given her in charity probably somewhere or other merely to get rid of them. There she sold coffee to the soldiers of the Legion. This little woman had a good eye for business. Her coffee was, 'tis true, merely coloured hot water and not especially good water at that, but the soldier of the Legion willingly drank it, for Manuelita's coffee was very cheap indeed, and a pretty smile and a coquette glance went with each cup. When business was slack the hostess would even chat a little. These tactics secured for the sly little Spaniard the faithful custom of the legionnaires. La Legion made love to Manuelita unceasingly. . . . The old legionnaires stole flowers for her, and if somewhere in Tonquin or on the Morocco border plundering had been going on, Manuelita would some months later be sure to receive the finest presents, stolen for her by her old friends of the Legion and carried about all the time in knapsacks. The Legion was grateful to Manuelita. She was the great exception. Besides her and Madame la Cantinière there was no woman in the town of the Foreign Legion who would even in her wildest dreams have deigned a legionnaire worthy of a glance.

ROSEN

6

NON-COMMISSIONED OFFICERS: OFFICERS

Sufferings of a recruit: a dishonest N.C.O., 1773

MATTERS changed with me much for the better when I joined my regiment, as far as regarded my personal feelings, but I had to experience other sufferings. I was put into a mess with a number of recruits. The non-commissioned officer who had us in charge received our pay every Saturday, and squandered the greater part of it in paying the expenses of his weekly score at the public house, by which means, we had to subsist upon a very scanty allowance, although at that time, provisions were very cheap in Waterford. We often complained in private among ourselves, but whenever we remonstrated with him he menaced us with confinement in the guard-house, and such was our inexperience, and apprehension of being punished by his interference against us, that we submitted in silence. If we had boldly stated our grievances to the officer commanding, we most certainly had been redressed. No doubt such an effect would have resulted from our complaints properly made.

SERJEANT LAMB

A regimental sergeant-major and 'the epaulette gentry.' Canada, late eighteenth century

WHILE I was Corporal I was made clerk to the regiment. In a very short time, the whole of the business in that way fell into my hands; and, at the end of about a year, neither adjutant, paymaster, or quarter-master, could move an inch without my assistance. The accounts and letters of the paymaster went through my hands; or, rather, I was the maker of them. All the returns, reports, and other official papers were of my drawing up.

Then I became Sergeant-Major to the regiment, which brought me in close contact at every hour, with the whole of the epaulette gentry, whose profound and surprising ignorance I discovered in a twinkling. The military part of the regiment's affairs fell under my care. In early life, I contracted the blessed habit of husbanding well my time. To this more than to any other thing, I owed my very extraordinary promotion in the army. I was always ready: never did any man, or anything, wait one moment for me. Being raised from corporal to sergeant-major at once, over the heads of thirty sergeants, I naturally should have been an object of envy and hatred; but this habit of early rising really subdued these passions; because everyone felt that what I did he had never done, and never could do. Long before any other man was dressed for parade, my work for the morning was well done, and I myself was on parade walking in fine weather, for an hour perhaps. My custom was this: to get up, in summer, at daylight, and in winter at four o'clock; shave, dress, even to the putting of my sword belt over my shoulder, and having my sword lying on the table before me, ready to hang by my side. Then I ate a bit of cheese, or pork, and bread. Then I prepared my report, which was filled up as fast as the companies brought me in the materials. After this I had an hour or two to read, before the time came for any duty out of doors, unless when the regiment or part of it went out to exercise in the morning. When this was the case, and the matter was left to me, I always had it on the ground in such time as that the bayonets glistened in the rising sun, a sight which gave me delight, of which I often think, but which I should in vain endeavour to describe. If the officers were to go out, eight or ten o'clock was the hour, sweating the men in the heat of the day, breaking in upon the time for cooking their dinner, putting all things out of order and all men out of humour. When I was commander, the men had a long day of leisure before them: they could ramble into the town or into the woods; go to get raspberries, to catch birds, to catch fish, or to pursue any other recreation, and such of them as chose, and were qualified, to work at their trades. So that here, arising solely from the early habits of one very young man, were pleasant and happy days given to hundreds.

About this time, the new discipline, as it was called, was sent out to us in little books, which were to be studied by the officers of each regiment, and the rules of which were to be immediately conformed to. Though any old woman might have written such a book; though it was excessively foolish from beginning to end; still, it was to be complied with, it ordered and commanded a total change.

To make this change was left to me, while not a single officer in the regiment paid the least attention to the matter; so that, when the time came for the annual review, I had to give lectures of instruction to the officers themselves, the Colonel not excepted; and, for several of them, I had to make out, upon large cards, which they bought for the purpose, little plans of the position of the regiment, together with lists of the words of command, which they had to give in the field. There was I, at the review, upon the flank of the grenadier company, with my worsted shoulder-knot, and my great high, coarse, hairy cap; confounded in the ranks amongst other men, while those who were commanding me to move my hands or my feet, thus or thus, were, in fact, uttering words, which I had taught them; and were, in everything except mere authority, my inferiors; and ought to have been commanded by me. It was impossible for reflections of this sort not to intrude themselves; and, as I advanced in experience, I felt less and less respect for those, whom I was compelled to obey.

But I had a very delicate part to act with those gentry; for, while I despised them for their gross ignorance and their vanity, and hated them for their drunkenness and rapacity, I was fully sensible of their power. My path was full of rocks and pitfalls; and, as I never disguised my dislikes, or restrained my tongue, I should have been broken and flogged for fifty different offences, had they not been kept in awe by my inflexible sobriety, impartiality, and integrity, by the consciousness of their inferiority to me, and by the real and almost indispensable necessity of the use of my talents. They, in fact, resigned all the discipline of the regiment to me, and I very freely left them to swagger about and to get roaring drunk.

To describe the various instances of their ignorance, and the various tricks they played to diguise it from me, would fill a volume. It is the custom in regiments to give out orders every day from the officer commanding. These are written by the Adjutant, to whom the Sergeant-Major is a sort of deputy. The man whom I had to do with was a keen fellow, but wholly illiterate. The orders which he wrote most cruelly murdered our mother-tongue. But in his absence, or during a severe drunken fit, it fell to my lot to write orders. As we both wrote in the same book, he used to look at these. He saw commas, semi-colons, colons, full points, and paragraphs. The questions he used to put to me, in an obscure sort of way, in order to know why I made these divisions, and yet, at the same time, his attempts to disguise his object, have made me laugh a thousand times. He at last fell upon this device: he made me write, while he pretended to dictate! Imagine to yourself, me sitting, pen in hand, to put upon paper the precious offspring of the mind of this stupid curmudgeon! But, here, a greater difficulty than any former arose. He that could not write good grammar, could not, of course, dictate good grammar. Out would come some gross error, such as I was ashamed to see in my handwriting, I would stop; suggest another arrangement; but this I was at first obliged to do in a very indirect and delicate manner. But this course could not continue long; and he put an end to it in this way: he used to tell me his story, and leave me to put it upon paper; and this we continued to the end of our connection.

COBBETT

Promotion: the duties of a non-commissioned officer, 1802

I HAD now attained the age of eighteen years; was healthy and active; a zealous, though very humble member of the profession I had chosen; and an ardent aspirant to share in my country's glory. With these feelings and qualifications, assuring myself that, now I was in India, I was in the wide field of promise, I began to revolve in my mind if I could not better my situation. I was then fifer and bugler in the light company, the kind captain of which, seeing my anxious spirit, generously undertook to improve me in reading and writing, of which I at that time knew but little. In the course of one year's close application, I so much improved as to keep his books of the company and his own private accounts. I then begged of him that I might be removed from the drummers to the ranks. I did not like the appellation drum-boy. As I have seen many a man riding post, who was at least sixty years old, still called a post-boy, so, if a drummer had attained the age of Methusaleh, he would never acquire any other title than drum-boy. Indeed, there were many other things I could never bring myself to relish in any eminent degree: such as flogging—to say nothing of being flogged—and dancing attendance on a capricious sergeant-major, or his more consequential spouse, who is queen of the soldiers' wives, and mother of tipplers, and an invitation-card from whom to tea and cards is considered a ponderous obligation.

In about a week after having made this request, I was transferred from the drummers' room, and promoted to the rank of corporal. This was promotion indeed—three steps in one day! From drum-boy to private; from a battalion company to the Light Bobs; and from private to corporal! I was not long before I paraded myself in the tailor's shop, and tipped the master-snip a rupee to give me a good and neat cut, such as became a full corporal. By evening parade my blushing honours came thick upon me. The captain came upon parade, and read aloud the regimental orders of the day, laying great stress upon, 'to the rank of corporal, and to be obeyed accordingly.' I was on the right of the company, being the tallest man on parade, when I was desired by the captain to fall out and give the time. I did so, and never did a fugleman cut more capers; but here an awkward accident happened. In shouldering arms, I elevated my left hand high in the air; extended my leg in an oblique direction, with the point of my toe just touching the ground; but in throwing the musket up in a fugle-like manner, the cock caught the bottom of my jacket, and down came brown Bess flat upon my toes, to the great amusement of the tittering company. I must confess, I felt queer; but I soon recovered my piece and my gravity, and all went on smoothly, till I got into the barracks, where a quick hedge-firing commenced from all quarters; such as, 'Shoulder hems!'—'Shoulder hems!'—'Twig the fugleman!' This file-firing increased to volleys, till I was obliged to exert my authority by threatening them with the guard-house, for riotous conduct; but this only increased the merriment, so I pocketed the affront, as the easiest and most good-natured mode of escape; my persecutors ceased, and thus ended my first parade as a non-commissioned officer.

In my new sphere of life I now felt that there was, unquestionably, some satisfaction derivable from being

'Clothed in a little brief authority.'

A corporal has to take command of small guards; is privileged to visit the sentinels whenever he pleases; his suggestions are frequently attended to by his superiors; and his orders must be promptly obeyed by those below him. There is certainly a pleasure in all this, and a man rises proportionately in his own esteem. In short, to confess the truth I now looked upon a drum-boy as little better than his drum.

Full of the importance of my situation and duties, thus passed the time for nearly six months, at the end of which I was advanced to the rank of sergeant, and, shortly afterwards, to that of pay-sergeant, in the same regiment. The post of pay-sergeant is certainly one of importance, and he who holds it is a personage of no small consideration. He feeds and clothes the men; lends them money at moderate interest and on good security; and sells them watches and seals, on credit, at a price somewhat above what they cost, to be sure, but the mere sight of which, dangling from a man's fob, has been known to gain him the character of a sober steady fellow, and one that should be set down for promotion. Thus, at least, good may sometimes be educed from evil; and, as it is not my intention to enter into a detail of the chicanery practised among the minor ranks in the army, let it suffice that I never served in a company in which every individual could not buy, sell, exchange, lend, and borrow, on terms peculiar to themselves.

JOHN SHIPP

A rifleman and General Hill in Portugal, 1808

IT WAS five or six days before the battle of Rolica, the army was on the march, and we were pushing on pretty fast. The whole force had slept the night before in the open fields; indeed, as far as I know (for the Rifles were always in the front at this time) they had been for many days without any covering but the sky. We were pelting along through the streets of a village, the name of which I do not think I ever knew, so I cannot name it; I was in the front, and had just cleared the village, when I recollect observing General Hill (afterwards Lord Hill) and another officer ride up to a house, and give their horses to some of the soldiery to hold. Our bugle at that moment sounded the halt, and I stood leaning upon my rifle near the door of the mansion which General Hill had entered: there was a little garden before the house and I stood by the gate. Whilst I remained there, the officer who had entered with General Hill came to the door, and called to me. 'Rifleman,' said he, 'come here.' I entered the gate, and approached him. 'Go,' he continued, handing me a dollar, 'and try if you can get some wine; for we are devilish thirsty here.' Taking the dollar, I made my way back to the village. At a winehouse, where the men were crowding around the door, and clamouring for drink (for the day was intensely hot), I succeeded, after some little difficulty, in getting a small pipkin full of wine; but the crowd was so great, that I found as much trouble in paying for it as in getting it; so I returned back as fast as I was able, fearing that the general would be impatient, and move off before I reached him. I remember Lord Hill was loosening his sword-belt as I handed him the wine. 'Drink first, Rifleman,' said he; and I took a good pull at the pipkin, and held it to him again. He looked at it as I did so, and told me I might drink it all up, for it appeared greasy; so I swallowed the remainder, and handed him back the dollar which I had received from the officer. 'Keep the money,' he said, 'my man. Go back to the village once more, and try if you cannot get me another draught.' Saying this, he handed me a second dollar, and told me to be quick. I made my way back to the village, got another pipkin full, and returned as fast as I could. The general was pleased with my promptness, and drank with great satisfaction, handing the remainder to the officer who attended him; and I dare say, if he ever recollected the circumstances afterwards, that was as sweet a draught, after the toil of the morning march, as he has drank at many a nobleman's board in Old England since.

RIFLEMAN HARRIS

A rifleman's observations on his officers

It is, indeed, singular, how a man loses or gains caste with his comrades from his behaviour, and how closely he is observed in the field. The officers, too, are commented upon and closely observed. The men are very proud of those who are brave in the field, and kind and considerate to the soldiers under them. An act of kindness done by an officer has often during the battle been the cause of his life being saved. Nay, whatever folks may say upon the matter, I know from experience, that in our army the men like best to be officered by gentlemen, men whose education has rendered them more kind in manners than your coarse officer, sprung from obscure origin, and whose style is brutal and overbearing.

RIFLEMAN HARRIS

Disappointment over promotion: an N.C.O.'s views

I was in a short time made drill-corporal in my own regiment, and afterwards drill-sergeant. This was a situation I was fond of, and a preparatory step to that of regimental sergeant-major. For a time this new toy pleased me, for I would, at any time, sooner command than be commanded; but the duties of a drill-sergeant are very laborious.

I went on tolerably well with the troubles and vexations of this arduous office, when, one fine morning, it was rumoured through the lines that the sergeant-major was defunct in hospital. I was congratulated from all quarters as his successor, as a matter of course, and the eye of the whole regiment was upon the drill-sergeant. I expected a summons every moment from the commanding officer. So sanguine was I myself, that I had directed that all my 'traps' might be put in moveable order; when, lo! another sergeant was appointed sergeant-major, leaving poor me the butt and jeer of the whole corps. I could not imagine what could possibly be the cause of this strange appointment. I say strange, for two reasons, first, that the situation had been promised to me; and, secondly, that the sergeant who was appointed was, of all others, the most unfit for it. I felt hurt beyond description, but my spirit was too proud to permit me to ask why I had thus been passed over. I bore it as patiently as I could, still trying to kill care by fagging at the drills; and no doubt some of the poor fellows under me felt the weight of my disappointed hopes, for I had them out late and early. I mentioned, however, the circumstance to my captain, and told him I would resign both my drill-sergeantship and also my three other stripes; but the captain, having more prudence and temper than his sergeant, advised me to put up with it, saying, that he had no doubt the colonel had something better in store for me. This supposition appeased my troubled mind, and I endeavoured to smother my grief by making myself a better drill; and in a short time the storm had blown over, and the event was nearly obliterated from my memory. After this affair I always avoided the colonel, and whenever chance threw me his way, I gave him the customary salute due to his rank, but accompanied with a few dark looks, as tokens of my gratitude.

JOHN SHIPP

The new sergeant-major, 24th Light Dragoons, 1813

ON THE following morning I moved into my new house, and published my own appointment. Here all the cares and anxieties of my past life were forgotten. The very idea of having the whole regiment under my special command at drill, was to me inexpressibly delightful, and I looked forward to the day as the consummation of my military glory.

As a groundwork for proceeding properly in my new office, I established an inseparable vacuum between my rank and that of the other non-commissioned officers, treating them with every respect consistent with theirs, and, in time, making them sensible that such a difference must be established between their station and that of the privates under their command. I enforced prompt obedience and attention from them, and they from those under them. This they at first construed into pride on my part; but, in time, that prejudice wore off, and they obeyed with pleasure. Those who proved refractory were removed from their situations, and those more obedient promoted in their stead. Thus things went on smoothly and pleasantly; and, in two or three months, I could trust them in the discharge of their duties with confidence, and they soon learned how far they could go with me. I had a strict and vigilant adjutant; he made a strict and vigilant sergeant-major; he made good non-commissioned officers; and they good private soldiers. Thus, discipline and good-will towards each other went hand-in-hand together. My situation was a respectable one, and, what was equally pleasant, a lucrative one.

JOHN SHIPP

Death of Sir Henry Lawrence

AND now about Sir H. Lawrence. On that day, while sitting with his Staff in his room in the Residency, a shell was fired into his room but without doing any damage, except the hole it made in the wall. His Staff urged him to leave his present quarters for fear of any harm occurring to him, but he treated the circumstance very lightly, saying, they will never fire another shell into the same place, but on the next day a shell came into the exact place and exploded, and a splinter of said shell hit Sir Henry in the groin and terminated his earthly career, which was not only a noble but a Christianlike and useful one, and the country lost not only a brave but a valuable servant, and the Garrison lost its right arm, indeed, for the foresight of Sir Henry, I am almost sure we would never be able to hold our position as long as we did, for by his judgement and tact he could see what was coming, and he set about provisioning the place from all sources, and well it was that he did so, and his loss cast a gloom on the whole Garrison. He, when he found his end was near, sent for Colonel Englis [Inglis] of my Regiment and Major Banks—handed over the entire Command to Colonel Englis and the Commisionership (which he held himself) to Major Banks. The latter was killed during the Siege and former survived the Siege and was promoted to Major-General and K.C.B. all in the space of five months. Quick promotion you will say, but it was nothing extraordinary in those days. Well, the last words he uttered were—'Dear Inglis, ask the poor fellows who I exposed at Chinut to forgive me. Bid them remember Cawnpore and never surrender. God bless you all.' And thus ended the life of a gallant soldier and a true Christian. He is in Heaven.

METCALFE

Dishonest N.C.O.s, 1843

DURING my stay at Chatham desertion was of frequent occurrence, and I understood to be to a greater extent than had ever been previously the case. This evil had its origin in a complication of causes, the major one being the manner in which recruits were treated on their joining, when not only was the bounty given them absorbed by the purchase of necessaries, but likewise the larger portion, and in many instances the entire, of the subsequent month's pay. Thus for two, or perhaps three months, the recruit would only receive two, at the most, threepence per diem, and young lads having good appetites, this trifling sum would be expended in procuring something by way of an evening meal, their ration meals only embracing a breakfast and dinner. Having accordingly no money to spend in amusement, and imagining they must continue to be similarly situated while in the service, young soldiers become quickly disgusted with it; and, when destitute of principle, desertion on the first opportunity followed almost as a matter of course.

There was also another cause tending to the same object, the harshness with which recruits were treated, in numberless instances, by non-commissioned officers, who tyrannized over them with the greatest impunity. These having sufficient art to veil their true character from their superiors, whose favour they propitiated by officiousness and servility, adopted out of very wantonness a system of domineering towards new-comers, sheltering themselves in the ignorance of the latter as to military laws and usages. I have frequently heard it stated since by every class of soldiers, and my own experience leads me to be of the same opinion, that the generality of the non-commissioned staff at Chatham are morally the lowest and most contemptible of their grade in the service. It is a fact, of the truth of which I have myself been often a witness, that some of them are perfect adepts in every species of fraud, and the larger part are of the most depraved habits otherwise—the necessary result of laxity of principle, and protracted stay in a vicious neighbourhood. On my joining, I was made to pay for clothing, which I should have got gratis: at the time of my discharge I compelled the sergeant who paid the depot then, and who is now pay and colour sergeant with the regiment, to refund the money he cheated me out of, by threatening to claim it before the board about to assemble for the purpose of recording my services, conduct, and cause of discharge. Others were treated in the same way who enlisted with me; but those died or volunteered in India, or were ignorant of what they were entitled to; at all events no claim but mine was ever made.

One mode of depriving the recruit of his pay, is to give him an old shattered musket, easily injured; thus there are ten chances to one, that some part of it gets broken, while it is in his possession; and he has in consequence a round sum to pay on delivering it into the store, when leaving the garrison. I have known this to be the case with many persons, some of whom had to pay ten shilling for stocking an old musket in use for the past forty years, and the intrinsic value of which might be ascertained, by weighing the barrel, and calculating its worth at two-pence per pound. Whether such were ever stocked is a question the armourer alone can decide; but in any case, he and the pay sergeants quietly arranged it all their own way.

MACMULLEN

A C.O. in India, 1844

THE writer cannot refrain here from saying a few words in favor of his old commanding officer, Colonel Brookes; it was generally admitted that he was severe and eccentric in weighing off prisoners, for he had scores brought before him almost daily; having under his command three troops of horse and artillery and two light field batteries, (he had a great variety of men to deal with) at the same time he was very forgiving, but in a bullying manner; for instance whenever he took the whole brigade out for a field day (about twice a week) and the manœuvring was executed to his satisfaction he would dismiss the brigade, by ordering his trumpet-major to sound the flourish, which meant the captains were to take their respective troops and batteries home, and he followed later. While the horses were being rubbed down he paraded himself up and down the horse lines until the horses were dry and cleaned, he then ordered his trumpet-major to sound dismiss: now comes the time for all defaulters of each troop to step out to their respective captains with a request to see the Colonel, their request is granted, they are marched up, each captain taking his squad before the Colonel, who puts the question, 'what do all these men want?' Each captain replies, 'They wish to see you, sir'—the Colonel asks each man, 'Well what do you want?' Each man has the same request to make, to have their sentence forgiven; some promise him to keep out of trouble for one month, others for two, others for six and so on. 'Now, if any of you vagabonds are brought before me within three months I will double your sentence. Go to your barracks and begin a new leaf.' But any morning the manœuvring displeased him, he rode off home without dismounting at the horse lines. He always rode from two to three horses at his field days, to keep them in good trim, he being a crack horseman. He was like a second father to me for he several times gave me a telling off, at the same time promoting me step by step when promotion was least expected.

BANCROFT

A lance-sergeant of Hussars, c. *1870*

MY NEXT promotion came to me far sooner than I could reasonably have looked for it, within a very short time Colonel T—— made me a lance-sergeant. In the ordinary course I would not have been due this step under two years, but it was given me in order that I might have more authority over the men in the young horse stables. Of course it made a vast difference in my life, for I passed from the benches and bare deal tables of the barrack-room to the luxury of a sergeants' mess. After six years of barrack life the change was a very marked one; the food was much superior, and there were mess waiters to attend to our requirements. I acquired a share in a room with two other sergeants; never again did I groom a horse, for I had a batman now to look after mine and furbish up my traps, and there were the club-like conveniences of the mess to make the evenings pass pleasantly.

On the other hand, a lance-sergeant's rank carried no extra pay with it, and was the hardest position of all to keep up, for there were extra clothes to provide, and as a sergeant never wore fatigue dress, his uniform had more wear and tear to stand. The subscription to the mess came to a shilling a day, and this, after paying my batman, left a very small balance for my other expenses. And so, although I had finer clothes on my back, my pockets were often empty. Still there was corn in Egypt somehow or other. My chum was caterer to the mess for a month, and of course during that time I wanted for nothing so far as liquid refreshment and other little extras were concerned. The nest-egg he put by tided him over for a month or two, and then it came his turn at the canteen, which was as good as a ten-pound note in his pocket; and as really good comradeship existed in the sergeants' mess in those days, it was always a case of share and share alike.

Where a lance-sergeant benefited most was in the matter of society for he could always get the choice of an upper servant in one of the tip-top families or a tradesman's daughter; being now in a position to give invitations to the frequent dances given by the mess. In return for this the young ladies would look after the sergeants out of barracks and lacked no liberality in returning our hospitality. Civilians can hardly understand the vast social difference that exists between the sergeant and the private soldier. The former is always expected to act as a gentleman, and treated as such, whereas the latter is often looked down upon as if he belonged to a lower caste altogether, although both originally came from the same class; nor is it always the really best man of the two who wears the stripe.

MOLE

The road to promotion

IN APRIL, 1879, or about a year and a half after enlisting, I was promoted full corporal. This was, for the time almost unprecedented rapidity of advancement in the cavalry, and it entailed my transfer to another troop under other superiors having other ways. Shortly afterwards the regiment was ordered to Brighton—a four days' march—and I was selected to go on ahead in charge of the billeting party to arrange for the accommodation of the men and horses of the troop at the various halting-places. It was in this way that I gained my first experience in those duties of Quartermaster-General which were to devolve upon me in the Great War.

Soon after arrival at York I was promoted lance-sergeant (or provisional sergeant), thus becoming a member of the sergeants' mess and terminating my barrack-room life with the men.

As sergeant, my horse, saddlery, and accoutrements were cleaned by a batman, who received six shillings a month from government for the additional work, as well as certain indulgences granted by his master. This was a welcome change, for there was no harder animal in the world to groom than a troop horse in winter, when, no part of him being clipped, his hair would be inches in length, and in spite of rubbing would remain wet from mud or perspiration for hours, and until he was dry the rubbing had to be continued. In winter, too, many men would be absent on furlough, which meant that two and sometimes three horses fell to the lot of each man present at stables.

After being employed for some weeks on mounted duty at the headquarters of the York district, I was placed in charge of the regimental remounts—about forty in number—and so occupied another semi-independent position. My selection for these different posts was probably due to the credit earned at Chatham.

The following August I was sent to the school of musketry at Hythe to qualify as assistant instructor of musketry. The curriculum was then about as unpractical and wearisome as it could well be, the greater part of the time—two months—being devoted to acquiring efficiency in repeating, parrot-like, the instructions laid down in the drill book. Little or no attention was paid to the art of shooting in the field, and the total amount of ball ammunition expended was restricted to the orthodox forty rounds per man. It was not till some years later, under such commandants as Ian Hamilton and Monro, that a more intelligent system, better suited to modern requirements, was introduced, and Hythe began to be a really useful institution.

Both in going and returning I travelled between Hull and London by boat, making the journey at each end by rail. This may not seem a very expeditious route, nor was it. For instance, when returning from Hythe I had to spend a day in London waiting for a boat; another two days were taken by the sea passage; and as I arrived at Hull late on a Sunday I had to stay the night there before being able to get a train for York. To the financial mind, however, the itinerary was

M

SANTA CLARA PUBLIC LIBRARY
SANTA CLARA. CALIF.

correct, for the travelling expenditure incurred was some pence and perhaps even some shillings, less than it would have been had I travelled all the way by rail.

January, 1882, saw me promoted full sergeant, by far the youngest of that rank in the regiment, both in age and service, and this led to my transfer to another troop. 'B' commanded by Major Garrett. He was a general favourite with his men, and I have pleasant recollections of my time under his command.

In June I was deputed to go through a course of instruction at the school of signalling at Aldershot. It was considerably more advanced in its methods than the Hythe establishment, but was nevertheless not as up-to-date as it should have been.

Whilst I was at Aldershot the regiment moved from York to Ireland, headquarters and three troops going to Dundalk, and the remaining five troops to four other stations, of which Belfast was one. On completion of the signalling course I was ordered to join at Dundalk.

Ireland was at this period, as at many other times in her history, suffering from the effects of being a political shuttlecock, the military were frequently called out to assist the police in the suppression of disorder. Evictions for non-payment of rent were the most common source of trouble, and some of them would be attended by thousands of sympathisers from the countryside, necessitating, in the opinion of the authorities, the presence of a considerable military force. I have known as much as a brigade of all arms employed on this duty, the evicted tenant being an old woman occupying a dilapidated hovel, and the unpaid rent amounting to a few shillings!

Having passed the examination at the signalling school, obtaining 282 marks out of a possible 300, I was made assistant instructor of the regimental signallers, whose standard was then very low. The annual inspection took place about two months later, and consequently there was not sufficient time to make much improvement. The regiment was reported as being only 'fair' and it occupied 44th place in the army 'order of merit'. The inspecting officer was pleased, however, to classify the assistant instructor, myself, as 'very good'. The commanding officer, now Schwabe in place of Whigham, was bent on achieving much better results, and he gave Lieutenant Dugdale, the 'instructor', and myself a free hand to do as we liked on the understanding that the necessary improvement should be made. In this we succeeded at the next annual inspection, when the regiment took 12th place in the army and 3rd place in Ireland. In 1844, we did still better, the regiment being first in Ireland and missing first in the army only by a decimal.

A month later (March 1885), I was promoted troop sergeant-major of 'E' troop. My predecessor had been a medical student before joining the army, and as he was well educated his prospects would have been good had he not been addicted to periodical spells of hard drinking. He had been promoted in the hope that his increased responsibilities might help to keep him straight, and he had promised to abstain from drink, but before many months had elapsed the troop accounts, for which he was answerable to his troop officer, were found to balance on the wrong side and he was accordingly ordered to revert to the rank of sergeant and to hand over his duties to me. I was directed to go to his quarters to discuss matters, and I there found him to be quite drunk and incapable of explaining anything. When his condition became known to higher authority he was placed 'in arrest' pending investigation by the commanding officer.

Next day a troop sergeant-major went to escort him to the orderly room, and finding his door locked he came for me. We returned together, and on breaking open the door discovered that the poor fellow had shot himself a few minutes before. Apparently he had felt unable at the last moment to face the ruin and disgrace which confronted him, and a round of service ammunition and a carbine had done the rest. For several days I was kept busy in unravelling the tangle into which the accounts had been allowed to fall, but beyond neglect and carelessness there was nothing seriously wrong with them, the actual deficiency in money amounting only to thirty-five pounds. For this miserable sum drink had claimed its victim, whose life, but for the one weakness, might have been so different.

'Paddy' Malone, the commander of my new troop, was a splendid specimen of manhood both in build and character, standing a good six feet six inches in height and made in proportion. Wyndham Quinn and Dugdale were the two subalterns, and from all three I experienced nothing but kindness during the three years I was their troop sergeant-major.

A troop sergeant-major occupies a position which enables him to exert, for good or for evil, great influence over his men. It is said that the non-commissioned officer is the backbone of the army, but it is equally true that he can do much harm unless he is strictly impartial and identifies himself with the interests of his men. Although the 'old soldier' as I knew him eight years before was rapidly disappearing, a certain number still remained who, with some of the younger ones, required firm and tactful handling. In not a few cases the worst characters were the best workmen—that is, the best grooms and best riders—when money was scarce; when it was plentiful they would fall under the spell of drink, and this would lead to absence, insubordination, and other military offences. Try as one might these men proved very hard to reform, and while I gained many gratifying successes I also had some failures in my efforts to make them see the folly of their ways.

The fault lay not nearly so much with the men—who were good fellows at heart—as with the authorities who neglected to provide them with congenial means of recreation, to place greater trust in their self-respect, and generally to call forth the better part of their nature. With the introduction of comfortable regimental institutes; the substitution, except when a really serious dereliction of duty had been committed, of 'minor offences' for 'crimes'; the abolition of the practice of imprisoning all offenders in the guard-room no matter how trivial the offence; greater liberality in the granting of leave; and the adoption all round of more intelligent and sympathetic methods, a marked improvement in the behaviour of the men quickly followed and their outlook on life automatically became quite different.

For some years before going to Dublin I had cherished the

hope of obtaining a commission, but at first there seemed no more chance of this hope being realised than of obtaining the moon. Apart from riding-masters and quartermasters it was very seldom that anyone was promoted from the ranks—not more than four or five a year on an average—and moreover the initial step lay with the commanding officer, a strong backing from whom was a sine qua non. Whigham was not friendly disposed towards me, and he happened to be, I think, one of those who held the view that promotion from the ranks was not to the benefit of either the man or the State. During his regime, therefore, nothing was or could be done.

The idea of trying for a commission had originated with Leslie Melville, the rector of my native village. Both he and his wife had taken a kindly interest in me from early boyhood, and the lady, who had several relatives in the army, was particularly keen that I should make a name for myself. Some officers of the regiment, Dugdale more than any, gave me similar encouragement, and when Whigham was succeeded by Schwabe, and I had come to the front a little as a result of the special duties I had been carrying out, my prospects seemed brighter.

Setting to work more systematically and with greater confidence, I commenced to study for a 'first class certificate of education', this qualification being necessary before I could be recommended for a commission. The certificate was duly secured in the autumn of 1883, and I then turned to the professional side, reading all the books on tactics, strategy, and past campaigns that I could lay hands on. They were few in number, as the regimental library did not cater for this kind of study—or for any other for that matter—and I could not afford to purchase many books. The deficiency had to be made up by reading very carefully those that were available. The ordinary drill books I knew from A to Z.

But there was another and much greater obstacle to be considered, about which I could not make up my mind for a long time. I had no private means, and without some £300 a year in addition to army pay it was impossible to live as an officer in a cavalry regiment at home. The infantry was less expensive, but I could not entertain the idea of leaving my old arm, the cavalry.

The money difficulty did not arise in the case of the so-called 'ranker' who sought a commission through the ranks because he could not, owing to lack of brains or industry, obtain one through Sandhurst or the militia. Such rankers as these usually possessed ample money, and, being backed by private influence, would be given their commission, if at all, a year or two after enlistment, and were then able to resume the social status which they had temporarily laid down. The true ranker, having no influence behind him, had to toil for several years before receiving a commission, and even then the chances were that he would, owing to the want of private means, be miserable in himself and a nuisance to his brother officers.

All officers were, quite rightly, expected to live up to the standard of their regimental mess, and to bear a due share of the expenses—at some stations a very heavy item—incurred by the entertainment of mess guests, balls, race-meetings, and so forth. Considerable contributions had also to be made towards the upkeep of the regimental band, which was maintained only to a very limited extent from public funds. An absurd amount of costly uniform had to be purchased and constantly renewed, while chargers had to be paid for out of the officers' pockets, and had to be of first-class quality. A subaltern's pay was about £120. per annum. Ten years or more might elapse before Captain's rank was attained, and then the pay was less than £200 per annum.

It had hitherto been possible, as well as convenient, to find room in each regiment for at least one ranker by appointing him adjutant, a post which he could hold for an indefinite time. This brought him useful pecuniary benefit, and by entrusting to him much of the elementary training of the men the other officers were able to enjoy increased facilities for leave. But this system was rapidly passing away. Troop and squadron officers were now being made really responsible for the training and administration of their commands; a higher degree of efficiency was being demanded; and the post of adjutant, now limited to five years, was no longer regarded as the perquisite of the ranker, but was being eagerly sought after by all young officers who aspired to rise in their profession.

It will be understood that in these circumstances the ranker was not as welcome to the officers of a regiment as before and as the financial obstacle seemed insurmountable I decided that I must give up all idea of realising my ambition, and I did.

This matter did not rest there for long, as one day in 1884 Schwabe expressed the wish that I should take a commission as soon as possible. Not having previously mentioned the subject to me, his generous offer came as a complete surprise, and I again went over all the old ground, wondering whether I dare accept the offer or not. Eventually, and with a sad heart, I reluctantly declined it, and I believe that Schwabe was as sorry as myself. He told me I was acting foolishly, and probably he was right. Soon afterwards he was succeeded in the command of the regiment by Colonel Maillard.

Sticking to my studies in the hope that something might yet turn up to justify going back on the decision to which I had come, I became more and more devoted to a military life and the old ambition soon reasserted itself. When, therefore, in 1886, Maillard made the same proposal as his predecessor had done, and appeared equally desirous that I should not refuse, I determined to put aside my fears and take the risk of failure owing to lack of funds. He allayed my anxiety in this respect by promising to get me posted to a regiment in India if possible, when the pay would be higher and the expenses much lower than in England. Thus the die was cast.

Before he could recommend me for a commission, however, I had the mortification of having to undergo a further educational examination, the standard of the first class certificate having been raised since I took it three years earlier. A few weeks' study overcame this stumbling-block, and in April 1887 the recommendation was at last sent on its way to the Horse Guards. The reply came back in August that the outfit allowance of £150. granted to rankers on promotion could not be given me during the current financial year, as the Treasury allotment for that purpose had already been promised. I was given the choice of taking a commission without the allowance, and as I could not afford to do that the only alternative was to wait for still another year.

These vexatious delays terminated early in February 1888, when I appeared before a board of officers of the 4th Dragoon Guards at the Royal Barracks, Dublin, to be examined in the subjects of qualifying for promotion to Lieutenant. The examination was very simple and was passed almost as a matter of course, for it would have been an unforgiveable breach of etiquette for officers of one regiment to plough a candidate sent up by another.

In March my squadron was ordered to the Curragh, and a few weeks later the whole regiment moved to Aldershot, where I had joined it as a recruit about ten and half years before. On the 27th June, I was gazetted 2nd Lieutenant in the 3rd Dragoon Guards, then serving in India.

It was with real great regret, not unmixed with anxiety as to what my future had in store for me, that I parted company with my comrades of the sergeants' mess, where I had spent many pleasant hours. Maillard, who had always shown the most kindly interest in my welfare, presented me with a sword; Dugdale insisted upon fitting me out with saddlery; the members of the sergeants' mess gave me a silver-mounted dressing-case; and from many others in the regiment, officers and men, I received expressions of goodwill. The 16th Lancers had become a home to me, and I am proud to think that I once had the honour of serving in so distinguished a regiment.

ROBERTSON

A difficult general in French Indo-China: Foreign Legion

Two days later I was back in my old place, my absence having lasted about a week, and the following morning General Pernot came up from Hanoi with his staff.

He was a short, fat, red-faced man with a very loud, disagreeable voice, and a temper that was worse; and his reputation with the men of being a crusty martinet was not altogether unjustified. The day following his arrival he came to the office and passed a review of the secretaries. On learning that I was in charge of the records, he came over to where I was standing at 'attention', and asked:

'You are naturalised, I suppose?'

'No, mon Général,' I answered.

'What! not naturalised yet! You have the intention of becoming so, of course?'

'No, mon Général,' I replied.

He glared up at me with an angry stare, and his face took a dull-red colour. I thought he was going to burst.

'Oh, indeed!' he blurted out at last. 'You must put in an application to become a French citizen, or go back to your battalion. I will have no foreigners in a post of confidence on my staff. Grand Dieu! what have they been doing to allow such a thing? It is shameful! Nom de nom!'

He almost shouted the last words, so great was his indignation, and from the expression he put into them one might have been justified in imagining that the Republic was in danger owing to my presence there. I did not become naturalised, and I heard nothing more about the question; and in justice to this cantankerous officer, I must acknowledge that, during the fifteen months he commanded the Brigade, he treated me with consideration on the rare occasions that I had any direct business to transact with him. He had risen from the ranks—indeed, I was told that he began his career as a sailor on a man-of-war and it is therefore probable that his modest origin and the hard times he experienced at his début accounted for his rough and rude manners.

MANINGTON

7

BILLETS IN PEACE AND WAR

Quarters on the march: Coventry, 26th August, 1642

THIS morning we cheerfully marched towards Buckingham in the rear of Colonel Chomley's regiment, by reason whereof we could get no quarter there, but were constrained to quarter ourselves about the country; whereupon I and three gentlemen of my company visited that thrice noble gentleman, Sir Richard Inglisby, where his own table was our quarter. And Sergeant-Major Burrif, and his son Captaine Inglisby, and several other noble gentlemen were our comrades. Saturday, early in the morning, I departed hence and gathered a complete file of my own men about the country, and marched to Sir Alexander Denton's park, who is a malignant fellow, and killed a fat buck, fastened his head upon my halberd, and commanded two of my pickets to bring the body after me to Buckingham, with a guard of musketeers coming thither. With part of it I feasted my captain, Captain Parker, Captain Beacon, and Colonel Hampden's son, and with the rest several lieutenants, ensigns, and sergeants, and had much thanks for my pains.

WHARTON

The occupation of Worcester, 1642

THURSDAY morning we marched in the front four miles towards Worcester, where we met one riding post from

Worcester, informing us that our troops and the cavaliers were there in fight; but it was false, only to haste the captains from Warwick. Upon this report our whole regiment ran shouting for two miles together, and crying 'To Worcester, to Worcester!' and desired to march all night: but after we had marched two miles further we were commanded to stand until our forces passed by, and then marched two miles further into Assincantlo, where we could get no quarter, neither bread nor drink, by reason of the Lord Compton's late being there. Friday we marched four miles on this side of Worcester, but our soldiers cried out for one hour together to go forward to set upon the enemy, but could get no commission. This day we had such foul weather that before I had marched one mile I was wet to the skin. This day our horse forces, namely, Sir William Belford, Col. Sands, Col. Vines, Col. Clarke, Major Duglas, kept all the passages over the Severn, and by that means kept in the Cavaliers, who often assayed to fly, but were repelled. Those commanders sent to His Excellency for three field pieces, and offered with them to keep them in on that side until we had surrounded them: but they were denied this day. Towards even Prince Rupert entered the city at a bye passage with eighteen troops of horse, most of the city crying 'Welcome, welcome!' but principally the mayor, who desired to entertain him; but he answered, 'God damn him, he would not stay, but would go wash his hands in the blood of the Roundheads', and immediately set some to lie in ambush, and with the rest sallied out upon our forces; and immediately Col. Sands came on bravely, even unto the breast of their chief commander, and discharged. The rest undauntedly followed, but their forces immediately fled, and our followed them, and by the ambushment were beset before and behind, so that the battle was very hot, and many fell on both sides. Some of our chief commanders, as Col. Sands and Duglas, was wounded, and are since both dead. The chief amongst the Cavaliers were Prince Rupert, who, I hear, was wounded, the Lord Craven, and the Lord of Northampton. Our wounded men they brought into the city, and stripped, stabbed, and slashed their dead bodies in a most barbarous manner and imbrued their hands in their blood. They also at their return met a young gentleman, a Parliament man, as I am informed—his name I cannot learn—and stabbed him on horseback with many wounds, and trampled upon him, and also most maliciously shot his horse. This even, our general's troop of gentlemen, going to quarter themselves about the country, were betrayed and beset by the enemy, and, overmuch timorous, immediately fled so confusedly that some broke their horses' necks, others their own; some were taken, others slain; and scarce half of them escaped; which is such a blot upon them as nothing but some desperate exploit will wipe off. Hearing this news, we immediately cried out to march unto them, and forthwith drew out a forlorn hope—some out of every company—and sent them before, intending to march after them; but about eleven of the clock, the enemies fled, and our hope returned. Here we abode all night, where we had small comfort, for it rained hard. Our food was fruit, for those who could get it; our drink, water; our beds, the earth; our canopy, the clouds; but we pulled up the hedges, pales and gates, and made some good fires; his Excellency promising us that, if the country relieved us not the day following, he would fire their towns. Thus we continued singing of psalms until the morning. Saturday morning we marched into Worcester—our regiment in the rear of the waggons—the rain continuing the whole day, and the way so base that we went up to the ankles in thick clay; and, about four of the clock after noon, entered the city, where we found twenty-eight dead men, which we buried—some of them Cavaliers—and these were all that we can find slain on our side. This evening, by lot, our company watched one of the gates, and also the day following, until even. This evening, his Excellency's guard entered the mayor's house, and took him prisoner, who is now more guarded than regarded. Sabbath day morning our soldiers entered a vault of the College, where his Excellency was to hear a sermon, and found eleven barrels of gunpowder and a pot of bullets. This day Mr Marshall Sedgewick & Co., preached about the city, but I, being upon the court of guard, could not hear them. This evening his Excellency proclaimed that no soldier should plunder either church or private house, upon pain of death. We shortly expect a pitched battle which if the Cavaliers will but stand, will be very hot; for we are all much enraged against them for their barbarisms, and shall shew them little mercy.

WHARTON

The price of unrationed provisions in Gibraltar during the Great Siege (1779 to 1783)

September, 1780. We have not received an ox from Barbary since June 12th, and every species of provision is now at a most extravagant price; a turkey cock was sold a few days ago for three guineas and a half, ducks are one guinea per couple, a goose one pound six shillings, a hen twelve shillings, powder sugar two shillings the pound, soap one shilling and four-pence ditto, charcoal half a guinea for 25lb weight, oil two shillings the pint, pork two shillings and six pence the pound, fish at the rate of eighteen-pence ditto, firewood five shillings and sixpence per hundred weight, tallow candles two shillings and six-pence per pound, made very different, onions eight-pence ditto, and all other articles proportionate dear. From this sketch you may form an idea of our present situation, and the consequences that are to follow, if some supplies are not sent from England.

October, 1781. Last night arrived with a fresh breeze at West, the *Unicorn* cutter, and four other vessels from Faro, laden with fruit and poultry, a very seasonable and excellent supply, as the garrison are very much necessitated for vegetables, fruit, and fresh diet. The New Mole wharf, this morning, was quite crowded, every one being anxious to buy something, although the articles sold at an exhorbitant rate; onions sold for six rials per pound, two shillings and five-pence farthing, and oranges and lemons one rial eight quarts each, seven-pence-half-penny sterling, the poultry at the usual prices, viz. three dollars and an half for an hen. Common green tea, brought by the *Unicorn*, sold for fourteen dollars per pound, two pounds five shillings and sixpence, and loaf sugar five dollars, nearly seventeen shillings per pound. This is rare traffic! We hope these times will not last long, and a communication will be opened, so that supplies may be brought in and sold at moderate price; or, should they continue, the garrison will, of course, be exhausted of all cash to support nature.

ANCELL

Bad billets in English inns

THE regiment was ordered to proceed to the barracks at Hilsea, Portsmouth. This was soldiering in clover; and good living, fresh scenes, faces and events, conspired to make me, in a measure, forget the stripes which I had lost. I was not long on the march, before I became as knowing as the best of them, and was soon well versed in the tricks of the road. I found that it was the practice of some of the landlords to give us fat pea-soup, and of others to regale us with greasy suet dumplings, as heavy as lead, by way of taking off the edge of our appetites. These dishes I invariably avoided, stating that they were injurious to my constitution, or that the doctors had forbidden me to eat such food. I therefore waited for the more substantial fare—the roast and the boiled—which I attacked with such zest, as could not fail to convince the landlord of the delicacy of my constitution, and of the absolute necessity of my refraining from less substantial diet. In two hours after dinner the duff and pea-soup eaters were as hungry as ever; but I kept my own counsel, and thus was enabled to go on my way with a smiling countenance that indicated good and substantial fare.

When we were treated in the scurvy way I have spoken of by the landlords on our line of march, we never failed to leave some token of our displeasure behind us. Thus, one day at Chelmsford, we were compelled to submit to dreadful bad quarters; and even the extreme delicacy of my constitution, which had so often succeeded with me before, could not, on this occasion, induce our host to give us anything but greasy puddings and fat stews, made of the offal of his house for the last month. The fat on top of this heterogeneous mixture was an inch thick; and I, for my own part, protested that I could not and would not eat it. Finding me so positive, he privately slipped a shilling into my hand to quiet me, which I did not think it expedient to refuse. This bribe tended, in some degree, to pacify me; but my comrades, on quitting the house, evinced their disapprobation of the treatment they had met with, by writing with a lighted candle on the ceiling, 'D—d bad quarters—How are you off for pea-soup?—Lead dumplings—Lousy beds—Dirty sheets.'

This was the mildest description of punishment with which we visited landlords who incurred our displeasure; for, in addition to this, it did not require any very aggravated treatment to induce us to teach some of mine host's ducks and geese to march part of the way on the road with us; to wit, until we could get them dressed.

JOHN SHIPP

Moscow, 1812

WE HAD hardly entered the outskirts of the town, when we met several of the miserable creatures expelled from the Kremlin; they had all horrible faces, and were armed with muskets, staves and pitch-forks. In passing over the bridge leading from the suburbs to the town itself, a man crept from underneath the bridge, and placed himself in front of the regiment. He was muffled up in a sheepskin cape, long gray hair fell on his shoulders, and a thick white beard came down to his waist. He carried a three-pronged fork, and looked like Neptune rising from the sea. In these accoutrements he walked proudly up to the drum-major, moving as if to strike him, no doubt taking him for the General with his smart uniform and gold lace. He aimed a blow at him with his pitchfork, which luckily the drum-major managed to avoid, and, snatching the miserable creature's weapon from him, he seized him by the shoulders; then, kicking him behind, he launched him over the bridge and into the water he had just left. He did not get out again, however, swept away by the current, we only saw him come up at intervals. Finally he disappeared altogether.

We met several others of the same kind, who fired at us

with loaded arms. There were even some of them who had nothing but wooden flint-locks to their muskets; as they wounded no one, we contented ourselves with taking their arms from them and breaking them, and if the creatures returned we got rid of them by blows in the back with the butt end of our muskets. Some of these weapons had been taken from the arsenal at the Kremlin; the muskets with the wooden flint-locks certainly came from that place.

We knew that these wretches had tried to stab an officer of Murat's staff.

After passing over the bridge, we marched along a large and beautiful street. We were astonished not to see anyone come out—not even a lady—to listen to our band playing 'La victoire est à nous.' We could not understand this total silence, and we imagined that the inhabitants, not daring to show themselves, were peeping at us from behind their shutters. Here and there we saw a few servants in livery, and some Russian soldiers.

After marching for about an hour, we got to the first enclosure of the Kremlin. Turning sharp to the left, we entered a larger and finer street than the one we had left, leading to the Place du Gouvernement. Just as we stopped, we saw three ladies at a ground-floor window. I happened to be on the pavement, and near one of the ladies, who gave me a piece of bread as black as coal, and full of long pieces of straw. I thanked her, and in return gave her a bit of white bread, which I had just got from Mother Dubois, our cantinière. The lady blushed, and I laughed; then she touched my arm—I cannot tell why—and I went on my way.

At last we arrived on the Place du Gouvernement. We massed ourselves together opposite the palace of Rostopchin, the Governor of the town, who ordered it to be fired. We were told that the regiment was to camp, and that no one on any pretence whatever was to absent himself. An hour afterwards, however, the whole place was filled with everything we could want—wines of all kinds, liqueurs, preserved fruits, and an enormous quantity of sweet cakes and flour, but no bread. We went into the houses on the Place asking for food and drink, but as we found no one in them we helped ourselves.

The fire began an hour after our arrival. On our right we saw a thick smoke, then a whirl of flames, not knowing from whence it came. We were told the fire was in the bazaar, the merchants' quarter.

'They are probably freebooters,' we were told, 'who have carelessly set fire to the shops in searching for provisions.'

Many people who were not in the campaign have said that it was the fire at Moscow that ruined the army. I, and many others with me, think just the contrary. The Russians need not have set fire to the town; they might have thrown all the provisions into the Moskowa, and wasted the country for ten leagues round—an easy thing to do, as part of the country is desert already. Had this been done, we should have had to leave in a fortnight. After the fire there were still houses enough to shelter the army, and, even supposing all the houses had been burnt, there were the cellars remaining. At seven o'clock the fire reached the back of the Governor's palace. The Colonel gave orders that a patrol of fifteen men should leave at once. I was among them. M. Cesarisse came with us, and took command. We went in the direction of the fire, but we had hardly gone three hundred steps before we heard some firing on our right. We did not pay much attention, thinking it was only a few drunken soldiers, but fifty steps further we heard it again. It came from a sort of blind alley, and was directed at us. At the same moment I heard the cry of a wounded man close to me. He had a ball in the leg; but the wound was not dangerous, as he could still walk. We had orders to go back at once to our regiment; but we had hardly turned round, when more firing from the same quarter changed our direction again. We advanced to the house where the firing came from; we beat in the door, and came face to face with nine great rogues, armed with lances and muskets to prevent an entrance.

Then we fought in the yard, the numbers unequal. We were nineteen against nine; but, believing there were more of them, we had started by knocking down the three first. A corporal was wounded between his shoulder-belts and his coat; feeling nothing, he seized his adversary's lance, which placed him at a disadvantage, as he had only one free hand, having to hold his musket with the other. He was thrown violently back against the cellar door, still holding the lance fast. At that moment the Russian fell wounded by a bayonet. The Officer had just wounded another in the wrist with his sword to make him drop his lance; but, as he still held firm, he was struck by a ball in the side, sending him to the shades. While this was going on, I with five men held the remaining four (for three had run away) so closely against a wall that they could not use their lances. At the first moment they made a move we could run them through with our bayonets held against their breasts. They kept striking their weapons with their fists out of bravado. These unfortunate fellows were drunk with the brandy they had found in quantities, so that they were like madmen. We were obliged at last to finish them off.

We hurried into the house, and in one room we found two or three of the men who had made off. They were so frightened when they saw us, that they had no time to seize their weapons, upon which we fell at once; while we were doing so, they jumped from the balcony.

As we had only found two men, and there were three muskets, we searched for the third, who was under the bed, and came out without being told, crying, 'Bojo! Bojo!' which means, 'My God! My God!' We did nothing to him, but kept him by us as a guide. Like the others, he was frightened and loathsome—like them, a convict clothed in a sheep-skin, with a leather belt round his middle. We left the house, and found in the street the two convicts who had jumped from the window—one was dead, his head being smashed on the pavement; the other had both his legs broken.

We left them as we found them, and set out to return to the Place du Gouvernement; but what was our surprise to find this impossible, the fire having spread to such an enormous extent! To right and left was one wreath of flames, the wind was blowing hard, and the roofs were falling in. We were forced to take another course. Unfortunately, we could not make our prisoner understand us; he seemed more like a bear than a man.

BOURGOGNE

Arrival in safety after the retreat from Moscow, 1812

WITHOUT losing time, we went to the town-hall for our billet; it was crowded with soldiers.

We noticed several cavalry officers far more wretched than we were, for nearly all had lost fingers and toes, and others even their noses; it was distressing to see them. The magistrates of the town did all they possibly could do for their comfort, giving them good lodging, and ordering that every care should be taken of them.

After an hour's waiting, we were given a billet for the five of us, and for our horse; we hurried off to the place at once.

It was a large tavern, or, rather, a low smoking den. We were very ill-received; they showed us a large corridor without fire for our rooms, and some bad straw in it. We expostulated, and were told that it was good enough for Frenchmen, and that, if that didn't suit us, we could go into the street. Indignant at such a reception we left the house, expressing all our contempt to the brute who had received us in such a way, and threatening to make him give an account of his behaviour to the town magistrates.

We decided that we must try to get our billet changed, and I was charged with the mission, my comrades waiting for me at an inn. . . .

BOURGOGNE

Soldiers and civilians: England, 1812

DURING my stay in England nothing surprised me more than the spirit of revolt displayed by the people in general against the government. At different times I was sent out with the command of escorts of ammunition, for the use of the local militia; this was most galling and disagreeable to me, for, go where we would, as soldiers we were hated and despised, insulted and loaded with the foulest epithets—in our different billets looked upon and received as if we had carried pestilence, robbery, and pillage with us. It would be a disagreeable task to enumerate the many instances of insult to which I was liable, in these times of disatisfaction with the government, and of utter insensibility to the blessings that Britain enjoyed, compared with the surrounding nations. Let one be a specimen of all the others.

It was in a place called Ware, where I halted my party, after a fatiguing day's march, in foul weather; it was in the month of May, 1812, at the time that Spencer Percival was shot. I was shocked and disgusted at the audacious language that was employed in speaking of the government, and the epithets that were applied to ourselves, for we were viewed as the off-scourings of the inhabitants of Britain. All in the public-house where I stopped were prophesying and wishing for a rebellion; many hesitated not to say that the melancholy event was an indication of its commencement, and approved of the murder, wishing that many of the ministers were served in the same way. —'D—n them, they ought to be, and will be so too, and that you will see, whoever lives to see it,' said one, addressing his discourse to me; others cursed the government for robbing and making slaves of them and starving the people, and this too at the same moment that many of them were tipsy, others eating cheese, bread, pork, and mutton, and all fat and fair; they appeared to be too well fed, and did not know it. I civilly put the question to one of them, who, with his son, was most vociferous, yet consumed a great quantity of mutton-chops all the time, if he really was starved, he looked in a rage at me, and swore, saying, 'It is you and such as you that enable them to starve us.' I smiled, and said, 'You are in a better way to die of a surfeit than of fasting, friend.' 'We cannot afford to pay for it, that's what a means,' he said; 'but d—n it, I'se an Englishman, and I will ha'e my rights too, and that's what I will, in spite of them, an' you to boot; what are they better than us? No, d—n it if they are, or half so good neither; and what are you but a slave yourself to them, a poor pitiful scoundrel, who has sold himself for a shilling a day; body and mind, you cannot have a will of your own, or do one thing but what you are bid, and must go to be shot at like a cock at Shrovetide; there is not a spark of spirit in thy body or thee would not wear that coat; d—n thee, I'll box thee for a farthing, and all thy company, one after the other. If thee has no money I'll box thee for love.' All eyes were upon us; I saw they wished for a quarrel; my blood boiled in my veins, yet the fear of being defeated in the character of champion withheld me, more than any consequences, for I was so very weak from my long and still unrecovered sickness it was with difficulty that I did my duty. Conscious of this, I restrained my temper, and turning from him and the rude and boorish men walked upstairs to bed, humbled and dispirited far more than such a low adventure ought to have made me. Weary as I was, sleep forsook my eyes; and I passed another night of melancholy retrospection.

ALEXANDER ALEXANDER

In conquered France, 1814

WE ENCAMPED upon the other side of the town; and next morning followed the line of march, until we came before a town called Aris. We had severe fighting before we got into it. We were led on by an aide-de-camp. The contest lasted until after dark. We planted picquets in different streets of the town; the enemy did the same in others. Different patrols were sent out during the night; but the French were always found on the alert. They retired before daylight; and we marched into the town, with our music at the head of the regiments. The town appeared then quite desolate, not worth twopence; but we were not three days in it, until the French inhabitants came back, opened their shops and houses, and it became a fine lively place. There was a good deal of plundering the first night; for the soldiers, going into the houses, and finding no person within, helped themselves. The people have a way of keeping their fowl in cans, full of grease, about the size of a hen. This we found out by accident; for, wanting some grease to fry, in cooking, we took one of these cans and cut out the fowl. We commenced a search for the grease cans and were very successful. The fowls were excellent.

'71ST'

A young soldier in the Antipodes, 1830 to 1836

I ENLISTED in the 17th Regiment of Foot at the 'Old Magpie', Leicester, on the 30th July, 1829, at the age of Sixteen years, and marched from there to Chatham, where I was kept at my preliminary drill for eight weeks, and was then sent to my duty as a trained soldier.

Life in Tasmania

We were sent out to Australia in the year 1830 on board the ship *Manlas* from Woolwich. We took on board 350 transports and sailed to Hobart Town, Van Diemen's Land (17,000 miles), and marched up the country to Oatlands, and from there to Hobb's Bluff, in the Blue Mountains.

Life in the bush

It took us three days to march twenty-one miles through the bush, and when we arrived we had to build huts for ourselves and the married people before we got any shelter.

There was not a house within twenty-one miles of us in the wild bush.

If anyone got lost we had to make fires in the high mountains and to fire off guns for signals, and if the lost party heard them they were guided by the direction of the sound until they could see the fire; however, we soon got used to it.

I was present and marched with the line which was formed —from Table Mountain to East Bay Neck—to put the natives down, Governor Arthur being in command.

The line was formed right across the country, and when it broke up we returned to Oatlands, and from there to Saint Paul's Plains.

Bushrangers

I was sent to Ben Lomond with two other men to guard a house occupied by a Mr. Bateman in case the natives should attack it, when they most probably would have burnt the house and killed the wife and children, the husband being away in the bush in pursuit of bushrangers and natives.

We stayed there nine months, and then returned to Saint Paul's Plains, and marched from there to Oatlands, and afterwards to Hobart Town.

Australia
We took ship from there to Sydney, stayed in Sydney for drill and left for Port McQuarrey, a settlement for political transports and cripples, from where we returned by ship to Sydney, and afterwards left for Springwood.

Capture of Jenkins the Bushranger
While at Sydney there were twelve of us sent in pursuit of Jenkins, the noted bush-ranger, and his party, who had murdered Doctor Wardle. We stayed at Mr. Parkes', at Cook's River, two days and nights. We stationed ourselves each side of the river on a Sunday morning, and one of our men went to an old man's hut, in the bush, to light his pipe, when the old man fired at him. He called and told him who he was. The old man said he thought it was Jenkins, and on being questioned it appeared that the bush-ranger had been in his hut all the previous night and had only left about twenty minutes.

On returning to our punt we found they had taken a boat and crossed the river.

We were quickly after them and soon came in sight of them crossing a paddock. Two mounted police saw us after them, and followed them down the Liverpool Road and captured them, we coming up at the same time.

There was £200. reward for whoever took them, dead or alive. The policemen got the reward and we got nothing.

I went to see them (the bush-rangers) hung in the old Gaol in George's Street, Sydney, in the year 1835.

We went to Springwood, in the Blue Mountains, to pick up bush-rangers.

Left there for Mount Victory with 300 convicts who worked in chains, to make a road through the mountains to Cox's River. We then marched back to Sydney and remained there until we got the route for India.

CLARKE

Aden (1842 to 1845)

NOW we go to Aden for a month.

It is a dirty place. Nothing but sand and shells and a kind of pumice stone. Not a bit of soil or anything green to be seen. We did not taste a bit of vegetables for three years.

Sometimes we got a few turnip radishes from the mainland in Arabia. We eat the bottoms and cut up the tops and eat them with vinegar.

We got the scurvy very badly and had to take lime juice and pickled limes.

It was brackish water we had to drink all the time.

Now that was the way we had to live for three years. What do you think of it?

Now there is talk about us leaving Aden. There is a ship at last signalled from Serra Island. It turns out to be a troopship with the 94th Regiment on board, from Madras, to relieve us.

They came on shore and we went on board at Back Bay, for Bombay.

We had a sad accident on board, with a large iron pot of pitch. Two sailors were lifting it off the fire when the rope broke, and the boiling pitch flew over the deck. About fourteen were scalded.

Two sailors were very badly burnt. One of our men was close against it when it fell. He had no shoes on. He fell, and the pitch went over him. He was in such agony that he begged to be thrown overboard. His clothes were cut off him, and the flesh came with them. He only lived a few hours and died in great agony, and was thrown overboard. He was a Leicester man, named Jones.

That finishes Aden, after three years in misery.

CLARKE

Hardships of a Crimean winter

MY FIRST impressions at the first sight of our men before Sebastopol I shall never forget, their appearance being appalling. The men were unshaven, unkempt, dirty-looking, ragged, and filthy, and as I saw them wading about up to the knees in mud and 'slurry', I could not discern whether they were British, Turks, or Russians, until getting speech with them their tongue disclosed the fact that they were indeed British; but soon we were as bad as they.

And now we had reached Sebastopol, the place which for so long had been our one topic of conversation, and were destined to remain in position before it for two long rigorous winters, with all their accompanying horrors, inseparable from men situated as we were. Our efforts to keep warm would have appeared ludicrous in any other situation, as for the first three months after landing we had nothing upon which to lie down but one grey blanket and big coat. The blanket we doubled like a woman's shawl, then cut two holes in it, put our arms through the holes and wrapped the rest of the blanket around our body, finally placing over this the big coat, afterwards putting on our accoutrements, this completing our toilet. But we got an improvement on this, for about the latter end of February, 1855, we were given some warm flannels, these proving very acceptable as we stood in need of a change of underclothing. The furniture of our tents at this time was also most luxurious, the only article to sit down upon being a stone.

PARSONS

Camp in North Africa: French Foreign Legion

AGAIN the slow progress past the milestones. At eleven o'clock in the morning we reached a little village. The marks on the last milestone said that we were fifty kilometres from Sidi-bel-Abbes. We passed by the old rickety houses of the village, and at a given signal the regiment halted, the companies forming up on the dry, sandy piece of ground to the left of the street.

Then followed the command: 'Halt!' and immediately afterwards the order: 'Campez!'

In a moment we had piled our arms. The knapsacks were thrown to the ground and the folding tent-supports and the tent-covers pulled out. Then the corporal of each section stepped out of the line, holding the tent-poles high above his head to mark the tent lines for the whole company. Again a short command, and in a few seconds the waste surface of sand was covered with little white tents.

It was a miracle. We were so well drilled and each individual knew his part so well that it only took a few seconds to pitch a tent. With surprising quickness the long rows of soldiers were turned into a tent encampment and five minutes afterwards the officers' tents were pitched in a final row. In the meantime Madame la Cantinière had hauled out of her sutler's cart folding tables and benches, ready to do a roaring trade with the tired-out legionnaires. The heavy Algerian wine was indeed a blessing after such a march and the poor devil who in these marching days did not possess a few coppers felt poor indeed.

In ten minutes the narrow trenches for cooking were dug out and in twenty places camp fires flared up simultaneously. The patrol marched round and round the white 'soldiers' city'. The food, consisting of macaroni and tinned meat, was greedily devoured.

After this the quiet of utter exhaustion reigned in the camp. The legionnaires lay huddled together in the tiny tents, on blankets spread out on the ground, covered with their cloaks, while the knapsacks served for a pillow. The rifles were brought into the tents and tied firmly together with a long chain by the corporal of each squad, who fastened the end of the chain to his wrist as a further precaution, for the Arabs had a habit of creeping through the lines on a dark night and stealing the much-coveted weapons from the tents. The patrols of the Legion have standing orders to challenge an Arab only once at night and then to fire. Even in this first night the watch caught a thief. The Arab was badly treated and he was delivered up to the civil authorities in the village the next morning in a horrible condition.

By seven o'clock in the evening the whole camp was fast asleep, sleeping the sleep of exhaustion.

ROSEN

8

ON THE MOVE IN PEACE AND WAR

Early troubles of a civilian army: Aylesbury, 16th August 1642

ON MONDAY, August the 8th, we marched to Acton, but being the Sixth Company, we were belated, and many of our soldiers were constrained to lodge in beds whose feathers were above a yard long. Tuesday, early in the morning, several of our soldiers inhabiting the out parts of the town sallied out unto the house of one Penruddock, a papist, and being basely affronted by him and his dog, entered his house, and pillaged him to the purpose. This day, also, the soldiers got into the church, defaced the ancient and sacred glazed pictures, and burned the holy rails. Wednesday: Mr. Love gave us a famous sermon this day; also, the soldiers brought the holy rails from Chiswick, and burned them in our town. At Chiswick they also intended to pillage the Lord of Portland's house, and also Dr. Duck's, but by our commanders they were prevented. This day our soldiers generally manifested their dislike of our Lieutenant Colonel, who is a Goddam blade, and doubtless hatched in hell, and we all desire that either the Parliament would depose him, or God convert him, or the Devil fetch him away quick. This day, towards evening, our regiment marched to Uxbridge, but I was left behind, to bring up thirty men with ammunition the next morning. Thursday, I marched toward Uxbridge; and at Hillingdon, one mile from Uxbridge, the rails being gone, we got the surplice, to make us handkerchiefs, and one of our soldiers wore it to Uxbridge. This day, the rails of Uxbridge, formerly removed, were, with the service book, burned. This evening Mr. Hardinge gave us a worthy sermon. Friday, I, with three other commanders, were sent with one hundred musketeers to bring the ammunition to Amersham in Buckinghamshire, which is the most sweetest country I ever saw; and as is the country, so also is the people; but wanting room for the regiment coming after us we were constrained to march four miles further unto Great Missenden, where we had noble entertainment from the whole town, but especially from S. Brian Ireson and the ministers of the town. Saturday morning, our companies overtook us and we marched together unto Aylesbury, and after we had marched a long mile, for so they all are in this country, we came to Wendover, where we refreshed ourselves, burnt the rails and, accidentally, one of Captain Francis his men, forgetting he was charged with a bullet, shot a maid through the head, and she immediately died. From hence we marched very sadly two miles, where Colonel Hampden, accompanied with many gentlemen well horsed, met us, and with great joy saluted and welcomed us and conducted us unto Aylesbury, where we have a regiment of foot, and several troops of horse to join with us. In this town our welcome is such that we want nothing but a good Lieutenant Colonel. Sabbath day, August the 15, in this town a pulpit was built in the market-place, where we heard two worthy sermons. This evening our ungodly Lieutenant Colonel upon an ungrounded whimsy commanded two of our captains, namely, Captain Francis and Captain Beacon, with their companies, to march out of the town, but they went not. Every day our soldiers by stealth do visit papists' houses and constrain them from both meat and money. They give them whole great loaves and cheeses, which they triumphantly carry away upon the points of their swords. I humbly entreat you, as you desire the success of our just and honourable cause, that you would endeavour to root out our Lieutenant Colonel; for, if we march further under his command, we fear, upon sufficient grounds, we are all but dead men.

WHARTON

An amateur army marches off to war, 1642

UPON Wednesday the 23 of August, our red regiment of the train'd bands marched into the new artillery ground, and from thence that night we marched to Brainford, and came thither about one o'clock in the morning; from whence the next day many of our citizens, who seemed very forward and willing at the first to march with us, yet upon some pretences and fair excuses returned home again, hiring others to go in their room; others returned home again the same night before they came to Brainford.

Upon Friday the 25 of August, we advanced from Brainford to Uxbridge, where our regiments were quartered there that night, and marched away the next morning.

Saturday the 26 of August we advanced to a town six miles beyond Uxbridge called Chaffan, where we were quartered that night; at this town a soldier belonging to Lieutenant Colonel Tompson was accidentally slain by shooting off a musket by one of his fellow soldiers, though at a great distance from him, yet shot him in the head whereof he died.

Sabbath day 27 August, we advanced from Chaffan near to a village called Chessun; this day the blue regiment of the trained bands, and the three regiments of the auxiliary forces met us upon a great common about three miles from Chessun, our whole regiment was quartered at one Mr. Cheyney's house, an esquire, where we were well accommodated for beer, having great plenty, two or three hundred of us this night lay in one barne.

Monday the 28 of August, we advanced from thence to a town called Asson-Clinton, a little village three miles from Alesbury, we continued here one day and two nights.

Wednesday the 30 of August, we advanced from thence to a village called Clayden; this day the lord general's army and our regiments of the trained band, together with the auxiliary forces, met at Alesbury; the great guns were fired at every fort about the town, as the lord general passed by; this was the fast day; our regiment was quartered this night at Sir Ralph Verney's house, a parliament man; his father the king's standard-bearer was slain at Edge hill.

Thursday the 31 of August, we advanced from thence to a village called Stretton-Ardley; this night all our brigade consisting of six regiments, viz. Colonel Manwaring's red regiment, two regiments of trained bands, and three of the auxiliary, were all quartered in this little village, it is conceived we were in all of this brigade about five thousand, here was little provision either for officers or soldiers, the night before we came hither, the cavaliers were at Bister two miles from this village and six miles from Oxford, but were beaten out of it by our soldiers and the lord general with his army quartered there this night.

Friday the 1 day of September, we advanced from hence to a place call'd Bayard's-greene in Oxfordshire, being three miles distant from Brackley, and eight miles from Banbury, where our brigade met my lord general with his whole army; whereat was great shouting and triumph as he passed by to take a view of our regiments; the whole army being drawn up in their several regiments, continued there about an hour and then we marched away; it was a goodly and glorious sight to see the whole army of horse and foot together; it is conceived by those that viewed our army well, that we did consist of (to speak of the least) fifteen thousand horse and foot, some speak of many more. This day good news was brought to us concerning Gloucester, and Exeter. From hence we marched this day to a village called Souldern, four miles from Banbury, where our six regiments that came from London were quartered; and my lord general and the rest of the army were quartered about a little mile from us, at a market town called Ano on the Hill; we were very much scanted of victuals in this place.

Saturday 2 September, we advanced from hence to Hooknorton, twenty-five miles from Gloucester, at which village our whole brigade was quartered. This day the lord general's troops had some skirmish with the cavaliers; it is reported there was eight slain of the enemie's party and one on ours. From hence we marched away the next morning.

FOSTER

Return to England, 1809

WE WERE not long till we came in sight of Ramsgate. I left my old firelock with the sailors. But in preparing to leave the ship, I went to my knapsack to put on my new shoes that I got when I came to Corunna, but to my sad disappointment they were stolen away by some one. I had to keep on my old shoes without stockings. When I landed, the regiment was on parade ready to march off for Canterbury. We joined our company with the same appearance as we came from Corunna. We marched off, and it was not long till it came on very wet. I went forward as well as I could, but my old shoes would not keep on my feet. I had then to take them off. I did the best I could for some time, but had to fall out of the ranks. A Corporal was ordered to go with me. The people were looking at the regiment passing, but when they saw me, I was looked upon as an object of pity. Well might they say, 'Here is a representative of what we have heard about Corunna retreat.' I was stopped; shoes and stockings were brought to me, and as I was putting them on, they were asking questions about me at the Corporal, for he was a countryman of their own. The English showed no small kindness to the soldiers that came from Corunna. When they came into the towns after marching, some of the people took them to their houses without billets. We came away, and I was very thankful for the kindness shewed to me. My comrade and I was billeted in a public house. After getting our supper, the people that came in to drink were asking us questions about what we had come through, and what we had seen. But we were wearied with the journey, and my comrade was complaining of pain in the head and we wanted to go to bed.

Next day we marched to Ashford, and this ended our journeying for a time. I said that my comrade was unwell, and when we came to Ashford, he was no better. He had to go into hospital, and it was not long till I heard that he was dead. A good number died of fever. Also our head surgeon, Doctor Evans. He was much respected. For a short time, we got coffee for breakfast. We had now to get our knapsacks renewed, and it was well for them that lost theirs for they got £2.2.0. I should have let mine drop off my back, for it was not worth two shillings. After receiving what things I was in need of, I was in debt about five pounds, but I received five pounds for my wound, and this paid my debt. In this place we were made a Light Infantry Regiment.

A BUGLER OF THE 71st FOOT

On the march: India, the Sikh Wars

WE STRUCK camp at 11 o'clock This was a very long day's march, over sandy deserts and plains. The water being short the horrors became past describing. We drew near to a well some time in the morning, and the confusion all round was fearful,—the men rushing and pushing to get at it, some letting their caps fall into it, and some their bayonets; and I quite expected some of the men would go in. One poor fellow, endeavouring to get up, had fallen, and was begging most pitifully that some one would give him a draught to save his life; but, God help him! he spent his breath in vain. The doctor seeing him in this deplorable state, asked a man to give him a drink, but was refused. Every one must take care of himself: all respect for one another was gone. I was very nearly done up myself. Here my tongue was swollen, and mouth parched up; and I felt very weak. My brain seemed to be on fire, and my eyes as if they would jump out of my head. I felt as if I were done; but I made a rush at the water and got some. God knows what a relief I felt, as if I had lost a great load! When most of the throng was over, I filled a tin flask which I carried with me for that purpose; so did all others who had them. Our officers were as bad as the men. What thousands there are in England who do not know the value of a drop of water!

Towards the end of the march the wind rose, and drove the sand in such clouds that it cut our faces, and drove in heaps like snow. We pitched camp at 5 o'clock on Monday morning.

We struck camp at 12 o'clock, p.m. To give a proper description of this day, is more than I can do. The wind blew a perfect hurricane and the sand rose in clouds, cutting our faces and eyes dreadfully, and completely darkening the air. The country all round was a barren desert.

Officers and men became frantic for want of water, and our guides informed us that we must go six miles further before we could get any more; those who had flasks filled them. Mine did not hold more than half-a-pint. I could have sold it for any money before we got far on the way. The wind blew fearfully, and the sand rose in clouds; so that we could not see one another. My company was on the advance guard, and we lost the regiment on the plains. The sand rose in such clouds that we could not see them, and the wind blew so strong that they could not hear our bugle sound 'the close'. Our officers rode in all directions in search of them; at length, they succeeded. The storm abated for a short time, but soon commenced again, and the sand rose in such clouds, and the wind was so hot, that the men fell by numbers. The want of water was past everything—the best and strongest men were beaten up—the cry of 'water, water,' 'well, well,' was heard on every side. Men were in the greatest agonies. I found my drop of water of more value than gold; but how I stood it more than the rest I do not know. I carried a bit of ginger in my mouth always—perhaps it was that. Although I was ill, very ill, and wished I was dead, yet God was good and merciful to me, and I pulled through.

We came to a well and a few Indian huts at 4 o'clock. All became disorder; men rushed out of the ranks like madmen, and all the officers could do to keep order was useless. I and two others got into the huts, and the natives gave us all the water they had; so we did pretty well. We halted here about three quarters of an hour, when the wind dropped to a calm. We saw a large, black, dismal-looking cloud rising to our right—for it was now daylight. In a short time after, a gentle breeze sprang up, and ruffled the sand as it came slowly along. We all expected it was going to rain; but alas! alas! we were mistaken,—the breeze began to be stronger and of a cool kind, which made us shudder—though not a cold shudder; something seemed to be awful about it.

The wind now got to the east, and began to blow stronger; and the men fell sick by numbers. I felt very bad. It was a sickly kind of a feel. There the men lay, groaning in the greatest of agony. The doctors and apothecaries were all bustle, bleeding the men as they lay upon the sand, until pools of black blood were spread all over the ground. It was a most shocking sight to behold. There they were,—some dead, and some dying. The dead were as follows:—one captain, one sergeant and four privates. One man shot himself, to put an end to his troubles; thus making a total of seven dead, and very near half the regiment sick. Luckily, the wind changed to the south-west, and the sickness abated. Those who were not so very bad revived all at once.

Our poor colonel was nearly distracted, not knowing what to do for the best. The wind by this time was blowing as bad as it did when we first started, and the sand rose in masses. One part of the regiment lost the other in the storm; but the officers rode all round, and the bugles sounding 'the close', we got together again.

We pitched our camp about six o'clock, with those tents at least which had arrived; for some of the tents and baggage did not come until late in the day; they got lost in the sand-storm. Two of our camp followers had fallen dead. Our colonel went all over the ground to see that his men were as comfortable as they could be. The wind dropped in the evening. We paraded at six o'clock, to bury our dead; they were sown up in their beds, and put altogether into a pit which was made for that purpose. The captain was put in a few boards, knocked up together, and buried by their side. We fired three volleys of blank cartridge over them. The colonel read the funeral service. The only thing that marked the spot was a few trees near an Indian village.

During the time we were burying them, a thunderstorm rose. The sky was one complete sheet of fire, and the peals of thunder were dreadful, as if the heavens were coming down. The whole of the men looked pale, sad, and downcast. The doctor told the colonel that he must halt the next day, as it was impossible to move the whole of the sick. One man went out of his mind, and ran through the jungle, and was not captured until a few days after.

RYDER

On the move: Indian Mutiny

WELL, we start from Cawnpore for Lucknow, which was to be the grave of many a fine man. We had our Christmas dinner (such as it was) at a place called Bonnie Bridge, the scene of one of Brave Havelock's gallant deeds or feats of arms on his famous march to the relief of the beleaguered Garrison. Well, after we breakfasted, my comrade and me took a stroll a little way from camp and came to a sort of hunting box of the old King of Oude. We walked in and the place was decorated with pictures of native art. Amongst the rest was a rough sketch of the massacre of the British Envoy and suite at Kabul in 1840. While we were commenting on this picture in walks a very consequential sort of native. I believe he was in charge of the building. Be that as it may, he told us in very marked terms that as we were going to Lucknow, our stay there would be very short. We asked him what he meant, and he very soon enlightened us on the subject, i.e. that we would be thrashed out of it, as badly as we had thrashed the Sikhs out of Goodgerat [Gujerat], an engagement in which my regiment took part. I thought this was rather strong on his part and was about the first intimation of the great struggle in which we were subsequently engaged in. So I thought I would commence the campaign on my own account and perform on my native friend who was going to help thrash us out of Lucknow. Consequently, I let him have a straight one from the shoulder (natives don't like straight ones from the shoulder). I repeated the dose several times, my comrade remaining neutral all the time. Well, we left Mr. Native, not in a very enviable position, but there was very soon a hue and cry in the camp that several soldiers had nearly killed a poor native. The 'Assemble' was sounded, so as to enable this poor native to pick the culprit from the ranks. I may here add that my regiment was very strict as regards the ill treating of natives, so that I thought I had put my foot in it, so to speak. Well when I saw all the preparations that were being made, I thought I might as well spare the regiment the trouble of parading, so I went to the Orderly

Tent, saw the Commanding Officer and stated the matter to him as it happened. The Commanding Officer asked who was by at the time, and my comrade corroborated my statement. He then asked the native if it was me who struck him, and he answered in the affirmative, and the verdict was—Serve you right. He was sent to the right about, and I was cautioned to be more careful in future.

METCALFE

Early days of a native war: New Zealand, 1860

FEBRUARY 11th.—We are busy in preparing for our expedition to the Waitara. Everybody knows something about it, but nobody knows the truth. I fear I shall yet see a few shots fired in anger before I leave the service, and I pray the Lord to give me a Christian's faith and courage. Then let balls and bullets fly; I shall still be safe to praise God on earth if I escape, and in heaven if I fall.

February 13th.—The settlement is in a state of excitement, principally caused by false reports. The Maoris are evidently expecting something unusual, for they are now making a great stir. The out-settlers are seeking protection from the Officer Commanding, and, as I understand, are about to build a stockade for self-defence. Several natives have come in from the south, and it is reported that hundreds more are on their way. The troops are busy practising the art of constructing entrenchments, and my gunners are daily at gun-drill. In fact, every movement has the appearance of a coming contest.

It is a difficult thing to please every one; for my part, I hope and trust it may please God to avert the coming struggle, and give us peace and prosperity. But it is not difficult to see that the natives are ten times more frightened than the Europeans; their inquiries and manner fully bear me out in this belief. They see that the settlers are preparing themselves for any emergency. One man is getting his revolver in order; another looking to his fowling-piece; a third arming as a volunteer; and all assuming a warlike appearance. The settlers at Bell Block are erecting a stockade for their defence.

These things make the natives look on with surprise. But we are not without a few amongst us who, with despair in their countenances, anticipate the horrors of Cawnpore, and believe that the natives are planning a second Indian revolt. Some foolish person has stated that there is an intention to murder secretly all the white people in Taraniki; and so easily are the fears of some people worked upon, that many believe in the rumour. I saw one man yesterday who had provided himself with a new bolt for his door. I asked him why he had bought it just at this time. He replied, with the utmost seriousness, 'It's the dreadful massacre I'm thinking about'; and, turning towards his only child, added, with a look of sorrow, 'I don't care so much about myself, but for that little one to fall into their hands would be horrible.' I replied, 'You may safely trust it with any native in New Zealand; they would take as much care of it as you would yourself.' But I might as well have talked to the wind, as have attempted to allay his fears.

February 20th.—The question of peace and war which has so long been in agitation in New Plymouth, has at length come to a decision. Unhappily war is inevitable. Where, how, and when it will end, it is difficult to determine. No one can imagine our present condition; whole families are flying here from the country, leaving their houses and lands to be destroyed by the savage natives. I have been compelled to quit my beautiful retreat, and take up my residence in town; and even at midnight, cart-loads of timid and trembling women and children may be seen making their way to some more secure abode. Armed men are patrolling the town and its suburbs during the night, and everything denotes the coming conflict. In a few days we expect martial law to be proclaimed, and hostilities to begin. This has been a doubtful, anxious day; for the surveyors were sent down to inspect the newly acquired land, and any interference on the part of the natives would have been considered a declaration of war. At noon they returned, stating that their chain and other instruments had been seized, and that they had had some difficulty in regaining possession of them. Just at this time the town was full of natives, who, as soon as they heard the result, left for their several pas.

Unfortunately we have no vessel in harbour to enable us to communicate with Auckland, but the steamer with the English mail is hourly expected. At length the worst has happened. Hitherto I have thought nothing of the affair, for I did not suppose that the natives would offer any resistance. But now I fear our out-settlers will suffer most severely, for the savages will not face the soldiers, but will aim at burning and destroying all before them at Bell Block, Mangorea, Tataraimaka, and other places. The settlers are building blockhouses and stockades, into which they may retreat on an emergency until assistance arrives. I am so far prepared to resist any invasion of my castle, that I sleep with a loaded pistol and a good bowie-knife at my head. This is, indeed, a pretty general precaution, for should we be first attacked, it will be a struggle for life, without hope of mercy. We are all expecting to see a man-of-war arrive shortly: this will greatly relieve our minds by insuring to us the welcome power of communicating with the rest of the world.

February 21st.—A messenger was sent to the chief rebel Wi Kingi, this morning, giving him twenty-four hours to consider the step he had taken, and offering him an opportunity to repent of his folly, and place himself at the mercy of the Governor.

February 22nd.— Wi Kingi's reply has just been received, stating his adhesion to his former policy. So we are now waiting for the order to march against him. Possibly, however, hostilities will not be commenced until a man-of-war arrives. A mounted troop of twenty civilians is being organized, under the command of Captain R——, 65th Regiment, and whole families are flocking into town with all their movable property.

February 23rd.—Late yesterday evening, martial law was proclaimed in this province.

February 28th.—Everything has been quiet for the last few days. We are awaiting the arrival of the steamer from Auckland with troops and orders. News has reached the town that the Maoris are entrenching themselves on the Devon line, near the Waitara, and many of our friendly natives are joining the rebel mob. Loads of furniture arrive in town every day from the bush, and the present delay will enable the settlers to save much of their corn, which otherwise would have been destroyed. Union prayer-meetings are being held in the various places of worship every night this week, to implore God to have mercy upon us, and to save us from the horrors that threaten us. Do Thou hear us, O Lord, and deliver us, for Thy great name's sake!

March 2nd.—Yesterday, the *Airedale* arrived from Auckland, bringing the Governor, with the whole of his staff, and about one hundred and ninety men of the 65th Regiment. In the evening, the war-steamer *Niger* came in with fifteen men of the Artillery, and two 24-pounder howitzers.

Camp, Waitara, March 6th, 1860.—We are now in camp; and as I have not been able to write for the last few days, I will state what has occurred. Sunday was a busy day with us. The usual bustle of packing up ammunition and camp equipage tended in no slight degree to disturb all Sabbath thoughts. At half-past two on Monday morning, we started on our march. The guns were in the centre of the line, and the baggage in the rear. We passed on through Bell Block, and on reaching Maori ground, we proceeded with greater caution, halting every now and then to enable the skirmishers to ransack the vast plain of fern-land around us. We exchanged the main road for one parallel with the beach. After crossing the Mowanaka and another river, we came up to a pa, which proved to be deserted. Just before we arrived at this spot, an accident occurred which nearly cost me the loss of a leg. Being much exhausted after the previous day's work and a sleepless night, I mounted the limber-box, but from some cause or other my foot got entangled in the spokes of the wheel, and before the bullocks could be stopped, it was completely twisted round. Even now, as I write this, I suffer great pain; but, thank God, no bones were broken, and I manage to hop about and do my duty.

Having arrived at noon at our camp-ground, we pitched our tents in a potato-field, having taken every precaution to prevent a surprise. We turned out twice on Monday night, but no appearance of an enemy was to be seen. On Tuesday morning we observed that a pa had been erected over against us during the night. Just at this time the man-of-war was starting for Auckland, so we fired a gun to detain her, and landed a portion of her crew. An orderly was also sent off to the newly-erected pa, to inquire what the natives meant by coming upon this land. They replied, 'They would fight us at all hazards'. When the news was brought to camp, it caused a shot which must have frightened the Maoris. Everybody was instantly in a bustle, preparing for the encounter; and as soon as the man-of-war had landed some rockets and a 12-pounder howitzer, we set off for the pa. Strong as it appeared to be, it was soon surrounded and entered, but not a soul could be found. After some difficulty, the stockade was pulled up and burnt, the rain falling heavily all the time. We soon discovered that the native courage had failed on our approach, and that, while the course was clear, the enemy had very judiciously bolted. During our advance against the pa, I could not walk, in consequence of the great pain in my foot; but, rather than be left behind, I mounted the limber-box and prepared the shell. As soon as we had set fire to the stockade, we returned to camp. Some of our men had some fine sport at a pig-hunt, killing two or three and bringing them into camp.

March 11th, (Sunday)—We are now getting settled in camp, and but for the scarcity of water should be comfortable enough. My foot is much better, and my health very good. Today I held my Bible-class in a tent kindly given me by the Brigade-Major.

March 15th.—Last night I held another service, which was well attended. This evening, as I was going out of the camp to hold a meeting, one of our officers said to me, 'What have you got there?' I replied that they were hymn-books, and asked him if he would take one to his tent and read it. He refused; but another gentleman present said, 'I will have one.' I told them that those books taught me my duty to my superiors, and my allegiance to God. Holding one out in my hand, I said, 'The Bible and these hymns have been my comfort for eight years, and I hope they will continue to cheer me till the day of my death'. My class was well attended, and the presence of God was with us. After it was over, I suggested that we should put by, while we were here, sixpence a week each for the cause of God—half to go to the Church-Mission Fund, the other half to that of the Wesleyans,—a proposal which was cheerfully agreed to.

March 18th, (Sunday)—On the afternoon of the 16th I went to New Plymouth by sea, arriving there at ten o'clock P.M. I got two 24-pounder howitzers, with ammunition, into the boats, and by one o'clock had everything ready for my return. My orders from the Colonel as I left the Waitara were, 'Mind what you are about. I depend upon you, and shall look out for your signal about three o'clock in the morning'. So far I had complied with his command, not even going to my own house, my dear wife having come down to the beach to see me. At one o'clock we put off, and by three A.M. the boatmen announced that we were off the mouth of the Waitara, and wanted me to communicate with the camp by sending up a rocket. But I knew very well that this report was incorrect, so I would not give the signal. However, we cast anchor, and waited for daybreak, when we had the mortification of seeing that the boat was off Bell Block, some five or six miles from the Waitara. We arrived there about seven o'clock, after crossing the 'heavy bar' in safety, when the guns were landed and conveyed to the camp. I had suffered a great deal from cold during the night, having had no clothing but a serge shirt and a pair of trousers, and when I arrived at camp I was very much fatigued. But I forgot the hardships when the Colonel met me at the gate and said, 'Well, you are back all right. I knew you could do it; I knew my man'.

I hoped now to get a few hours' rest, but soon found out my mistake; for we had to march at once against the newly-erected pa; and as we passed it, we saw the natives eyeing us from the interior. On we went, however, to a hillock about one thousand yards from the stockade. Taking up our position, we opened fire with three guns and one rocket-tube. The latter was manned by sailors. We poured in torrents of shell, and expected every minute to see the besieged fly from their garrison. After firing about a dozen rounds per gun, we advanced upon them, and they opened fire in return. The position taken up by my gun was about two hundred yards from the pa, and I fired every shot through the place. After halting here for a short time, we advanced still nearer, but more towards our left. While we were making our last move, some of our mounted civilian troops rode up to the pa, taking away the flag, which had been shot down and was hanging over the stockade. This was a very daring act, and brought forth a volley which flew about us like hail. One poor fellow was killed near me; I heard his mournful cries as he lay in the fern, hid from our view; another was brought down from his horse, and a third was shot through the thigh. The cries from the pa were terrible in the extreme, and I could not make out why the rebels remained there so long. Our ammunition being now expended, and night having come on, we assembled our forces about two hundred yards from the pa, and lay down in the fern while ammunition was being brought from the camp. Meanwhile the enemy kept up at intervals a well-directed fire, some of the shot striking my gun, and whizzing past my ears, others entering the ground close to my feet; and yet, through God's mercy, I was spared. We lay upon the ground until daybreak, without coat or blanket, trembling with cold.

MARJOURAM

On the march (*Confederate Army*)

TROOPS on the march were generally so cheerful and gay that an outsider, looking on them as they marched, would hardly imagine how they suffered. In summer time, the dust, combined with the heat, caused great suffering. The nostrils of the men, filled with dust, became dry and feverish, and even the throat did not escape. The 'grit' was felt between the teeth, and the eyes were rendered almost useless. There was dust in eyes, mouth, ears, and hair. The shoes were full of sand, and the dust, penetrating the clothes, and getting in at the neck, wrists, and ankles, mixed with perspiration, produced an irritant almost as active as cantharides. The heat was at times terrific, but the men became greatly accustomed to it, and endured it with wonderful ease. Their heavy woollen clothes were a great annoyance; tough linen or cotton clothes would have been a great relief; indeed, there are many objections to woollen clothing for soldiers, even in winter. The sun produced great changes in the appearance of the men; their skins, tanned to a dark brown or red, their hands black almost, and long uncut beard and hair, burned to a strange color, made them barely recognizable to the home folks.

If the dust and the heat were not on hand to annoy, their very able substitutes were: mud, cold, rain, snow, hail and wind took their places. Rain was the greatest discomfort a soldier could have; it was more uncomfortable than the severest cold with clear weather. Wet clothes, shoes, and blankets; wet meat and bread; wet feet and wet ground to sleep on, mud to wade through, swollen creeks to ford, muddy springs, and a thousand other discomforts attended the rain. There was no comfort on a rainy day or night except in 'bed'—that is, under your blanket and oil-cloth. Cold winds, blowing the rain in the faces of the men, increased the discomfort. Mud was often so deep as to submerge the horses and mules, and at times it was necessary for one man or more to extricate another from the mud holes in the road. Night marching was attended with additional discomforts and dangers, such as falling off bridges, stumbling into ditches, tearing the face and injuring the eyes against the bushes and projecting limbs of trees, and getting separated from your own company and hopelessly lost and no sympathy. If he dared to ask a question, every man in hearing would answer, each differently, and then the whole multitude would roar with laughter at the lost man, and ask him 'if his mother knew he was out?'

Very few men had comfortable or fitting shoes, and fewer had socks, and, as a consequence, the suffering from bruised and inflamed feet was terrible. It was a common practice, on long marches, for the men to take off their shoes and carry them in their hands or swung over the shoulder. Bloody footprints in the snow were not unknown to the soldiers of the Army of Northern Virginia.

McCARTHY

Escort for Queen Victoria, Scotland

THE next day the Queen visited Melrose Abbey, and we were formed up fronting the entrance, in a rather confined strip between the royal carriages and a stand erected in our rear for spectators. When the Queen appeared she seated herself in the leading carriage, and whilst waiting for the suite to enter the others, my trooper, a clever mare, with an inquisitive turn of mind, poked her nose forward, and there being no room for me to back, managed to reach the door of the royal carriage. Her Majesty immediately stretched out her hand and stroked Biddy's muzzle. I was half inclined to pull my horse's head up, but the Queen looked at me with such a pleasant smile that I thought I might be giving offence if I brought my horse to attention, and so Biddy enjoyed the highest honour, that ever fell to a Hussar's horse, for it was not until the cortège moved on that her Majesty ceased stroking her, whilst I sat frozen in the saddle, cold and stiff as marble.

The proceedings of to-day were a repetition of what had taken place yesterday. During the journey to Abbotsford, where the Queen was to rest for the night, some of the remarks made by the Scotch countrywomen were very comical, and I remember one forcing her way close to the carriage and calling out, 'Ay, woman, but you're lookin' bonnie the day,' at which her Majesty smiled very kindly.

At last the gates of Abbotsford were reached, and passing through them the Queen found protection from the excited enthusiasm of her loyal Scots. The next day we escorted her Majesty to Jedburgh, and here our duty ended, and we returned to Edinburgh, carrying in our minds the remembrance of a Royal week, rich in incidents, such as none of us were ever likely to experience again.

MOLE

Marching: the French Foreign Legion

THE legionnaire can march. Forty kilometres a day is the fixed minimum performance. He must be able to do that, day by day, without interruption, without a day of rest, for weeks on end. That is the object of his training from the very beginning—the daily 'pas gymnastique,' the 'double timing' in the long springy running stride of the Legion, the initiatory practice for marching. Several times every week the men must make practice marches over a distance of at least twenty-four kilometres, with full equipment, at the Legion's pace of five kilometres per hour, which has always remained the same. The only object of the practice marches is to teach the recruits steady quick marching. They neither end with a small manœuvre, nor have they exercises such as scouting, or exploring the country by means of patrols. It is nothing but simple marching at a prescribed pace, a tramping onwards to fulfil a given task. The 'marches militaires,' as the practice marches are called, usually commence at midday, when the sun is at its hottest, after a hard morning's drill, so as to represent a practical exercise. On one of the military roads which branch off from Sidi-bel-Abbes in all directions, the march goes on until the twelfth kilometre is reached, and then the men are marched back again.

On the march a legionnaire may carry his rifle as he pleases, either shouldered or by the strap, just as is most comfortable to him; he may take off his knapsack if it hurts him, and carry it in his hand; he is not ordered when to open his coat or when to shut it. The officers do not worry the marching legionnaires with paltry orders, and they are allowed to sing or to smoke as they please. When there is a large puddle on the road, or when one side of the road is stony, the column turns off of its own accord and marches where the road is best. In the course of many a whole-day march I have not heard a single word from the officers, no orders, except the short whistle signals, which mean: 'Column, halt!' and 'Column, forward march!' As soon as the signal sounds for a halt, the front rows form front without orders, and every man sits or lies down during the halt as suits him best. The marches are regulated by the one principle: March as you like, with crooked back or toes turned in, if you think that nice or better, but—march!

It is always being drummed into the legionnaire that he is

intended for nothing else in this world except for marching. If the pangs of hunger are gnawing at his stomach or thirst parches his tongue, that is so much the worse for him, but is no sort of a reason for his not marching on! He may be tired, dead tired, completely exhausted—but he must not stop marching. If his feet are bleeding and the soles burn like fire, that is very sad—but the marching pace must not be slackened. The sun may burn till his senses are all awhirl, he must go on. His task in life is to march.

The greatest crime that he can commit is to fail on the march. There is no such thing as an impossible marching performance for the regiment of foreigners. Each individual is inoculated with the one idea, it is hammered into him, that he has to march as long as he can control his legs. And when he can no longer control them, then he must at least try to crawl.

It is a merciless system, which, however, produces wonderful soldiers.

Inseparable from the march of the Legion is the baggage of the legionnaire.

The French foreign soldier marches with an equipment called the 'tenue de campagne d'Afrique.' He wears splendidly made laced boots, white duck trousers held together at the ankles by means of leather gaiters, and the 'capote', the heavy blue military cloak. The cloak is put on over the shirt, without any coat underneath, and its tails are buttoned back behind, so that thighs and knees are left free, and an untrammelled gait rendered possible, just as with the French soldiers. The only difference is that the legionnaire wears the 'ceinture' round the body, the blue sash, about four metres long, of fine woollen cloth, which not only gives the body a firm support, but also does service as a tropical belt, indispensable in the sudden changes of temperature in Africa, where the glowing hot day is followed by an icy cold night. The red 'kepi' has a white cover, and, as further protection against the sun, a thin linen cloth—the 'couvre-nuque,' neck-cloth—is buttoned on to the 'kepi', covering the neck, ears and cheeks. There are consequently in the Legion comparatively few cases of sunstroke, which may sound rather surprising.

He carries a rifle and a bayonet, two hundred to four hundred cartridges, cartridge pouch and knapsack, and the 'sac.' This knapsack is made of black varnished canvas with a unique system of straps, and has hardly any weight of its own. On the march it contains two complete uniforms, the legionnaire's linen and polishing cloths, partly in the inside and partly in 'ballots,' in carefully prescribed bundles. Tent canvas and blanket encircle the knapsack in a long roll. The collapsible tentsticks are stuck in at the side. On the top is fastened the 'gamelle' and fuel for the bivouac fire. In addition each man also carries one of the saucepans of the company or pioneer's implements. Knapsack, rifle and equipment altogether weigh almost fifty kilogrammes; no soldier of any other army carries such a load.

With this kit he marches over sand under a burning sun, on very scanty rations. In barracks he gets a cup of black coffee on rising in the morning. At ten o'clock he gets his forenoon soup, at about 5 p.m. his afternoon soup. Two meals a day, both consisting of soup, in which are boiled all sorts of vegetables as an extra, spinach, carrots or such-like. With this he eats the French military bread, a grey kind of bread which is very easily digested, undoubtedly nutritious, sufficient and palatable. When marching, however, the meat rations are dropped, and food consists almost exclusively of rice and macaroni. As a substitute for the bread he is served with a kind of hard ship's biscuit.

Marching always commences in the early hours after midnight. It then goes on uninterruptedly, with the hourly halts for the rest of five minutes, until the task has been completed. This is a peculiarity of the Legion from which there is no deviation, even when in the field. Be the distance ever so great, it is covered in one march.

The Legionnaire marches. . . .

ROSEN

9

SOLDIERS AT SEA

Attack on the French coast, 1800

WE LEFT Chelmsford on the 14th April, [1800] and marched to the Isle of Wight, where we lay until the 27th May. I was once in the Methodist meeting-house, while we lay in the town of Newport. On the 27th May, 1800, we embarked on board the *Diadem* 64 guns, and the *Inconstant* frigate, both armed 'en flute' [i.e. partially armed], and fitted for the reception of troops. We left all our women and heavy baggage in the Isle of Wight, and as we were not informed where we were going, this circumstance led us to conjecture, that we were destined for some desperate, and secret enterprize. We were joined by some more ships with troops, and sailed down the English Channel, until we fell in with the Channel fleet, under the command of Sir John Jervis. Sir Edward Pellew, (now Lord Exmouth) was sent along with us, with a squadron of eight ships of war. It was a magnificent sight to see the Channel fleet in regular order. They were in number forty-four ships of the line (a large proportion of them three-deckers) and a number of frigates. We sailed along the coast of France until we came to the bay of Quiberon, where we came to an anchor on the 2d June, near a small Island called Houet, lying betwixt the isle of Belleisle and the main land, about four or five miles from the latter, and six or seven from Belleisle.

'G.B.'

Transport to India, 1803

We marched from Chatham to Gravesend, on the 7th February, 1803;—and a very severe march we had, for it snowed all the way, with a high wind. We embarked on board the *Walpole*, East-Indiaman, Captain Sandilands commander. And were sent down below to the orlop deck, in the midst of darkness, cold, and confusion; but such a torrent of swearing, grumbling, and blasphemy, I did not think it possible for human beings to pour forth; it made my very heart tremble within me, much as I had heard since my fatal enlistment. During this long and tedious voyage, I was often afraid the wickedness and profanity that prevailed on board would sink the ship, or bring some dreadful calamity upon us. The vessel was very much crowded, and we were packed together like negroes in the hold of a slave-ship; and what made matters worse for us, our officers and non-commissioned officers were very strict as to our personal appearance, when it was our watch on deck. One comfort I enjoyed above my companions in suffering, was, that being so young I did not require to shave. The want of light, and the place being so crowded, rendered this a very serious operation to the men, besides we were on short allowance of water. There were a good many cabin passengers on board who were rioting in plenty of water and every luxury, but who looked upon us poor soldiers as if we had been animals of an inferior creation, and seemed afraid lest any of us should come near them. Keenly did I feel how low in the estimation of mankind I had fallen; and bitterly did I lament my folly in leaving Carriacou and the West Indies.

At length, to our great joy, we came to anchor in Madras roads, upon the 15th of June. We received orders to be transshipped next morning, and to sail immediately for Ceylon, as the war was at this time going on with the King of Candy.

ALEXANDER ALEXANDER

The Army on naval discipline, 1803

WE WERE put on board the *Dedinouse* frigate, still under the command of Captain Rogers. Captain P. Heywood, the captain of the frigate, had been a midshipman in the far-famed *Bounty*. He took little concern in the ship, leaving all to his first lieutenant, who was a very severe officer, and the crew were very low spirited and unhappy. We were told off in watches; he soon began to strike and knock about the soldiers, as he did his own sailors and marines. Complaints began to pour in to Captain Rogers every hour; and he told us he could not help it, as we were on board of a king's ship, under the command of her captain, and not under his, advising us to put up with it the best way we could, as it would soon be over. However, it became at length unbearable, so much so, that one day six of our men seized this tyrant lieutenant, and would have thrown him overboard, had not Corporal James Walker interfered, who with difficulty, rescued him, and, at the time, explained to him his Majesty's regulations respecting the army, and that there was no such thing as striking or canes allowed, especially in the artillery. He walked aft to the quarter-deck, and never took any notice of the affair, nor beat any of us after this; his boatswain's mates and petty officers carried rope ends, and used them at their discretion. I have heard him call to them to use them, and they were constantly in play; indeed, it was dreadful to see the manner in which these poor men were beat, both sailors and marines. His speaking trumpet was the weapon he used; one day a great hulking fellow of ours, went to Captain Rogers and said, 'Sir, please your honour, the lieutenant has beat me with his speaking horn.' 'D— the speaking horn,' replied Rogers, 'I can get no rest for it night nor day;' he went and remonstrated with the lieutenant; but it did no good, until the threat of throwing him overboard put a stop to it.

ALEXANDER ALEXANDER

Convoy for India: storms and scurvy

WE HAD not been long at Portsmouth, when the headquarters of the regiment were ordered to embark on board of the *Surat Castle*, East Indiaman, a fifteen-hundred-ton ship, then lying off Spithead, and the remainder of the corps on board of other ships at the same place. Our destination was the Cape of Good Hope. The *Surat Castle* in which I was doomed to sail, was most dreadfully crowded; men literally slept upon one another, and in the orlop-deck the standing beds were three tiers high, besides those slinging. Added to this, the seeds of a pestilential disease had already been sown. An immense number of Lascars, who had been picked up in every sink of poverty, and most of whom had been living in England in a state of the most abject want and wretchedness, had been shipped on board this vessel. Many of these poor creatures had been deprived of their toes and fingers by the inclemency of winter, and others had accumulated diseases from filth, many of them having subsisted for a considerable time upon what they picked up in the streets. The pestilential smell between decks was beyond the power of description; and it was truly appalling to see these poor wretches, with tremendous and frightful sores, and covered with vermin from head to foot, many of them unable to assist themselves, left to die unaided, unfriended, and without one who could perform the last sad office. The moment the breath was out of their bodies, they were, like dogs, thrown overboard as food for sharks. To alleviate their sufferings by personal aid was impossible, for we had scarcely men enough to work the ship. These circumstances were, I suppose, reported to the proper authority; but whether this was the case or not, in three or four days we weighed anchor, with about sixty other ships for all parts of the world. The splendid sight but little accorded with the aching hearts, lacerated bodies, and wounded minds of the poor creatures below. It was about four o'clock in the afternoon when the signal was fired to weigh. Immediately every sail was waving in the wind, and in a quarter of an hour after we stood out from land, each proud bark dipping her majestic head in the silvery deep, and manœuvring her sails in seeming competition, to catch the favouring breeze.

Such firing, such signals, such tacking and running across each other now prevailed, that our captain resolved to run from it; and the evening had scarcely spread her sombre curtains over the western ocean, and the golden clouds begun to change their brilliant robes of day for those of murky night, when our crew 'up helm', and stole away from the motley fleet, plying every sail, and scudding through the blue waters like some aerial car or phantom-ship, smoothly gliding over the silvery deep. In three or four hours we had entirely lost sight of our convoy. We were running at the rate of eleven knots an hour, and, as it seemed, into the very jaws of danger. The clouds began to assume a pitchy and awful darkness, the distant thunder rolled angrily, and the vivid lightning's flash struck each watching eye dim, and, for a moment, hid the rolling and gigantic wave from the sight of fear. The wind whistled terrifically, and the shattered sails fanned the flying clouds. All was consternation; every eye betrayed fear. Sail was taken in, masts lowered and yards stayed—preparations which bespoke no good tidings to the inquiring and terrified landsman. I was seated on the poop, alone, holding by a hen-coop, and viewing the mountainous and angry billows, with my hand partly covering my eyes, to protect them against the lightning. It was a moment of the most poignant sorrow to me: my heart still lingered on the white cliffs of Albion; nor could I wean it from the sorrowful reflection that I was, perhaps, leaving that dear and beloved country for ever. During this struggle of my feelings, our vessel shipped a tremendous sea over her poop, and then angrily shook her head, and seemed resolved to buffet the raging elements with all her might and main. The ship was shortly after this 'hove-to' and lay comparatively quiet; and, in about a couple of hours, the wind slackened, and we again stood on our way, the masts cracking under her three topsails, and fore storm-staysail. However, she rode much easier, and the storm still continued to abate. I was dreadfully wet and cold, and my teeth chattered most woefully; so I made towards the gun-deck, some portion of which was allotted for the soldiers. There the heat was suffocating, and the stench intolerable. The scene in the orlop-deck was truly distressing: soldiers, their wives and children, all lying together in a state of the most dreadful sea-sickness, groaning in concert, and calling for a drop of water to cool their parched tongues. I screwed myself up behind a butt, and soon fell into that stupor which sea-sickness will create. In this state I continued until morning; and, when I awoke, I found that the hurricane had returned with redoubled fury, and that we were standing towards land. The captain came a-head to look out, and, after some consideration, he at last told the officer to stand out to sea. The following morning was ushered in by the sun's bright beams diffusing their lustre on the dejected features of frightened and helpless mortals. The dark clouds of sad despair were in mercy driven from our minds, and the bright beams of munificent love from above took their place. The before downcast eye was seen to sparkle with delight, and the haggard cheek of despondency resumed its wonted serenity. The tempestuous bosom of the main was now smooth as a mirror, and all seemed grateful and cheerful, directing the eye of hope towards the far-distant haven to which we were bound.

A great number of the fleet were the same morning to be seen emerging from their shelter or hiding-place, from the terrific hurricane of the day before; but our captain was resolved to be alone; so the same night he crowded sail, and, by the following morning's dawn, we were so much a-head that not a sail was visible, save one solitary sloop, that seemed bending her way towards England.

Some three weeks after this we were again visited by a most dreadful storm, that far exceeded the former one, and from which we suffered much external injury, our main top-mast, and other smaller masts, being carried away. But the interior of our poor bark exhibited a scene of far greater desolation. We were then far from land, and a pestilential disease was raging among us in all its terrific forms. Nought could be seen but the pallid cheek of disease, or the sunken eye of despair. The sea-gulls soared over the ship, and huge sharks hovered around, watching for their prey. These creatures are sure indications of ships having some pestilential disease on board, and they have been known to follow a vessel so circumstanced to the most distant climes—to countries far from their native element. To add to our distresses, some ten barrels of ship's paint, or colour, got loose from their lashings, and rolled from side to side, and from head to stern, carrying everything before them by their enormous weight. From our inability to stop them in their destructive progress, they one and all were staved in, and the gun deck soon became one mass of colours, in which lay the dead and the dying, both white and black.

It would be difficult for the reader to picture to himself a set of men more deplorably situated than we now were; but our distresses were not yet at their height: for, as though our miseries still required aggravation, the scurvy broke out among us in a most frightful manner. Scarcely a single individual on board escaped this melancholy disorder, and the swollen legs, the gums protruding beyond the lips, attested the malignancy of the visitation. The dying were burying the dead, and the features of all on board wore the garb of mourning.

Every assistance and attention that humanity or generosity could dictate, was freely and liberally bestowed by the officers on board, who cheerfully gave up their fresh meat and many other comforts, for the benefit of the distressed: but the pestilence baffled the aid of medicine and the skill of the medical attendants. My poor legs were as big as drums; my gums swollen to an enormous size; my tongue too big for my mouth; and all I could eat was raw potatoes and vinegar. But my kind and affectionate officers sometimes brought me some tea and coffee, at which the languid eye would brighten, and the tear of gratitude would intuitively fall, in spite of my efforts to repress what was thought unmanly. Our spirits were so subdued by suffering, and our frames so much reduced and emaciated, that I have seen poor men weep bitterly, they knew not why. Thus passed the time; men dying in dozens, and, ere their blood was cold, hurled into the briny deep, there to become a prey to sharks. It was a dreadful sight to see the bodies of our comrades the bone of disputation with these voracious natives of the dreary deep; and the reflection that such might soon be our own fate would crush our best feelings, and with horror drive the eye from such a sight. Our muster-rolls were dreadfully thinned: indeed, almost every fourth man amongst the Europeans, and more than two-thirds of the natives, had fallen victims to the diseases on board; and it was by the mercy of Providence only, that the ship ever reached its destination, for we had scarcely a seaman fit for duty to work her. Never shall I forget the morning I saw the land. In the moment of joy I forgot all my miseries, and cast them into the deep, in the hope of future happiness. This is mortal man's career. Past scenes are drowned and forgotten, in the anticipation of happier events to come; and, by a cherished delusion, we allow ourselves to be transported into the fairy land of imagination, in quest of future joys—never, perhaps to be realised, but the contemplations of which, in the distance, serves at least to soothe us under present suffering.

When the view of land first blessed our sight, the morning was foggy and dreary. We were close under the land, and were in the very act of standing from it, when the fog dispersed, the wind shifted fair, and we ran in close to the mouth of Simon's Bay. The now agreeable breeze ravished our sickened souls, and the surrounding view delighted our dim and desponding eyes. Every one who could crawl was upon deck, to welcome the sight of land, and inhale the salubrious air. Every soul on board seemed elated with joy; and, when the anchor was let go, it was indeed an anchor to the broken hearts of poor creatures then stretched on the bed of sickness, who had not, during the whole voyage, seen the bright sun rising and setting—sights at sea that beggar the power of description. For myself I jumped and danced about like a merry-andrew, and I found, or fancied I found, myself already a convalescent.

JOHN SHIPP

Escape by sea from Corunna, 1809

SECURE within the wooden walls, bad as our condition was, I felt comparatively happy in being so fortunate as to be on board the same vessel with Donald. In relieving his wants, I felt less my own, and was less teased by the wit and ribaldry of my fellow-sufferers; who, now that they were regularly served with provisions, and exempt from the fatigues of marching and the miseries of cold, were as happy, in their rags and full bellies, as any men in England.

For two days after we came on board, I felt the most severe pains through my whole body: the change was so great, from the extreme cold of the winter nights, which we had passed almost without covering, to the suffocating heat of a crowded transport. This was not the most disagreeable part: vermin began to abound. We had not been without them in our march; but now we had dozens for one we had then. In vain we killed them; they appeared to increase from the ragged and dirty clothes of which we had no means of freeing ourselves. Complaint was vain. Many were worse than myself: I had escaped without a wound; and, thank God! though I had not a shirt upon my back, I had my health, after the two first days, as well as ever I had it.

'71ST'

Shipwreck, 1839

The wreck of the Ann, *17th March, 1839, off the River Indus*

WE GET orders the next day to pack up the tents ready to put on the ship *Ann.* She was waiting for us, and we all went on board ready for Bombay.

We set sail with the breeze and at eight o'clock that night, as soon as we had relieved the watch, bump went the ship on a sand-bank, and we were wrecked at the mouth of the river Indus on the 17th March, 1839.

We tried all night to get the ship off, but were unable to do so.

We fired guns of distress, and burnt blue lights all night, but not one of the country boats would come near us, and there we were sinking.

We threw everything over to lighten the ship, but all to no purpose.

Two of our men volunteered to take a boat on shore to see if they could get any relief.

We tried to get ashore with the ship's boats, but they leaked, so we had to turn back.

The men who went in the boat for help went up the river, and saw a bungalow and a flag staff.

They ran up the river shouting. They thought they heard a noise, and found it was from two gun-boats going to Crutchee.

The Lieutenant had gone before them. The Captain said they were bound to come to assist us.

They pressed all the country boats, and made them come and put in.

One gunboat came to the ship, and the other had to stay on the other side of the tide to pick us up at the beacon or land mark.

We were at it all night. When it got dark we fired our guns, and they fired pistols from the gunboats till we got to the boats.

We had to wade and get in the best way we could, and had to help one another in.

One boat went back to the ship, and the other put us in the native boats, and they put us on an island, and the next day we all got off.

When the last lot left, they were up to the knees in water on the deck.

That left us three days fasting, but we had plenty of good water, and that assisted us.

The next day we got some salt fish and rice.

The second morning we were on the island, some of the men were looking for the ship. They could not see it, but saw a smoke. All hands came to look, and it was the *Burneese* steamer towing a small steamer to run up the river Indus. It was not long before it came close to us. We told the Captain who we were, and he said he would signal to the Captain of the *Burneese*, as he was going to sail in half-an-hour.

The answer came to bring us on board quick. The first lot got on board and the steamer came to fetch the others. We all got on board and sailed to Bombay.

There was plenty to eat, but we could not eat; we wanted to sleep. The Captain gave us a good dram of grog each and that sent us to sleep.

We landed in Bombay a miserable lot, both officers and men. We had lost everything but what we stood up in, and that was not much, I can tell you.

CLARKE

The loss of the Birkenhead *(26th February, 1852)*

(i) By John O'Neil (then a corporal, 91st Regiment, Argyll and Sutherland Highlanders)

THE drafts on board included 100 of the Argyll and Sutherlands and an officer of ours, Major Wright.

I and my escort had only been on board half an hour when the vessel struck on a rock between Simon's Bay and Port Elizabeth, somewhere near Danger Point. She struck a mile and a quarter from shore. It is fair to suppose the disaster was caused by reckless navigation, because outside the breakers the sea was as smooth, almost, as this floor; there was scarcely a ripple on the surface of the water. It was a strange scene when she struck. The Captain of the ship, ah! I recollect well the last words he uttered. He rushed down below and told the sailors to man the boats. 'Lower your boats, men,' said he, 'we are all lost!' I never saw him again. Major Wright gave the order, 'All hands fall in on deck,' and we fell in, every man. He told off so many soldiers, and so many sailors to each boat, to get them out and save the women and children. I forget how many boats there were, but every boat available was got over the side. No man was allowed to leave the ranks till the boats were pushed off. Major Wright threatened to shoot any man who stepped towards the boats, but no one thought of doing it. Any rush would have swamped the boats for certain. Discipline was maintained till the last. The ship went down twenty minutes after striking. It was a terrible time, but we stood on. We all expected to die, but the women and children were got safely off. Not one of them was drowned, thank God! They and their escort comprised the greater part of the 179 who were saved. The water rose as the ship was sinking. Before we left her we were up to our necks in water on the top deck. Just before the end came Major Wright addressed us. 'You men who cannot swim,' said he, 'stick to some wreckage—

whatever you can lay hands on. As for you who can swim, I can give you no advice. As you see, there are sharks about, and I cannot advise you how to avoid them,' which of course he could not. There was many a quiet hand-shake and silent goodbye. Few of us hoped to live through it. The breakers between us and the shore were awful. At last the ship sank. There was a lurch and a plunge, and all was over. I found myself in the water and struck out for shore. I had next to nothing on in the way of clothing. It was a fight for life. We were not above a mile and a quarter from land, as far as my eye served me; but that is plenty far enough when there are breakers and sharks! The breakers were so big. Luckily I knew how to swim breakers, or I should not be here now. Any one not knowing how to would have been drowned, as sure as fate! They would smother him. With proper management a breaker will sometimes sweep you in for hundreds of yards. The backwash was the worst. I stuck to it, and got ashore at last, escaping the sharks. I saw nothing of the rest, or of the ship's boats. All the trouble was not over when I got ashore. I had to walk sixteen miles stark naked under a blazing sun before I met any one or obtained any assistance. I shall never forget Major Wright. If it had not been for him all hands would have been lost, women and children and all. You may know that he was afterwards granted an annuity of £100, and he deserved it. I believe there was a lot of treasure on board the *Birkenhead* when she foundered. The military chest was on board for the troops—so we were led to understand. I think it is true, because for some time afterwards we were paid with Mexican dollars. They never recovered anything from the wreck.

O'NEIL

(*ii*) *By John Smith* (*2nd Regiment*, *Queen's Royals*)

I WAS asleep below when I was aroused by a tremendous crash. I at once realised that something serious was amiss, and calling to my mate, a Romford man, I told him I thought we must be ashore. We ran up on deck with the rest, and afterwards I stood at the gangway and assisted to hand the women and children into the boat. The men all stood back until they had got safely away; but there was no 'falling in' on deck. When the vessel went down I was in the long boat. There were about a hundred of us in it altogether, but when the ship broke in two the falling funnel caught our boat, and smashed it, throwing us all into the water. I managed to swim about until the ship went to pieces, when I got hold of a bit of forecastle and clambered on to it, afterwards picking up two other men and helping them on to my raft. It was an awful experience. There were men in the water all around. We could hear them struggling and occasionally came shouts of 'Boat ahoy!' but the shouts became fewer and the struggles feebler, until at last everything was quiet. We were fourteen hours in the water before we drifted to the shore. When we got in there was a man about 200 yards off floating on a barrel. He couldn't get off without help, and my two mates managed to get him ashore. Many were killed close to the shore, and we afterwards buried no less than 45 in the sand. We landed at a place where there was not a soul to be found. We set off to find some one, and part of the time I assisted in carrying Ensign Lucas, of the 73rd Regiment, who had been injured on the rocks. We came upon three black fellows fishing, but could not make them understand anything, and it was two days before we came to a place belonging to Captain Smales, who had been in the Army, and got something to eat. A schooner (the *Lioness*) came for us when they knew where we were, and we had to go back to the shore to meet it. We were taken back to Simon's Bay, and from there went on to East London, and were sent up to the front. I was in the Kaffir War of 1852–53, under Sir Harry Smith and Sir George Cathcart. I returned to England in 1861, on a merchant ship called the *Belvedere*. After getting back I went into the service of the Great Eastern Railway Company, and served them for 37 years and six months. I am now superannuated from the railway, and have a small pension from them of five shillings per week, which is my principal source of income.

SMITH

An unlucky shipwreck, 1857: Indian Ocean

IT WAS a fine morning April the 6th, 1857 when the left wing of our regt., under command of Major Barnston, embarked on board H.M.S. *Transit* at Portsmouth for the purpose of proceeding to China. All were agreed that great misfortunes were in store for us during the voyage out.

Our first mishap took place at the mouth of the Needles. On the morning of the 7th after anchoring for the night, we found, a little to the surprise of all on board, that there were four feet and a half of water in the forehold. The captain therefore immediately on the discovery weighed anchor and put back into Portsmouth. We ran [*sic*] alongside the old *Bellerophon* and, as soon as the authorities could send a sufficient number of men on board to man the ship's pumps, the whole of the troops commenced taking their kits from the *Transit* and placing them on board the *Bellerophon* and, after the whole of the kits and the mess utensils had been placed safely on board the *Bellerophon*, we went on board ourselves.

The *Transit* was immediately taken into dock for the purpose of being botched up. Soon it was evident that she was not properly repaired and in fact was never seaworthy from the time she was launched. This done, and it took six days to do it, we again started on our road, but ill-luck was all we were to meet with, for in passing through the Bay of Biscay, we met with strong head winds. Our jibboom was carried away and the jib-sails flew into ribbons. The ship was leaking in several places and the troops had never a dry berth to sleep in. No one knew the extent of the danger save the captain and the sailing master.

We put into Corunna on the Spanish Main on the 21st of April and after getting things in a little order, we started with a little more success. But the ship was in a deplorable state; she was continually leaking and the pumps were going night and day. May the 4th we put in for coal at the Isle of St. Vincent, one of the Cape de Verd Islands on the western coast of Africa. May the 21st we arrived at the Cape of Good Hope. Here we again had to take in coal and provisions. I may mention that it is a very unpleasant thing taking in coal. You must know that soldiers have to work as well as sailors on all occasions on ship board and we invariably have a full share of all the dirty work going on.

We left Simons Bay on the 4th June and we had rough weather and on the 22nd of June we met with a severe storm, which lasted five days, during which time the *Transit* appeared a complete wreck, having lost her jibboom, jib sheets and foretopsails, her main yard snapped in two, lying on the deck. The pumps were constantly at work. The ship's Carpenter was daily reporting to the captain that more rivets had given away and that he had discovered fresh leaks in the hull of the ship and another in the head of the vessel, so large that the men stuffed their blankets in to keep the water out. The ship's carpenter was busily engaged for several days splicing the main yard and when it was spliced all hands were required to sling it, which was done just in time to be a little respectable to run on a sunken reef on the morning of the 10th of July in the Straits of Banka.

In the ten minutes after the accident the ship was in a sinking state. Water covered her engines. The whole of the fires were put out. The stokers were up to their armpits in water and she was fast sinking astern. The boats were lowered and filled with provisions and landed on a rock three miles from Banka Island and three miles from the wreck. It was very fortunate for us that the tide was low at the time of the wreck, otherwise we all must have been lost. We remained on the rock until the tide rose, when we were taken off in boats and landed all safe with the exception of one man. The troops lost all they were possessed of.

The land is a very pleasant spot and very productive. Fruit of every description grows in abundance. The natives were very kind to us. They sent us fresh bread, a couple of oxen and several young pigs, which were of very little use to us, for they were very fat and we had scarcely any biscuit. We therefore had to throw the greater part of it away. They also brought us tobacco in abundance and for an old knife or a button they would give us a pound of the finest shag tobacco that ever was smoked in a yard of clay. There are a great many venemous insects and reptiles, also a number of wild beasts, but we were not without arms, though we had but little ammunition, for the whole of the ammunition or nearly so was spoilt, but we could have stood a brush with any party of natives or wild bears who might have attacked us. Scarcely a man amongst us had but one shirt to cover his back and every morning the whole of us had to strip to our buff to wash the same and the skin was often taken off our backs by the sun, being so nearly under the line.

On the morning of the 20th the H.M. Ship *Actæon* came in sight and we got orders to embark immediately and the boats were soon filled with our men and we pushed off to the ship. Glad enough we were, for we had not had any coffee since the wreck, neither had we had a sufficient amount of biscuit to satisfy a hungry belly. And now as one after the other leaves the boat and embark [*sic*] on the *Actæon* they seem taken aback. They first looked at the clean white decks, so different from the *Transit* and then at their bare feet, dirty with sand and mud and then at their ragged shirts without a covering to hide them, when a blush would mount their cheek and it was evident that one and all felt ashamed either more or less. But the first lieutenant soon put us to rights. He said the captain was at China, but he had ordered to give us every liberty we required and he did so. Although we often got in his way, he never complained.

WICKINS

Cholera at sea: after the Indian Mutiny

WE EMBARKED on the 17th April and were towed out to sea on the 19th and 20th and on the evening of the 17th there was one of the ship's company sent ashore from the ship for refusing to work or sail in the ship, for he swore there was cholera in the ship, which was only too true. The cholera did break out in the ship and the boatswain of the ship was the first who was attacked and died. The ship's cook was the next, and he got over it. It next broke out amongst the troops, and it was—well, you may imagine that fell disease breaking out in a crowded ship of somewhere about 11 or 12 hundred tons burden, and about 500 men and women on board, exclusive of the ship's company. Why, it beggars description. I would go through the Siege of Lucknow again sooner than experience the same, for in Lucknow, what with the excitement from shot and shell, and mines, etc., as the man said, there was scarcely time to get sick, and there was an end of it, but this way we were cooped up in a dirty ship. Bear in mind this was not one of H.M.'s troopships, but an old tub of a merchant ship that was hired in a hurry for the occasion, for there was so many troops coming home from India at that time that they were glad to get any sort of tub to transport the troops in, and as for the crew, well, the less said about them the better, only they were composed of all sorts.

Well, the cholera continued to make havoc, throwing overboard every day at the rate of four and five, till the ship had to lay at the Sand Head, till the General Doctor signalled for, came from Calcutta. He came, and previous to his coming the troops were ordered to bring everything from the troop deck up the main deck; give the ship a thorough overhauling from stem to stern as the saying is, and then disinfected. All the men who were suffering at the time were taken up and placed under an awning on the poop. The pumps were set to work, salt water pumped into the ship and pumped out again, and it is almost impossible to conceive the filth that was got out of the ship. However, by the time the General Doctor came on board the ship had assumed a pretty tidy appearance, and when he did come on board and saw the arrangements he said that we could not have done better if we were trying for a twelve month and told us, that the only chance we had was by proceeding on our voyage.

And now for a couple of instances in connexion with this disease. There was on board an old Sergt. Major who belonged to the Company's Service and whose term of service had expired. He was pensioned off from the Service and was homeward bound to rest after his well earned pension—for in those days if a man enlisted in the Company's Service you had to remain in India the whole of the time that would entitle you to a pension and that would be the whole term of 21 years. Well, this man had no doubt been the whole of that time there and you would say long enough too. Well, when the General Doctor was about to step into his boat which was to take him to his steamer, this Srgt. Major went to him and said, 'Will you kindly allow me, Sir, to go back to Calcutta in your steamer? I don't wish to remain any longer aboard this plague-stricken ship.' The General Doctor stared at him (and well he might) for such a strange request. He said, 'My good man the only chance you have is to go on in your ship.' The man said, 'The only chance I have is to accompany you back to Calcutta and that I'll do right or wrong.' He tried to persuade him but it was no use. At last the Doctor said to him, 'I think you are afraid.' The man said, 'You have just hit it. Sir, I have been in many a rough scene and many a bloody engagement and never felt the least dread or uneasiness till now.' And I believed that man. However, the General Doctor humoured him and took him in his boat, and, as he was descending the ship's side the Doctor made the remark, I believe he has it now—and sure enough before the steamer was out of sight the Signal was made from her mast head that this man had died. Such is the force of fear. I believe that man would have faced the Cannon's Mouth in action without the least hesitation and often done so, yet acknowledged his fear of the Cholera and I have not the least hesitation in saying that fear was the cause of his death.

METCALFE

Sea transport: Foreign Legion

ON BOARD the *Bien-Hoa* the troops were submitted to the same discipline as the crew. We were divided into messes and watches, and had to take a turn at scrubbing the decks in the morning, hauling in and slacking the lead ropes at sail drill, and aiding in the several other duties of the ship, which a landsman can safely do without imperilling life and limb. We grumbled a great deal, for that is a soldier's prerogative; and were grumbled at still more for our clumsiness; but the work kept us fit, and was an excellent cure for those disposed to sea-sickness.

Frequent parades and kit inspections were also held by our

own officers, and these did away with the tendency to slackness and loss of discipline which are the consequent results of the tedium and inaction of a long voyage. The food was good and plentiful. Fresh meat, vegetables and bread were served out four days in each week; salt beef or pork, dried beans or lentils, and ship's biscuits formed the menu of two days' meals; and Friday being a fast-day—for at that time the French navy still retained many Catholic institutions—meat was replaced by sardines and cheese. There was an abundance of good coffee and pure water at the disposal of thirsty men, and each private drew a daily ration of a pint of red wine.

Defaulters, however, were deprived of this wine during the term of the disciplinary punishment they had incurred.

All the military passengers, from the sergeants downwards, slept in hammocks slung in the 'tween decks, and, judging by my own experience, it is certain that many of us found this mode of accommodation far from comfortable during the first week or so. However, we all seemed to become reconciled to it in the long run, although, even towards the end of the voyage, I would have preferred to sleep on the deck, and I know there were many more of the same mind; but this was strictly forbidden.

There is certainly, if one can depend on what the sailors say—and they ought to know—a way of obtaining as much rest in a hammock as in a bed if only one knows how; but I am convinced, from experience, that to gain that knowledge one must serve a long apprenticeship and begin it when young.

Some very good concerts were organised on board, and these, together with the exciting games of draughts, dominoes or loto, were of great help in assisting us to pass the time when we were not at drill, on duty, or undergoing inspection.

Our journey was a long one, for the ship, though a very seaworthy craft, could not steam more than twelve knots at her best. The engines broke down on two occasions, once in the Red Sea, when we were delayed for two days, and again in the Indian Ocean, where the trooper lay like a log for seventy hours before the necessary repairs could be effected.

For coaling purposes we touched at Colombo and Singapore, but remained only a few hours in these ports.

The *Bien-Hoa* arrived at Saigon on 13th April, and stayed there for four days, during which we were quartered in the barracks of the 11th Regiment of the Infanterie de Marine.

Here we were able to stretch our legs a little by going out and visiting the town, which is a fine one, and possesses a splendid Botanical Garden and zoological collection. Most of us were specially delighted at being able to sleep for a few nights in a cot again.

We sailed early in the morning of the 18th and anchored in Along Bay (Tonquin) on the evening of the 21st April (1891).

MANINGTON

Troopship to Cape Town: 1900

THE following details as to diet, etc., on board a troopship, may serve to remind us of our journey out. Here is a typical day:

BREAKFAST.—About three-quarters of a pint of a curious infusion called by courtesy coffee; half-a-pound of dry bread, with now and again some half-dozen tablespoons of porridge. This is oatmeal porridge in the strictest sense, there being no other legitimate ingredient save water.

DINNER.—Three-quarters of a pint of soup (I suspect this to be water masquerading as soup on the somewhat inadequate grounds that it has been used to boil meat, puddings, or to wash greasy dishes). The meat itself is—well, we generally leave it untouched. (I never knew before where all that unwholesomely fat meat one sees at Christmas time goes. I think I know now. It is used to feed the fishes on the Cape route.)

TEA.—This meal consists of a pint of 'tea'—a brew which has considerable claims to be called 'special'. It is certainly like nothing I have ever tasted before. This, with half-pound of dry bread, constitutes the last meal of the day.

No beer or spirit is procurable. There is, however, a 'dry canteen', a sort of coffee shop, which opens thrice daily for an hour.

With 1,300 hungry customers, it does a roaring trade. Getting at the bar is like getting into the pit of a theatre on a first night. A 'queue' of fifty or sixty patient (!) Tommies waiting their turn is not at all an uncommon sight.

The troop deck at night is a weird picture, and it is impossible to move about save on one's hands and knees—the hammocks swing so near the deck. The deck itself is covered with sleeping forms in more or less picturesque attitudes.

Beyond the usual duties of swabbing, mess-work, guards, pickets and fatigues, there is little else to record.

After a couple of parades a day, comprising physical drill and kit inspections, the troops are at liberty to spend their time as they wish. To some, the monotony of the voyage weighs disagreeably, whilst others divide their time between reading and gazing at the wonders of the deep—spouting whales, sporting dolphins, and porpoises, flying fish and the gaudy miniature ship-like nautilus.

Perhaps the majority are absorbed in the gaming schools of cards, 'house-on-the-line' and the 'crown and anchor'. The proprietors of the last-mentioned game, invite the Tommies to 'roll up and back the lucky crown'; 'win gold, wear gold'; or cry 'the more you puts down the more you picks up'. Business of this nature had to be carried on under the special difficulties of settling disputed claims and keeping a sharp look out for the ubiquitous provost-sergeant and his men.

A concert, or a free and easy sing-song at night, whiles away the voyage. And as the days come and go, the Southern Cross and other strange constellations shortly appear at night, telling us unmistakably that we have left our northern hemisphere behind.

MOFFETT

THREE

IN ACTION

If any question why we died,
Tell them, because our fathers lied.

Rudyard Kipling

10

LIFE ON CAMPAIGN

In the enemy's lines: foraging in King William's War

DURING this siege, which was not more bravely attacked than defended, as I was one day a-foraging, I entered a château, deserted by the enemy, and found in it a basket of eggs, and another of cocks and hens (in the camp language, corporals and their wives), which I made free with; the eggs I presented to the Duke of Argyle, and the fowls to some officers. The next day I returned to the same place, and got corn, hay, and straw, for my mare. The third visit I made with a resolution to search more narrowly, for something of greater consequence, but some of our men had been there, and deceived my hopes; for I could meet with nothing more valuable than what I had before carried off; therefore I was forced to content myself with provender for my mare. In the time I was searching, some of the French army came in upon me, and took both myself, my mare, and my forage. The soldiers were quarrelling about the right to my clothes, when their officer came in, whom by good fortune I knew. He asked me, what had brought me thither, and who I was. I answered, that I thought he ought to know me, being a son of Captain Maclaughings of Clare's regiment (for I was in man's clothes). 'Well now, honey,' said he, 'I vawsh not after knowing you before, but give my humble service to my cushin and naamshake; but heark'ye now, joy, are you Richard or John?'

'Fait,' said I, in the brogue, 'I am Richard.' 'Well, now, cushin,' replied he, 'what will I do for you? But indeed, honey, nobody shall meddle wid your tings, joy, but go in te name of Cott.' I made the best of my way to the Duke of Argyle's quarters, where I found his grace and the Lord Mark Kerr at chess. I asked them with some warmth, in a language which only became a soldier, and a freedom allowed my sex, what they meant by having no better intelligence, and idling their time at chess while the French were on the point of cannonading us. I had, in returning from my château, observed all the hedges lined and the cannon ready to play upon us. The Lord Mark Kerr, surprised to see his grace pay any regard to what I had said, told him, I was a foolish drunken woman, and not worth notice: to which the duke replied, he would as soon take my advice as that of any brigadier in the army. He then asked me my reasons: I told him, and had hardly done it, when he found my intelligence true, and that we had scarce time to get into the lines of safety.

MOTHER ROSS

Soldiers and their beaten foes: Ireland, 1798

AS OUR regiment had not been in the country during the outbreaking of the rebellion, we had received no injury to provoke our resentment. We were called into the services of suppressing this unhappy and calamitous rebellion, after it had begun to decline, and we were rather witnesses of its ruinous and distressing effects, than active hands in suppressing it by force. For it so happened, that although we several times pursued considerable bodies of the rebels through the mountains, we were at times pretty close upon them, yet no one of us fired a musket, with the exception of one or two, who did it without orders, on the morning of the 5th July, at the White Heaps, neither was a musket fired at us; and the only loss the regiments sustained during this service, occurred one morning, when we were pursuing a body of rebels among the mountains. One of our men having fallen behind through weakness, was met by two or three rebels in women's clothes, carrying pails of milk on their heads, as if returning from milking. They offered him drink, and while he was drinking, one of them seized his musket, and after threatening to kill him, they allowed him to proceed to the regiment, with the loss of his musket and ammunition.

The sight of so many houses and villages, and parts of towns, burned and destroyed, and the great number of women and children, who were in a destitute state, because their husbands and fathers were either gone with the rebels, or were fled for safety, touched most powerfully the sensibilities of our hearts, and diffused a feeling of generous sympathy through the regiment. It so happened at that time, that we had newly received a more than ordinary balance of arrears of pay, so that every man was in possession of money, less or more; and although we were very fond of milk, because we had been long living upon salt provisions, before our arrival in Ireland, yet there were none, who would accept of a draught of milk for nothing, but would pay its price. And if the people of the house would not take payment, they would give the value of what milk they received, to the children.

When we entered the town of Gorey, it was, in great part, deserted by the inhabitants. Nothing was to be procured for money. After the very fatiguing march we had on the day we entered it, we received one biscuit, and one glass of whisky. On the next day, we marched to a considerable distance, in quest of the rebels, and returned back; we got a draught of milk, and one day's allowance of boiled beef, which had arrived from Arklow; but no bread.—The day was very warm, and I was considerably exhausted. That day passed over, and the next day, until the evening, without any word of any more provisions. The dread of having to pass another night, in our present hungry state, determined other two and myself, to go in quest of something that we could eat. We saw some who had purchased some old potatoes at the mill of the place. We made all haste to the mill; but the potatoes were all sold. We felt disappointed; but, observing that the mill was at work, we entered it, to see what was grinding. We found a man attending the mill, who said he was not the miller, but had just set the mill to work to grind some barley. There were but a few handfuls ground; and we resolved, rather than want, that we would wait until some greater quantity was done, when we would endeavour to get it cleaned, so as to be capable of being turned into food. After stopping a few seconds in the mill, I began to look about, when I perceived a number of sacks, that were less or more filled with something; I said to my comrades, 'Perhaps there may be something in some of these sacks that will serve us: we had better examine them and see.' We were indeed loath to touch any thing; but we were in absolute want of food, and were willing to pay for it. Observing a sack about half full, standing beneath another that was full, and was bent over it, we thought we would see what was in the broken sack first. We instantly removed the full sack, and to our great joy, we found the other was about half full of excellent oat meal, ready for use. The miller's wife came in, in great agitation, and said, that she durst not sell it, for it belonged to a gentleman in the neighbourhood, who was a Captain of the Yeomen. I replied, that we were in absolute need, and must have it; but that we would pay a fair market price for it, which she could give to the gentleman who owned the meal; that he would likely be able to procure a supply to himself elsewhere; that he was perhaps not in the immediate want of it, but that we were, and did not know any where else to find it; and that she might state this to the owner, and that would remove all blame from her. She assented to the justice of this, and said, that One shilling and Sixpence was a fair price for the stone weight. The weights were quickly erected; we weighed a stone, paid the price, and set out to get it cooked, leaving a number more of our comrades, who had come to the mill, to be supplied in the same way as we had been. While passing along the street, looking for an inhabited house, where we might get our meal cooked, we met other three of our comrades, who had gone to the country in quest of provisions, but could get nothing but milk, of which they had their canteens full. We agreed that we would give them a share of our meal for a share of their milk. We then went into a house, in which was a woman with one child. She said her husband was a blacksmith, and that the rebels had forced him to go with them, to forge their pikes. We told her that we wanted her to make us some porridge and that she would get a share of them for her trouble. She instantly cleaned her pot, (which was but a small one), and got it on the fire. We procured some wood for fuel, and, the first pot full being soon made, and poured into a dish to cool, we desired her to make haste, and get the second ready, for we were very hungry, and what was in the dish would do little to fill us: we then sat down, all six, to satisfy our hunger. What was in the dish, would have been a very scanty meal for three; yet after we had eagerly swallowed a few spoonfuls, we began to slacken our speed, and (although the milk and porridge were exceedingly good) to swallow them slowly, and with difficulty; and we were all reluctantly compelled to leave off, before our little mess was nearly finished, and the poor woman got the remains, and the second pot-full for her trouble. We told her, that we would call back next day after parade, to get another meal. On returning to our quarters, we found that our provisions had arrived in our absence; but as we could not know that they were to arrive that night, we felt satisfied with what we had done. We did call back at our cook's next day: and, after taking a little more porridge, desired her to make use of the rest of the meal as she needed it, for that we had now got plenty of other provision, and were not likely to require it.

'G.B.'

In India: among the enemy's outposts

ABOUT the 18th of December [1804] we took up a position before the fort of Deig, and in two days after broke ground against it. The two companies to which I belonged led the column, carrying tools for working. The night was as dark as pitch, and bitterly cold. Secrecy was the great object of our mission, and we slowly approached the vicinity of the fort, steering our course towards a small village about eight hundred yards from the spot, where we halted under shelter from their guns. This village had been set on fire two days before, and its inmates compelled to take shelter in the fort. Small parties were dispatched in search of eligible ground for trenches, and within breaking distance. I was dispatched alone through the desolate village to see what was on the other side. I was yet but a novice in soldiering; and, believe me, reader, I had no great fancy for this job; but an order could not be disobeyed; so off I marched, my ears extended wide to catch the most distant sound. I struck into a wide street, and, marching on tiptoe, passed two or three poor solitary bullocks, who were dying for want of food. These startled me for the moment, but not another creature could I see. I at one time thought I heard voices, and that I could see a blue light burning on the fort, from which I inferred that I was getting pretty close to it. Just as I had made up my mind that this must be the case, I distinctly heard a voice calling out 'Khon hie?' in English, 'Who is there?' I was riveted to the spot, and could not move till the words were repeated; when I stole behind one of the wings of a hut close on my right. Soon afterwards I heard the same man say, 'Quoi tah mea ne deckah;' which is, 'I am sure I saw somebody.' Another voice answered, 'Guddah, Hogah;' which signifies, 'A jackass, I suppose;' for there were several wandering about. I fully agreed with the gentleman who spoke last, but was determined to throw off the appellation as quickly as possible, by endeavouring to find my way back. In attempting to make my retreat with as little noise as possible, I put my foot into some fire. This compelled me to withdraw rather precipitately, and they heard me, when one of them said, 'Hi quoi;' which is, 'There certainly is somebody.' The other replied, 'Kis wastah nay tuckeet currah?' 'Why don't you ascertain it, then?' Hearing this, I dashed into another hut, and squatted myself down close, resolved at least to have a fight for it. A man passed the door of the hut twice, but, at last, crying out, 'Cally ek lungrah bile hie,' which signifies, 'There is only one lame bullock,' he rejoined his party. The attempt to steal away in so dark a night would have been impracticable; I must infallibly have been heard. I resolved, therefore, to have a run for it, and off I bolted, up the same street through which I had come, when a whole volley of matchlocks was sent after me, but they did not attempt to follow—at least, as far as I know, for I did not stop to look behind me. I arrived safe at the division, not a little frightened; and I can venture to say that I never ran so fast before in my life. This afterwards proved to be a strong cavalry piquet.

JOHN SHIPP

Opening of the Peninsular War, August, 1808: Mondego Bay, Portugal

WE BEGAN to disembark on the 1st August. The weather was so rough and stormy that we were not all landed until the 5th. On our leaving the ships, each man got four pound of biscuit, and four pound of salt beef cooked on board. We marched, for twelve miles, up to the knees in sand, which caused us to suffer much from thirst; for the marching made it rise and cover us. We lost four men of our regiment, who died of thirst. We buried them where they fell. At night we came to our camp ground, in a wood, where we found plenty of water, to us more acceptable than any thing besides, on earth. We here built large huts, and remained four days. We again commenced our march alongst the coast, towards Lisbon. In our advance, we found all the villages deserted, except by the old and destitute, who cared not what became of them.

On the 13th, there was a small skirmish between the French and our cavalry, after which the French retired. On the 14th we reached a village called Alcobaco, which the French had left the night before. Here were a great many wine stores, that had been broken open by the French. In a large wine cask, we found a French soldier, drowned, with all his accoutrements.

'71ST'

Battlefield plunder, 1808

AFTER the battle (Vimiero) I strolled about the field in order to see if there was anything to be found worth picking up amongst the dead. The first thing I saw was a three-pronged silver fork, which, as it lay by itself, had most likely been dropped by some person who had been on the look-out before me. A little further on I saw a French soldier sitting against a small rise in the ground or bank. He was wounded in the throat, and appeared very faint, the bosom of his coat being saturated with the blood which had flowed down. By his side lay his cap, and close to that was a bundle containing a quantity of gold and silver crosses, which I concluded he had plundered from some convent or church. He looked the picture of a sacrilegious thief, dying hopelessly, and overtaken by Divine wrath. I kicked over his cap, which was also full of plunder, but I declined taking anything from him. I felt fearful of incurring the wrath of Heaven for the like offence, so I left him, and passed on. A little further off lay an officer of the 50th regiment. I knew him by sight, and recognized him as he lay. He was quite dead, and lying on his back. He had been plundered, and his clothes were torn open. Three bullet-holes were close together in the pit of his stomach: beside him lay an empty pocket-book, and his epaulette had been pulled from his shoulder.

I had moved on but a few paces when I recollected that perhaps the officer's shoes might serve me, my own being considerably the worse for wear; so I returned again, went back, pulled one of his shoes off, and knelt down on one knee to try it on. It was not much better than my own; however, I determined on the exchange, and proceeded to take off its fellow. As I did so I was startled by the sharp report of a firelock, and, at the same moment, a bullet whistled close by my head. Instantly starting up, I turned, and looked in the direction whence the shot had come. There was no person near me in this part of the field. The dead and the dying lay thickly all around; but nothing else could I see. I looked to the priming of my rifle, and again turned to the dead officer of the 50th. It was evident that some plundering scoundrel had taken a shot at me, and the fact of his doing so proclaimed him one of the enemy. To distinguish him amongst the bodies strewn about was impossible; perhaps he might himself be one of the wounded. Hardly had I effected the exchange, put on the dead officer's shoes, and resumed my rifle, when another shot took place, and a second ball whistled past me. This time I was ready, and turning quickly, I saw my man: he was just about to squat down behind a small mound, about twenty paces from me. I took a haphazard shot at him, and instantly knocked him over. I immediately ran up to him; he had fallen on his face, and I heaved him over on his back, bestrode his body, and drew my sword-bayonet. There was, however, no occasion for the precaution as he was even then in the agonies of death.

It was a relief to me to find I had not been mistaken. He was a French light-infantry man, and I therefore took it quite in the way of business—he had attempted my life, and lost his own. It was the fortune of war; so, stooping down, with my sword I cut the green string that sustained his calabash, and took a hearty pull to quench my thirst.

After I had shot the French light-infantryman, and quenched my thirst from his calabash, finding he was quite dead, I proceeded to search him. Whilst I turned him about in the endeavour at finding the booty I felt pretty certain he had gathered from the slain, an officer of the 60th approached, and accosted me.

'What! looking for money, my lad,' said he, 'Eh?'

'I am, sir,' I answered; 'But I cannot discover where this fellow has hid his hoard.'

'You knocked him over, my man,' he said, 'in good style, and deserve something for the shot. Here,' he continued, stooping down and feeling in the lining of the Frenchman's coat, 'this is the place where these rascals generally carry their coin. Rip up the lining of his coat, and then search in his stock. I know them better than you seem to do.'

Thanking the officer for his courtesy, I proceeded to cut open the lining of his jacket with my sword-bayonet and was quickly rewarded for my labour by finding a yellow silk purse, wrapped up in an old black silk handkerchief. The purse contained several doubloons, three or four napoleons and a few dollars. Whilst I was counting the money, the value of which, except the dollars I did not then know, I heard the bugle of the Rifles sound out the assembly, so I touched my cap to the officer, and returned towards them.

RIFLEMAN HARRIS

The North-west Frontier, 1839

Now we entered Afghanistan. We had to fight our way every day for six weeks through the Crugates heights.

We were attacked the first day from a large mountain. We sent the Sepoys all round it and stopped with the treasure. The Afghans could be seen running all over the mountain, but the Sepoys repulsed them in every way they went. In an hour not an Afghan could be seen.

We were put upon short rations. One quarter pound of meat, one quarter pound of flour a day, when we could get it. Hard times that!

We had to march twenty miles, and sometime more a day, and never saw a bit of tea, or sugar, or coffee all the eighteen months we were out.

When we arrived at Candahar the whole army had to halt through sickness.

We had to march to Ghuznee and arrived there on July 21st, 1839, the Bengal army leading, followed by the Bombay army, and Shaw Suger's army next, the man that we were again to put upon the throne at Cabul.

The Bengal army arrived hours before us.

They had to move camp as the Afghans could fire into their camp with their long gun, which is now at Woolwich. We took it and sent it home to England.

When we got in at four o'clock in the afternoon after eighteen hours forced marching, we had to halt our camels to unload them. We had yet had nothing to eat.

We got orders to march to the opposite side of the fort to a camping ground. We started again with the whole army, some one way and some another, and got in about four o'clock in the morning, but the camels did not get in till six hours later.

Nothing to eat yet! but some natives formed a bazaar and we bought some flour, but had not time to bake it, so we had to cook it in the short way.

On the 22nd there was a battle with the Afghans' cavalry and artillery. We could see them in the mountains from our camp. We were in readiness but were not engaged. There was no infantry with them, so our cavalry and artillery had to face them.

They allowed the enemy to come down into the plain and then they got the command to charge. Out they started and were soon engaged.

The Afghans could not get away, and all that were left alive were taken prisoners with everything they had.

The prisoners were all turned over to Shaw Suger, the Ameer who we were to put upon the throne at Cabul, in place of Dus Mahomet, who had fled to Herat.

The Ameer commenced to try the prisoners the same day. Some were sentenced to be beheaded, and others to be shot.

I saw as fine a man as could be wished, and who was a chief, being marched by our tents, and some of us went to see what they would do with him. They took him to a walled-in place, opposite our Light Company's tents, shut the door, and in a few minutes shot him. Lord Kean heard of it, and sent word to Shaw Sugar that he would not allow the executions to be carried on in a British camp.

I saw two men blown from a gun in the palace of Candahar, by order of the Shaw.

Assault on Ghuznee

That night the whole army had to parade at eight o'clock and were served out with sixty round of ammunition, and flints each, with orders to fall in at twelve o'clock on the same ground. There was not a word to be spoken above a whisper, and we were to turn our belts inside out and also the scales of our caps, in order to make everything as dark as possible. The artillery had their horses' hoofs muffled and also the wheels of the guns and chains.

We all had to lie flat on the ground till the gate was blown open, which was done with two 'Mussacks' of gunpowder, screwed on the gate.

At the end of the draw-bridge was a mortar to fire red-hot shot. Now the whole army got the silent word to march, and not a word could be heard from the men. Our regiment, the 17th, were first after the storming party. The 13th Light Infantry went to the opposite side of the city to fire blank cartridge to take the attention of the enemy.

The whole of the army had to lie down, until crossing the draw-bridge, the artillery firing from the heights and also firing from the batteries and from the citadel, with rockets shooting, bullets and cannon-balls flying about our heads like a swarm of bees.

Now the work began, the bugle sounded the advance, up we got, charged the drawbridge and took it, and got into the fort the best way we could.

The first man we saw was General Seale, wounded with a sabre cut across the cheek. He led the storming party.

We were the first company into the fort. Colonel Croker asked the General for orders, and was told to use his own judgement, but to clear the battery.

The Company faced about and fired a volley, and when the smoke cleared away not a man could be seen standing. All either killed or wounded.

We had about eight hours' work now in front of us, and made for the citadel. The colours of the 17th were first upon it, and when they were once placed there, there was no taking it from us, but it had taken some time to take it. It was a very strongly fortified place.

After we had taken the citadel, the remainder of the city had to be taken, and that took up the remainder of the day. We had not much time to look about. We were at it 'till about three o'clock in the afternoon. When we had possession of the citadel and forts, we took Dus Mahomet's son, and a number of chiefs prisoners, and others surrendered and that finished the fighting; but what a sight to see!

Now to camp for something to refresh us, for we wanted it bad enough I can tell you.

The end of the taking of Ghuznee, 23rd July, 1839.

Now we start for Cabul!

Every day's march the Chiefs begin to come in and give themselves up. Dus Mahomet has bolted to Herat, and his army begin to desert and give themselves up.

About the fifth day's march (we were on the advance guard) our artillery came galloping up to us about daylight.

We halted to let them pass, and they told us there was a battery on the plain and they were to take it. They went through a little pass to Paradise Valley. When we got to the pass we heard a loud report and thought they were engaged, but when we got through nobody was in sight but our own artillery. We hastened up to them and found a beautiful half-moon battery formed round the pass.

The report we had heard was caused by one of our artillery-men, who had got on the ammunition-box and was lighting his pipe when a spark got into some loose powder. This had exploded and blown him away.

We examined the guns that were left (six brass rifled ones), and loaded to the muzzles, and then went on to the end of the day's march.

The next day we got to Paradise Valley and found plenty of everything we wanted. It was more like home than any other place I had been in. The natives brought melons, pears, cherries, apples, and other fruit, the same as at home, but no gooseberries—they will not grow there. Water-melons could be picked up by the roadside.

The Chiefs came in droves to give themselves up.

Cabul

Next day to Cabul, a very long march. We had not much fighting there. Some big guns were fired from the forts, but they soon ceased.

It took the whole army all day to march round it. It was a beautifully rich city.

We got to camp at last, pitched tents and made everything ready for a good rest, but got no rest at night, for the mountain robbers were all about the camp.

Afghan robbers in camp

Every night about ten o'clock the shots began with the out-lying picquets. The robbers mostly made for the officers' tents and would strip everything out of them if they were asleep The in-lying picquets were continually firing, sometimes you would think a battle was going on all over the camp. It extended about four miles, and all in darkness. We could not get any light to burn, but we set traps for them, and when we caught them they seldom went home to tell the tale.

We had some men killed through going out of camp. We buried one the morning we left Cabul.

Good-bye to Cabul!

The Bengal army is to stop there, and the Bombay army is to go to Beluchestan to take Khelat.

Now we start from Cabul for a two months' march through the Gilghee Mountains. When we arrived there it was bitter cold, for the winter was setting in.

After we entered the mountains we filled our water bags, but the second day they were frozen and kept so until we got out of them. We were six weeks in them and nothing but frost.

After every day's march, if there was a village within two or three miles of us, we had to march to it to get forage for the artillery horses, and if we could not buy it we took it, after which we had to pitch the camp.

There was very little of anything to eat for the poor horses, and they kept dying daily, and at last we had to pull the guns ourselves.

We could not pitch the tents, as we were unable to drive the pegs in, but when we came to a place where there were any large stones we had to tie the ropes round them.

It was bitter cold the whole way. There was no wood to be got to make a fire. Nothing but stones. The cooks had to follow the camels to pick up the dung to cook the bit we had to cook. Not much I can tell you.

Every day we kept thinking we should get out, but the further we went the higher the mountains got and the colder it seemed.

We were nearly starved to death, for the clothing we had was worn out and we were nearly bare-footed, and could get no fresh supply for a couple of months yet. At last we got them.

About ten days before we got out we found a change in the air, and a little warmer, and two days before, it got quite warm, and we were able to pitch the tents and had the first night's good sleep for about six weeks. The next day we got out and arrived in the valley of Shall, Near Quitta.

So good-bye to the Gilghee Mountains.

CLARKE

Loss of a brother in action: Sebastopol, 1855

ONE night in particular I remember, and that was the night we took the quarries. That night we had a hard tussle and lost a lot of our poor fellows, the enemy turning out in very strong force. But eventually we drove them back and succeeded in taking the quarries, although both sides lost heavily. In this attack I had a brother killed, belonging to the 7th Royal Fusiliers. I knew he was in the engagement, and after it was over made enquiry and finding no trace of him, next day—the flag of truce being hoisted—I went out amongst the dead to search for the body, in this being successful. Obtaining a pick and spade I buried him alone, the other bodies being placed in heaps. I had another brother belonging to the marines, also engaged in this action, but he fortunately escaped. It is after the battle when the field is strewn with the dead and wounded, that the full horror of war makes itself felt; a horror which words but feebly express, and entirely fail to describe, were you bold enough to attempt to describe such scenes; but the soldier has no place for fine feeling, and at the call of duty he must do or die, and leave the sentiment for others.

PARSONS

On campaign: Indian Mutiny, November, 1858

AFTER this we had a month's rest and then broke up camp and marched to join the Commander-in-Chief's army at a place called Sultanpore. We were here some time, and the enemy appeared in force at a place called Doudpore. (The places in India are nearly all poors or bads.) We were ordered out to smash them. We did so and I shall never forget it. On one night before the action I put on a new pair of Wellington boots (boots could be purchased very cheap in India). Well, I put on these boots and we were told we would start very early in the morning so that we could get the action over and get back again to camp before the sun would attain a very high altitude. We were told we would have to go about five miles, thrash them, and be back again. We started in the morning, me keeping the new boots on all night so that I might have no trouble in putting them on in the morning. Well at the end of the five miles we halted and sent out videts, but no enemy were to be seen. A spy came in and informed the General that the enemy were about three miles in advance, strongly posted in a beautiful position, and indeed they were, but the three miles turned out to be nearer eight. Be that as it may, away we went for them. After being marching some time we came to a very dense jungle and my regiment were ordered to skirmish through it. I forgot to mention that my regiment was partly filled up from home by this time by drafts sent out to us.

Well, we skirmished through this jungle. Sometimes we could not see our right or left files, and indeed our front rank men (I was in the rear rank). Well, we got out of this at last and formed up on what appeared at first sight to be a beautiful plain, but when we got into it and the action commenced, I thought we got into a pretty puddle, for the beautiful plains, as we thought, turned out to be a large field of rice, where the natives had been inundating with water from wells, and when we got into it and the enemy commenced peppering us with grape and round shot I thought a great many of us would bite the dust before we got out of it. Every step we took we would sink ankle deep and more sometimes. Meantime the cavalry and horse artillery (splendid arm of the service) got up on our flanks and it took them a long time to come up for they could not get through the jungle the same as the Infantry, and when they came up and commenced operations the enemies fire was drawn from the Infantry. Well, we got out of the mud after a while and went in with the bayonet, headed by our gallant Colonel Carmichael. It was a grand sight to see him. Like a giant he was, about 6 ft. 2½, and built in proportion. We, I mean the Infantry, turned the enemy's flank and they soon shewed the back seams of their jackets, and the cavalry and the R.H.A. completed the game. The Infantry were called off and highly complimented by the General, and they well deserved it, for their advance through the morass and the enemy peppering them all the time, their steadiness and coolness deserved all praise. The cavalry and artillery also deserved great praise which they got on their return.

Well, we were served, each man, with a tot of grog, and ordered to lay down under the shade of the trees for the morning's fatigue was too much for the Infantry to march back again after the action. We remained under the trees for a considerable time, and I fell asleep, and these beautiful boots that was flidedeflop on my feet when we were going through the mud of rice field were many degrees too big for my feet (for country leather will stretch when wet, it not being properly tanned). When the sun got at them when I was asleep they shrank up again so that I could scarcely move in them, as hard as they could possibly be. When the bugle sounded the fall in I rose up, and Oh, such a stinging headache. I thought my head would burst, and those beautiful boots made matters worse. I thought I should never reach camp, and indeed, I wished a friendly bullet would find its billet in my then miserable body. I could not help it, for I really was bad, and still so bad I would not give in and be carried on the elephant which we captured from the enemy, though frequently urged to do so by the officer and comrades, for I believe they were sick of looking at me in my misery. No, I would not give in. I believe my stubbornness kept me up on that occasion. At length a halt was called, and Oh with joy I heard the sound. I believe I hailed that sound with more joy than the remainder did the sound of the subsequent sound for grog, and that is saying a great deal. As soon as we halted I asked one of my comrades to cut off my enemies (the beautiful boots). 'Nonsense, Harry, if you do you won't be able to march to camp.' I said never mind, do as I tell you. He did so and after I got my allowance of grog and a little rest I was ready for the road again. We were then about 7 miles from camp. A nice job for bare feet, which were already sore enough, but I did it, and I afterwards heard my comrades say that it was as good as a pantomime to watch me picking soft parts of the road to walk upon. I did it however, and got back all right, but how I felt the next morning I will not say. On arriving in camp we were served with an allowance of grog. The Captain of my Company asked me how I felt, and I told him I did not know. He said, 'Could you do with another allowance of rum?' and I said I thought I could, and he gave it to me and he remarked that I was the most persevering little man he ever knew. He asked me why, when I felt so bad, that I did not give in; I said if I did my comrades would laugh, and it was. I was too proud to wear the ordinary soldiers' boots. I must needs wear Wellingtons, going into action, but I said I would never wear Wellingtons again, and indeed I have kept my word, for they are rather too expensive out of India. 'Well,' the officer said, 'What became of the Wellingtons?' I said I had thrown them away. He then gave me what would have bought two pairs of Wellingtons, and thus ended the action of Doudpoor on the 14th November, 1858.

METCALFE

The old camp-ground: war between the states

OUR camping-ground was a small pine knoll at 'Stoneman's Switch,' near Falmouth, Virginia, and but a few miles from the city of Fredericksburgh, where the great battle was fought. Here our regiment passed its first winter in Virginia. The tents of our company were built on both sides of our company street. The walls were of logs, and some three feet in height, and the sharp roofs were covered with thick cotton cloth. They were each about eight feet square, and usually contained four men. In each tent was a small fire-place made of sods cut from the muddy soil, and in these little huts, through the cold, chilling storms of that long winter, our regiment found but poor protection. Wood was so scarce that it had to be carried a long distance, and then it was of the poorest quality. At first the men could obtain sapling pine and white-wood trees by carrying them two miles, but this supply soon failed. When the trees were all gone, they were obliged to dig out the stumps and roots, and carry them that long distance for firewood. Our regiment suffered severely from exposure and sickness, and as I recall those long, dreary weeks, I can only wonder that the little graveyard on the hillside does not contain the ashes of a great number of our men than it does. We buried some of the bravest of our men there,—noble fellows, who had hoped that if they were to die for the country they might have the privilege of dying on the field of battle, but that boon was denied them.

A few of us visited this old camp-ground after the close of the war, as we were marching from Richmond to Washington in 1865. The tents were all destroyed, the streets were overgrown with weeds, the parade-ground was covered with grass—all was changed; the only places that remained in any degree in their natural condition were the little sacred mounds containing the remains of our comrades. Those hillsides of Virginia contain that which is far more precious to our nation than all the gold and silver of its mines—the priceless ashes of our noble dead.

GERRISH

Washington, 1862: after Second Bull Run

IT WAS the Sabbath day when we entered the city. At home it had been a day of quiet rest, or delightful worship. How strange the surroundings seemed to us as we marched along the streets of Washington. Every one was excited over the recent defeats suffered by the Union Army, and the rapid advance of General Lee.

The demoralization of war was visible on every hand. Regiments of soldiers filled the squares, squadrons of cavalry were dashing along the streets, batteries of artillery, long lines of baggage wagons and ambulances were seen in every direction. We marched to the United States Arsenal, and here everything reminded us of war. Great piles of dismounted cannon looked grimly upon us, stacks of shot and shells surrounded them, the building itself was packed with fire-arms of every design, from the old flintlock musket of continental times to the rifle of most modern make. Our regiment was equipped and armed with Enfield rifles, and there was dealt out to each man forty rounds of ammunition. We now supposed we were model soldiers, and marched proudly away. That night we encamped near the arsenal grounds.

GERRISH

Negotiating with the Zulus

SOME negotiations had now to be undertaken with the Zulu nation, and General Sir Evelyn Wood was entrusted with them. He took with him three squadrons of cavalry, each consisting of two troops from the three regiments at Ladysmith, and a full band. I was told off to accompany ours, and when we mustered I could not help observing that the squadrons illustrated two different theories of how a regiment should take the field for active service. We wore serge coats and khaki pants, with Indian puttees, or long strips of cloth, bound round and round the leg below the knee, in lieu of jack-boots: they were much more comfortable and supporting. Our helmets and belts were rubbed over with red clay to harmonise with the colour of the ground, and our steel work was all dulled. The squadrons from the Inniskillings and 15th Hussars adopted quite a different style; they were as spick and span as could be, helmets and gloves white and clean, and steel and brass work all sparkling in the sun. It was a queer contrast altogether and represented two widely different schools of military opinion.

We marched in light field order, but with tents and baggage-waggons drawn by mules. Our route was almost the same as that followed by the army under Lord Chelmsford's command during the Zulu war, and we saw many evidences of the numerous fights that had taken place, especially at the fatal field of Isandlana, where some grim relics still strewed the ground, with here and there a few bleached bones, and human skulls half hidden in the grass.

Crossing a high range of hills, we encountered snow and intense cold, and several of the men suffered severely from frost bites. Our destination was Conference Hill, which we reached after a ten days' march. Here we found the Zulu army, or nation, formed up in a huge crescent, their chiefs at their head, ready for the palaver. A ragged tent was pitched, and in front of this we took up our station, with the assembled Zulus facing us. They were strangely apathetic at first, and remained squatting on the ground in their crescent formation, while Sir Evelyn Wood and his staff dismounted and entered the tent. For some time we sat at attention on our horses. Presently the general came out and ordered the band to play 'God save the Queen' and the men to give a cheer. As we did this, the Zulus half rose in an almost threatening way, but their head men remaining seated, they squatted down again. There seemed to be some hitch in the negotiations, for the chiefs remained very grave and quiet. At last an order came to the bandmaster to strike up something lively, and he, being an Irishman, treated them to 'Patrick's day in the Morning'.

Never have I seen any tune produce such a magical effect as this one did. First a few of the Zulus rose, then a few more, and then the whole lot, as if the Pied Piper of Hamelin was after them, and they could not help themselves. In less than five minutes the whole of that dusky host were swaying and dancing to the music. When it was over they swarmed round us, patting our horses, laughing and talking, all in the best of humours. Above all things, they admired the big drummer, who could sit on his horse, and whack out such a fine tune. In the end the negotiations were successfully completed, and the Zulu army escorted us during the first day of our return march, and then left us with every token of amity.

MOLE

On the Veldt

We had won Bloemfontein with men on half rations or quarter rations, and whole-day marches, 220 miles in a month. In our long marches we existed on bully beef and hard biscuits, with very little water.

We once halted for a rest near an abandoned Boer farm, and discovered potatoes and pumpkins etc., while a few comrades captured a goat which was unceremoniously killed, cut into chunks, including skin, which we put into our canteen or mess-tins with our share of vegetables, and cooked over a slow fire. While my lucky 'feed' was cooking a few of us went over the farmhouse, in case there might be spies etc. On going upstairs we discovered a coffin on the table in one of the upper rooms covered with a white sheet. On removing this we found the coffin was empty. It had evidently been used to camouflage a consignment of rifles from the nearest seaport. We tore the sheet up into squares, and we lucky ones had clean handkerchiefs, the first for many a long day. The bugle just then sounded 'fall in', which was most annoying, for my South African 'Irish' stew was just coming on to boil, so I had to carry it in one hand with my rifle shouldered with the other, until we came to the next halt, about two hours later. It was still warm and I don't think I ever enjoyed a meal better; it only needed some of that Bloemfontein bread to complete it. . . .

It was very heavy going and the bullocks could not travel very fast, the wheels of the gun carriages sinking so deeply into the veldt, and what with forced marches on half, and sometimes even quarter rations, it was a wonder we were so successful in our advance. . . .

We never got down to hand-to-hand fighting, it seemed to us such a different kind of warfare from that we had previously experienced. For instance, as we advanced towards a range of hills north of Bloemfontein the oxen-drawn guns were firing over our heads at the enemy on the hill-tops, who looked to us like hundreds of tiny matches silhouetted against the skyline. We advanced about 100 yards or so and then were signalled 'halt and flatten out', which meant 'flat on our stomachs' as close to Mother Earth as we could, so as to make ourselves as small a target as possible. Then, after our artillery had ceased fire we went on and on until we made the final charge up the hill-side with our bayonets fixed. This was no use, because when we took their position all we could find was thousands of empty cartridge cases and no sign at all of any Boers. They were by now miles away on their horses (their horses being tethered on the other side of the hill) and they did not wait for close quarters because they had a decided aversion to cold steel. . . .

Well! we were on another forced march again, sometimes on half rations, and sometimes on quarter rations, and sometimes no drinking water available. Many a mile have I trudged along with a small stone in my mouth, the streams and wells being poisoned by the carcasses of dead horses and cattle having been thrown there by the retreating Boers in order to poison us. The stone helps to keep one's mouth moist when there is nothing to drink.

CORBETT

South African blockhouse, 1901

THE work of Blockhouse building along the Basutoland Border was commenced. These blockhouses proved just the thing required to meet the enemy's guerilla tactics in this region, for in addition to cutting off the Boer food supply from Basutoland, they formed an effectual barrier against bands of the enemy attempting to break through to the mountains in the rear. Each blockhouse is enclosed with barbed wire sloping down inwards and outwards from iron standards. This effectually prevents the citadel from being rushed by a superior force of the enemy. In the centre of the wire entanglements is the citadel, which consists of a large cylinder about twelve feet in diameter, and which is surrounded by a two foot wall of loose stones packed in the shell of the cylinder; these stones in turn being banked up by earth, sloping down to a trench four feet in depth. The trench surrounding the citadel may be thus safely used by troops, who stand and fire from this position. Usually about six men and a non-commissioned officer are left in charge of a blockhouse, and for their use the blockhouse is fitted with a cylindrical tank holding fifty or a hundred gallons of water. They are usually victualled for a fortnight, with a reserve supply both of ammunition and food, to be used only in cases of emergency. The whole line of blockhouses was ultimately put in telephonic or telegraphic communication with one another. In cases of continued attack, when ammunition and food may be running low, rockets are fired to attract attention of troops who may be operating in their neighbourhood. At special strategic points, forts are built, which are on a larger scale than the blockhouses, accommodating a larger garrison and at the same time capable of withstanding artillery attacks.

During the building of this blockhouse line, opportunity was taken to round up farms for horses, cattle and forage.

MOFFETT

II

FIRST TIME IN ACTION

An early skirmish in the Civil War, 1642

WE PILLAGED the minister, and took from him a drum and several arms. This night our soldiers, wearied out, quartered themselves about the town for food and lodging, but before we could eat or drink an alarum cried 'Arm, arm for the enemy is coming!' and in half an hour all our soldiers, though dispersed, were cannibals in arms, ready to encounter the enemy, crying out for a dish of Cavaliers to supper. Our horse were quartered about the country, but the enemy came not, whereupon our soldiers cried out to have a breakfast of cavaliers. We barricaded the town, and at every passage placed our ordnance and watched it all night, our soldiers contented to lie upon hard stones. In the morning early our enemies, consisting of about eight hundred horse and three hundred foot, with ordnance, led by the Earl of Northampton, the Lord of Carnarvon, and the Lord Compton and Capt. Legge, and others, intended to set upon us before we could gather our companies together; but being ready all night, early in the morning we went to meet them with a few troops of horse and six field pieces; and being on fire to be at them we marched through the corn and got the hill of them, whereupon they played upon us with their ordnance, but they came short. Our gunner took their own bullet, sent it to them again, and killed a horse and a man. After we gave them eight shot more, whereupon all their foot companies fled and offered their arms in the towns adjacent for twelvepence a piece. Their troops, wheeling about, took up their dead bodies and fled; but the horses they left behind, some of them having their guts beaten out on both sides. The number of men slain, as themselves report, was fifty besides horses. One drummer, being dead at the bottom of the hill, our knapsack boys rifled to the shirt, which was very lousy. Another drummer we found two miles off with his arm shot off, and lay a-dying. Several dead corpses we found in corn fields, and amongst them a trumpeter, whose trumpet our horsemen sounded into Coventry. We took several prisoners, and amongst them Capt. Legge and Captain Clarke. From thence we marched valiantly after them toward Coventry, and at Dunsmore Heath they threatened to give us battle, but we got the hill of them, ordered our men, and cried for a mess of Cavaliers to supper, as we had to breakfast; but they all fled, and we immediately marched into Coventry, where the country met us in arms and welcomed us, and gave us good quarter both for horse and foot.

WHARTON

A first brush in the Civil War

SABBATH day, 3 September, 1642, we advanced from hence to a little village called Addington about a mile from Stow the Old, the hither-most town in Gloucestershire, and about twenty miles from Gloucester; where, in our march this day, we again met the lord general's army, upon a great common about half a mile from Chippingnorton; at which place also our five regiments departed from his army, and marched to the village aforesaid. The blue regiment of the train'd bands marched in the van and took up the first quarter in the town; the other three regiments of the auxiliary forces were quartered at the adjacent villages; whereupon our red regiment of the trained band was constrained to march half a mile further to get quarter. We were now in the van of the whole army, having not so much as one troop of horse quartered near us; but we were no sooner in our quarters, and set down our arms, intending a little to refresh ourselves; but presently there was an alarm beat up, and we being the frontier regiment nearest the enemy, were presently all drawn up into a body, and stood upon our guard all that night. We were in great distraction, having not any horse to send out as scouts, to give us any intelligence; my lord general with his army lay at Chippingnorton, about three miles behind us; who had an alarm there given by the enemy the same night also; our regiment stood in the open field all night, having neither bread nor water to refresh ourselves, having also marched the day before without any sustenance, neither durst we kindle any fire though it was a very cold night.

Monday, 3 September, we got some refreshment for our soldiers, which was no sooner done, but news was brought to us, that the enemy was within half a mile of the town, which proved to be true; for presently one rid down to us having his horse shot in the neck all bloody, and told us the enemy was at the town's end; also one trooper slain a quarter of a mile above the town, one of our soldiers stript him, and brought his clothes to us: It was a little open village, the enemy might have come in upon us every way, therefore we conceiving it not safe to abide in the town, drew up our regiment presently into a body, and marched into a broad open field to the top of the hill. The blue regiment of the train'd bands were quartered within less than half a mile of us, but came not up to us: Being come into the field we saw about four or five thousand of the enemy's horse surrounding of us, one rid post to my lord general to inform him of it. One great body of their horse stood facing of us upon the top of the hill at our town's end, within less than a quarter of a mile from us. Another great body of their horse was in the valley, upon our right flank as we stood: and a third great squadron of their horse were going up to the top of a hill, in the rear of us; by all which appears, they had an intent to have surrounded our city regiments, and to have cut us off; we stood and faced one another for the space of half an hour; then six or seven of our men who had horses, rode up to them, and came within less than musket shot, flourishing their swords, daring them, and one or two of our men fired upon their forlorn hope: we had lined the hedges with musketeers, which they perceiving did not move towards our body, but only stood and faced us. Then some of the auxiliary forces came up to us, at whose coming we gave a great shout: and then by and by after we saw my lord general's forces coming down the hill about a mile and half behind us: my lord drew out the forlorn hope upon the hill as they came down; who fired three or four drakes against the enemy's horse that were near them on the top of the hill, that were coming upon the rear of us, and made them retreat to the rest of the body; their intent was to have compassed us in on every side, but the Lord prevented them. They might have spoiled our whole regiment, had they in the morning come down upon us when we were taking a little food to refresh ourselves, the enemy being then but half a mile off; a great many of the cavaliers lay all night within less than a mile of us, which we perceived in our march the next day. I hope the mercy of that day will not be forgotten.

FOSTER

First encounters before Quebec, 1759

THE first Push we made was on the 31st of July, 1759, with 13 Companies of Grenadiers, supported by about 5 Thousand Battalionmen. As soon as we landed we fixed our Bayonets and beat our Grenadier's March, and so advanced on. During all this Time their Cannon play'd very briskly on us; but their Small-Arms, in their Trenches, lay cool 'till they were sure of their Mark; then they pour'd their Small-Shot like Showers of Hail, which caus'd our brave Grenadiers to fall very fast. Brave Gen. Wolfe saw that our attempts were in vain, so he retreated to his Boats again. The number of kill'd and wounded that Day was about 400 Men. In our Retreat we burnt the two Ships, which we had ran ashore on that side to cover our Landing.

The 3rd Day of August a Party of Capt. Danks's Rangers went from the Island of Orleans to Quebec Side, a little down the River; they were attack'd by a Party of French, and was smartly engag'd for the Space of half an Hour; but the Rangers put them to flight, kill'd several and took one

Prisoner. The Rangers lost one Lieutenant, who died of his Wounds soon after, and 2 or 3 others. They got a great deal of Plunder.

THE SERGEANT-MAJOR OF GENERAL HOPSON'S GRENADIERS

A seventeen-year-old volunteer at Valmy, 1792

THE battle began about 8 o'clock, and was fought obstinately on both sides up to 9 o'clock. At that moment, the enemy having unmasked a fresh battery near the houses on the Lune, General Kellermann brought up his artillery, and the cannonade recommenced. That of the enemy did us great damage. Kellermann had his horse killed under him by a cannon ball, and his aide-de-camp was mortally wounded. At ten, several of our ammunition waggons blew up, which caused some disorder in our ranks. Our light artillery was then placed near the mills, and opened fire; more ammunition arrived and we regained our positions.

We manœuvred in close columns by battalions. Three Prussian columns moved forward, and marched towards the mill. General Kellermann galloped up, and ordered us to extend in line. 'Comrades!' he cried, 'victory is ours. Let the enemy come without our firing a single shot. Long live the Nation!' These words electrified us; we raised our hats on our bayonets, and cried, 'Long live the Nation!' The Enemy advanced nearer and nearer, as steadily as though on parade. At this moment, the mist cleared, and we gave them a terrible volley, which knocked over the front ranks of the Prussians. The others crushed one another in their anxiety to bolt, and their officers had immense trouble to rally them.

General Clerfayt, who had crossed the Bionne to attack the camp at Sainte Menehould, was beaten and driven back by General Beurnonville, which prevented us from being surrounded, and completed the victory. This first success redoubled our ardour.

We of the volunteer battalion, although in line with veterans, lost few men. We manœuvred like our comrades, and did some shooting, which much amused us, and made us wish the enemy would take his revenge. He did not fail to try. About 4 o'clock in the afternoon, having received reinforcements, he came on in the same order as in the morning, but was received with such a hot fusillade that he was obliged to retreat with heavy loss. A battery of twenty-four guns—eight- and twelve-pounders—at the Valmy mill, crushed them, and completed the victory. Firing ceased about nine in the evening, when the Prussians were in full retreat, which was difficult for them, for they were shut in to such a degree that some of them had to lay down their arms, and we nearly captured the King. I do not know why we did not profit by our success, pursue them, and capture their train. The enemy was beaten, and surrounded on every side; it was said that we might have made the King of Prussia sign a peace. Instead of pursuing them, we remained on the field of battle, which was covered with dead and wounded. The battalion to which I belonged had twenty-seven killed and sixty-seven wounded. We of the 5th Paris battalion afterwards returned to the camp at Sainte Menehould; but there were absolutely no provisions for us. I even had to pay five francs in cash for a loaf of bad army bread.

I received a ball just above the right ear, which, however, only just grazed the skin and went clean through my hat. I was very proud of that hat, and kept it for a long time. Thus, after serving only sixteen days, we were amongst the victors of Valmy.

FRANÇOIS

Outside Montevideo, 1806

THIS was the first blood I had ever seen shed in battle; the first time the cannon had roared in my hearing charged with death. I was not yet seventeen years of age, and had not been six months from home. My limbs bending under me with fatigue, in a sultry clime, the musket and accoutrements that I was forced to carry were insupportably oppressive. Still I bore all with invincible patience. During the action, the thought of death never once crossed my mind. After the firing commenced, a still sensation stole over my whole frame, a firm determined torpor, bordering on insensibility. I heard an old soldier answer, to a youth like myself, who inquired what he should do during the battle, 'Do your duty.'

'71ST'

Bugler in action: Rolica, 1808

THE sun was very hot, the sand was deep, the water we had with us was warm, and we could not drink it. We halted and took up our camp. We had to go a long way before we got water; we got our provisions from the shipping, salt beef and biscuit. As water was precious, I was sent on the outlying picquet, and when we came back, the camp was removed. The inhabitants gave us a pint of wine and some fruit. The troops were now forming into a regular army. We got under arms before daylight in the morning in full marching order without the beat of drum or sound of bugle, Sir Arthur and his staff in front of the line. On the 17th August we came up with the French on the heights of Rolica. Our brigade was ordered to form line under the command of General Craufurd. Our light companies was sent out to skirmish. We were on the left. The right of our army attacked the left of the French, our brigade moving onwards sometimes to the right and left. At last the French was repulsed and had to give way. We then moved to the right. A cannon shot was fired at us; it went over our heads. It was very warm, and we had need of water, Some of our men got sick. It was said the French had poisoned the water, but I do not know. We marched forward to get to the front on a rising ground to the right. Death had been doing its work; the 94th Regiment lost a great number. As we went on, we came to a narrow road. There was a French soldier lying shot. He appeared to be of the Grenadiers. There was a Portuguese dragging him off the road to strip him naked, for this is what they did. This gave us something to think about. After we were out of this narrow road, we saw others lying wounded, crying for water to drink and looking to us for protection, for they were afraid of the Portuguese. We formed into line, but the French were retreating. We then took up our camp for the night. This ended the Battle of

Rolica. A few of us sat down to talk of what we had seen that day for our conversation was more serious than it had been before. The French soldier that we saw shot through the head was above all, but we were soon to see more than what we had seen.

A BUGLER OF THE 71ST FOOT

First alarm: Federal Army, 1861

WE FIRST heard the dreadful name of Jackson the very night we arrived in Hagerstown, Maryland, from Chambersburg, Pennsylvania. It was past midnight, perhaps between two and three in the morning, when the long roll of the regimental drum corps startled the still air of our new camp. The rebels, it was said, led by Jackson, were crossing at Williamsport in force, and we, perhaps the only bulwark between them and the nation's life—we six miles away! It was a time to try men's souls and men's patience. What a scramble for cartridge boxes, pistols and dirks, for the pistol and bowie-knife era was still upon us! The officers bade us be calm, but they needed the advice not less imperatively than we. At last we had formed line, and the Colonel, on the ground probably that more battles are won by marching than by fighting, started us, raw levies, with six long miles and probably a battle before us, off on a double quick. We ran a mile, puffing, sweating, straining our eyes to see that foe we so longed to annihilate. 'Halt!' What for? Why, the line officers have held a council of war while trotting along upon their horses, and have concluded that if we are to fight it maybe well to have our muskets loaded. No one had thought of it before. We had supposed that our brave Colonel, in whose skill as a tactician we had the most unhesitating confidence, intended on meeting Jackson, to charge with the bayonet? We conclude that he now alters his mind. At all events he commands to 'load'. But we have had no instructions in loading. Which end of the cartridge shall go downwards? About a third of the men, reasoning apriori that the bullet was the main thing, put it in first. A good number of those who did not do this failed to tear the cartridge paper. Several put two or three cartridges in; some even more. It was the work of a week to empty those muskets. Having loaded and breathed, we began to race again. The sun rose. Was it the sun of Austerlitz? It was as bright and as hot. Men fell from the ranks. Some fainted physically, others in heart, some wanted to go home. Perhaps a tenth of the regiment reached Williamsport together; the rest came straggling in all the rest of the day. No enemy was there, the more's the pity for the enemy, for a brave dozen of cavalrymen could have captured the whole of us. However, Jackson fell back toward Martinsburg, and we flattered ourselves with the hypothesis that he had heard of our advance and considered discretion the better part of valor.

ANDREWS

12

SKIRMISHES AND SAVAGE WARFARE

Perils of a Civil War

THURSDAY, Sept. 21, after we had buried our dead, we marched from this field with our whole army to a town called the Veal, eleven miles, and four miles from Redding; where in our march this day, our enemy pursuing of us, fell upon our rear in a narrow lane about a mile and halfe from a village called Aldermason; they came upon us with a great body of foot and horse: our London brigade marched in the rear, and a forlorn hope of six hundred musketiers in the rear of them, besides a great number of our horse: but our horse which brought up our rear, durst not stand to charge the enemy, but fled, running into the narrow lane, routed our own foot, trampling many of them under their horse feet, crying out to them, 'Away, away, every man shift for his life, you are all dead men;' which caused a most strange confusion amongst us. We fired ten or twelve drakes at the enemy, but they came upon us very fiercely, having their foot on the other side of the hedges; many of our waggons were overthrowne and broken: others cut their traces and horse-harnesse, and run away with their horses, leaving their waggons and carriages behind them: our foot fired upon the enemy's horse very bravely, and slew many of them; some report above one hundred and not ten of ours: some that we took prisoners our men were so enraged at them that they knocked out their brains with the butt end of their muskets. In this great distraction and rout a waggon of powder lying in the way overthrowne, some spark of fire or match fell among it, which did much hurt; seven men burnt and two kill'd: the enemy had got two of our drakes in the rear, had not our foot played the man and recovered them again: this was about four or five o'clock at night; many of our men lost their horses, and other things which they threw away in haste: we marched on and came to the Veal about ten o'clock at night.

FOSTER

Red Indian warfare, 1759

8th July, 1759

The 8th, we landed on Quebeck-Shore, without any Interception, and marched up the River about two Miles; when the Louisbourg Grenadiers being order'd out to get Fascines, they had scarce set down to take a small Refreshment, and detach'd a small Party of Rangers to guard the Skirts of the Wood, before a large Party of Indians surrounded them, kill'd and scalp'd 13, wounded the Captain-Lieutenant and 9 Privates; they likewise kill'd and wounded 14 of the Royal Americans, wounded 2 of the 22d and one of the 40th Regiment: we got only 3 Prisoners, and kill'd 2 of the Savages.

August, 1759

The 11th Instant there was an Engagement between our Scouting-Parties and the Indians; our People drove them off; we had a great Number wounded, several very badly, but the most slightly; there was but few kill'd: There was one of the 35th Reg. told me, he saw an Indian who fir'd at him, but miss'd him; that he levelled his Piece and fir'd at the Indian and miss'd him likewise; upon which the Indian immediately threw his Tomahawk at him and miss'd him; whereupon the Soldier, catching up the Tomahawk, threw it at the Indian and levell'd him, and then went to scalp him; but 2 other Indians came behind him, and one of them stuck a Tomahawk in his Back; but did not wound him so much as to prevent his Escape from them.

August, 1759

On the 20th the Louisbourg Grenadiers began their March down the main Land of Quebec, in order to burn and destroy all the Houses on that Side.—On the 24th they were attack'd by a Party of French, who had a Priest for their Commander; but our Party kill'd and scalp'd 31 of them, and likewise the Priest, their Commander; They did our People no Damage. The three Companies of Louisbourg Grenadiers halted about 4 Miles down the River, at a Church called the Guardian-Angel, where we were order'd to fortify ourselves till further orders; We had several small Parties in Houses, and the Remainder continued in the Church.—The 25th, began to destroy the Country, burning Houses, cutting down Corn, and the like: At Night the Indians fired several scattering Shot at the Houses, which kill'd one of the Highlanders and wounded another; but they were soon repulsed by the Heat of our Firing.

It was said that the Number of the Enemy consisted of 800 Canadians and Indians. Sept. 1st we set Fire to our Houses and Fortifications, and marched to join the Grand Army at Montmorancy; the 3 Companies of Grenadiers ordered to hold themselves in Readiness to march at a Minute's Warning.

THE SERGEANT-MAJOR OF GENERAL HOPSON'S GRENADIERS

The Kaffirs, 1795

THE Kaffirs may unquestionably be considered as a formidable enemy. They were inured to war and plunder, and most of them are such famous marksmen with their darts, that they will make sure of their aim at sixty or eighty paces' distance. When you fire upon them they will throw themselves flat upon their faces, and thus avoid the ball; and, even if you hit them, it is doubtful whether the ball would take effect, the skins worn by them being considered to be ball-proof. Added to this, as they reside in woods, in the most inaccessible parts of which they take refuge on being hard pressed by their enemies, an offensive warfare against them is inconseivably arduous.

Before they deliver the darts with which they are armed, they run side-ways; the left shoulder projected forward, and the right considerably lowered, with the right hand extended behind them, the dart lying flat in the palm of the hand, the point near the right eye. When discharged from the grasp, it flies with such velocity that you can scarcely see it, and when in the air it looks like a shuttlecock violently struck. They carry, slung on their backs, about a dozen of these weapons, with which single men have been known to kill lions and tigers.

From this harassing warfare, travelling through almost impenetrable woods, over tremendous hills, and through rivers, we were soon in a terribly ragged condition. Our shoes we managed to replace from the raw hides of buffaloes, in the following manner: the foot was placed on the hide, which was then cut to the shape of the sole, and fastened to the foot by thongs made of the same material, sewed to the sole instead of upper-leathers. In two or three days this dried, and formed to the shape of the foot, and was sure to be a fit. When we had remained at this station about two years, it was truly laughable to see the metamorphosis of the once white regimental trousers. Here and there pieces had been sewn in to patch up holes, and, these pieces being of materials of other texture as well as other colours, we looked at a distance, like spotted leopards. During these two years I had sprung up some six-inches, outgrowing, of course, both my jacket and trousers; and, when I was in full case for parade, my figure must have been exceedingly ludicrous. My jacket was literally a strait jacket; for, from its extreme tightness, I could scarcely raise my hand to my head. My pantaloons or trousers had been, during the whole period, continually rising in the world, and now they would scarcely condescend to protect my protruding knees. I was but a novice at the needle, so that the patches I put on were either too small or too large. In this predicament I had to march nearly fifteen hundred miles through Africa. The rest of the men were but little better off; and we might well have been compared to Falstaff's ragged recruits, with whom he swore he would not march through Coventry.

JOHN SHIPP

The horrors of the Irish Rising, 1798

DURING the time we lay in Dublin, the rebellion was raging in various parts of the country, and much blood was shedding. Dublin itself was kept in a state of tranquility, by the vigilance of the police, and the power of the military. Our stay in it was short. On the first July, the volunteer cavalry were employed in going through the city, pressing all the coaches, gigs, and other vehicles, and collecting them in one of the squares. At six o'clock at night we paraded, and went into them, and set off for Arklow. We travelled all night. We were all accommodated at the outset but fell into considerable confusion on the way, by some of the coachmen getting drunk, and striving to get past one another; which caused several of the carriages to break down, and others by running into ditches, to upset. It was conjectured that some of the coachmen did this wilfully from aversion to the service they were upon. Numbers had thus to walk in the rain which was heavy, and several had their muskets damaged, by the breaking down or upsetting of the carriages. One man had his firelock completely bent; and when he was asked by the people of the villages through which we passed, what kind of a gun that was, he told them it was one of a new construction, for the purpose of shooting round corners.

As we advanced into the country, we began to see the effects of the rebellion. Burnt houses began to make their appearance in the villages, and their number increased as we proceeded. The coaches carried us about three miles from Arklow, and then returned to Dublin. We entered Arklow in the evening. The place had been attacked, by a large body of rebels a few days before, who had been repulsed with great slaughter. They had some pieces of artillery, with which they had dismounted one of the guns of the military and damaged some of the houses. They had also burnt that part of the town that lay next the sea side, which was composed of low thatched houses, and was inhabited by fishermen. It was a very pitiable sight, to see this scene of destruction: and those of my comrades, who went to the ground where the rebels had stood during the action, said it was disgusting. Numbers of bodies were still unburied, some of them lying in ditches, and the swine feeding on them. There was a number of prisoners in the place, who had been taken, whom they were trying to court-martial and hanging; but I was not an eye witness to any executions in this place. A part of the regiment was stationed in the church, which was not a large one. This was a new kind of quarters, but every part was occupied, pulpit and all; and the grave stones were the place where we cleaned our arms.

The rebels were still in a body upon one of the hills in the vicinity, and kept the place in alarm; and we had frequently to stand to our arms during the night. On the fourth of July, we paraded in the street at 12 o'clock at night in great haste. The right wing of the regiment got three days bread served out, when we marched away in a great hurry, without giving the left wing any. I was in the left wing, and had only a few crumbs left of that day's rations. We marched very quickly through bye roads; and when day began to break, we made a short pause and loaded our muskets—the first time I had done so in the expectation of fighting. There was a high hill before us (called White Heaps) whose top was covered with mist, and that side which was next to us was very steep. The rebels were said to be on the top of it. Their number we afterwards learned, was 5000 of whom 1500 had firelocks, the rest pikes. There were about six troop of cavalry along with us: but our whole number did not amount to 1200, without artillery. We ascended the hills with difficulty, without being perceived by those on the top, the mist concealing us from each other. When we had nearly reached the summit, and had entered into the mist that covered it, our front was challenged by the rebel sentinels, who demanded the counter-sign, to which the Lieutenant Colonel replied, 'You shall have it in a minute.' We moved a little further and formed our line. The fog cleared up a little for a minute, when we found that our left was near the enemy, who were collecting themselves into three bodies. The ground betwixt us and them was a wet bog and the commander of the cavalry told our commanding officer, that if he advanced, the cavalry would not be able to act in such marshy ground as that before us. The fog again covered us, so that we could not see them, and a gust of wind with a shower of rain induced us to stand still. The rebels then gave a loud cheer, and then a second, and they began a third, but it died away, and was not so full or loud as the others. We expected to be instantly attacked, as this was their signal of attack. They, however, had imagined that we were much stronger than they were, and being terrified by the suddenness of our appearance, in place of coming forward to attack, they fled in great haste down the opposite side of the hill. We stood in uncertainty for some time, as we could see nothing; then hearing the fire of two guns, we moved in that direction, and got out of the fog, and descended the hill, on the side opposite to that which we had ascended. We then learned that the rebels had gone down the hill and, having fallen in another division of the army, had come upon them before they could get fully formed, and had come close to the guns; when they were fired upon and repulsed. It had been arranged that different bodies of troops should have mounted the hill, on opposite sides at the same time, but we had been sooner than the others, which disarranged the plan. The rebels continued to fly, the cavalry went forward in pursuit, and we followed with all possible haste. When we reached the foot of the hill, I saw four of the rebels lying dead. We continued to march with great haste, and frequently changed our route. We heard firing at no great distance, but the parties were always gone, before we came up. The road was strewed with old clothes, oatmeal, oat bread, and dough, thrown away by the rebels in their flight. The dragoons killed a great number of them in the fields. The rebels, in their flight, fell in with some baggage, belonging to some of the other divisions, attacked the guard, and killed and wounded several, before the rest of the army could come to their assistance, the rebels were then totally dispersed, and a great many killed & wounded; but our regiment never could arrive in time, to take share in any of the actions. We had a most fatiguing march, of upwards of thirty Irish miles. In the evening, we arrived at the town of Gorey, as did also two other divisions of the army.

One thing I would particularly notice here, is the ferocity

of civil war. It has barbarities, not now practised in the national wars of Europe. Among those whom I saw lying dead, numbers had their foreskins cut off. In one spot, where seven had fled to a house, in which they were killed, their bodies had been brought out to the roadside, where they lay, shamefully uncovered, and some of them greatly mangled:—particularly one lusty young man; in which case, it was said to have been done by a yeoman, who was personally known to the individual, and who had done it, as he was alleged to have wantonly said, to see how fat he was. Barbarities were committed on both sides, sometimes originating in animosity, sometimes in wanton cruelty, and at other times in retaliation.

I was witness to a scene of the latter kind a few days after, in the town of Gorey. A man was brought to the back of the camp, to be hanged upon a tree on the roadside, by a party of an English fencible regiment. The man was scarcely suspended when the officer of the party fired the contents of two pistols into the body, and then drew his sword and ran it into it. I then turned from the sight with disgust, but those of my comrades who staid told me, that the body was lowered down from the tree, upon the road, and the soldiers of the party perforated it with their bayonets, cut off the head, cut it in pieces, and threw them about, tossing them in the air, calling out, 'Who will have this?' They then dug a hole on the opposite side of the road, and buried the body and the mangled pieces of head in the presence of a few of the unhappy man's friends. I was informed, that he had been a judge in the rebel army for trying their prisoners; that a brother of the officer of the party had been taken prisoner by the rebels, and had been sentenced by this man to be piked to death: and that this was the reason why he had been so used.

'G.B.'

Assault on a Maori pa, 1860

SEPTEMBER 10th, 1860.—Troops with baggage arrived within two miles of this place at noon, where they encamped, preparations having been made for a double attack tomorrow. A few of the rebels came to the dismantled and bleak looking pa at Puketakauere, to watch our proceedings, but a company of the 40th Regiment soon put them to flight.

September 11th.—Early this morning, three hundred men belonging to this camp marched off under the command of Major N—— to a place appointed near the river, about two miles from camp. Two 24-pounder howitzers, (under my charge,) two eight-inch guns, and a few sailors, in charge of a naval officer, left camp at about half-past five, to join the main body under General P——. We arrived at the L pa, where we were joined by the first division, composed of the General, the staff, commissariat, artillery, (consisting of two 24-pounder howitzers, and two 3-pounder guns, under the command of Captain S——,) and a force of about three hundred and fifty men of the 65th with volunteers. A second division, under the command of Colonel L——, 40th Regiment, had taken another route, and was intending to cut off the rebels' retreat, should an opportunity be offered. We now advanced towards the bush, over as fine a country as ever was seen. We soon saw some pas in the distance, and fully expected to meet with a stout resistance. We fired a few shells into the first of these which we reached on our march, but received no reply. Then a detachment charged it, but, as usual, found it empty. It contained several wharras, which were instantly set on fire, the stockade sharing the same fate. We soon came up to another and much stronger one. This was carried by storm, and burnt. These pas were frequently seen at Bell Block, and supposed to be very strong; but their position was not good for defence, as they were situated in a flat, open country. We were on the point of leaving this place, and continuing our march, when a shot was heard at a pa, on the edge of the bush, supposed to be Wi Kingi's stronghold. This we considered to be a challenge. Leaving here a large reserve under the command of Major H——, of the 12th Regiment, we proceeded on our march, until we came to the pa in question. We went up to within a hundred and fifty yards of the stockade, and, as no resistance was offered, a small body of friendly natives, who had accompanied our force, made a splendid rush, and entered the place, in conjunction with a company of our own men, who had seen the Maoris

Sword drill (cavalry fight) by Rowlandson, 1793

A Highland regiment at Vimiero,

Battle of Waterloo, 1815

The cavalry action at Balaklava, October 25th, 1854

Boarding: soldiers at sea, *c.* 1830

Troops on the march in India during the Mutiny

Charge of Hawkins's Zouaves, Roanoke Island, American Civil War

press forward, and were determined not to be outdone. As soon as these had entered the stockade, about three hundred men, with two 24-pounder howitzers, under the command of Major N——, made their way through a narrow clearing in the bush, with the intention of destroying a pa supposed to be in that vicinity. They had proceeded but a few yards, when the rebels opened a very heavy fire of musketry, which compelled them to retire with the loss of one man, (killed,) who fell into the enemy's hands. The Maoris proved to be much nearer and far more numerous than we had expected; and in less than five minutes the artillery were pouring into the bush torrents of shell and cannister, which created awful destruction and confusion among the tender branches, and must have occasioned great loss to the rebels, some of whom were seen to fall from the trees where they had concealed themselves. Their balls flew over and around us in all directions; and had they understood the art of taking a cool and steady aim, they might have picked us off at one hundred and fifty yards' range at pleasure. The bush here is very dense throughout, and, consequently, affords a splendid cover. Here, unseen and protected by rifle-pits, they took shelter, and kept up a constant fire, which broke into furious volleys when they saw the pa in flames. But our cannister and shell, ploughing through the bush with rapidity and precision, soon silenced them. We maintained our attack for almost two hours, and as the rebels seemed to have had quite enough of it, the order was given to return to the camp at Waitara. Our loss was very slight indeed, considering the number of men scattered about, and the heavy fire kept up. It consisted of only one killed and three wounded,—one of the latter, a bombardier, being severely injured in the foot. Too much cannot be said in favour of the friendly natives, who were in the thick of the fight during the whole time, and stuck manfully to the guns. The General, with indomitable courage and coolness, sat on his horse, calmly watching the progress of events, utterly heedless of the balls flying about him. The lion of the day was Major N——, who, having put on his war cap, appeared delighted at the prospect of paying the rebels off for their butcheries on the 27th June. He is indeed a brave and noble officer, and his men worship him. Captain S—— was also there, and displayed his usual contempt for Maori balls, never feeling satisfied unless in the midst of danger. A company of the Taraniki volunteers, under the command of Captain W——, and a few militia men, under Captain S——, were in rear, ready to do their work as soon as their turn came. The order to retire having been given, we were enabled to practice retreating with the prolong,—a manœuvre well adapted to protect a body of retiring troops. Inexperienced and injudicious criticisms have been vouchsafed, condemnatory of the General's conduct in ordering the troops to withdraw when they did. Some, indeed, have gone so far as to insinuate that the retreat was compulsory. I must, however, enter a respectful protest against these various judgments. We did a good day's work, and taught the enemy a lesson they will not readily forget. And now, O Lord, I thank Thee for sparing me again. Many were the narrow escapes I had; but still Thou didst not suffer me to fall. May I love Thee more, and cling more closely to Jesus; and may the rest of my days be spent to Thy glory, for Jesus Christ's sake!

MARJOURAM

Rifleman G. H. Gilham in Ashanti, 1874

WE PROCEEDED to Momsey, eleven miles nearer Coomassie. Here we saw two white men, a woman and a child, whom the King had released after a long captivity. The march on the following day took us over the Adansi Hills, a height of about one thousand five hundred and sixty feet above sea-level. We were disappointed in the view, for we could see nothing but tree-tops. On descending the hills and entering the forest we found pieces of white rag fastened to several trees, which we took as signals of peace; and here we came upon some more chiefs who had an interview with Sir Garnet, after which they were marched out of the camp, the men lining the road, and the buglers sounding the 'General Salute.'

Soon afterwards we captured a prisoner from whom the General gained some valuable information. After several days' advancing, our skirmishers, on the 31st, came upon a large body of the enemy, who opened fire upon them causing them to fall back and rejoin the main body. Upon this we received the order 'Chin-straps down, open out, and push on through the jungle'. I was one of the leading four of the front company, and as our skirmishers came in, I noticed one with the bones of his arm broken by slugs from the enemy's muskets.

We cut our way right and left into the jungle with our cutlasses, lying down in the underwood, standing behind trees for cover, pegging in where we could, and forming a semi-circle to the front; but the foliage was so dense that it was like being in a net, and the farther we went the thicker it seemed to get, so that I don't believe we advanced a hundred yards during the whole of the fight.

The enemy were all armed with flintlock muskets, obtained from the old Dutch settlers, and they fired at us with rough bits of lead, old nails, pebbles and rusty iron, which at first passed over our heads and showed us that the enemy were on a slope below us, whereupon we fired low and did terrible execution among them, although we could only catch sight of them here and there. Our men numbered about two thousand, while the Ashantis were believed to muster something like twenty thousand. They outflanked us on several occasions, but we changed front, first on one side and then on the other, so that we were always ready for them.

We had not been in action long before a slug crashed into the breast of a marine on my right hand. Poor fellow, I shall never forget how he fell back, and curled himself up in his agony. Directly afterwards a man belonging to the Naval Brigade, on my left, was hit in the shoulder and went down like a log. The doctors were continually passing up and down behind us, and two came along just afterwards and cut the slug from the chest of the marine, but they could not get at the bullet that hit the sailor. Both men were carried to the rear.

Soon afterwards my front-rank man, Richards an old chum of mine, was shot just by the side of his right eye, the bullet passing round the side of his head under the skin and coming out at the back. I had to help him to the sick-tent, which the

Engineers had hastily erected. I got back to my place in time to see an officer close to me shot through the arm, and several others were either killed or wounded near me; and after about six hours' fighting, I got a shot just above my right hip, which caused a flesh wound, about three or four inches long. I was attended to by a doctor, and resumed my firing.

A small field gun which was got into position did good work among the enemy, as did also the rockets which were sent among them, and no doubt astonished them. When at last they retreated, we went after them as well as we could, and we found that they had dragged their dead into heaps. Pressing on beyond their dead, and driving the fugitives before us, we captured their village, Amoaful. We rested here that night, but were alarmed once by the enemy making an attack upon our sick and baggage. However we drove them off, and heard no more of them. Our losses in the fight in killed and wounded, were—Naval Brigade 29; 42nd Highlanders, 114; Rifle Brigade, 23; Welsh Fusiliers, 53.

On the following day we continued our march towards Coomassie, and drove the natives from several villages through which we passed. Before we started the next morning our scouts brought in five or six chiefs who had been sent by the King with a flag of truce to ask for four days' grace, but Sir Garnet Wolseley wanted to get us all out of the country before the commencement of the rainy season, he would not agree to their proposal, and the troops were formed up in line to see them safely out of the camp.

We rested that night on the south side of the river Dah, and spent one of the most miserable nights we had during the campaign. The thunder, lightning, and rain were incessant, and the darkness was so intense that the sentries could only be posted by the aid of a compass, a candle, and a box of matches. The heavy rain, no doubt, prevented the enemy from attacking us by damping the priming of their old muskets.

Crossing the river early the following day we encountered a large body of Ashantis drawn up to oppose us for the last time, for we were then very near the capital, and intended making short work of it. They made a good stand for a few hours, and while the fight lasted it was hot work, for the firing on both sides was terrible, but they had to give in at last and make for the bush behind the town, King Coffee going away with the first of them.

To get to the town we had to pass through a shallow river about three hundred yards wide, the water reaching a little above our knees. The General, who was going through at the same time, on a mule I think it was, said, 'Come on, my lads, you will have a house to sleep in to-night, perhaps a palace.' We pushed on with a cheer, and soon the British flag was flying over the miserable old town. We drove out all the natives, taking away all the arms we could find, and breaking them up. We found a good many wounded natives, whom our doctors looked after.

Our Fantee bearers, who had all along been afraid to advance into the enemy's country, were now particularly bold, and we had to keep a sharp lookout to prevent them looting; and on this point English discipline is always severe. The first man caught offending, after having been previously cautioned, was hung on a tree, by the General's orders. I shall never forget the poor wretch's struggles. He was soon overpowered, bound hands and feet, a rope with a slip knot was put round his neck, and he was hoisted well off the ground. The more he struggled the worse it was for him, and there we left him as an example to the others.

SMALL

Broken Square at Abu Klea, 1885 (*Harry Etherington, of the Royal Sussex Regiment*)

ON JANUARY 16th we approached Abu Klea Wells, which are situated in a defile between some low hills. We brought up for dinner three miles off in the desert, and sent forward a party of Hussars to see if the wells were occupied. As they did not return, General Stewart ordered an advance, when all at once there were shouts of 'Dismount! Undo ammunition!' and we saw the Hussars riding back for their lives, and announcing that the Mahdists were thousands strong at the wells.

We were at once formed into a three-sided square, with the camels in the middle; one man being told off to look after six camels. Then we began to advance over the broken ground. About two miles from the wells it became dusk, and just as the sun was setting on the skyline, we saw the gleam of hundreds of native spears on the brow of a low hill. Some sharp shooting followed, but we were too far off to do any good, and in a few minutes it was dark.

Then commenced a night of terror. We formed a zereba of bushes and crouched behind it; many a man prayed that night who was not in the habit of doing so, I can assure you. You see it is one thing to face a foe in the field, and quite another to lie awake at night expecting to be killed every minute. All the while the Mahdists kept up a desultory firing—for they had two thousand Remingtons, captured from Hicks Pacha—and we lost several men and a number of camels.

All night long we could hear the native tom-toms beating, and every moment we expected a charge. I was told off for outpost duty, which was not very pleasant under the circumstances, but we did not go more than a hundred yards from the column. My regiment was in the rear, the heavy Camel corps being in front. Colonel Burnaby came round to us all, and said, 'Don't strike a light, and don't fire on any account, or you will show the enemy where you are; wait till you see the white of their eyes, and then bayonet them.'

By this time we were almost maddened with thirst, for our supply of water was nearly exhausted and we had only a pint per man left. Hence it was absolutely necessary that we should capture the wells before we went any farther.

The next morning we had one of those glorious sunrises that are only seen in the tropics. At eight o'clock we again formed square, for the Mahdists were beginning to descend from the hills. We sent out skirmishers to attack them, and Lieutenant de Lisle was shot while we were forming square.

The enemy then formed in three columns of five thousand men each, with riflemen on each side, the rest being armed with spears, and all thoroughly well disciplined.

We were only two deep in square till within fifty yards of the enemy, when our skirmishers retired, and we opened square to let them in. At that moment the Mahdists charged, but were repulsed. A second charge failed, but at the third they succeeded in breaking one corner of the square, and then the position became very serious indeed. Probably their success was due to the fact that our men at that corner were not used to the bayonet but to the sword. Anyhow, the Soudanese broke a British square, and that is something to their credit.

Our seven-pounders were thus left outside, and Colonel Burnaby rushed out of the square to recapture them. He fought like a hero, but was thrust in the throat by a Mahdist spearman and killed. We dragged him back to the square, but it was too late.

It was at this point that Gunner Smith won the only Victoria Cross of the campaign. When the square was broken, Major Guthrie stuck to the guns, and fought till he fell wounded. Then Gunner Smith rushed to the rescue. He had lost his rifle, but he caught up a gun spike, beat off the Soudanese, and dragged the Major back into the square.

When the square was re-formed a lot of the Mahdists were inside, but you may be sure that none of them lived to get out again. One odd incident happened inside the square. We were carrying a number of chests of bullion for Gordon, and these were knocked open in mistake for ammunition, so that the ground was literally strewn with sovereigns.

At last the Gatling guns were got into action, and that practically ended the battle. The Soudanese were simply mown down. Their bodies flew up into the air like grass from a lawn-mower. But their pluck was astonishing. I saw some of the natives dash up to the Gatling guns, and thrust their arms down the muzzles, trying to extract the bullets which were destroying their comrades! Of course, they were simply blown to atoms.

The battle lasted off and on from eight in the morning till five in the afternoon, when the Soudanese finally fled. We did not pursue them, but with a ringing cheer we dashed to the wells, for we had drunk nothing all day, and were nearly maddened with thirst. Altogether sixty-five of our men were killed, and a hundred and eighty wounded, while about two thousand natives lay dead upon the sand.

We buried Colonel Burnaby where he fell, and every uninjured man brought the biggest stone he could find, and so we built a great cairn over the man who died as a volunteer in the service of his country.

SMALL

Private George Pridmore of the Bedfordshire Regiment in the relief of Chitral, 1895

I WAS on convoy duty, much to my disappointment, so that I took no active part in storming the Malakhand Pass, but I had a fine view of the engagement. For five hours the Swats faced a most deadly fire without flinching, although we used mountain batteries, and they were largely armed with old flintlocks, and in some cases had to actually apply lighted matches to their rifles to make them go off. It is true that a certain number of them were armed with Martini-Henris and Sniders, but they could not use them to much effect.

How did they get these? Well, most of them were probably stolen from our troops in North India. These hill tribes are most expert thieves. They enter the camp at night without a sound, and, if any bungalow door has been left unlocked, something will be sure to have vanished before morning. I have known many a man to lose his rifle in this way. The thieves come naked and well oiled, so that if caught they nearly always wriggle out of our clutches and escape.

But they were wonderfully plucky in the fight. After the battle a good number of wounded natives came into camp for treatment, for I suppose you know that it is the custom in the British Army to render full medical assistance to any wounded foes who care to avail themselves of it. Well, the number of wounds that some of these men carried was simply astonishing. One man had six bullets through him, and then walked nine miles to a village, where he was treated by one of our army surgeons, and actually recovered!

One man stood on the top of a hut and beat a tom-tom to encourage his comrades. Several times he dropped wounded, but each time struggled up again, until at last he was shot through the heart and fell headlong down the cliff. One of their standard-bearers was knocked over by our bullets again and again before he was finally killed.

One incident which occurred during the fight was especially remarkable. We noticed a man standing on a high peak with a signalling flag. He had evidently belonged to some of our native troops, for he was an expert signaller, and as he watched our operations with the batteries—which were now aimed at the sangars—he signalled the result of each shot for the benefit of his comrades. Thus we saw him making the usual signals for 'too high' 'too low' 'on the right' and so on, as the case might be. Of course that sort of thing was not convenient, so we sent a shell where we thought it would do most good, and blew the signaller all to pieces. The moment he was hit, another native sprang to the spot, caught up the flag and signalled Bull's eye!

SMALL

A bayonet charge in Dahomey: French Foreign Legion

IT WAS five o'clock in the morning. Reveille had just sounded though it was still quite dark, and we of the 2nd Group were fumbling and groping around to get ready for our march when a shot rang out from an outlying picket, which was composed of Marine Infantry. We rushed to our arms and formed up, there were a few more shots, and then the picket came bounding into camp with thousands and thousands of black shadows close at the men's heels—the Dahomeyans had surprised us. As fast as we could ram the cartridges in and loose off we fired into the moving black shadows and saw them topple over like corn falling under the sickle. They checked momentarily and then moved sideways towards the staff tents.

'Now, legionaries, let us give 'em the bayonet,' shouted Commandant Faraux.

Before he had finished this remark we were on the run towards the threatened side of the camp, and in a few seconds more were in the thick of them, ramming our bayonets into their bodies until the hilt came up against the flesh with a sickening thud, and then throwing them off to make room for another, like a farm labourer forking hay, until we had to clamber over dead and dying men piled two or three high to get at the living.

For the moment there was no question of those of the enemy who were receiving our special attention running away. They couldn't run away, for the great mass behind was pushing them on to our bayonets. It was a terrible slaughter. And above the yells and curses of the combatant, above the shrieks and howls of the wounded, we heard the voice of Commandant Faraux shouting, 'Come on, legionaries, come on.'

After driving the bayonet charge well home we retired to re-form, and the enemy came on again. The legionaries then charged a second time, and, after a severe hand-to-hand tussle, again pushed them back.

Previous to the commencement of the fight many of the enemy's sharpshooters had been hoisted with ropes to the tops of the tall palm trees which fringed the open space on which the camp stood, and from these points had been pouring a plunging fire into us from the first moment of the attack, a sub-lieutenant of the Marine Infantry, the first man killed on our side, having been shot as he lay asleep in his tent before the alarm was given.

It was light when we charged for the second time, and the Dahomeyans in the tree-tops seemed now to be picking their marks instead of firing at random, and their special attention appeared to be directed to the officers. In general the enemy were wretched shots, which was in part explained by the fact that they rested the butt of the rifle on the thigh when firing, so that the bullets for the most part passed over our heads, but these men in the trees made good practice and must have been the crack shots of the Dahomeyan army.

Commandant Faraux was quite close to me as we were moving on the enemy, and I suddenly heard him exclaim, as, for a moment, he stopped cheering us on: 'Je suis bien touché' (I am well hit). That was his reception of what turned out to be a mortal wound. He continued to advance and encourage us notwithstanding; but presently he was hit again and fell to the ground. When the enemy had once more retired before the points of our bayonets, and we were again re-forming, the commandant was carried past us on his way to the ambulance.

Then, without anybody giving the order, and while the enemy was pouring a heavy fire into us, every legionary spontaneously presented arms as the wounded officer was borne by.

MARTYN

In ambush: French Indo-China

I GLANCED at the tirailleurs. They were kneeling now, and throwing eager glances through the foliage. In a low voice I told them to fix bayonets and load, and noticed that the man next to me trembled like a leaf as he did so. Excitement, I thought—or was it fear? From a deep bronze his skin had changed to a dirty yellow. I should have known and taken away his weapon, but this was my first experience.

Mechanically I slipped my right hand into the pouch of my belt, took out a cartridge, and after wetting the bullet with my tongue, slipped it into the open breech of my rifle and closed it. Now nothing moved, and the only sounds that struck the ear were the song of the cicadas, the whistle of the kite, and the gentle rustle of the bamboos in the breeze.

Suddenly, round the corner of the last hillock, came a man; then, a yard or so behind, another. Though expected, their actual appearance produced an impression of surprise; perhaps because we had waited so long.

Both wore a kind of uniform of green cotton cloth, and putties of the same colour. Their long hair was rolled in a silken turban of similar hue. Hanging on his shoulders, suspended by a string which passed round the front of his neck, each man had a big palm-leaf hat.

The sun glittered on their brass cartridges fixed in a belt round the waist, and on the Winchesters which they carried on the shoulder, as a gardener carries his spade; the end of the muzzle in the hand, the butt behind them.

On they came at a sort of jog-trot, and we could hear the pad! pad! pad! of their naked feet on the hot path.

Now they were within 100 yards of us, and I fancied I could perceive a look of relief on the ugly flat features of the first as he glanced towards the pagoda.

The first of the long string of bearers with their bamboo and baskets were now visible, coming along at a jerky run. I felt something touch my left elbow, and glanced round to find that Hellincks had come down from his perch and was kneeling beside me.

The two armed men were quite near now. We could see a bead of perspiration on the face of the first as it came from his hair and trickled down his forehead. We could hear the regular, short pant of his hard breathing, note his half-open mouth, and distinguish his black-lacquered teeth.

Pad! pad! pad!—a soft puff of breeze brought to my nostrils the acid odour of the perspiring native. Another few seconds, and by thrusting my rifle through the leaves I could have touched his breast with the muzzle.

These two will surely be ours; nothing can save them!

Unable to control himself, mastered by excitement or fear, the tirailleur on my right suddenly sprang to his feet, and shouted in the vernacular:

'Toi!' ('Stop!') 'Adow di?' ('Where go you?')

From the pagoda behind us I heard an angry murmur, and could distinguish the corporal's voice. 'Kill the swine! Oh, kill him!'—Hellincks cursed and groaned like a man struck with fever. I felt that I had stopped sweating, and a big lump rose from my chest into my throat, and seemed to choke me. I gave a great sob of disappointment and surprise.

The next instant we were on our feet, for Hellincks rose with me, and as he shouted 'We can yet catch one,' I knew that he had a similar thought to mine. But we had hardly taken the first step forward, prior to forcing our way through the bushes and jumping down into the paddy field, than we were blinded for a second by two bright flashes from a few feet in front of us, and half deafened by the close report of the rebels' Winchesters. The Linh (native soldier), the cause of all the racket, pitched head foremost into the foliage. There was no time to lose, so both of us rushed through the little cloud of smoke, through the bushes, and the next instant we were down in the field.

Fifteen, perhaps twenty, yards away I saw the backs of the two green-clad natives who were running for dear life. They were side by side in the field, for the path was littered with the baskets and bamboos of the coolies, who had disappeared as if by magic. 'Too late!' I shouted. Hellincks jerked up his rifle and covered the native on the left. The next instant, acting on his example, I was peeping along my sights and bringing them in line on to the middle of the palm-leaf hat, which bumped as it hung on the receding back of the man to the right.

Before I could press the trigger Hellincks had fired, and a cloud of smoke floated across the line of vision. It was gone in a second, and I got my chance. Through the white puff from my rifle I saw a dark figure spring into the air with the pose of a marionette of which all the strings have been jerked together; and, as I brought down my weapon, jerked out the empty cartridge and reloaded, I saw a dark mass lying motionless on the damp ground amongst the bright green stalks of young rice.

'Vite! vite! you fool, mine is winged, and will escape if you do not hurry!' cried my comrade as he started off at the double.

On we ran for about 30 yards; then Hellincks stopped, and, pointing to the ground, jerked out: 'I told you so'; and I saw a small blotch the size of a man's hand, which, as the bright sunshine played upon it, glittered red like a splendid dark ruby.

'These fellows have as many lives as a cat,' he continued hurriedly. 'He was done and up again in a second; limped away across the path into that tall grass on the right'—pointing in that direction. 'Come! we may have him yet.'

On we went a few more yards, when the Belgian came a cropper, having tripped over the foot of the thing spread-eagled in the rice field. In his hurry he had passed too close. I had given it a wide berth. I came back to help him up, and had to look at it. There was a small round hole in the back of the neck, just below the base of the skull.

Hellincks scrambled up, panting. How he cursed!

'What are you staring at, man? Take his gun—quick!'

Bending down, I picked up the Winchester. In doing so I almost touched the body, and with difficulty suppressed a murmered, 'I beg your pardon,' because I was dominated by a sentiment of awesome respect for the thing that had been, and was no more. I wished to walk softly, on tiptoe, and felt so thankful that he had fallen face-downwards.

All this had passed in the space of a few seconds. 'Come back! come back!' It was the corporal shouting to us, and there was a note of warning in his voice.

Before turning to go I glanced up, and saw a puff of white smoke arise, float for a second over the top of the hillock ahead, and I heard a report. Something struck the wet ground a little in front and to my right. A speck of mud hit me on the chin; then, along a distance of 50 yards or so, the crest was covered with smoke, and there was a rattle of musketry.

As we ran, the ground and the air seemed to me to be alive, and I could not go quickly enough to please myself.

Hellincks said between pants: 'We forgot the cartridges.'

'Oh! d—n the cartridges!' I replied and it was as if some one else had said it . . . How far it seemed!—there were not more than 40 yards. How hot the sun was! I believe I was terribly afraid during the few seconds it took us to get back to shelter again.

How we got back I don't remember; I only know that I felt quite surprised to find myself standing, somewhat blown, behind the big tree, telling my 'non-com' what had happened, and feeling very anxious not to appear flustered.

MANINGTON

13

SIEGE

Formal siege in the Low Countries

THE Army from the Seige of Roremont encampt on the other side of the Maes by Mastricht for the convenience of fforrage, and the next day being the 1st day of October, His Lordship took a vew of the Right wing of the Army, after the Review both Officers and Soldiers concluded the campaigne was ended, Wee having been then seaven months in the ffeild, but to our great surprise by two in the afternoon our Train and Wheel baggage was ordered for Mastricht, and the Army to be ready to march by three in the morning, which Decampt according to order and comenced our march to the Left, leaving Mastricht on our Left, bore our front to St. Peters Hill, from whence Wee marched directly for Leige the which His Lordship had a Designe to had Invested that Evening, but by reason of great Rain that day, and the badness of the Roads, Wee were oblidged to Encamp a League and a halfe short of the ground His Lordship intended to have taken up.

Leaving the prisoners of the Cittadel under the care of the Regiments that had marched in out of the Trenches, at w.ch time there was orders given out in the Camp for ten Battalions, of w.ch the English Regim.ts were Hows and Godfreys to march next morning by 7 cross the Maese, and Invest the Chartreuse, as also 50 men of each Regim.t to Levell the Trenches and Batteries, and twenty men of each Regim.t to

Carry the Faschines from thence near to the Place designed for Opening the Trenches agst the Chartreuse wch orders was all putt in execution next morning, and the ten Regiments were encamped by eleaven a Clock, at wch time they were ordered to be opened that night, which was accordingly don under the cover of three Battalions, which Regimts were Hows, Prince of Hesse's and Nassau Waloons, comanded by Brigadeer Withers, and 700 workmen under comand of proper Officers, the which Trenches were carried on all night with great success with very little or no loss, and being supplyd with all manner of necessarys for the work, they advance the same the next day by ten a Clock the batteries were mounted, and ready for fireing, wch the Governor perceiving, and very well knowing the dreadfull callamity ensued upon the Obstinacy of the Governr of the Cittadel, a few days ago was resolved that he would not putt himself in such a hazard, whereupon he ordered a Chamade and a flagg to be hung out to signifie his inclination to come to a Treaty, the which being observed, Hostages were exchanged and the Articles were in a very short time agreed upon, and the Garrison marched out the next day upon Honble Terms, being 24th of Octobr and were safely conducted to Antwerp, and the day following the 10 Battalions repast the Maese, and encamped with the Army in their former Ground.

WILSON

The Siege of Ghent, in King William's War: by a soldier's wife

My husband in the siege was one of the forlorn hope, a body of men under the command of a lieutenant, ordered to lay the ropes and to direct the cutting of the trenches: we seldom expect to see any of these return again; but here the danger was greater than customary, as the night was clear, and they were soon descried by the sentinels; but so remarkably expeditious were our men, that they were all covered before the enemy had got their forces together to oppose them. As I always accompanied my husband, however dangerous it was, I, as usual, followed him this time, but Colonel Hamilton stopping me, and saying, 'Dear Kit, don't be so forward', I lost sight of him, and was some time hunting about before I could find him; for the ropes being lain, he with his companions were retired into a turnip field, and lay flat on their bellies, expecting the trench, which the workmen were throwing up, to cover them. Major Irwin told me where he was; and both the major and Lieutenant Stretton begged hard of me for some beer; but as I had but three flasks, and feared my husband might want, I had no pity for any one else: as the night was very cold, and the ground wet, I had also provided myself with a bottle of brandy, and another of gin, for my dear Richard's refreshment. When I left these officers, I met a lieutenant known by the nick-name of A—— and Pockets; a spent musket-ball had grazed on, and scratched his forehead, which his fright magnified to a cannon-ball. He desired I would show him to a surgeon; but his panic was so great, that I believe, had he been examined at both ends, he stood more in need of having his breeches shifted than his wound dressed. In his fright he left his hat and wig, but they being found and restored him, and he at length assured his wound was no way dangerous, recovered his small share of spirits, but never his reputation; for he was called by every one poltroon, and soon after broke as a coward. Leaving this Cotswold lion, I went to the turnip field, where I found my husband in the front rank, to whom my liquors were very comfortable. We stayed here till the trench was ready for us. The next morning, as I was standing by Colonel Gossedge, he received a shot through the body; I gave him some beer, and a dram, and carried him, though it was very dangerous, to Colonel Folke's quarters, for which piece of service the gentleman was extremely thankful, and promised, if he recovered, to reward me handsomely; but he died in three days. On my leaving him, I was sent for by the Duke of Argyle, to inform him what men we had lost. The next day, a drum of our regiment went into a very dangerous place to ease nature; I cautioned him against it, as I had observed the enemy pointed at or near that place: he did not heed my advice; but when he was buttoning up his breeches, a cannon-ball took off both his arms. The place where he rashly exposed himself was so very dangerous, that not a man would venture to go to his assistance. I ran, therefore, and carried him off to a surgeon, under whose care he was in a fair way of doing well, but a cold he got killed him.

At a mile's distance from the town, out of danger, as I thought, of any shot from thence, and near the camp, I pitched my tent, which I stored from a garden belonging to a deserted brewhouse, that I had taken possession of. I had filled my tent with so many potatoes, carrots, turnips and co., that I left but just room enough to sit down close by the door. One day a drake-shot from the enemy came in there, went through my tent into my garden, where I had turned my mare and an officer's horse, and killed the latter; I was luckily then a-foraging, or I had infallibly been killed, as I was always sat directly fronting my tent door. This obliged me to remove my tent farther off, that I might be out of danger. While the siege continued, we had, one day, so severe and incessant rain, that not a man in the army had a dry thread on his back, which was followed by so severe a frost in the night, that a fire I had made before my tent, to dry myself and husband, I really believe, saved the lives of a number of our men. I burnt no less than forty faggots that night, which Colonel Godfrey gave me leave to take from a stack in his quarters. Two of our sentinels were found frozen to death.

MOTHER ROSS

Under fire in Gibraltar, July 1781

YESTERDAY and today they fired incessantly. Our batteries made but a trifling return, as it is almost madness to fire at their works, they being so thickly covered with sand, that our shot finds very little penetration.

The enemy continue firing, and seem determined if possible, to batter down all our works—their gun and mortar boats again visited us, without effecting any damage. We are really in a dismal situation—between the land and sea fire, we scarce dare close our eyes. On your part you must not expect correct letters; the hurry of times, the noise of mortars, howitzers, cannon and the bursting of shells, render the mind so confused that it would be a task; let it suffice that I am alive: That shot and shells are my near companions, that smoke, and wounded brothers, soldiers, are constantly in view; that we have heavy duty, hard watchings, and little rest; that our comforts are groans; that our nightly repose is turned to harassing alarms, that our pastimes are destruction, that every hour, we or the enemy are inventing some horrid stratagem; and that the next we behold each other plunged thereby into the most excruciating anguish.

Such, dear Brother, are Gibraltar exhibitions, and perhaps while you are reading this, and feel a sensible pang at your heart for my situation, I may be performing my part with convulsive struggles in this tragical scene.

ANCELL

The Great Assault on Gibraltar, September, 1782

September 9th, 1782

THIS morning between four and five o'clock the enemy opened their sixty-four and other batteries (amounting to about one hundred and thirty pieces of cannon and eighty mortars) with the greatest spirit upon the garrison, which we immediately answered. Their sixty-four gun battery was an incessant volley the whole time, which lasted most of the day, and the distance being so short, their shot reached the wall, almost as soon as you perceived the flash; so quick was the discharge that the balls rolled along the streets by dozens; this was by way of retaliation, for the unexpected compliment we paid them yesterday. Lieutenant Wharton, of the 73rd regiment and several men wounded. The enemy remove their floating batteries to the Orange Grove as fast as they get them ready—there are two of them that have not got their sails bent.

Wind E. Their line of battle ships, nine in number (viz. seven Spanish and two French, accompanied by a xebec and frigate) stretched over in a line from the Orange Grove this forenoon, and fired upon the garrison until they passed Europa, when they tacked again and returned firing the same way; they then stood on the opposite side, where they again stretched over, and under a gentle sail directed their fire on the southward, in the same manner as before, continuing their course to the eastward, at which time their gun-boats came over, and rowed in a line under the King's Bastion, and began a fire; but our batteries gave them such a smart reception, that they found it convenient to withdraw. The 97th regiment which landed last March, are ordered to do duty.

About one o'clock this morning, the nine line of battle ships returned from the eastward, and fired upon Europa and the southward encampments: They continued a brisk cannonade until they came near the King's Bastion, when they stood over to the Orange Grove and anchored—several seamen at Europa and others, were wounded thereby. They repeated this maneovre again this forenoon, but they having been frequently struck by our shot, they have come to an anchor on their own side, where we observe two of them repairing. From the land side they also maintain a brisk cannonade, and their sixty-four gun battery represents an entire blaze—It is apprehended that we shall suffer considerably from this work.

Between nine and ten o'clock this evening, the enemy advanced to Bay-side, and set fire to the Pallisadoes at that place, which burnt very freely for some time, when one of them again advanced, observing it rather decaying, and put fresh fire to those that were not consumed, notwithstanding the guards in the lines and at the advanced posts, discharged their musquetry upon him. The gun and mortar boats came over at the same time, and poured in a brisk salute of shells and shot for above two hours. Some few killed and wounded upon the occasion.

This morning we perceived a great part of the pallisadoes burnt down, sufficient to admit eight men abreast. From this circumstance we imagine will not be long before they make the assault. From the isthmus and forts they keep a constant fire, and this morning as I came off Landport Guard, crossing the Esplanade, I observed a soldier before me, lying on the ground, and his head somewhat raised, and supported on his elbows; I ran to him (imagining the man had life) and lifted him up, when such a sight was displayed to my view, that I think I never shall forget. A twenty six pound ball had gone through his body, and his entrails as they hung out from the orifice were of a most disagreeable resemblance; whether it was from the force of the ball, or their natural colour, I cannot pretend to determine. The shot from the enemy was dropping on every side, and as I found his life was gone, I left him on the same spot, and made the best of my way to the southward. A party of men buried him soon afterwards. The floating batteries at the Orange Grove have been taking in stores, etc., yesterday and today. The other two have also arrived there.

Several boats have been brought out of the rivers to the Orange Groves; some of them seem to have a kind of cover, which we suppose is to shelter them from our musquetry, when they come near the shore. The wind being westerly, we shall expect the junk ships to embrace this opportunity. The enemy have erected stands or booths around the shore, lined with crimson or scarlet, where the nobles and grandees will take their seats.

A report is just circulated that a fleet are observed in the gut—we hope it is the British coming to our relief—every one seems impatient to discover their colours: A gentleman who has been taking a view says they are French and Spanish men of war; if so our fate is inevitable.

The fleet are now distinguishable by the naked eye. They are ships of force, under French and Spanish colours, standing for the bay. The garrison are greatly agitated and disappointed in their expectations. Will you believe me, Brother, there is forty-four sail of the same line, exclusive of the nine already on the station, who are now anchoring between Algaziras and the Orange Grove. If we can withstand this force we may bid defiance to all the world.

This afternoon the gun and mortar boats came daringly on, as much as to say, 'Ye dogs, surrender,' but luckily a shot struck one of them, when she disappeared—the rest soon afterwards retired. Major Lewis of the Royal Artillery was wounded this day.

A reinforcement is ordered to Queen's lines and to the different picquets, nine of which are ordered to take post in town.

That our enemies may be defeated is the sincere and hearty wish of Your loving Brother.

To Arms! to Arms! is all they cry—the enemy's floating batteries have weighed anchor, and are now under sail with a fine breeze at N.W. Their colours wanton in the wind with gaudy decorations for the battle, while thousands of spectators from yon glittering shore, impatient wait to triumph in their success. They have now tacked with their heads towards the garrison, and what is remarkable, they work them without a man being exposed or seen.

The floating batteries have just brought too, between the Old Mole and South Bastion, within eight hundred yards of the walls, a very bold manœuvre. Adieu! Victory or Death will crown our cause. The garrison have begun firing upon them. The bay and rock cannot be ascribed by words.

Tired and fatigued I sit down to let you know that the battle is our own, and that we have set the enemy's ships on fire. When they came on at nine o'clock this morning, they proceeded successfully to their different stations, and as they moored began to fire with the utmost vivacity; at the same time we began a discharge of cold shot upon them, but to our great astonishment we found they rebounded from their sides and roofs. Even a thirteen-inch shell would not penetrate one! However, we were not much disheartened, although we had several killed, but with all possible speed we kindled fires in our furnaces, and put in our pills of thirty-two pound weight to roast. If you could have peeped over the rock, and viewed our several employs, you could not have forbore smiling; some stationed to work the guns like Ethiopians, black by rubbing their faces with their hands dirtied with powder—the sons of Vulcan were blowing and sweating, while others were allotted to carry the blazing balls, on an iron instrument made for that purpose; but as these did not afford a sufficient supply for the batteries, wheel-barrows were procured fill'd with sand, and half a dozen shot thrown into each. The fire was returned on our part without intermission, and equally maintained by the foe, but the continual discharge of red hot balls, kept up by us, was such, as rendered all the precautions taken by the enemy in the construction of the flotantees of no effect, for the balls lodging in their sides, in length of time spread the fire throughout. This we found to be the case repeatedly during the day, though the foe frequently kept it under, but a continuance of the same inconvenience rendered it impossible at last to work their guns. Just at the close of day-light we observed one of the largest to be on fire in several places, and soon after another in the same condition. This gave the troops additional courage, and the fire was redoubled upon the remaining eight. The Spanish land batteries co-operated with a view of dividing our attention, and to flank the different batteries that were pouring their discharges on the Junk ships, but this did not effectually accomplish their designs, as the ordnance mounted on the heights of Willis's, etc., supported a hot cannonade upon their works, which tended to abate their fire. We had the inconsiderable loss of Capt. Reeves of the Royal Artillery, killed; Captain Grove Seward, and Lieutenant Godfrey of ditto, Lieutenant Witham of 58th and Captain Alexander McKenzie of 73d regiments, wounded, beside several non-commissioned officers and men killed and wounded. What with the heat of the day, the forges, furnaces and piles of flaming shot, amidst clouds of smoak and sulpher, accompanied with heavy toil, you may judge we found ourselves very feeble and thirsty, and in this situation a drink of water which was all the allowance could scarce be procured. An Officer (who commanded a battery) observing the men at the guns almost exhausted with drought, he chearfully took a keg (which holds about a pail) went to the fountain, filled it with water and brought it through the enemy's fire to the men on the battery.

One o'clock in the morning
The floating batteries have ceased firing, and one of them has just broke out in flames. The hands on board them are throwing rockets as signals for assistance—Captain Curtis with a body of seamen has just arrived at the New Mole, to man our gun boats to prevent the enemy from escaping. A report

is now received that an officer and eleven men were drove on shore, upon a piece of timber, being part of a floating castle that was sunk by a shell from the garrison, as she was steering to co-operate with the flotantees.

Day-break
Our bay appears a scene of horror and conflagration. The foe are bewailing their perilous situation, whilst our gun-boats are busily employed in saving the unhappy victims, from surrounding flames and threatening death, although the enemy from their land batteries inhumanly discharged their ordnance upon our tars to prevent their affording them relief. But never was bravery more conspicuous, for notwithstanding the eminent dangers which were to be apprehended from so daring an enterprize, yet our boats rowed along side of the floating batteries, (though the flames rushed out of their port holes) and dragged the sufferers from their desperate state—the contempt paid by the British tars to the enemy's fire, of round and grape shot, and shells, will ever do honour to Old England. Our gun boats have been chasing two of the enemy's small craft, who had left the floating batteries, but have only captured one.

The enemy's ships are blowing up one after another half full of men, and our boats having staid as long as possible, they are now returning with a body of prisoners. A remarkable instance of providence I cannot help mentioning—A young boy on board one of the floating batteries (which was almost in an entire blaze) observing our boats making for shore, got upon the head, wept and cry'd, and in the Spanish tongue called for help; his intreaties prevailed, and one of our boats notwithstanding the immense danger which threatened, rowed towards him, which he perceiving jumped into the sea, and at that very instant the ship exploded, with the greatest part of the hands on board—the boat soon after took the boy up.

Eight o'clock
Captain Curtis is arrived at New Mole, with about four hundred prisoners including officers, some of them miserably

wounded and scorched. The boat that he was in overset in the explosion of the first floating battery, by which his coxswain was lost. As the Spanish officers came past a furnace at the New Mole, in which there was about one hundred red-hot balls, and some of them melted with the excessive heat, they shrugged their shoulders and gave a pitious groan at what their eyes beheld.

Our seamen are bringing the trophies of victory on shore. One has just landed with the Royal Standard of Spain, which was intended by the foe to be hoisted on these battlements. The hills and heights were covered with spectators. When the tars began their procession, incessant shouts and repeated acclamations continued from the Mole to the South parade, where the Governor and principal officers were congratulating each other on the occasion, to whom they carried the colours, which sensibly pleased our gallant chief, who joined the crowd in three cheers, and presented the tars with some gold as a reward.

The prisoners are by a guard landed, and escorted to Wind-Mill-Hill; except the wounded who were conducted to the Naval Hospital, where every care and tenderness will be shewn them. Some of them really were most horrid spectacles. One in particular I cannot help mentioning who was carried by four men on a handbarrow; He had received a wound on his face, so that his nose and eyes were separated from his head, hanging by a piece of skin, and the motion of the men that carried him, occasioned its flapping backwards and forwards much resembling a mask, though he must have felt the most sensible agony, yet he looked round him with great complacency, as he passed the numerous crowds of people.

Ten o'clock

The floating batteries have not yet all exploded. One of them has almost burnt to the waters edge, the crew having thrown the powder overboard. The enemy's land batteries maintain their cannonade upon the garrison, spitting forth their venom'd rage, while on the opposite shore confusion and consternation visibly appears. The Nobles and Grandees who had assembled to view the capture of the place are withdrawing from the Spanish camp, to carry the direful news to Philip's court, who impatient waits to hear the expected joyful tidings. But what will be his surprize when he hears that the all victorious impregnable flotantees are lost, and that flaming balls effected their ruin!

It must be a galling vexation to our foes, to behold their Royal Standard displayed upon our South Parade, where it is tied to a gun and reversed.

Four o'clock in the afternoon

The last battery has just exploded off the Old Mole Head; our red hot shot had not fired her, and it being found impracticable to warp her in here, it was judged expedient to detach a boat to set her in flames, which accordingly they effected without any injury from the land batteries. Those formidable machines, the admiration of Spain, and in whose achievements centred all their pride, are no longer dreadful, nor appear with threatening aspect.

While Princes, Dukes, and Grandees on yon hills, Behold the sad effects of our hot pills.

The enemy during the day extinguished the fire, by the assistance of engines, which supplied them with a vast quantity of water, but the continual and excessive discharge of red-hot balls, intirely frustrated their purpose, and they were constrained to desist from the use of water, as it was found that the battering they had received, opened the caulking, and let the water run between their decks, instead of the channels that were made in their sides to receive it, so that they were apprehensive of their powder being damaged. The construction of these machines was excellent, for the enemy being sensible that we should fire red-hot balls, (though they did not imagine so fast, nor unless the gun was elevated) had judiciously contrived conveyances in the larboard sides for continual circulation of water, which was furnished by working of the engines. From the nicest calculation the floating batteries received upwards of five thousand red-hot balls of twenty-four and thirty-two pounds weight.

ANCELL

Assault: the capture of the Fort of Deig, 1804

THE storming party consisted of about seven hundred men, composed of two companies of his majesty's 22nd regiment, two of the Company's European regiments, and the rest native troops, the whole under the command of Colonel Ball, a brave old hero, but so feeble, that he was obliged to be pushed up the track of glory. The two flanks companies to which I belonged led the column. Sergeant Bury, of the Grenadier company headed the foremost; but being wounded at the moment, he was compelled to leave the battery. I volunteered to take his place. The enemy had a strong intrenchment between our batteries and the breach, with innumerable guns, so placed as to have a cross fire on the storming party. However, we soon fought our way through their intrenchments, our gallant captain (Lindsay) cheering and boldly leading us on. Crossing these trenches, this brave officer was cut with a spear in the arm, and also received a severe wound from a sabre; but his gallantry and zeal were so great, that he could not be prevailed upon to retire from the scene of action. A little on our right I saw some of the enemy point a gun at us. Immediately, with three or four comrades, I rushed out to spike it; for which purpose, I was in the act of searching for the touchhole, to put a nail in it, when one of the enemy's golandauze (artillery-men) fired the gun off, and I was thrown on my back in the trench, and the same man was in the act of cutting me to pieces, when a grenadier of our company, named Shears, shot him, and I once more escaped. Fortunately for us, the whole of the enemy's great guns were elevated too much, owing to which the shots passed over our heads. If they had been properly directed, we must have been annihilated to a man. Within fifty or sixty paces from the breach, I received a matchlock ball in the head, which dropped me to the ground, the blood flowing profusely. When I came a little to myself from the stun, I found myself impelled onward by one of our companies, who were close together, and running stooping, to avoid the shots, which, being near the breach, were uncomfortably thick; but we reached, and soon planted the British flag on the summit of the bastion which was breached. Our opponents fought hard to resist our entrance, throwing immense stones, pieces of trees, stink-pots, bundles of straw set on fire, spears, large shots, &c.; but resistance was in vain: we were determined to conquer. In spite of this laudable resolution, however, we found some hard work cut out for us on making good our ascent. The streets in the fort were narrow, running across each other, and every ten yards guns were placed, for the purpose of raking the whole streets. Added to this, many of the enemy had got into high houses, in which were loopholes, from which they could fire down upon us, without the possibility of our getting at them. Near the corner of a street, in a kind of nook, I saw our dear Captain Lindsay attacked by five or six of the enemy. He was on one knee, and quite exhausted, having lost much blood from his former wounds; but, to our great joy, we were just in time to save him, and punish some of his assailants. From the intricacy of the place, we were afraid of shooting our own men, and were therefore obliged to keep pretty close together. At midnight I again met Captain Lindsay clearing one of the streets, when he asked me how I felt myself. I complained of a wound in my side, but said that I could find no hole; but this was not a time for talking. In turning sharp down a street rather larger than those we had cleared, we met a column of the enemy, with a person of rank in a palanquin. We soon stopped his black highness; and, to ascertain who was inside the palanquin, which was an open one, I, with several others, probed our way with our bayonets, when a tremendous fat zemindar (an officer) roared out most lustily, and began to show fight. He fired a matchlock at me, which went through the wing of my coat, but did not touch my person. Before I could retaliate, my comrades had finished him, and we then commenced at the column; but I took from the palanquin the gun which had nearly robbed me of life. It was like the barrel of a gun, about two feet long, with a round handle; at the handle end was a sharp hatchet; at the other extremity a sharp hook. This extraordinary instrument I presented to the commander-in-chief; but he refused the present, saying it was my trophy. His lordship was afterwards prevailed on to purchase it, at the price of two hundred rupees. We at this time got information that the five companies which had deserted from the Honourable Colonel Monson, in his masterly retreat from Jeypore, were standing, dressed in the full uniform they deserted in, outside the principal gate of the fort, with their arms ordered, without apparently making any resistance, and frequently crying out, 'Englishmen, Englishmen, pray do not kill us; for God's sake, do not kill us.' As these supplications proceeded rather from fear than from penitence for the crime they had been guilty of—that of deserting to any enemy—these men could expect no mercy. We had positive orders to give them no quarter, and they were most of them shot.

JOHN SHIPP

Relief of Lucknow: ingratitude of the rescued

WE KNEW that we were to advance at 6 a.m. but long before this we had formed up and were awaiting orders to move off at 5.30. Sir Colin and his staff rode by the column. Sir Colin called for the officers of the various corps. He told them that the enemy was to be attacked that morning and that the men could be sparing of their ammunition, thereby intimating that the bayonet would be used as much as possible. Sir Colin said that the officers and men would have an opportunity of distinguishing themselves before noon. He then gave the word to advance.

We crossed the river and were soon in a very narrow, intricate and circuitous lane with houses on either side, through which it was very difficult to pass. At length we arrived at an opening in the lane on the south west side of Secunder Bagh. The enemy opened a brisk fire upon us from a little loophole or two a little past the opening and we were ordered to rest our rifles against the wall of a mud building. We were then ordered to man two large ropes attached to an eight-inch howitzer, which we immediately drew up a steep embankment under a very heavy fire, but thanks be to God not a man of us was hurt.

The guns were soon in position and were ranging away in

first-rate style. A breach was soon made on the south side. A few horses were killed and a few artillery men wounded, when we got the word to storm the place and in two minutes the building which was one hundred and twenty yards square was surrounded. The 93rd lost a good many men, and the detachments under command of a Major Barnston also lost a few killed and wounded. But the awful retribution that this day fell upon the sepoys, 16th November, exceeded the expectations of all engaged that morning. For in the Secunder Bagh was [*sic*] upwards of two thousand of the enemy; these two thousand and upwards met with all sorts of deaths; some were killed by the explosion of our shells, others were killed by the shot from our cannon and our Enfields, others met with these deaths—by jumping off the tops of the walls and breaking their necks, some were cut down by the sword; others were burnt alive and many were run through with the bayonet. Not a man escaped to tell the tale.

The following few days were occupied in bringing such of the guns that were serviceable out of the old palace and in bursting upwards of two hundred guns of native manufacture and also in making a covered way, whereby the women and children might be brought out in safety. The whole of the men available were engaged day and night in making this covered way for the ladies and need I say that they ran great danger. For the enemy had got the range of more than one or two places, where there was no covering whatever from the enemy's shot, which we had got pretty well acquainted with and to which we paid but little attention however. We soon had a trench thrown up, that protected us from imminent peril. Tent walls, or more properly speaking tent canauts, were brought out and so arranged that the enemy could not see anything that was going on. Everything was carried out in style that totally deceived the enemy. Engineers and sappers were employed in running a mine which was to blow up the Kaiser Bagh and all that were in it. The Naval Brigade had a mortar battery playing on and into the new place. The heavy guns were likewise employed in making a breach in the western side of the palace walls. But all this time our army was employed in making every preparation for retiring from Lucknow. The guns and treasure, which amounted to 23 lacs of rupees or two hundred and thirty thousand pounds, were safely brought out of the Residency and taken to the Dilkoosha Park.

The Ladies, women and children were all brought out in safety without a single casualty. And now let us see what were the thanks we got from the ladies for all that we had done for their safety and for their personal comfort. We, the relieving force, were called all sorts of foul names—dirty, ill-looking fellows, not in any way to be compared to the clean, respectable and ever-obliging sepoy. The reader will scarcely believe that in 1857 there were at Lucknow Englishwomen who actually refused help to a poor fellowcountryman to a drop of water. Yea, I assure you it is a fact, these Englishwomen, who had been rescued from a fate too horrible to think of and had been protected during their imprisonment with the beleaguered garrison of Lucknow by the ever-brave and generous English soldier! And so protecting them he had met with his death wound and now he is unable to rise from his cot. He calls on his countrywomen for a drop of water, either to quench his parched lips or otherwise to wash his wounds. But what must have been the consternation of the poor dying soldier to have these women reply to him in words to this effect? Pointing to the well they said, 'There is the well, my man, and you can get the water yourself.' And this to a dying man! And all likewards this man had his death wound through rendering some assistance to his ungrateful countrywomen.

Another thing I may as well mention is this, that there was not a woman who would wash a shirt for a wounded man for less a sum than two or three rupees. Think of this—four or six shillings for washing a shirt in a little water and hanging it up to dry, taking it down when dry and handing it to the owner! Six shillings for five minutes work! And then they consider they were rendering a favour to the men. These poor fellows now found to their sorrow that it was useless fighting for women that were completely destitute of gratitude. Really this was a striking contrast to the ladies that went out to the East under that amiable lady Miss Florence Nightingale during the Crimea campaign to tend the wants and comfort of the sick and wounded. All honour be to these ladies. But what can be said in favour of those women, whose lives were saved in Lucknow and different parts of India. On one hand these brave men had done nothing to receive the kindness which was proffered so disinterestedly, and on the other hand they had risked their lives to save the lives of those who were so utterly destitute of every practice of gratitude.

WICKINS

14

VICTORY

After Newbury, 1643

THE next day I viewed the dead bodies: there lay about one hundred stript naked in that field where our two regiments stood in battalia. This night the enemy conveyed away about thirty cart load of maimed and dead men, as the town-people credibly reported to us, and I think they might have carried away twenty cart load more of their dead men the next morning, they buried thirty in one pit. Fourteen lay dead in one ditch. This battle continued long; it began about six o'clock in the morning, and continued till past twelve o'clock at night; in the night the enemy retreated to the towne of Newbury, and drew away all their ordnance; we were in great distress for water, or any accommodation to refresh our poor soldiers, yet the Lord himself sustained us that we did not faint under it; we were right glad to drink in the same water where our horses did drink, wandering up and down to seek for it.

FOSTER

Before Blenheim: the Schellenberg, 1704

UPON the 19th of June the Army continued their march in sight of the Elector of Bavaria then encampt at Dillinghem on this side of the Denbie, and encampt again with our Right at Almordingen and our Left at Onderingen, whereupon the Elector of Bavaria sent a Detachment of the Best of his Troops under the command of Gen^{ll} Lee, to reinforce Count de Arco who was posted at the Pass of Schelinberg on a rising ground betwixt Donawort and a wood about a mile from it, who arrived there upon the 21st by times in the morning, as also a sufficient number of Pioneers, who fell to work immediately to Intrench their Camp, notwithstanding the Duke of Marlborough was resolved to Drive the Enemy from this important post, and accordingly all necessary orders were given and Disposition made of the Army upon the 21st, which was as follows, vizt all the Grenad^{rs} of the Army and twenty Battalions of ffoot, thirty Squadrons of English and Dutch Cavalry, with three Battalions of Imperial Grand^{rs}, the English Troops of the Infantry, were the Battalion of the 1st Regim^{t} of Foot Guards, the 1st Battalion Royall, Ongoldsby's and Meredith's, all which had orders to parade at 10 o'clock at night upon the Left of the Front Line, as also a Sufficient number of the Train of Artillery, and likewise the Country Waggons with ffaschines were to follow in the Rear of the Train. We continued upon the Parade till 3 in the morning at which time We commenced our march, the Duke of Marlborough being at our head, and continued on the same towards the River Werentz, the Grand Army having orders to follow with all expedition, but by reason of the Length of the way and the badness of the Road, We did not come to the River till about two of the Clock, and about four o'clock We had laid our Boats and passed the River with Our Artillery, and all within Sight of the Enemy, upon which His Grace advanced at the head of the Cavalry in order to veiw the Enemys Intrenchm^{ts}, at which time the Earl of Orkney and Gen^{ll} Gore, used all their endeavours to form the English and Dutch Grenadiers, and the rest of the Battalions of ffoot in Line of Battle, and Brigadier Blood used his utmost Diligence in posting the Artillery to the Best advantage and comenced Cannonading the Enemy with all the vigour imaginable which they answered as bravely from their Batteries, which gave us to understand the Action would be what indeed it was both bloody and Hott, but there being no time of looking back we resolved to Attack them, and the first Line which was made up by the Grenad.rs the Guards, the Royall and Ingoldsbys Battalions had orders to throw down all their luggage upon the ground. The Country Waggons at the same time had come along the Front of the Line and thrown ye ffaschines down in parcels, and also the Cavalry were then formed in Battalia under the comand of Gn.ll Lumley, Gen.ll Ross and Gen.ll Humphesch. And His Grace having taken the most advantageous ground in order to Disperse necessary orders from time to time, it being then about Six o'clock at night, the Attack was ordered to begin in the manner following, the ffront Rank had orders every man to Sling his firelock and take a Faschine in his Arms in order to break the Enemy's Shott in our Advancing, after w.ch we advanced with all the Courage and Vigour in Life, and the Enemy received us, with such warmth, both from their own Shott, and a prodigious fire of Cartridge Shott from their Batteries, that they obliged Us to retire with considerable Loss, and w.ch had likely to have been of great damage further, by the retreat, to putt our Second Line into Confusion and Disorder, but the Gen.lls at their Head using all Diligence to keep their troops in order, as also Gen.ll Gore and Gen.ll Bonheim who commanded the Front Line used all Diligence to compleat that Line, and to Rally again; but about that time it began to Rain which by The Slipperyness of the ground rendered the procedure of the Action very Difficult. Notwithstanding of all those difficulties the Grenadiers made a Second Attack, with as great Courage as the former, and was as vigorously received, our Right being intirely beat back again with as great loss if not greater then before, but Our three English Battalions, afores.d which made up the Left of the Front Line, and the Companies of Grenadiers of the 2.d Battalion Royall, How's, Rues, and Primrose's Regim.ts which joined the said three Regim.ts haveing in the Attack (though not without Great Loss) obliged the Enemy to give way, by which they made themselves masters of the Wood upon the Enemy's Right and stood their ground, which His Grace perceiving ordered the Action to commence in Gen.ll which held for the space of three Quarters of an hour with continued fire and great slaughter on both sides. At which time Gen^{ll}. Humpech and Gen^{ll}. Ross advanced with the English and Dutch Dragoons on the Enemy's Right, as also the Prince of Hesse Cassell, commenced his attack upon the Enemy's Left and our Right near the walls of Donevart, by the three Regim^{ts}. of Imperial Grenadiers as before mentioned, being Seconded with three other Battalions of the Imperial Infantry, under the comand of Major Gen^{ll}. Pallandt, which were immediately sustained by 10 Squadrons of Imperial Cavalry and Hussars, under the command of Count Horn, at which time Prince Lewis of Baden advanced from the Grand Body of Our Army, and came in the Heat of the Action, who like a wise and experienced General dispersed his necessary orders. And by this time the Action was very hott, We sometimes obliging the Enemy to give way, and they in their turn obliging us to retire. But at last our English Troops obliged the Enemy to quit the Trenches on the Right, upon which Humpass and Ross charg'd their Right wing of Horse both with Courage and good success, which the center of their Line perceiving gave way, and Gen^{ll}. Lumley and Gen^{ll}. Wood advanced with great Courage and Charged the Enemy so briskly that there ensued a violent slaughter, the Enemy retiring towards the River, and our Horse pursuing them so hard, that by the crowd of the Enemy, their bridge broke, and great numbers were glad to escape as well Generals as Private Soldiers to save themselves by swimming the River.

Night coming on put an end to this Terrible Engagem^{t}., which was fought with a great deal of Courage and Resolution; to the Glory of all the Confederate troops under His Grace the Duke of Marlborough's Command, and in an Eminent manner to His Grace's own particular Honour, who during the whole behav'd himself like a wise and experienced General, and undauntedly exposed himself every where to disperse orders as he judged necessary. But as the engagem^{t}. was commenced with the English and Dutch troops, it was believed they were the greatest sufferers, especially those three Battalions and four Companies of Grenadiers before mentioned who maintained their ground and stood the force of the Enemy's fire on the Right, dureing the interval of ye Second and third Attacks.

It was computed that the Enemy in this action, had killed and drowned 6000 men, being at the commencement of the Engagement about 14,000 strong, all Choice troops Commanded in Chief by Count d'Arco, and under him three Bavarian and two French Lieut-Generals. By this it must be believed that our Loss was also very considerable, and especially by the loss of Genll. Gore and Genll. Beinheim and sevll. other Officers of note killed upon the Spot. Prince Lewis, the Prince of Hesse, Count Horn, Major Genll. Wood, Major Genll. Pallandt, were all (with sevll. other Officers of note) wounded. We took in this Action Sixteen pieces of the Enemy's Cannon; 13 Colours and Standards, as also all their Tents and Camp Equipage. After which our Troops continued all night in the ffeild of Battell, the Battell being thus ended.

WILSON

Cavalry battle at Almanara, Spain, 1710

THAT night that our reinforcement joyned us thare was private orders given that when the tattoo was bett Boots & Saddels to be beat at the same time, and four regments of Dragoones were ordered to march directly, the Royal Regiment and Pepers of the English and Matta's and Kittenburk of the Dutch, which we did in order to secure a pass, for the enemie was getting out of Cattalona as fast as they could in order to get under their cannon at Lerrada, but our Genll thought it more convenient to come at them a more nearer way, for the strong party of Dragoones that was sent out that night secured that pass. It lay upon the New Nager, which is the name of the river. On Sunday the 16 of July just as the sun was rising we got over the river, then we refresht our horsses and ourselves, and abought one in the afternoone good part of our Horss was got over the river and we had orders to mount our horsses, which we did and marching into the plaine a party was ordered out to goe with Brigadier Peper to see if he could discover the enemie, which he soone did for they did begin to appeare, so they kept bickering abought one with the other sum time. Now abought this time our Horss being almost all over and our foot makeing all the haste they could in gitting over, but the enemies squardroones began to apeer very thick upon the hills, which was strong ground. And had their army come all up and had lay thare all night they would have intrencht themselves & made it so strong that we should have lost a good part of our army in beating them out of their works. But our Genll was very carefull abought it and a Councel of War was held in what they should do in the matter. Starinburk was for staying until all the foot was come up but Stanhope, he was our Genll and being counted a man of understanding, it was agreed to what he proposed, for he tould the King & all the Generals that if they gave them the liberty to come to that ground that they would so entrench themselves to that degree that there would be no driveing them off. So he begged the command of the enterprise, so the English that day had the two posts of honour, for they had both the right & the left of the army, Raby's & Pepper's Dragoones on the right and my Lord Rochford's to the left of the front line, with Harvey's Horss & Genll Stanhope's on ye reare line.

On Sunday, about an hour before sun sitt on the 16 day of July 1710, our squardroons had orders to advance as fast as our hor[s]es could goe. The sun then was not above a quarter of an hour high when ye left began to engage & the right was soon up with them, which made the enemie in a maze to see & behold how like lions our men fel upon them with sword in hand. And we advancing so fast after the enemie that our foot could not keep up with us, likewise our traine could not no way beare up with their cannon to doe the enemie any damage but they came so neare that they saw a squardoone of our Horss & took it to be the enemie & kild Count Nassau, a Cornet and a private Dragoone. But accion was soone over for ye enemie turnd taile and run in a confused manner, for had we but two houres more daylight we had with the blessing of God undoubtedly gained the crown of Spaine that night, for thare was not above 16 squardroones of our army that did engage their body of Horss that night, which their owne men did justifie that ware taken prissonners did affearme, and the most or all their Horss was thare besides a great many of their foot was come up & that their cannon was come very near them, but they were all so amazed and runing all that could get off under the walls of Lerrada, leaving behind them seven or eight peaces of cannon and several waggons laded with provision for their army and a great deale of baggage. They being so soone gone overnight and we could not see to follow them, we did expect they would have rallied againe & got to a head on the next morning, so we lay on our armes all that night but on the next day they ware safe under the walls of Lerrada & thought themselves better off than to run the other hazzard and fare worss, so when we found that they did not come we formd our camp, the King's quarters being at Almenar which was the name of the battle.

We lost but very few besides Count Nassaw, a Cornet and very few privit men but them that we lost was brave fellows: the Lord Rochford was in this, likewise many more fine offecers. So on Munday the 13 of July all the dead was buried & the wounded take care of well.

A ROYAL DRAGOON IN THE SPANISH SUCCESSION WAR

The Plains of Abraham, 1759

September, 1759

12th. By this day's orders it appears the General intends a most vigorous attack, supposed behind the town, where to appearance a landing is impracticable.

Our disposition terminates thus: that the Light Infantry are to lead and land first, in order to maintain a bicquering with the enemy (as also cover the troops' debarkation) till the army take a footing on the heights.

We are to embark on board our flatt-bottomed boats by 12 o'clock and upon the *Sunderland* man-of-war shewing a light, we are to repair to that rendevouze, where the boats will range in a line and proceed when ordered in the manner directed; viz. the Light Infantry the van, and the troops to follow by seniority. The army compleated to 70 rounds amunition each man; and the flatt-bottomed boats to repair to the different vessells, and proportionably divide according to the number on board the ship.

By 10 o'clock Colonel How called for the whole of the volunteers in the Light Infantry, signifying to them, that the General intends that a few men may land before the Light Infantry and army, and scramble up the rock, when ordered by Capt. Delaune, who is to be in the first boat along with us; saying that he thought proper to propose it to us, as he judged it would be a choice, and that if any of us survived, might depend on our being recommended to the General. Made answer: We were sensible of the honour he did, in making us the first offer of an affair of such importance as our landing first, where an opportunity occured of distinguishing ourselves, assuring him his agreeable order would be put in execution with the greatest activity, care, and vigour in our power. He observing our number consisted only of eight men, viz:—

1st.	Fitz-Gerald	5th.	Makenzie
2nd.	Robertson	6th.	McPherson
3rd.	Stewart	7th.	Cameron
4th.	McAllester	8th.	Bell

Ordered we should take 2 men each of our own choice from three companys of Lt. Infantry, which in all made 24 men. Which order being put in execution we embarked in our boat. Fine weather, the night calm, and silence over all.

Waiting impatiently for the signal of proceeding.

September 12th and 13th. Morning, 2 o'clock, the signal was made for our proceeding, which was done in pretty good order, the same disposition formerly mentioned. When we came pretty close to the heights we rowed close in with the north shore, which made the *Hunter* sloop-of-war, who lay off, suspect us to be an enemy, not being apprised of our coming down. However, we passed two sentries on the beach without being asked any questions. The third sentry challenged, 'Who is there?' Was answered by Capt. Fraser in the French tongue, 'French,' saying, 'we are the provision boats from Montreal', cautioning the sentry to be silent, otherwise he would expose us to the fire of the English man-of-war. This took place till such time as their officer was acquainted, who had reason to suspect us, ordering all his sentrys to fire upon us; but by this time the aforesaid volunteers was up the eminence, and a part of the Light Infantry following. After we got up we only received one fire, which we returned briskly, and took a prisoner, the remaining part of the enemy flying into a field of corn. At same time we discovered a body of men making towards us, who we did not know (it being only daybreak), but were the enemy; we put ourselves in the best posture of making a defence: two of us advanced, when they came close, and challenged them, when we found it was Capt. Fraser with his co. who we join'd and advanced to attack this party of the enemy lodged in the field, who directly fled before us; by pursuing close the Lieut. and his drummer came in to us. In this interval the whole of the Light Infantry were on the heights, and a part of the regts. We remained till the whole army took post, when we were detached to silence a battery who kept firing on our shipping who were coming down the river. This was effected without the loss of a man; the enemy placed one of the cannon to flank us crossing a bridge, which they fired, drew off, and got into the woods which was within forty yards of the battery. We demolished the powder and came away.

On our return we saw our army forming the line of battle; we (Light Infantry), who stood at about 800 paces from the line, were ordered to face outwards, and cover the rear of our line, as there was a body of the enemy in their rear and front of the Light Infantry. About 6 o'clock observed the enemy coming from town, and forming under cover of their cannon; we saw they were numerous, therefore the General made the proper disposition for battle; they marched up in one extensive line. When they came within a reconoitring view they halted, advancing a few of their Irregulars, who kept bicquering with one or two platoons, who were advanced for that purpose, at the same time playing with three field pieces on our line. On which the General ordered the line to lay down till the enemy came close, when they were to rise up and give their fire. The enemy, thinking by our disappearing, that their cannon disconcerted us, they thought proper to embrace the opportunity; wheeling back from the centre, and formed three powerful columns, advanced very regular with their cannon playing on us. By this time we had one field piece on the right, and two howats on the left who began to give fire; the enemy huzza'd, advancing with a short trott (which was effectually shortened to a number of them) they began their fire on the left, the whole of them reclining that way, but received and sustained such a check that the smell of gun-powder became nauseous; they broke their line, to all parts of the compass.

To our great concern and loss General Wolfe was mortally wounded; but the Brigadiers, who were also wounded, excepting Murray, seeing the enemy break, ordered the Grenadiers to charge in among them with their bayonets, as also the Highlanders with their swords, which did some execution, particularly in the pursuit.

During the lines being engaged, a body of the enemy attacked a part of the Light Infantry on the right, were repulsed and thought proper to follow the fait of traverse sailing. As I was not in the line of battle I can't say what the latest disposition of the enemy was before engaging.

How soon this action was over we received a part of our intrenching tools, and began to make redoubts, not knowing but next morning we would have another to cut, as the enemy expected 13 companies of Granadiers to join, and about 2000 men who occupy'd a post near Point au Treamp, but it seemed they were not recovered of the former morning's portion; not liking English medicines.

This affair gave great spirit to the whole army, notwithstanding the loss of the much regretted Life of the Army, General Wolfe. The men kept sober, which was a great maxim of their bravery.

Towards the evening a part of the enemy, who were of the Regulars, formed, who seemed to make a shew of standing; Colonel Burton, 48th regt. was drawn opposite with a field piece in their front, which disputed them. We took post in our redoubts; not having the camp equipage on shore, part of the army lay on their arms in the field till next morning. All quiet during the night of the 13th.

AN N.C.O. OF FRASER'S REGIMENT

Near Egmont, Holland: 2nd October, 1799

THE firing ceased sometime before sun-set. I was much in want of water, and went, along with another, to search for it. We found it at last, in the hollow of the opening of the sand hills, into which we had wheeled when we left the beach and engaged the enemy. There had been a good deal of rain some days before: and the tramping of our feet upon the surface of the sand, had brought water to it, which being observed by some who came to place afterwards, they dug a small hole in the sand, and put in the sides an empty ammunition box, which served for cradling; and the hole was soon filled with good water. A number more of such kind of wells was presently made, and plenty of water got which supplied both horse and foot. We filled our canteens, and then went to look among the dead and wounded for a comrade, of whom we could get no certain account. The spectacle of the dead, the dying, and the wounded, greatly affected me. The dead were lying stiff on the ground, in various postures; but death had so altered their countenances, that of all that I saw, belonging to the regiment, with many of whom I had been familiar, I knew only two; and it was by peculiar marks such as death could not alter, that we distinguished them. The groaning of the wounded was very afflicting; for they were mostly bad cases, all that were able to walk or crawl having removed farther to the rear; and all the assistance, that could be given to those who were unable to move, was to carry them from the spot where they were lying, to a place of greater shelter. This had been in part already done, and the wounded were lying in groupes in the best sheltered hollows adjacent to the beach. The universal cry of these poor men was for water. I supplied them as far as I was able, both enemies and friends; and amongst the rest, one of our own officers, who was most severely wounded. I had to hold him up, and put the canteen to his mouth, for he was unable to help himself; he died during the night. We did not find the object of our search; but we got afterwards certain account of his having been wounded, and probable accounts of his death; and we never heard more of him.

I returned to join the regiment, ruminating on the affecting sights I had seen, and grieved for the loss of comrades and acquaintances. When the regiment was mustered, in the evening, about one-half were missing; but about thirty joined in a day or two after, who had lost the regiment. We were upwards of 600 strong; and our loss in killed, wounded and prisoners (of whom there were 40) was 288. The company to which I belonged, entered the field with 59 rank and file, and 3 sergeants, out of which, 5 were killed on the field, and 24 were wounded, 5 of whom died in a few days and 3 shortly after. Of the rest, few recovered so as to be fit for service. The regiment had suffered this severe loss in about three-quarters of an hour.

'G.B.'

Vimiero, 1808

Nothing to speak of took place till we came to the hills of Vimiero. We were in camp on the side of these hills on the 21st August. We got under arms before daylight. This was the Sabbath. We were to parade again at ten o'clock for Divine Service. We were all cleaning ourselves, and a good many of the men was washing their shirts, when the drums beat to arms, the bugles sounded. Our picket on the top of the hill called down that the French were advancing. Our Colonel ordered us to fall in. It was not long till the advance posts were engaged. The French were moving in two large columns, one to the front and the other to our left. We were ordered to the left until we got in front of these lines. We got orders to prime and load, and lie down. The firing on the right was kept up on both sides at the same time. The French artillery was firing shot and shell at us; our artillery was on the right of our regiment firing at them. While laying down, we had a little time to reflect there was very many of us ill prepared for leaving this world. Our Major was behind us; he said there was a good number of bees flying about (the musket balls he meant). The French was still advancing towards us and our skirmish was ordered to their company. The General called our 71st advance. We got up and moved a few steps forward. I saw the French before us, marching toward us, and we toward them. I thought they had a fine appearance.

Our Colonel called out not to fire till we were closer. The French fired on us. A man not far from me was shot through the head. Some of us turned our heads to him, for he was crying. The Colonel cried 'Take him away. Do not be looking round, men.' This man died. One of the balls struck my firelock or bayonet. When we got nearer, we fired on them, and they on us. At last, they turned and made off. We cheered, and went on. They turned round and fired on us. We returned the fire, they made off, it turned into a race. They went over the hill, and left three guns and waggons behind. We halted and piled our arms. In the pursuit, a good many of the French threw away their knapsacks. They were soon opened to see what they could find. Some of the men went down the hill to look for water. They found a French General and an Officer lying wounded. Corporal Mackay took them up to the Regiment. The French appeared on the hill. They came down upon us, cheering and firing. We ran to our arms. I was wounded, and our Adjutant, and many others. Our General gave orders to charge them. They retreated up the hill, the regiment after them. One of the pipers was wounded. He sat on the ground and played the charge. I went and got my wound dressed, and came back to the Regiment. They were on the top of the hill. Sir Arthur Wellesley rode up to the Regiment. Our Colonel went and met him. We gave him three cheers. This ended the Battle of Vimiero. It is said the French lost 3,000 men and nearly all his artillery. We marched back to the old camp.

A BUGLER OF THE 71ST FOOT

A Charge, 1808

DURING the battle [Vimiero, 1808], next day, I remarked the gallant style in which the 50th, Major Napier's regiment, came to the charge. They dashed upon the enemy like a torrent breaking bounds, and the French, unable even to bear the sight of them turned and fled. Methinks at this moment I can hear the cheer of the British soldiers in the charge, and the clatter of the Frenchmen's accoutrements, as they turned in an instant, and went off, hard as they could run for it. I remember, too, our feeling towards the enemy on that occasion was the north side of friendly; for they had been firing upon us Rifles very sharply, greatly outnumbering our skirmishers, and appearing inclined to drive us off the face of the earth. Their lights and grenadiers I for the first time particularly remarked on that day. The grenadiers (the 70th, I think) our men seemed to know well. They were all fine-looking young men, wearing red shoulder-knots and tremendous-looking moustaches. As they came swarming upon us, they rained a perfect shower of balls, which we returned quite as sharply. Whenever one of them was knocked over, our men called out, 'There goes another of Boney's Invincibles.' In the main body immediately in our rear were the second battalion 52nd, the 50th, the second battalion 43rd, and a German corps, whose number I do not remember, besides several other regiments. The whole line seemed annoyed and angered at seeing the Rifles outnumbered by the Invincibles, and as we fell back, 'firing and retiring,' galling them handsomely as we did so, men cried out (as it were with one voice) to charge. 'D—n them!' they roared, 'charge! charge!' General Fane, however, restrained their impetuosity. He desired them to stand fast, and keep their ground.

'Don't be too eager, men,' he said, as coolly as if we were on a drill parade in Old England; 'I don't want you to advance just yet. Well done, 95th!' he called out, as he galloped up and down the line; 'well done, 43rd, 52nd, and well done all. I'll not forget, if I live, to report your conduct to-day. They shall hear of it in England, my lads!'

A man named Brotherhood, of the 95th, at this moment rushed up to the general, and presented him with a green feather, which he had torn out of the cap of a French light-infantry soldier he had killed; 'God bless you, general!' he said; 'wear this for the sake of the 95th.' I saw the general take the feather, and stick it in his cocked hat. The next minute he gave the word to charge, and down came the whole line, through a tremendous fire of cannon and musketry—and dreadful was the slaughter, as they rushed onwards. As they came up with us, we sprang to our feet, gave one hearty cheer, and charged along with them, treading over our own dead and wounded, who lay in the front. The 50th were next us as we went, and I recollect, as I said, the firmness of that regiment in the charge. They appeared like a wall of iron. The enemy turned and fled, the cavalry dashing upon them as they went off.

RIFLEMAN HARRIS

Bayonet and Loot: Sobral, 1810

NEXT morning, the French advanced to a mud wall, about forty yards in front of the one we lay behind. It rained heavily this day and there was very little firing. During the night we received orders to cover the bugle and tartan of our bonnets, with black crape, which had been served out to us during the day, and to put on our great-coats. Next morning the French, seeing us thus, thought we had retired, and left Portuguese to guard the heights. With dreadful shouts, they leaped over that wall before which they had stood, when guarded by British. We were scarce able to withstand their fury. To retreat was impossible; all behind being ploughed land, rendered deep by the rain. There was not a moment to hesitate. To it we fell, pell-mell, French and British mixed together. It was a trial of strength in single combat; every man had his opponent, many had two. I got one up to the wall, on the point of my bayonet. He was unhurt: I would have spared him: but he would not spare himself. He cursed and defied me, nor ceased to attack my life, until he fell, pierced by my bayonet. His breath died away in a curse and menace. This was the work of a moment: I was compelled to this extremity. I was again attacked, but my antagonist fell, pierced by a random shot. We soon forced them to retire over the wall, cursing their mistake. At this moment, I stood grasping for breath; not a shoe on my feet: my bonnet had fallen to the ground. Unmindful of my situation, I followed the enemy over the wall. We pursued them about a mile, and then fell back to the scene of our struggle. It was covered with dead and wounded, bonnets, and shoes trampled and stuck in the mud. I recovered a pair of shoes: whether they had been mine or not I cannot tell, they were good.

Here I first got any plunder. A French soldier lay upon the ground dead; he had fallen backwards; his hat had fallen off his head, which was kept up by his knapsack. I struck the hat with my foot, and felt it rattle; seized it in a moment, and, in the lining, found a gold watch and a silver crucifix. I kept them; as I had as good a right to them as any other. Yet they were not valuable in my estimation. At this time, life was held by so uncertain a tenure, and my comforts were so scanty, that I would have given the watch for a good meal and a dry shirt. There was not a dry stitch on my back, at the time, or for the next two days.

'71ST'

Waterloo infantry

WE WERE going out for a field-day on the 16th June, 1815, when we were ordered back and formed on the one side of the village. We stopped here a short time; then were sent to quarters to pack up everything and march. We immediately marched off towards the French frontier. We had a very severe march of sixteen miles, expecting to halt and be quartered in every town through which we passed. We knew not where we were marching. About one o'clock in the morning, we were halted in a village. A brigade of Brunswickers marching out, we took their quarters, hungry and weary.

Next morning, 17th, we got our allowance of liquor and moved on until the heat of the day; when we encamped, and our baggage was ordered to take the high road to Brussels. We sent out fatigue parties for water, and set a-cooking. Our fire were not well kindled, when we got orders to fall in and move on along the high road toward Waterloo. The whole length of the road was very much crowded by artillery and amunition carts, all advancing towards Waterloo. The troops were much embarrassed in marching, the roads were so crowded. As soon as we arrived on the ground, we formed in columns. The rain began to pour. The firing had never ceased all yesterday and today, at a distance. We encamped and began to cook; when the enemy came in sight, and again spoiled our cooking. We advanced towards them. When we reached the heights they retired; which caused the whole army to get under the arms and move to their positions. Night coming on, we stood under arms for some time. The army then retired to their own rear, and lay down under arms, leaving the 71st. in advance. During the whole night rain never ceased. Two hours after daybreak, General Hill came down, taking away the left subdivision of the 10th. Company to cover his reconnaisance. Shortly afterwards we got half an allowance of liquor, which was the most welcome thing I ever received. I was so stiff and sore from the rain, I could not move with freedom for some time. A little afterwards, the weather clearing up, we began to clean our arms and prepare for action. The whole of the opposite heights were covered by the enemy.

The artillery had been tearing away, since day-break, in different parts of the line. About twelve o'clock we received orders to fall in for attack. We then marched up to our positions, were we lay on the face of a brae, covering a brigade of guns. We were so overcome by the fatigue of the two days' march, that scarce had we lain down until many of us fell asleep. I slept sound for some time, while the cannonballs plunging in amongst us killed a great many. I was suddenly awakened. A ball struck the ground a little below me, turned me heels-over-head, broke my musket in pieces, and killed a lad at my side. I was stunned and confused, and knew not whether I was wounded or not. I felt a numbness in my arm for some time.

We lay thus, about an hour and a half, under a dreadful fire, which cost us about 60 men, while we had never fired a shot. The balls were falling thick amongst us. The young man I lately spoke of lost his legs by a shot at this time. They were cut very close: he soon bled to death. 'Tom,' said he, 'remember your charge: my mother wept sore when my brother died in her arms. Do not tell her all how I died; if she saw me thus, it would break her heart: farewell, God bless my parents!' He said no more, his lips quivered, and he ceased to breathe.

About two o'clock, a squadron of lancers came down,

hurraying, to charge the brigade of guns: they knew not what was in the rear. General Barnes gave the word, 'Form square.' In a moment the whole brigade were on their feet, ready to receive the enemy. The General said, 'Seventy-first, I have often heard of your bravery, I hope it will not be worse than it has been to-day.' Down they came upon our square. We soon put them to the right about.

Shortly afterwards we received orders to move to the heights. Onwards we marched, and stood, for a short time, in square; receiving cavalry every now and then. The noise and smoke were dreadful. At this time I could see but very little away from me, but all around the wounded and slain lay very thick. We then moved on in column, for a considerable way, and formed lines, gave three cheers, fired a few volleys, charged the enemy, and drove them back.

At this moment a squadron of cavalry rode furiously down upon our line. Scarce had we time to form. The square was only complete in front when they were upon the points of our bayonets. Many of our men were out of place. There was a good deal of jostling, for a minute or two, and a good deal of laughing. One quarter-master lost his bonnet, in riding into the square; got it up, put it on, back foremost, and wore it thus all day. Not a moment had we to regard our dress. A French General lay dead in the square; he had a number of ornaments upon his breast. Our men fell to plucking them off, pushing each other as they passed, and snatching at them.

We stood in square, for some time; while the 13th dragoons and a squadron of French dragoons were engaged. The 13th dragoons retiring to the rear of our column, we gave the French a volley, which put them to the right-about; then the 13th at them again. They did this, for some time, we cheering the 13th, and feeling every blow they received. When a Frenchman fell, we shouted, and when one of the 13th we groaned. We wished to join them, but were forced to stand in square.

The whole army retired to the heights in the rear; the French closely pursuing to our formation, where we stood, four deep, for a considerable time. As we fell back, a shot cut the straps of the knapsack of one near me: it fell, and was rolling away. He snatched it up, saying, 'I am not to lose you that way, you are all I have in the world;' tied it on the best manner he could, and marched on.

Lord Wellington came riding up. We formed square with him in our centre, to receive cavalry. Shortly the whole army received orders to advance. We moved forwards in two columns, four deep, the French retiring at the same time. We were charged several times in our advance. This was our last effort; nothing could impede us. The whole of the enemy retired, leaving their guns and ammunition, and every other thing behind. We moved on towards a village and charged right through, killing great numbers, the village was so crowded. We then formed on the other side of it, and lay down under the canopy of heaven, hungry and wearied to death. We had been oppressed, all day, by the weight of our blankets and great coats, which were drenched with rain, and lay upon our shoulders like logs of wood.

Scarce was my body stretched upon the ground, when sleep closed my eyes. Next morning, when I awoke, I was quite stupid. The whole night my mind had been harassed by dreams. I was fighting and charging, re-acting the scenes of the day, which were strangely jumbled with the scenes I had been in before. I rose up and looked around, and began to recollect. The events of the 18th came before me, one by one; still they were confused, the whole appearing as an unpleasant dream. My comrades began to awake and talk of it; then the events were embodied as realities. Many an action had I been in, wherein the individual exertions of our regiment had been much greater, and our fighting more severe; but never had I been where the fighting was so dreadful, and the noise so great. When I looked over the field of battle, it was covered and heaped in many places; figures moving up and down upon it. The wounded crawling along the rows of dead was a horrible spectacle; yet I looked on with less concern, I must say, at the moment, that I have felt at an accident, when in quarters. I have been sad at the burial of a comrade who died of sickness in the hospital, and followed him almost in tears: yet I have seen, after a battle, fifty men put into the same trench, and comrades amongst them, almost with indifference. I looked over the field of Waterloo as a matter of course—a matter of small concern.

In the morning we got half an allowance of liquor; and remained here until mid-day, under arms; then received orders to cook. When cooking was over, we marched on towards France.

'71ST'

Battle in India: Ferozeshah, 22nd December, 1845

IT WAS now getting dusk; the troop was in a frightfully crippled state from the loss it had sustained in men and horses, there being only a young lieutenant (W. A. Mackinnon) in charge. Still the troop advanced, and in the advance the writer took his seat on the trail of a wagon, and felt for a short time pretty comfortable. But only for a very short time: the gun on his right halted in consequence of its two polemen being literally cut in two, the lower portions of their bodies still remaining in the saddle, the upper portion of the right poleman's body being on the ground, while that of the left was suspended by the head over the collar bar. The sergeant major brought up a spare man to take the place of the near poleman, at the same time emptying the two saddles of their ghastly burdens. It must be said that the spare man hesitated to jump into the saddle—for one of the mangled bodies was that of his brother! The sergeant-major seeing there was no time to be lost, freed the collar-bar from the half body hanging over it, and threatened the spare gunner with his pistol if he did not jump into the saddle immediately, and he did so. The gun on the writer's left had now halted; the off poleman having been struck by a round shot in the face, which carried away the left half, the body still sitting erect in the saddle. Here another spare man ran up, tilted the body out of the saddle, and sprang up into his seat, which he had scarcely attained when a shot broke the off fore-leg of the horse he had just mounted. The horse was sent adrift, but appeared loth to leave his mates on the advance of the battery, for he hobbled after it, and as ill-luck would have it, came blundering up to the wagon, on the beam of which the writer was seated, and poked himself between the wheels of the limber and wagon, putting an end to all progress for a time. Holding on with his left arm the writer tried his utmost to keep the brute off with his feet, but a cannon ball soon solved the difficulty. It struck the horse on the hind quarters causing him to bound forward, and knock the writer off his perch, placing him in imminent danger of being run over.

BANCROFT

Battle in the Sikh Wars: Gujerat, 1849

A LITTLE before four, a.m., on the morning of the 21st, the orderly sergeant came to call the corporals to go and see the rations drawn, and get them cooked immediately. This order had not been given many minutes, before another came, for us to strike our camp and pack our baggage upon the cattle, as quickly as possible. This was sufficient to convince us what kind of parade we were going to have, and was a good sign of a general fight, too. Our hungry cattle had cropped off the growing corn close to the ground, for a mile or more all round the camp. We had just made fires, and got our frying pans on, and our baggage was not packed, nor the camp struck, when the well-known sound of the bugle was heard, ringing through the camp, for us to stand to arms. All now was confusion: we got a dram of grog served out per man, and a pound of bread for every two comrades. Our accoutrements were soon upon us, and muskets in our hands. Some might be seen with a slice of raw meat in their grasp, which they had snatched up as they went by; and others were running with their bread in their hands, eating it as they went. I caught hold of some meat out of the frying pan, as it was upon the fire, which had not been on long, so it was raw or nearly so; but I was hungry enough to eat my boot soles, if it had been possible. I had often heard talk of a hungry army; but none could be more hungry than this. We were reduced to nothing but skin and bone. My bones were ready to come through my skin; and as some of the men remarked, their ribs would make gridirons; yet our men were all in high spirits, and appeared eager for the battle. As the whole army on both sides was here, we determined to make this a finishing stroke. Had the Commander-in-chief only told us there was a good breakfast in the enemy's camp, it would have been all he needed to say. We left our camp and baggage upon the ground, and our cooking utensils on the fire, with no one with them but the tent men, and a small guard to bring them forward.

The whole army was now formed for battle, in a line fronting the enemy, who appeared to be watching us very closely, for we could see them upon every rising ground, and on the tops of the houses at the village. We could discern a great stir in their camp, as if they were preparing to receive us. Horsemen were riding about at full speed, as if to carry orders to the different parts of their position. As we now stood formed for battle, awaiting further orders to advance, I took a survey of the country all round us. It was a level plain, well cultivated, the corn a little above knee high, with here and there a fresh ploughed piece of ground. In our front were topes of trees and numerous small villages, scattered about the plain, which the enemy appeared to make good use of; as we could see them strongly posted in them. The city of Goojerat was visible about four miles in our front. This was the enemy's head-quarters, and the centre of his position, from which he had a good view, and so could watch all our movements.

The morning was fine and clear, and as the sun rose it cast forth its golden rays in great splendour upon the two opposing armies, as they stood with glistening accoutrements, waiting to commence the deadly strife. It was about six o'clock, a.m., when the line advanced, covered by skirmishers, who soon became engaged with the enemy. They retired, as we came up, out of most of their advanced villages. Our line kept good order, as if on a common parade. The artillery was now ordered forward, and a most fearful cannonading commenced, such as had never been heard before; the whole artillery of both armies being now in full play upon each other. We were ordered to lie down, so that the enemy's shot might pass over us; and over us they did pass, tearing up the ground all round us, until it looked as if it had been fresh ploughed, and we were covered with earth, though not many were killed. The enemy's artillery deserved great credit; for their guns were served in good style, and very regularly. They made some fine shots. Two of our ammunition wagons were blown up by them, and many of our artillery-men killed at their guns; while several of the artillery horses and bullocks were carried away at one shot, and some of our guns disabled. On our side, the shots were thrown in a masterly manner, and shell was pitched very skilfully, killing every man at their guns, blowing up their magazines, and committing woeful havoc. Our shot dismounted their guns, and swept the men away wholesale, leaving them quite helpless.

Our loss was not so great as might have been expected; but I must here mention Captain Anderson, of the Horse Artillery, belonging to my brigade, who had been with us through the whole war, and was as kind-hearted an old gentleman as ever drew sword. His battery was exposed to a heavy cross fire, and he and nearly all of them were killed. He was wounded first by a round shot, and was requested to go to the rear; but he said he would have another shot or two first, when he was struck by another and killed, and his brave men never flinched from their guns, although exposed to such a destructive fire.

The artillery had been in play for about two hours, when the enemy's guns began to slacken. We had most of this time been lying down upon the ground, and the enemy's shot had been flying thick about us, and two anxious hours they were; they appeared more like two years, and many were the thoughts that crossed the mind. We got impatient, for all the cry was, 'Let us be at them'. The infantry was now ordered to advance; and, as we went forward, we could see the enemy forming their line to receive us. They commenced firing at a long range of musketry. We advanced, and did not discharge a shot till within 150 yards or less, when we opened such a murderous and well-directed fire that they fell by hundreds. They, on their part, kept up a good fire, but it was badly directed; as most of their balls went over our heads. They also showed great skill in their movements; for they made a gallant attempt to turn our right flank. To oppose this, our right was thrown back, and the right brigade of cavalry was ordered to charge, which they did in a splendid style, cutting the enemy down in all directions, and driving them back in disorder. By this time, the fight had become general along the whole line: roll after roll of musketry rent the air, and clouds of smoke rose high and thick, while death was dealt out without mercy; and now was heard the well-known shout of 'Victory'. With levelled bayonets we charged; but they could not stand the shock of cold steel. They gave way in all directions; although some of their officers showed the most daring courage. They tried to rally their men by waving their swords, and going in front of them, to urge them forward; but these brave men were soon shot down, and on we went, clearing the fields before us; while all the cry was, 'We'll finish them today.' The enemy formed several squares, to keep us in check, whilst they got their guns away; but our field artillery galloped to the front, and opened a most destructive fire of grape and canister, which swept them down by whole battalions. On we rushed, bearing all down before us, charging and cheering. We took every gun we came up to, but their artillery fought desperately: they stood and defended their guns to the last. They threw their arms round them, kissed them, and died. Others would spit at us, when the bayonet was through their bodies. Some of their struggles were desperate. Some of the guns and carriages were streaming with blood. An aide-de-camp now rode up with orders from Lord Gough, to say that the right of the line was too forward, and that we were to halt. The left now appeared to be getting the worst of it, the villages being thicker and more strongly occupied by the enemy, and every one having to be taken by storm. The East India Company's Bengal native regiment of Europeans suffered severely, as a number of those villages fell in their front; and this regiment deserves the greatest credit for its bravery, for it carried all before it. This was a very trying time for the right of the line. While standing, waiting for orders to advance, the enemy were boldly re-forming their line in our front, and keeping up a fire upon us; although it was nearly harmless, as they (as usual) fired high. Our men were with the greatest difficulty in the world kept in check by the officers. Lord Gough sent a second order for the right to keep back, as the left could not get up; and the brigadier told the aide-de-camp that he could not keep the men back, nor did he, until he rode at all hazard in front of the line, telling the men to cease firing and to halt. The enemy now had brought some guns to bear upon us with grape. The first round they fired fell just in front of us, and as the ground was fresh ploughed, the shots buried themselves in it; but the second round came, and it fell rather short, slightly wounding one of our men, and severely wounding another. They also made a gap in the 51st regiment of native infantry, which was upon the point of giving way, had it not been for the exertions of the officers, who pressed it to go forward; and I was told one of the officers cut down a man for refusing. One of the Sikh cavalry regiments, bearing a black flag, then deliberately formed line in front of us, as if about to charge us, when our men could stand it no longer. We opened fire upon them, and whether any word 'forward' was given or not, I do not know; but forward we went, and when near to them, and just as they were about to spring forward upon us, we opened such a well-directed fire, and poured it into them with such deadly effect, that it fetched down man and horse by scores to the ground, while numbers of saddles were emptied, and the horses went off leaving their lifeless riders behind. On we went, charging and cheering, bearing all down before us; and the black flag fell into our hands, which we bore from the field in triumph. Everything was carried before us, and the dead and dying lay strewed all over the ground in heaps. In some places might be seen men lying in whole ranks, as they fell; and in more than one place I saw artillerymen and horses one upon another, as they had been shot down by whole batteries, at the time their guns were dismounted. The carriages lay broken and scattered in all directions. The enemy, as they retreated, made daring attempts to stand at the villages; but they were stormed, and very few escaped, for they were all either shot or bayonetted. The left of our line suffered the most, the villages lying the thickest in their front. However, nothing could daunt the courage of the British soldiers, nor resist the shock of the levelled bayonets. We drove them before us in disorder through their camp, which was pitched round Goojerat. We captured all their tents and camp equipage, with all their stores and magazines, and nearly all their artillery.

We stormed Goojerat, where all their principal stores and treasure were. Sheer Sing himself had but a narrow escape: he had been upon a high building, so as to see and direct the battle. It was reported we had entered the town before he left it. We came up to one place, where a strong guard was posted over some treasure, and spare arms. We called on them to surrender, and give up their arms; but they would not—they said, 'No, we will not give up to any English.' One of our men was going up to the sentinel, to disarm him, but the sentinel shot him dead on the spot. One of our officers then told them they had better surrender, as it was useless to resist; and he was going to disarm the sentinel, when he wounded him. We were then obliged to fire into them, and they were nearly all killed before the rest would surrender. The enemy were now driven from the field, and were in full retreat, in the greatest disorder, with nothing left but what they carried. Our cavalry was in full chase after them, cutting them down in all directions; and the ground for miles was strewed with dead. Such a slaughter never before was made. One of our cavalry told me they followed them for upwards of ten miles, sabring them as fast as they came up to them.

Our cavalry continued the chase after the flying enemy until darkness put an end to it. Some of the cavalry did not find their way back until the morning, as the night was so dark.

It was now about four o'clock, p.m., when we halted, and the Commander-in-chief ordered us a dram of grog per man; and we cheered our aged general as he rode along the ranks. Our next thing was to collect the captured guns, stores, horses, elephants, camels and bullocks. We set fire to the camp, and destroyed the powder, the quantity of which was enormous. I never could have believed that they had so much. Tons upon tons were buried in the ground, which we blew up. Lord Gough came amongst us, and was very full of jokes. He said that the enemy's teeth were drawn, and that they were totally defeated.

RYDER

Hand-to-hand: Indian Mutiny

WELL, there happened to be a great tall soldier of the Grenadiers with the party. There were two ladders placed against the two windows, and the word 'Forward' was given. We all rushed off together, and whether me being light or small, or what, I reached one of the ladders just as the tall Grenadier reached the other, and it was a race between him and me, and although I reached every rung of my ladder as soon as he reached his, still he seemed to be higher than I was, and so he was, and I never allowed for his height. However, I believe he got in at his window before I got in at mine, and when I got in I could not see anyone in my room. Consequently I concluded that the enemy did not wait for us but took to their heels as soon as we rushed forward. Well, I looked round the room to see if there was anything worth laying hands on in the shape of provisions etc. Well, there was a very large box, something about or nearly resembling a large flour bin. The lid was partly up so I threw it entirely up, and what was my astonishment to see three of my sable friends sitting on their haunches in this big box. Well, I shot one and bayonetted another, but the third was on me like mad and before I knew where I was he had hold of my musket by the muzzle so that I could not use the bayonet at him. So there I was, he chopping away at me with his native sword, and me defending myself the best way I could by throwing up the butt of my musket to protect my head and trying to close with him, which I knew was my only chance. In doing this I received a chop from his sword on the left hand which divided the knuckle and nearly cut off my thumb. Well, he had his sword raised to give me, I suppose, the final stroke, when in rushed the tall Grenadier. Tom Carrol took in the situation in a glance and soon put an end to my antagonist by burying the hammer of his musket in the fellow's skull, and when he saw me all covered with blood he shouted out a great hoarse laugh and said, 'You little swab, you were very near being done for,' and indeed, so I was. I then showed him the box and its contents, and I can tell you it rather astonished him.

METCALFE

Little Round Top, Gettysburg, 1863

THE conflict opens. I know not who gave the first fire, or which line received the first lead. I only know that the carnage began. Our regiment was mantled in fire and smoke. I wish that I could picture with my pen the awful details of that hour,—how rapidly the cartridges were torn from the boxes and stuffed in the smoking muzzles of the guns; how the steel rammers clashed and clanged in the heated barrels; how the men's hands and faces grew grim and black with burning powder; how our little line, baptized with fire, reeled to and fro as it advanced or was pressed back; how our officers bravely encouraged the men to hold on and recklessly exposed themselves to the enemy's fire—a terrible medley of cries, shouts, cheers, groans, prayers, curses, bursting shells, whizzing rifle bullets and clanging steel. And if that was all, my heart would not be so sad and heavy as I write. But the enemy was pouring a terrible fire upon us, his superior forces giving him a great advantage. Ten to one are fearful odds where men are contending for so great a prize. The air seemed to be alive with lead. The lines at times were so near each other that the hostile gun barrels almost touched. As the contest continued, the rebels grew desperate that so insignificant a force should so long hold them in check. At one time there was a brief lull in the carnage, and our shattered line was closed up, but soon the contest raged again with renewed fierceness. The rebels had been reinforced, and were now determined to sweep our regiment from the crest of Little Round Top. . . .

Our line is pressed so far that our dead are within the lines of the enemy. The pressure made by the superior weight of the enemy's line is severely felt. Our ammunition is nearly all gone, and we are using the cartridges from the boxes of our wounded comrades. A critical moment has arrived, and we can remain as we are no longer; we must advance or retreat. It must not be the latter, but how can it be the former? Colonel Chamberlain understands how it can be done. The order is given 'Fix bayonets!' and the steel shanks of the bayonets rattle upon the rifle barrels. 'Charge bayonets, charge!' Every man understood in a moment that the movement was our only salvation, but there is a limit to human endurance, and I do not dishonor those brave men when I write that for a brief moment the order was not obeyed, and the little line seemed to quail under the fearful fire that was being poured upon it. O for some man reckless of life, and all else save his country's honor and safety, who would rush far out to the front, lead the way, and inspire the hearts of his exhausted comrades! In that moment of supreme need the want was supplied. Lieut. H. S. Melcher, an officer who had worked his way up from the ranks, and was then in command of Co. F., at that time the color company, saw the situation and did not hesitate, and for his gallant act deserved as much as any other man of the honor of the victory on Round Top. With a cheer, and a flash of his sword, that sent an inspiration along the line, full ten paces to the front he sprang—ten paces—more than half the distance between the hostile lines. 'Come on! Come on! Come on, boys!' he shouts. The color sergeant and the brave color guard follow, and with one wild yell of anguish wrung from its tortured heart, the regiment charged.

The rebels were confounded at the movement. We struck them with a fearful shock. They recoil, stagger, break and run, and like avenging demons our men pursue. The rebels rush toward a stone wall, but, to our mutual surprise, two scores of rifle barrels gleam over the rocks, and a murderous volley was poured in upon them at close quarters. A band of men leap over the wall and capture at least a hundred prisoners. This unlooked-for reinforcement was Company B whom we supposed were all captured.

Our Colonel's commands were simply to hold the hill, and we did not follow the retreating rebels but a short distance. After dark an order came to advance and capture a hill in our front. Through the trees, among the rocks, up the steep hillside, we made our way, captured the position, and also a number of prisoners.

On the morning of July 3d we were relieved by the Pennsylvania reserves, and went back to the rear. Of our three hundred and fifty men, one hundred and thirty-five had been killed and wounded. We captured over three hundred prisoners, and a detachment sent out to bury the dead found fifty dead rebels upon the ground where we had fought.

GERRISH

End of a War: near Appomattox Court House, April, 1865

WE SAW a white object flutter in an orchard up in the rear of their line of battle. A signal for their infantry to open fire, growled the boys as they saw it. Then we expected to see their line of battle mantled in fire and smoke as they poured volleys of death upon us; but a moment passed and not a gun had been fired. We looked again; we saw the object we had supposed to be a signal flag, but it had changed its position. It was advancing almost down to their line of battle. It continued to advance, and passed their battle line. Three men accompanied it. What could it mean? It was a white flag. We could not believe our eyes. At a brisk gallop the officers rode to within twenty rods of our line, then turned down to our right where Sheridan had disappeared. We advanced. A staff officer came out from the woods; his spurs were pressed hard against the smoking flanks of his noble horse. He was swinging his hat like a madman, and yelling—'Lee has surrendered! Lee has surrendered!' 'Halt, halt, halt!' came the order, and the last charge was over. But such a scene! I cannot describe it. Seventeen years have passed, but the blood tingles in my finger tips now, as I think of it. There was such a change in the situation, such a transition in our experience! Men laughed and shouted, shook hands and actually wept for joy. Could it be possible? It seemed more like a dream. Had Lee actually surrendered, and was the war about to close?

The joy of that hour will never be forgotten. We forgot the long, weary marches, the hours of suffering, the countless exposures, and many sacrifices, and for the time, even forgot our disappointment in not drawing rations at nine o'clock that morning. Many of the boys were even then skeptical as to the actual surrender of Lee, and contended that he only sent in the flag of truce to gain time, and thus steal a march upon us; but in the afternoon all doubts were removed. The advanced lines of the enemy had been withdrawn soon after the white flag came within our lines, and now large numbers of the rebel soldiers came over to us. We were glad to see them. They had fought bravely, and were as glad as we that the war was over. They told us of the fearful condition General Lee's army was in, and we only wondered that they endured the hardships so long as they did. We received them kindly, and exchanged pocket knives and sundry trinkets, that each could have something to carry home as a reminiscence of the great event. To our division was assigned the honor of staying to receive the remainder of the arms, while the rest of the army moved back toward Richmond. We had three days' rations of food in our baggage wagons, and this was divided with our prisoners; and thus for the day or two intervening between the surrender and the final stacking of their arms, we camped on the same hillside, ate the same hard-tack, and almost drank from the same canteen. The rebels were all loud in their praise of General Grant, for the generous terms of the surrender, and pledged themselves to go home, and live and die under the shadow of the old flag. They had fought for four years, been completely whipped, were sadly disappointed, but, like men, were determined to go home and work to regain the fortunes they had lost.

GERRISH

Sergeant Taffs of the 4th Foot at Magdala, 1868

It is not often a soldier knows much about the cause of the war in which he is engaged, but I managed to learn a few facts which caused me to take additional interest in the expedition. A missionary named Stern had been beaten and imprisoned in 1863 by order of King Theodore, and on the 3rd of January 1864, Captain C. D. Cameron, the British Consul, and all the British subjects and missionaries were imprisoned and kept in chains, like criminals, for alleged insults to the King, who called himself the King of Kings. The British Government sent a Chaldee Christian named Rassam, with Lieutenants Prideaux and C. Blanc, and after considerable negotiations the prisoners were released on the 25th February 1866, but were subsequently seized and re-imprisoned.

Our work, therefore, was to release the prisoners, and teach Theodore a lesson in humanity, and we pushed forward through the country with a strong determination to do so.

We made a grand show on the march, for we employed over 14,000 camels and bullocks, 13,000 mules and ponies, and about 50 elephants, and over 800 donkeys, besides the large number of natives engaged in transport work.

We arrived below Magdala on the 2nd April 1867, and learned that the captives had been relieved of their chains three or four days previously.

A week after our arrival below Magdala, Theodore massacred about three hundred native prisoners; and the following day, which was Good Friday, his troops attacked our First Brigade, but were defeated with much slaughter at a place called Arogee. I saw very little of the fighting, as I was behind with the Medical Staff, attending to the sick and wounded; but the next day I saw Lieutenant Prideaux come with a message from the King to Sir Robert Napier, who sent him back with a letter, to which the King sent an insulting reply.

On the 13th of April we bombarded and stormed Magdala, which was built on a high tableland, access to which was only possible on one side by what was called the King's Road. Theodore's troops made a pretty good stand; but when he found we were gaining the day, he shot himself with a pistol, which some years before had been sent him as a present from Queen Victoria. I saw him lying dead with the pistol beside him, and I read the inscription engraved upon it, but I forget exactly what it was.

We took possession of the town, and collected a large number of casualties. I brought away one or two vases from the palace, and a drinking-horn, which would hold about a quart.

We set fire to the place, and burnt it to the ground, on the 17th April, and set off at once for the coast, taking the Queen and her son with us. She died on the march back, but the boy was brought to England, where we arrived about the 21st or 22nd of June.

The expenses of the war were over eight million sterling, and having assisted the country in this pleasant little extravagance, I took my discharge.

SMALL

Atbara, 1898

On reaching rail-head we commenced our march over the desert and arrived at Wady-Halfa. During the march the only water we had to drink was carried in galvanised iron tanks on the camels' backs, and which was quite hot, owing to the blazing sun. I remember on one occasion coming to a large pool of water, the colour of milky coffee, where half a dozen peaceful natives were bathing. As soon as we halted for a rest there was a rush for what appeared to be a cool drink. The doctor, on horseback, rode amongst us shouting, 'Don't drink it men, you'll die of enteric fever,' but to no avail. Thirst, especially desert thirst, does not permit its victim to listen to reason, and many of us chased the natives away, and dipping our helmets in the pool, drank voraciously. I forgot to mention that, while at Wady-Halfa, I happened to be one of a guard over the native women, to keep prowlers away, although I never discovered why I was chosen or what special qualifications I may have had for this job.

At the battle of Atbara we had been marching all night, our brigade being under General Catacre, whom some of our men nicknamed, 'Bach-acher', owing to his apparent fondness for forced marches. We were only four British regiments in this action, viz, Seaforth Highlanders, Warwicks, Cameron Highlanders and the Lincolns, all the others being Egyptians.

At about 7 o'clock in the morning, Good Friday, 8th April, 1898, we surprised them having their breakfast; and what a surprise it was—bayonets instead of hot cross buns. In less than no time they were rushing about, yelling, the native women screaming—what a pandemonium! There was much hand to hand fighting and bayonet work in this action, and the Dervish women being dressed so much like their men,

SANTA CLARA PUBLIC LIBRARY
SANTA CLARA, CALIF.

they could not easily be distinguished many of them raising their Jebbahs or smocks to prove they were women and so save their lives.

The Dervish Commander, General Nahmud, in preparing for defence, had dug several trenches, which were protected from bayonet or hand-to-hand fighting by prickly bushes, or 'Zarebas', six feet high, and to prevent his force in the trenches retreating, had chained them by the ankles so that they would be compelled to fight to the last. It happened that some of our shells had set fire to their 'Zareba', which must have roasted a few of the poor wretches alive, as they could not get away.

CORBETT

Omdurman, 1898

'REVEILLE' sounded at 4 a.m. and we stood to our arms till daybreak, maintaining the same square formation as on the previous night, for we felt sure the Dervishes would take the initiative and attempt to drive us back. All day yesterday the gun-boats were shelling the town and performed excellent work.

Shortly after 5 o'clock our cavalry scouts came galloping back with the information that the enemy were advancing in thousands, and a few minutes later we were able to distinguish them coming round the base of the hill in vast hordes with their flags fluttering in the morning breeze. Their line seemed to extend about as far as the eye could reach. When about 2,000 yards away they started chanting their war song. Such a din of shouting and yelling from so many throats is better imagined than described. The noise, so far distant, seemed to fill the air. We allowed them to get within 1,000 yards of us, when—boom! The first shell was fired and burst in their midst with splendid effect. Then another and another followed, till the whole army became involved in the struggle. The Dervishes advanced to within about 600 yards of our position, and their bullets commenced to whistle about us, some at our feet, some flying overhead. Then our Maxims started—200 shots per minute from each machine-gun, while at the same time we were pouring deadly volleys amongst them. They carried their flags—to turn our bullets into water, as the Khalifa made them believe—but as they rallied round them, shells and volleys fell amongst them with deadly effect. The spectacle was an awful one, never to be forgotten. It was a treat to watch the shells flying through the air and bursting right into their midst. Once their cavalry made a desperate charge round the base of the hill, but ere they had advanced 100 yards, two or three shells exploded amongst them, and one could see horses and riders dashed to the ground in fifties at a time. Riderless horses were rushing away in terror in all directions, but the fight was not entirely one-sided. Some of their bullets found their mark. As soon as a comrade dropped, the stretcher-bearers rushed to the firing line picked him up and carried him a few yards at the rear, ascertained the nature of, and bandaged the wound, and then conveyed him to the field hospital, some 300 yards to the rear, where the doctors did whatever they could. The Dervishes' fire was either too high or too low, the bullets either striking the ground in front of our fighting line, or passing harmlessly over our heads. Had they the correct range we should have sustained many more casualties. We had been at it almost two and half hours when the Sirdar performed a splendid feat of manœuvring. I cannot describe it correctly being one amongst thousands. I didn't even notice the ingenuity of the scheme, but a message was heliographed from Lord Kitchener to retire from our position and proceed round the base of the hill at the opposite side to that on which we had been attacked. This was where the Khalifa fell into the trap. Thinking we were actually retiring, he advanced his whole force, including those in the trenches. In the meantime the 1st Brigade had come right round the hill completely cutting him off and preventing him retiring on Omdurman. Thus we had him between a murderous crossfire, which drove the remainder of his army into the desert. As we now advanced we stepped over thousands of dead and dying, lying in mangled heaps, and some of the fellows were terribly mutilated.

Very little remains to be told, for shortly afterwards the

fugitives fled in all directions, being scattered in the desert and pursued by our cavalry. The charge of the 21st Lancers was indeed a gallant one, that will be long remembered. They went right into the Dervishes' trenches alone, the native cavalry being unable to assist them, as they were on reserve flank. Such tremendous odds have scarcely ever been equalled, but they did their duty nobly.

After forming up again we marched into Omdurman, reaching there about 6.30 p.m. Then we had breakfast, dinner and tea, all in one. After which we lay down in a large square and enjoyed a well-earned rest. We had avenged General Gordon at last. Queen Victoria thought a lot of him. 'His bones are dust; His good sword rust; His soul is with the saints I trust.'

There is one incident which, though forgotten in my hurried account sent home after the battle, still stands out in my memory. It was when, after the guns had bombarded their positions and we were advancing to the attack, we had to step over numbers of Dervishes' bodies lying around which we imagined were dead, but we very soon found out that they were very much alive. They had cunningly been shamming 'dead', and as soon as we had stepped over them in our advance, some of them jumped up and speared or knifed some of our men in the back.

The incident referred to was when, after stepping over some of these bodies, I sensed some unusual movement behind me, and on looking round, caught a huge Dervish, about 6 ft. 4 ins. tall, with a thick bushy beard, getting up with a large double-handed sword. I shouted out: 'Look out, chaps', when three of my companions turned just in time to see this great fellow preparing to wield his sword with both hands, which could have sliced of at least two of our heads in one sweep. But before he could poise himself for the blow he was surrounded and our bayonets found their way into him in four different directions. I shall never forget the look in his eyes as he dropped his heavy sword and fell. I wish I could have taken a snapshot of this little 'incident'. After that, we were compelled to look into the eyes of every body on the ground, and if there was the least sign or flicker of life, he was disposed of in a similar manner, because it meant 'It's you or me, chum, and it's not going to be me'.

We took Omdurman and found that our guns had smashed the Mahdi's Tomb thus destroying the fanatical belief that he was immortal.

The next morning many of our officers went on a mission of mercy in order to relieve those who were still alive in the desert and dying from thirst etc. Everything that could hold water was filled and sent out on camels, donkeys, or anything on four legs, as it was impossible for anyone to go far on foot owing to the intense heat in the desert. Medical supplies, bandages etc., were also sent out to their relief. This time, if there should be any sign of life in the wounded enemy, instead of finishing them off, which we had to do during the battle, the Christian spirit prevailed, and we acted on the principle of 'Do unto others as you would they should do unto you', not as 'Do others as they would do you', as there would be no doubt as to what they would have done had the position been reversed.

All during the day our job was to search every native hut, etc., for hidden arms or ammunition, some which we discovered under the native beds.

CORBETT

15

RETREAT

Retreat to Corunna, 1808–9

WE CAME to Astorga. We expected to get into it, but it was full of Spanish troops, and the fever had broke out there, we halted outside, and got some bread served out. We went further on till we came to some houses and halted for the night. The weather was very changeable, sometimes rain, then frost and snow. It was difficult to get houses to shelter us for the night. We went off the road to a small village. There were six or eight of us put into one house. The people were baking bread, and got it into the oven, but they were keeping watch over it, and we were watching them. But it was managed to divert them off their guard and a loaf of bread was stolen out. It would be six or eight pounds weight. It was carried out, and by the light of the moon, divided into shares. They soon found out that one of the loaves was stolen. We had to march early in the morning. I put a pair of dry stockings and shoes on to keep my feet comfortable. But we had not gone far when we came to a river. There was no bridge. We had to go into it, and pass over. One of our officers got his servant to carry him on his back. Our Colonel came riding to him, crying out 'Put him down, put him down,' for he was very angry. We were well pleased at it. The French were keeping close behind us, and if the men did not keep up, they were sure to be taken prisoner. The roads were very bad, if they could be called roads. Many of us put on new shoes in the morning, and before night, had no shoes. Our marching was in the night as well as in the day. We had a blanket each of us to carry. But we made one blanket to serve two, and many of the men had none. I had a good comrade. He was abler to keep up with the Regiment than I was, and he carried the blanket. We came to what we called the Snow Mountains. We had a long day's march. It was 1st January, 1809. There were very few houses to be seen. Some of the men ran into them, but they soon came out. There were Spanish soldiers in them, sick, and some lying dead. We were now descending the mountains, and owing to the snow melting, the road was deep with mud and dirt. It was very dark. In going to the one side, it was so deep that I could not get out. The Regiment was passing, and another coming up. To cry for help it was in vain. I made one effort after another, and to save myself from falling in, I had to throw down my firelock, and in this way I got out. I then got hold of my firelock, for it was not so deep down. But it was not easy to get my shoes, but I got them. I came off with my firelock over my shoulder, covered with mud, and my shoes in my hand. While I was standing, and not able to extricate myself, I could not help weeping, for I was not eighteen years of age.

There was a small village at the foot of the mountain. The Regiment halted there. I went into the house where the Company was in. It was a miserable looking place, but I was glad to see it. I took off my knapsack, and out I went to a running stream, to wash my clothes and shoes and my firelock, and went back to where the Company was. They had a fire on the floor. We lay down round about the fire and slept. We were not long till we had to get up again. We now had to pass through between two high mountains, said to be about nine or ten miles long. There was so many turnings this way and that way that we could not see far before us. On the left of the road there was a steep precipice. The water rolling down from the mountains made the river to run very rapid. Into this river were thrown ammunition, guns, shoes, it was said dollars too. Now and then a shot went off. This was one of the cavalry or artillery horses shot, for when we went forward, we saw them lying on the road bleeding. I did not proceed far till I had to take off my shoes. They were hard and my feet was sore. I could not keep them on. I had to fall behind, and get forward the best way I could. At last I got to the other end of these two mountains. There was a bridge over the river. They were calling to us to make haste for they were waiting to blow it up. I moved on to get up to the Regiment. They went off the main road to a village to stop all night. I had to march a good way before I got there. Some of the men had taken from the inhabitants honey and potatoes. The Colonel paid for them, and we had to pay for them afterwards, three halfpence each man. I got some of the potatoes, but no honey. We marched next day. I took a few of the potatoes with me, but as I was not very able to march, I came on the best way I could. I did not go far till I had to throw away my potatoes. When I came to the main road, I saw my old comrade, Daniel McInnes. He had nothing, carrying no knapsack, no firelock; he had not been able to get up to the Regiment for two or three days past. He had nothing on but his regimentals.

Some of the staff officers was in the rear of the army, trying to get the men forward telling them that the French cavalry was cutting the men down when they came up to them. The staff officers cut the knapsacks off some of their backs to get them forward. But Daniel was taken prisoner, and I never saw him more. We came to Lugo. This was not a long day's march. I had in my knapsack cloth to make a pair of trousers. One of the tailors belonging to the company made them for me, for I had much need of them. I was put on the Provost guard. One of the 95th Regiment came into the guard house, lay down before the fire, and died. This was the way with many.

But all the army in the town was to march out the way we came in to take our position. The guard was ordered to fall in with our regiments. It was said that Sir John Moore was going to risk a battle. It was now dark. Our regiment was posted behind a low stone wall, where we sat down on our knapsacks. But it came on a tremendous thunder-storm, the rain falling on us in torrents, and the lightning flashing with one peal of thunder after another. My comrade and I put the blanket over our heads, and one or two with us. We sat with our heads close to each other. We got little or no sleep. Daylight came in, and it still rained. We got up on our feet, and saw before us the French, no better than ourselves. There was two or three farm houses between the French camp and ours. The French and our men were taking what they could find that was needful, meeting each other, and passing each other. Our Colonel went out on horseback. He saw a field of turnips, he came back, and called a man of each mess for turnips and water. Our Colonel knew that we had need of something to eat. Wood was sought after, and fires kindled. Afterwards, we got some flour served out. We made dumplings, or round balls, and boiled them. This was done as soon as possible, for we were hungry. After the cooking was over, we were drying our clothes on us.

We saw the French beginning to move towards us. We on with our knapsacks, and ran to our arms. We were ready for them, the 4th and 10th Companies, and many belonging to the other companies were sent out. My comrade was one of them. They fired on us with their cannon, and we lay down under cover. Night was coming on. The French retired, and so did ours. My comrade came back in safety. He saw a dead French soldier, opened his knapsack, and took out two or three napkins and a watch. We got beef served out, and we were preparing to get it cooked, and then to get a good night's sleep, when orders was given to fall in. Our beef was left lying on the ground. We were to march for Corunna. We would have about forty miles to go. We took the road, and as we went on, there was bonfires to be seen, of gun carriage carts, and anything that could not be taken away. After we left the town, we came to a house here and there. The men were running out of the ranks into them. Some of the officers were trying to get them out, but they could not. When the Army was drawn up for battle, as they were at Lugo and at other places, they appeared to be well pleased. But at this time, the officers lost all their authority. We got no sleep the night before, and none through the day. I saw that I was not able to go forward. I ran out of the ranks into one of these houses. There was a good number of men in it of different regiments. A large fire was on the floor. At first, I did not see where I could get a place to lie down. At last I saw a ladder or stair. I went up, and found a place. There was one or two before me. I took off my knapsack and lay down. I heard them crying to the men to turn out, the house was on fire. But I soon slept. The next I heard was one of the men saying 'Get up, for I think we are prisoners.' We on with our knapsacks. We looked down, and saw nobody. We took the road, and on we went. I thought that I *had* made a narrow escape. We came up to one or two more. We saw before us a village. Some of the houses had been set on fire through the night. When we came up to it, I went to one of the houses that was on fire. I saw potatoes lying in the ruins. I took up some of them to eat them, and found they were too hard. I thought of getting some of them boiled for I was very hungry, when the cry was made, 'The Cavalry! The French Cavalry!'

I took up my firelock, and ran, for they were not far from me, and as we went on, our numbers increased. The cry was 'Stop, stop, or they will cut us down.' We went outside of the village, and came to a small bridge, and then we turned round. But we had no officer to take the command of us. We saw a Sergeant belonging to one of the Highland Regiments. He was making his way forward. We brought him back. He took the command. We formed in line, and waited till they would come forward. They then came down towards us from the village. We then commenced firing on them. They put to the right-about, and into the village. We turned about and came on. The French cavalry came after us. They extended themselves on each side, their main body on the road. We thought they were going to surround us. We sent out skirmishers to the right and left, and kept firing on them. However, they did not try to get round us. We kept as close together as we could. We came up to some of our baggage, and those that could not get forward had to leave it behind. We marched this way for a long time. When Sir John Moore heard the firing, he halted the rearguard, and sent back the 18th Light Dragoons to our assistance. When we saw them, we were glad. When they came up, we halted, and the commanding officer ordered some of us to go forward, and he kept the rest. When I came up to the guard, there was a sergeant on the road to search and see if we had any dollars, for there were some of this description. He took hold of my knapsack and said 'What is this?' It was ten rounds of ammunition in addition to what we had in our cartridge box, that was 70 rounds altogether. I had no dollars. I went forward, but very weakly, for the want of food. There were some empty flour barrels off the road. I went over to them, for there were some before me, scraping the barrels with their fingers to see if we could get any flour. But Sir John Moore's staff officers came riding in amongst us, and drove us away. I went on a little further, and saw a blanket lying on the road. Some of the men had been carrying flour in it. The blanket being wet, the flour was sticking to it. I sat down, and made the best of it I could. I got up and moved on, and came to a part of the Army in camp. They were cooking the flour they got served out, but our regiment was not there. They were to march on to Betanzos, nine or ten miles farther. This was a sore disappointment, but there was no help for it.

We had plenty of company. There was officers as well as soldiers. We came to Betanzos. I found out where my company was. An allowance of bread and rum was served out. I got my bread, but no rum. My comrade laid it aside for me, but it was lost. It was not very long before I was ordered to turn out for picket. It was not my turn. There were so many absent they had to take those that were present. I had to put on my knapsack, and turn out. I could scarcely stand on my feet. The sergeant-major took pity on me, and put me on the inlying picquet to be ready to turn out when we were called on. The regiment was to march next morning, and those that were not able to keep up were to go away sooner. I was one of them. We marched off, and in leaving the town, they were waiting till the Army would pass, to blow up the bridge. We moved slowly on for some time, but we got orders to fall in with our regiments as they came up to us. We came at last in sight of the sea and Corunna, but saw no ships to take us away. We were put into a store house for the night. It was not a good place, but we were glad to see it. My comrade and I lay down under our blanket and slept. But I was a little disturbed in my sleep. There was another one under the blanket behind me. I said 'Who is that?' He said 'Whist, whist.' I looked round to see who it was. It was one of our officers belonging to the company. He had no servant, for he could not get one. We did not think much of him.

The next morning, we marched back, and took up our position. This was the eighth or ninth of January that we came to Corunna. While here, we were employed in various ways of cleaning ourselves, for we had much need of it. I do not remember when I had my clothes off. Had the ships been ready for us before we came, we would soon have got away. I got a pair of shoes served out, but they were of no use to me, owing to my feet being bruised. I put them in my knapsack. A few men of each company was sent to Corunna to bring new arms to the camp, and those that had bad ones could take a new one. I took one of them, and left my old one. The sailors that came on shore took up some of the old ones. Afterwards, the store, with many hundreds of barrels of powder and arms were blown up. It made a tremendous noise.

At last the ships hove in sight. Preparations were making for the accommodation of each regiment. All the cavalry horses were shot on the morning of 16th January. Our company was sent to the advance post to relieve one that was there before us. It was not long till the firing commenced. One of the cavalry was sent to the officer commanding us to come back. It was strange to be going back. Some of the men said we should go where the firing was, and join the skirmishers. The other officer agreed with us, but he would not. Another order was to make haste. We had to obey. When we came forward, we saw two guns on the road pointing towards the enemy. This might be the reason for us to make haste. Our division was commanded by Sir John Hope. We were on the left of the Army. The French commenced to attack on our right. At the same time, they were watching our left. There was skirmishing and cannonading with us, while the French was endeavouring to force the right of the Army towards the sea. But in this they were disappointed, for our Army kept their ground, and at last drove them back. The firing was kept up till near dark, and we heard that Sir John Moore was mortally wounded, and General Baird lost his arm. General Hope now had the command. Orders were given for the troops to embark, and some of the men was left behind to keep fires burning. When we came to the beach, the sailors were there with the boats. It was dark. The wind was blowing strong, and it was not easy to keep the boats from striking each other. My comrade and I got into one of the boats, but he went out of it into another and wanted me to come with him but I would not. I thought the one as good as the other. For this, I did not see him till we came to England.

The sailors got off, but the next thing was to find out the ship where the regiment was in. They rowed from one ship to another, but could not find out. We got orders to get into any ship. At last we got into one. There were not many on board, some women, and sick soldiers, but there was plenty of us afterwards. We were very hungry and had nothing to eat. They began to serve out to us biscuits and cheese. The French saw we were getting on board, for it was daylight. They brought their guns to bear on the shipping. Off went one shot, then another. There was no more biscuit or cheese served out then. I got mine. All was in a bustle, getting up on deck. But I sat down, and was eating my bread and cheese, for what could we do but to put out to sea as fast as possible. The ships were at anchor, and there was no time to take them up. They had to cut their cables. This caused some of the ships to run foul of each other, and some went on the rocks. Our ship came close to one. The men jumped out and into ours. We had two warships in harbour, but the sailors were employed in taking the troops on board or they would soon have silenced the French guns, but they did so afterwards. At last we got out of the harbour, and if they did not drive us into the sea, they drove us out to sea.

A BUGLER OF THE 71ST FOOT

The Retreat from Moscow, 1812 (1)

With a boot and an old shoe on my feet, a crutch in my hand, and dressed in a pink cloak lined with ermine and a hood over my head, I marched along with my faithful soldier and my two horses, which strayed at will without ever losing sight of us.

We ate the horses which died every day, and, as I was in the rearguard, we never found anything but the remnants of those; happy was he who could even get that.

Thus did I live till we reached Vilna, except for a pound of oatbread, that a Grenadier of the Guard sold me for a napoleon.

I ate horseflesh half-cooked, and was sprinkled with grease and blood from the chin to the knees. My face was begrimed, my beard long, and I looked like a Mayence ham; and, in spite of my condition, I often laughed at my own costume and those of my comrades. We marched with long icicles on every hair of our beards; the skins which half covered us, singed at the few bivouac fires we were able to light.

Dead horses were not sufficient for three-fourths of a starving army, and it was only the more courageous who could get that. Those who had neither knife, sabre, nor axe, and whose hands were frozen, could not eat. I have seen soldiers on their knees, and others seated near these carcases, and biting the flesh like hungry wolves. Thanks to my soldier, I was never short of horse-flesh, and every day I ate two to three pounds of this meat, without salt or bread.

For drink we had snow, melted in a saucepan, which my soldier carefully guarded, both for us and for the horses.

In spite of their demoralization, the soldiers of all ranks had still the humanity to respect the horses of the wounded, although their owners could not use them; for in that region and at that season, a man on horseback, in spite of the warmest garments, would have been frozen in a few hours.

Such was the condition of the army in the early days of this month, and I leave to the imagination the situation of the unfortunate wounded, sick, and amputated, huddled pell-mell in carts, of which the horses died of fatigue and hunger. These poor wretches were abandoned at the bivouacs, and on the road, and died insane. Those who had the strength killed themselves. The companions and friends of these sad victims could give them no help, but turned away their eyes in order not to see them.

The Cossacks, who, seeing this confusion, laughed like madmen.

(November 11th). The weather became dull and cloudy; the sun never appeared, and a strong wind covered us with flakes of snow which froze on us. The snow soon covered the ground; rivers, lakes, and ditches disappeared from our view. We could not find our road, except by the corpses of the unfortunate wretches who had preceded us, for this cold increased the number of stragglers, who followed with difficulty, and a great number of whom, not having the strength to march, fell. They fell with their arms in the air, and died, frozen, in that position.

That there were so many stragglers arose from the fact that these poor fellows, having their hands frozen, could not hold their weapons, wandered about, and were driven from the bivouacs and the fires, because they did not contribute any food to the stock. They died behind the groups of those who were warming themselves, and who, seeing them 'playing the bear' (that was the expression used) stripped them, without ever thinking that their turn might come. Many of these stragglers took refuge also in the houses they found still standing, set fire to them, and often perished in the flames, not having the strength to get away.

I have seen this effect produced by the cold; soldiers whose hands were frozen, fell down, and the fingers and thumbs snapped like glass. One of my friends, Captain Chidor, of the 9th Regiment of the Line, had his feet frozen. When he arrived at Smolensk, and took off the bandages in which his foot was wrapped, three toes came off with it. He removed the rags from the other foot, and taking hold of the great toe, twisted it round and pulled it off, without feeling any pain. He went through the rest of the retreat thus mutilated, and died in Italy from the result of his wounds.

For my part I had my ears and chin frozen, and the hands

slightly. The skin came off like that of a rabbit. One foot that was bare except for the shoe was not affected, but my wounded leg turned black, and I had no feeling in it. I did not have it dressed till I got to Gora; on removing the bandage, the skin, from the knee to the instep, came off, and the flesh under it was black and marbled. I felt no pain. Ever since then my left leg has been smaller than the other, but it is just as strong, and I never suffer from it.

Some days before we reached Smolensk, our cavalry had almost entirely disappeared. A good part of our artillery and baggage had been abandoned on the road. All our cavalry men left, who had looked so fine six months previously, were on foot with the stragglers. There was no discipline; all military rank was destroyed. Generals, superior officers and subalterns no longer cared for the soldiers who had contributed to their glory. The men themselves asked nothing but death. Such a request was often made to me, and I had not the strength to recommend them to take courage, or even to weep for them.

Those who, like myself, had still a little strength, were tortured by hunger, and we ran after the horses, watching for them to fall; when we threw ourselves upon them like wolves, fighting for bits of flesh. To cook this miserable food, we had to seek everywhere for wood. Often it refused to light, or else the wind blew it out. This search for food took all the time we had for rest. Worn out for want of sleep and long marches, we had nothing but the snow to lie on. Generals, officers, and privates were mixed pell-mell, huddled against one another. There were some, who, nearly dead with fatigue, stood all night like spectres, round the faggots, when they had been able to light them.

(November 12th). The army continued its march, and arrived this evening at Smolensk, where we found no resources, the Guard having take the little there was. And they sold us bits of bran or oatcake at five or six francs each.

I, with many others of my unfortunate brothers-in-arms, lodged in sheds or buildings outside the town; but none of us had the strength to drag ourselves about to seek for provisions, which were very rare, the Guards having seized everything.

They sold spirits, sugar and oat or bran bread at its weight in gold. I paid one of these egoists six francs for an ounce of oat-bread, and a napoleon for a quarter of a bottle of spirits. These Guards, at Smolensk as at Moscow, were unworthy of their name, and disgusted the whole army.

I will describe our situation as it was before crossing the Beresina.

For a long time past, officers of all grades had been accoutred like the soldiers. Nothing could look more extraordinary than our clothing of skins, half-burnt, and smothered with grease. Our long beards had icicles on every hair. Everybody marched in a dazed state, with haggard eyes, and insensible to the sufferings of others. When a man fell, those who could speak, said, 'Hallo! another one "playing at bear!" ' and a few instants later, one of those who had spoken played the bear in his turn. We marched anyhow. Our misfortunes had levelled all ranks. Some of the men bore on their shoulders a sack or nosebag containing a little flour, and had a pot hanging by their side by a cord; others dragged by the bridle ghosts of horses which carried a few provisions and cooking utensils. If one of these horses fell, it was quickly cut up, and the flesh packed on the backs of the other horses. The different corps of the army had almost ceased to exist, and their fragments were formed into small societies of six, eight or ten men, who marched together, had their stock of food in common, and drove away any person who did not belong to their gang. All these poor wretches marched huddled together like sheep, and taking great care not to separate in the crowd, for fear of losing their own gang, and being ill-treated. If a man strayed away from one of these companies, another gang took his provisions, if he had any, or drove him without pity from the fires, when the wind permitted us to make any, and from any place where he tried to take refuge. He did not cease to be assailed till he had rejoined his own comrades. These men passed in front of Generals, and even the Emperor himself, without taking any more notice of them than of the poorest wretch in the army. And the commanders saw all this without being able to say a word.

What could they say, in fact? Imagine 60,000 wretches,

each carrying a sack, supporting himself with a stick, clothed in dirty rags, and eaten up with vermin. Our faces were hideous, yellow and smoked, smeared with earth, blackened by the greasy smoke of pine fires, the eyes hollow, the beard covered with snot and ice. We could not use our hands to button our trousers, and many fastened them with a cord. We were all indescribably filthy, and I journeyed several days without being able to wash myself, or still less change my clothes. Such was the spectacle presented by an army, which, eight months before, had been the finest in the world.

All the way along, could continually be heard the sound of dead bodies being crushed under the feet of horses, or under the wheels of carts. On all sides were heard the cries and groans of those who had fallen, and, struggling in terrible agony, were dying a thousand times whilst awaiting death.

When we were near a town or village, everybody rushed for the houses, and in a moment they were so crowded, that one could not get out again. Those who could not get shelter under a roof—for the more fortunate drove the others away—lighted fires outside, and often burned down the habitation and those who had taken refuge in it. Sometimes the houses were set on fire purposely, out of revenge.

This was not infrequently done, especially to houses in which generals were living. Or, sometimes, the houses, which were all built of wood, were pulled down bodily, carried away to the bivouacs, and used for making rough shelters. When these shelters were finished, a fire would be lighted, and everybody would set to work to prepare the meal. Flour and water were kneaded together, and these 'dampers' cooked on the ashes. Each gang took from its sacks the horse-flesh, and threw it on the embers to get cooked. I lived on this fare for twenty-three days, without salt or bread, though I occasionally had some barley, rye, or oat cake, which my soldier procured for me. He had joined one of these gangs for the sole purpose of procuring me provisions. The dough was made of any sort of flour, mixed with snow water. It was a black mixture, and full of sand. Some gunpowder from the cartridges was mixed with it, for powder is salt, and, at all events, made the food prepared under such circumstances less insipid.

The meal being finished, everybody crowded round the fire, and soon went to sleep, to get some strength to resist the morrow's sufferings. At daybreak, without drum or trumpet, the army resumed its march.

From the Beresina to Wilna, more than 30,000 soldiers of all ranks—demoralized, stolid, wounded, frozen, sluggish, unarmed—marched in a troop, with their heads down, without saying a word. Many died on the road, and others, taken prisoner, died of want.

A thick snow darkened the air that day. We could hardly see the way, and the army had much difficulty in getting to the foot of the mountain, which is about a league from Wilna. We were surrounded by Cossacks, and, as many of their officers spoke French, they said to us, 'You will need frost-nails to climb that mountain. Wait a bit, and Tchitchagow and Platow will bring you some.' As a matter of fact, owing to the frost and the steepness of the path, we despaired of being able to follow it. The horses we had left were badly shod, slipped, fell, and had not the strength to rise again. We were obliged to abandon the remainder of our materials, the baggage, and the Emperor's treasure, of which he had, it was said, fifteen millions and his gold and silver plate. The soldiers kicked away the dishes and jugs, or threw them far into the snow, The wardrobe was burned. When I was on the top of the mountain I saw the Grenadiers of the Guard defending the last few chests against the Cossacks, who, however, finally carried them off.

The army had much difficulty in climbing this mountain. As for me, with my crutch, and my arm in a sling, I do not know how I managed to get to the summit. I fell more than a hundred times, and dragged myself along the ice. I cursed my fate, though I laughed sometimes at the oaths of those who, like me, kept falling down. When I got to the top, I was covered with bruises, my wounds had re-opened, and I was covered in blood; it was, I am sure, nothing but the intense desire to escape at all costs from so many misfortunes that sustained me.

FRANÇOIS

The Retreat from Moscow, 1812 (2)

The beginning

October. DURING the evening of October 18th, when, according to our daily custom, several non-commissioned officers were assembled together, stretched at full length like pashas on ermine, sable, lion and bear skins, smoking costly tobacco in magnificent pipes, an enormous silver bowl filled with punch before us, above which a huge loaf of sugar was melting, held in its place by two Russian bayonets—just as we were talking of France and of the glory of returning there as conquerors after so long an absence, just as we were composing farewells and promises of fidelity to our female Mongol, Chinese, and Indian friends—we heard a tremendous noise in the large room where the soldiers of our company slept. And who should enter but the Quarter-master with the announcement that we must hold ourselves in readiness to leave. The next day (the 19th) the town was filled with Jews and Russian peasants—the first-named to buy of the soldiers what they could not carry away, the last to pick up what we threw into the streets. We heard that Marshal Mortier was to remain at the Kremlin with 10,000 men to defend it if necessary.

We set out in the afternoon, packing some liquor from our stores on Mother Dubois's cart, as well as our large silver bowl; it was almost dark when we got outside the town. We found ourselves amongst a great number of carts and waggons, driven by men of every nationality, three or four in a line, and stretching for the length of a league. We heard all round us, French, German, Spanish, Italian, Portuguese, and other languages also, for there were Muscovite peasants, among them, and a great number of Jews. This crowd of people, with their varied costumes and languages, the canteen masters with their wives, and crying children, hurried forward in the most unheard of noise, tumult, and disorder. Some had got their carts all smashed, and in consequence, yelled and swore enough to drive one mad. This was the convoy of the whole army, and we had a great deal of trouble in getting past it.

We marched by the Kalonga road (we were then in Asia); soon we stopped to bivouac in a wood for the rest of the night. As the hour was already far advanced, we had not long to rest.

We resumed our march at dawn, but before we had gone a league we again met a large party of the fatal convoy, which had passed us while we were asleep. Most of the carts were already shattered, and others could not move, the wheels sinking deep in the sandy road. We could hear screams in French, oaths in German, entreaties to the Almighty in Italian, and to the Holy Virgin in Spanish and Portuguese.

After getting past this babel we were forced to wait for the left of the column. I spent the time in making an examination of my knapsack, which seemed too heavy. I found several pounds of sugar, some rice, some biscuit, half a bottle of liqueur, a woman's Chinese silk dress, embroidered in gold and silver, several gold and silver ornaments, amongst them a little bit of the cross of Ivan the Great—at least, a piece of the outer covering of silver gilt, given me by a man in the company who had helped in taking it down. Besides these, I had my uniform, a woman's large riding cloak (hazel colour, lined with green velvet; as I could not guess how it was worn, I imagined its late owner to be more than six feet high): then two silver pictures in relief, a foot long and eight inches high; one of them represented the Judgement of Paris on Mount Ida, the other showed Neptune on a chariot formed by a shell, and drawn by sea-horses, all in the finest workmanship. I had, besides, several lockets and a Russian Prince's spittoon, set with brilliants. These things were intended for presents, and had been found in cellars where the houses were burnt down.

No wonder the knapsack was so weighty! to lighten it, therefore, I left out my white trousers, feeling pretty certain I should not want them again just yet. I wore over my shirt a yellow silk waistcoat, wadded inside, which I had made myself out of a woman's skirt; above that a large cape lined with ermine; and a large pouch hung at my side, underneath the cape, by a silver cord. This was full of various things—amongst them, a crucifix in gold, and silver, and a little

Chinese porcelain vase. These objects seemed to escape the general ruin by a sort of miracle, and I still keep them as relics. Then there were my powder-flask, my fire-arms, and sixteen cartridges in my cartridge-case. Add to all this a fair amount of health, good spirits, and the hope of presenting my respects to the Mongol, Chinese and Indian ladies I hoped to meet, and you will have a very good idea of the Velite sergeant of the Imperial Guard.

I had scarcely finished reviewing my treasures, when in front of us we heard a report of fire-arms; we were ordered to set off in double-quick time. We arrived half an hour afterwards at the place where part of the convoy, escorted by a detachment of red Lancers of the Guard, had been attacked by partisans. Several of the lancers were killed, also some Russians and many horses. Near a cart was a pretty woman, stretched on her back on the ground, killed by the shock. We marched on by a fairly good road, and stopped in the evening to bivouac in a wood.

Early the next morning, we resumed our march, and met at noon a party of Cossacks of the regular army. The artillery made short work of them. We marched for most of this day over fields, and at night encamped on the banks of a stream.

The church at Smolensk

I stopped, and, raising my head to listen better to the music, I saw a light in front of me. As I walked on towards the light, the road descended rapidly and the light disappeared. In spite of this, I continued, but was stopped almost directly by a wall in front of me, and was forced to retrace my steps. I turned first to the right, then to the left and found myself in a street of ruined houses. I strode on quickly, still guided by the music. At the end of the street there was a building lighted up, from which the sounds evidently came. There I was stopped by a wall surrounding the building which I now saw was a church.

Tired as I was, I wished to avoid going all round the wall to find an opening, and decided to climb over it, feeling the depth on the other side with my musket. As it was not more than three or four feet, I climbed to the top and jumped down, and striking some round object with my feet, I fell. I was not hurt, however, but on walking a few steps I felt the ground uneven under my feet, and had to steady myself with my musket. I then became aware of the fact that more than 200 dead bodies lay on the ground, barely covered with snow. As I stumbled along, picking my way among the legs and arms of the bodies, a melancholy chant arose—like the Office for the Dead. I broke out into a cold sweat, not knowing where I was and what I was about. I found myself at last leaning against the church wall.

I came to myself in a bit, in spite of the diabolical noise, and walked on with one hand against the wall, at length finding an open door through which came a thick smoke. I went in, and saw a great number of people, who in the dense smoke looked like shadows. Some of them were singing, and others playing on the organ. All at once a great flame burst forth and the smoke disappeared. I looked round to see where I was; one of the singers came up to me and cried out: 'It's our sergeant!' He had recognized my bearskin, and I saw, to my immense surprise, all the men of my company! I was on the point of questioning them when one of them offered me a silver cup full of brandy. They were all fearfully drunk!

One, rather less drunk than the others, said that they had been on extra duty when first they came, and that they had seen two men with a lantern coming out of a cellar; that they had banded together to go there after the distribution of rations, to see if they could find something to eat, and then spend the night in this church. In the cellar they had found a small cask of brandy, a bag of rice, and a little biscuit, besides ten capes trimmed with fur, and some Rabbis' fur caps.

With the men of the company were several musicians of the regiment, who had started playing the organ—being half seas over, as they say. This explained the harmony which had puzzled me so much.

They gave me some rice, a few pieces of biscuit, and a Rabbi's cap, trimmed with magnificent black fox fur. I put the rice carefully away in my knapsack. The cap I placed on my head, and pulling a plank in front of the fire, I lay down on it. I had scarcely laid my head on my knapsack when I heard shouts and curses from the door, so we hastened to see what was the matter. Six men were driving a cart drawn by a worn-out horse. The cart was filled with dead bodies to be left behind the church, with the others I had seen there. The ground was much too hard to dig graves, and the cold preserved the bodies in the meanwhile. These men told us that, if this sort of thing went on, there would soon be no room anywhere for the bodies; all the churches were used as hospitals, and were filled with the sick, whom it was impossible to help. This was the only church not full of them, and the dead had been laid here for the last few days. From the time that the column of the Grand Army had made its appearance, they had been unable to supply transport for the men who died as soon as they arrived. After hearing all this I lay down again. These ambulance men asked us if they might spend the rest of the night with us; they unharnessed their horse and brought him into the church.

I slept pretty well for the remainder of the night, but was awakened before daylight by the shrieks of an unfortunate musician, who had just broken his leg in coming down from the organ-loft, where he had slept. The men below had taken away some of the steps during the night to make a fire. The poor devil had a terrible fall. It was impossible for him to walk; most probably he never left the church. When I got up, nearly all the men were roasting meat on the points of their swords. I asked them where the meat came from, and they replied it was the horse who had drawn the dead-cart, and they had killed him while the ambulance men were asleep. I don't blame them for doing it; one must live somehow. An hour afterwards, when a good quarter of the horse had disappeared, one of the undertakers told his companions what we had done. They were furious, and threatened to inform the chief director of the hospitals. We went on eating calmly, saying it was a pity he was so thin, and that half a dozen like him would be wanted for rations for the regiment. They went off threatening us, and in revenge they threw the seven corpses they had in their cart right in the doorway, so that we were obliged to climb over them to get out.

These ambulance men had not been through the campaign, or felt the want of anything, and they did not know that for the last few days we had lived on any horses we could find.

When I got ready to go back to my regiment it was seven o'clock. I told the fourteen men that were there that they must collect together and arrive in good order. We first had some very good purée de cheval au riz. After that, giving them the bag containing the Jew's fur capes to carry, we left the church, which was already filling with new-comers—some miserable wretches who had spent the night where they could, and many others who had left their regiments, hoping to find something better. They prowled about in all the corners, looking for food. They did not seem to notice the dead bodies in the doorway, but walked over them as if they had been wood, so stiff were they frozen.

The Grand Army during the retreat

After the Grenadiers came more than 30,000 men, almost all with their feet and hands frozen, a great number of them without firearms, as they were quite unable to make use of them. Many of them walked leaning on sticks; generals, colonels, other officers, privates, men on horseback, men on foot, men of all the different nations making up our army, passed in a confused rabble, covered with cloaks and coats all torn and burnt, wrapped in bits of cloth, in sheepskins, in everything they could lay their hands on to keep out the cold. They walked silently without complaining, keeping themselves as ready as they could for any possible struggle with the enemy. The Emperor in our midst inspired us with confidence, and found resources to save us yet. There he was —always the great genius; however miserable we might be, with him we were always sure of victory in the end.

I had more than an hour to wait before the column had passed by, and after that there was a long train of miserable wretches following the regiments mechanically. They had reached the last stage of destitution, and could not hope to get across the Berezina, although we were now so near it. Then I saw the remains of the Young Guard skirmishers, flank men, and some of the light companies, escaped from Krasnoe. All these regiments mingled together marched in perfect order. Behind them came the artillery and several waggons. The bulk of the artillery, commanded by General Negre, had already gone before. Next came the Fusiliers-Chasseurs. Their numbers were greatly diminished. Our regiment was still separated from me by some pieces of artillery, drawn by poor beasts with no power left in them. After that I saw my regiment marching to left and right of the road to join the Fusiliers-Chasseurs. The adjutant-Major, Roustan, saw me the first, and cried out, 'Hallo, poor Bourgogne! Is that you? We thought you were dead behind us, and there you are alive in front! This is first rate. Have you met some of our men behind?' I told him that for the last three days I had been in the woods to avoid being taken by the Russians. Mr. Cesarisse said to the Colonel that he knew I had stayed behind since the 22nd, and that he was surprised beyond everything to see me again. My company came at last, and I took my own place in it before my friends were aware of it. They marched with their heads bent, their eyes fixed on the ground, hardly seeing anything; the frost and the bivouac fires had nearly ruined their sight.

A change of clothing

Considering my deplorable condition, I felt it would be impossible to walk further without changing my clothes. It may be remembered that in a portmanteau found on the mountain of Ponari I had some shirts and white cotton breeches—clothes belonging to an army commissary.

Having opened my knapsack, I drew out a shirt, and hung it on my musket, then the breeches, which I placed beside me on the tree. I took off my jacket and overcoat, and my waistcoat with the quilted yellow silk sleeves that I had made out of a Russian lady's skirt at Moscow. I untied the shawl which wrapped round my body, and my trousers fell about my heels. As for my shirt I had not the trouble of taking it off, for it had neither back nor front, I pulled it off in shreds. And there I was, naked, except for a pair of wretched boots, in the midst of a wild forest, at four o'clock in the afternoon with eighteen to twenty degrees of cold, for the north wind had begun to blow hard again.

On looking at my emaciated body, dirty, and, consumed with vermin, I could not restrain my tears. At last, summoning the little strength that remained, I set about my toilet. With snow and the rags of my old shirt I washed myself to the best of my power. Then I drew on my new shirt of fine longcloth, enbroidered down the front. I got into the little calico breeches as quickly as I could, but I found them so short that even my knees were not covered, and my boots only reaching half-way up my leg, all this part was bare. Finally I put on my yellow silk waistcoat, my riding jacket, my overcoat, over this my belts and collar, and there I was, completely attired, except for my legs.

The remnants of a regiment

A large-sized sledge, drawn by two powerful horses, passed close by us. It was going swiftly that we could not distinguish to what regiment the men in it belonged. In about half an hour's time we caught sight of a good house. It turned out to be a posting-station, and an inn also. There were several soldiers of the Guard at the door, setting out on sledges that had been procured for them.

We dismounted and entered, asking for wine, as we had been just told that there was plenty of it and very good. The men who told us seemed to have themselves partaken copiously; they were both in a state of wild gaiety. This happened to almost all those who, like ourselves, had endured so much misery and privation. The least amount of drink went to our heads. One of them asked us if we had met the regiment of Dutch Grenadiers who had formed a part of the Imperial Guard.

We said, 'No.'

'It passed you,' said the Velite, 'and yet you didn't see it? That big sledge that overtook you contined the entire Dutch regiment! There were seven of them!'

BOURGOGNE

16

DEFEAT

Defeat at Brihuega, 1710

ON MUNDAY the 27 of November, 1710, about 9 of the clock in the morning thare advance-gaurd did begin to appeare upon the mountaines looking at us, but yet we thought ourselves secure· enough & we had been if we had marcht out of the towne then, but our offecers livd so well besides all the money they got, if they did not make a great deal more for our skins, for there came a pisan to our commander & tould him that thare was coming up after the advance gaurds their whole army & that they would soone be with us with their traine. But our Genll said he was sure of it that thare was no enemie neare us that could harme us nor neare us that they card for, so put the poor pisan to prisson, but it is my thought that the offecers ought to have been thare themselves. Now I come to tell you of our vissetors for they begin to come faster, faster & fuller in sight, so abought 12 of the clock we had orders to saddel our horsses and to be in a readyness for to mount when ordered, which we did and at 3 o'clock we had orders to mount & to draw up in the castle yard, thinking still they could not harme us, but an hour before sunset their cannon did appear upon the hills and began to tell us what we must stand to.

They keept on playing & trundling their great shott at us until sunset and then we had orders to goe to our quarters but to keep in readyness, not much minding the danger, and at that time all the Horss & and the best of the Foot could safley have got off, but instead of that the foot was ordered to defend the walls & we eating & drinking & making as much of ourselves as we could, for we found what would be our portion by & by, though indeed our Genll Sanhope did send one of his aiddecamps to Genl Starinbourg to give him of the same, which lay on the other side of the river sum leagues from us, but (at) 10 of the clock at night they sent out another aidedecamp but by this time the enemie had secuerd all the passes that led to Genll Starinbourg, so that the aiddecamp could no more goe to him to let him know the full of the matter.

So on Tuesday the 28 of November 1710 we had all of us orders to make fassens and to carry them into the market place & then to goe with our armes in order to keep the enemie from comeing into the town. We presently did and we ware posted at a gate of the towne whare our offecers thought it to be the weakest of all the towne's and as the enemie knew, for they sit the gate on fire three times, but we did put it out as fast & keept them out to that degree that could not be well expected, considering we had no cannon to defend us nor to offend them, and we should have keept them out longer but now our ammunition began to be wanting that our men was forst to be carefull of it, and the enemie finding it made them the brisker & the boulder. Thus we keept defending ourselves so well as we could but there was a stallage (in English a public-house or inn) that joynd to the walls of the towne that our people knew not of but the pisans or ye people of the towne gave the enemie notice of it and how that they might come in to the towne so that by 3 or 4 of the clock in the afternoone great part of their army was got into the towne & houses and made holes in the walls of the houses & knockt us downe as fast as they could shoot. We blockt up the street that led into the market-place but it was all in vaine, for by this time the enemie began to march in all strets and we had no ammunition, it being all spent, [so] that they came up within a dozen yards of our bristwork and stood and look upon us. This was abought 9 of the clock at night and Genll Carpenter stod at the bristwork & it was supposed a muskit ball was shot from sum house afare off, for it was a dead ball and shott Carpenter in the mouth and just made the blood come, but I believe that that man that shott it had the curss of a great many men that the ball had no more force. But presently thare was orders for our drum-major to beet a parley, but it was not heard the first nor second time, but third time it was heard, and the enemie stod before all the time & and when the parly was heard they came to our breast work & talkd with us, for our Genlls had all the writings ready & the Duck of Vandome readily signed them. The conditions, as I understand, was that the offecers should march out with their swords on horseback with all their baggage & baggage horsses, and all the men to leave & lay down armes & to leave their horsses and to march out with all their close & linning, and this was all agreed on by 10 of the clock on the 28 of November in 1710, but it was said that the reason that we got so good quarters was that the enemie knew that our General Starimbourg was coming to our releiff but we did not know any thing of it.

A ROYAL DRAGOON IN THE SPANISH SUCCESSION WAR

Defeat at Waterloo, 18th June, 1815: the fight at Wavre

WE MARCHED forward at 3.0 p.m. crossed the three bridges and attacked Wavre. Horse and foot performed prodigies of valour. General Vandamme finally made himself master of the position. The battle was of little use to us, and made us lose 1,100 men. It did little honour to our generals, who seemed to be groping in the dark; and all day long we heard the cannon on our left, in the direction of Waterloo. We ceased to hear it about 10.0 p.m. Nothing can describe the uneasiness this cannonade caused us. The soldiers were melancholy, and had the presentiment of a misfortune. They boldly declared that the Emperor was beaten, because the sound of the cannon was always in the same direction. Contrary to my custom, I was sad also, but inwardly I was raging. (June 19th). We of the 30th at the outposts, were attacked at three in the morning by the troops of the Prussian General

Thielmann. General Pecheux sent us forward, and we surprised a Prussian guard of about 300 men, some of whom we bayoneted, and the rest we took prisoners. I was the last to cut and slash in the enemy's ranks, being enraged, and wanting to avenge myself, I did not know on whom, whilst cursing most of our generals, whom I considered traitors. This affair being over, we advanced noiselessly, and when daylight came, formed a line of skirmishers; then we fired on Messieurs the Prussians, who retired without making great resistance, towards Wavre and the woods, to draw us on. These boasters seemed to know of the disaster at Waterloo. Many of them, after having fired, retired, crying in German; 'Come along with us, brave Frenchmen. You have no army left; Napoleon is dead.' I, and several of my comrades who understood German, did not know what to think of these rumours.

Our generals gave few orders, and let the men shoot if they liked. Their conduct puzzled us. We took and retook Wavre several times, without being able to keep it. The Prussians came out of the woods, and our sharpshooters fell back. Many of the officers had retired to the divisions, and the men were fighting without any leaders. About 1 o'clock in the afternoon, the generals sent for the superior officers, for the soldiers were grumbling, saying they had been betrayed, for they had noticed that, since the previous evening, no cannon had been heard in the direction of Brussels. Was the Emperor beaten?

At 2.30 p.m. orders were given to cease firing. The enemy's fire also ceased.

FRANÇOIS

Return home after defeat: Richmond, Va., 1865

TWO foot-sore, despondent, and penniless men stood facing the ruins of the home of a comrade who had sent a message to his mother. 'Tell mother I am coming.' The ruins yet smoked. A relative of the lady whose home was in ashes, and whose son said, 'I am coming' stood by the survivors. 'Well, then,' he said, 'it must be true that General Lee has surrendered.' The solemnity of the remark, coupled with the certainty in the minds of the survivors, was almost amusing. The relative pointed out the temporary residence of the mother, and thither the survivors wended their way.

A knock at the door startled the mother, and, with agony in her eyes she appeared at the open door, exclaiming, 'My poor boys!'—'Are safe, and coming home,' said the survivors. 'Thank God!' said the mother and the tears flowed down her cheeks.

A rapid walk through the ruined and smoking streets, some narrow escapes from negro soldiers on police duty, the satisfaction of seeing two of the 'boys in blue' hung up by their thumbs for pillaging, a few hand-shakings, and the survivors found their way to the house of a relative where they did eat bread and with thanks.

A friend informed the survivors that farm hands were needed all around the city. They made a note of the name of one farmer. Saturday night, the old blankets were spread on the parlor floor. Sunday morning, the 16th of April, they bid farewell to the household, and started for the farmer's house.

As they were about to start away, the head of the family took from his pocket a handful of odd silver pieces, and extending it to his guests, told them it was all he had, but they were welcomed to half of it! Remembering that he had a wife and three or four children to feed, the soldiers smiled through their tears at him, bade him keep it all, and weep for himself rather than for them. So saying, they departed, and at sundown were at the farmer's house, fourteen miles away. Monday morning, the 17th they 'beat their swords' (muskets, in this case) into plow-shares, and did the first day's work of the sixty which the simple farmer secured at a cost to himself of about half rations for two men. Behold the gratitude of people!

MCCARTHY

Disaster at Biddulphsberg, May, 1900 (by Trooper F. J. B. Lee, captured there)

WHEN nearing Senekal I was despatched to the main body with a message, and reached Senekal about three hours after the company had entered the town. On my arrival about 1.30 p.m. I found that pickets had been placed in the town as well as on the hill on the Bethlehem Road, which overlooked Senekal from the Biddulphsberg direction. While the destruction of surrendered arms was in progress, firing commenced to our rear, near the road by which I had just entered the town, and directly after a cossak post came in with the report that the enemy were in force in that direction.

Thirty of our men were out in many directions around the town and a similar number were in the town under the command of Major Dalbiac and Lieutenant Kennard.

The Major, to whom I at once reported myself, sent an order to Lieutenant Kennard for him to join forces immediately and attack the enemy in the direction from which the firing was heard.

It suddenly ceased however, but immediately broke out on the hill, east of the town.

As we wheeled about and extended to gallop up the hill, the side of which was both rocky and steep, the firing at our rear again commenced, and the 'sign' of the bullets with the little spurts of dust around us, told of good practice. Owing to the utter impossibility of scaling the almost inaccessible hillside with anything approaching proper formation, some reached the tabletop before others, among the first being the Major.

My horse was a good climber, so even though I had to go crab-fashion awhile to get up, I was about the sixth after him. Several horses fell during this scrambling climb and four men were hit.

With even so few as had successfully made the ascent, the Major ordered the advance at the gallop, with the object of holding the hill-top. I glanced round and saw poor Shells, my sergeant, walking, for his horse had come down. Immediately he was shot in the back. The short crack of the Mauser seemed now general on all sides, while the musical 'ping' of the bullet was incessant.

A sharp gallop brought us right upon the enemy, who were coming over the further crest in a group, dismounted. My first sight of the enemy was one leading three horses, two of them being greys. I remember this, for the thought of how, in contrast to them, we had coloured our white horses with Condy's crossed my mind as I dismounted to fire. Had we been cavalry at that moment, armed with sword or lance, our sudden appearance having doubtless surprised them, our pace would have taken us through and through them.

'Hold the hill!' cried the Major; but as the group of Boers in front fell behind the cover of the crest-line of rocks, they opened point blank on us. Our effective strength was about twenty, and on our left flank, we were raked by the enemy at short range. Sergeant Meek, who had been through the Afghan and Chitral campaigns, had by now succeeded in getting to the hill-top, and almost immediately had his horse shot; he however, succeeded in getting a stray Boer pony, but had not proceeded ten yards when that also was shot.

The Major was the first to fall, shot dead through the neck; then poor old Dean, who that morning had got his commission, and who was firing from the knee.

Personally, I was crawling between shots to an ant hill, my mare being led by the reins round my left wrist. She stood perfectly still, and at the finish was untouched.

Our remaining officer, Lieutenant Kennard, was shot through the face and leg, and exposed as we were, men were hit one after another until thirteen were left.

Seeing we were surrounded in an untenable position without supports, further resistance was thought by the Lieutenant, who had handed the command over to Sergt. Tomlin, not only to be hopeless against such odds, but a useless further sacrifice of life.

Thirteen of us laid down our arms, after which I was allowed, under escort, to go to one part of our position to bring away greatcoats and blankets off the dead horses. The Major was lying chest downwards with his face on one side, while Dean, who still wore his spectacles, was huddled in a heap.

With Sergeant Meek, I obtained the Major's wristwatch to give to his relatives should we reach England, but it was demanded from us by a Boer, to whom we handed it. In the aager to which we were taken, however, we mentioned the matter to the Commandant, who ordered its return to Sergt Meek. Having collected as many coats and blankets, and helmets, as I could carry, for we had discarded the last-named whilst firing, I rejoined my comrades.

A dozen horses were shot, some sitting on their haunches, being wounded in their hindquarters, while others were vainly trying to rise. These poor brutes were forthwith killed.

The wounded were left for the Boer ambulance, while we were marched away under strong escort towards Biddulphsberg. What our feelings were few who have not been under similar circumstances can know. Where is C? What has become of T? Who saw O last? These questions in the main eliciting doubtful or unsatisfactory replies, the thirteen surviving prisoners of the war of the 34th Company Imperial Yeomanry trudged slowly, heavily laden in mind and body, to their first night's resting place in an enemy's laager.

MOFFETT

Scots Guards at Biddulphsberg, May, 1900

We arose shortly after 4, and having received orders to be ready to move off at any moment, partook of a hasty breakfast, consisting of half a pint of coffee minus sugar and milk, and a small cake, whose sole ingredients were flour and water.

By 4.30 we were ready, although we did not move off until 7, having to pace up and down in a biting, frosty wind for two or three hours to keep warm.

Our force was directed by General Rundle, and consisted of General Campbell's Brigade, viz, the 2nd Grenadier Guards, 2nd Scots Guards, and the 2nd East Yorks, strengthened by the 2nd Royal West Kents. The mounted troops were under the command of Colonel Blair, and the Artillery comprised the 2nd and 79th Batteries of R.F.A., under the command of Colonel Pratt.

The ground over which we had to march was covered by a dense growth of tall dried grass of a very inflammable nature. In the distance huge volumes of smoke were rising from fired grass, through which we were shortly to pass. In addition to this parched vegetation, were considerable patches of mealies, the results of native industry, which, when fired, speedily became a charred desolation.

A straggling march of about five or six miles soon brought us to the Boer stronghold—Biddulphsberg. Field glasses were soon at work scrutinising the slopes and rocky faces of the mountain, but not a single Boer could be seen. However, the guns were unlimbered and were quickly searching its kloofs and seams with shrapnel, but failed to reveal the fact that the Boer position was still strongly held.

Many were the speculations as to whether the enemy had withdrawn during the night—a favourite Boer dodge—or whether they were keeping out of sight with the object of laying a trap and encouraging an unwary advance. Evidently General Rundle suspected their presence in spite of their absolute silence.

The veldt was now burning for miles round, and with the wind veering, the flames were carried fiercely and rapidly towards the kopje. Much has been said about the careless dropping of pipe-lights—this may have been the case—but from what I observed the veldt seemed to have been fired very early in the morning, and we had to traverse large areas of already blackened, and burned veldt.

For a while we halted under cover of a mealie field, while the artillery searched every likely place on the face of the mountain. It was now seen that an attack was to be made.

The 2nd Grenadiers under Colonel Lloyd were ordered to move forward in attack formation, while the 2nd Scots Guards under Colonel Romilly and the West Kents were to support them. At the same time, the 2nd Battery opened fire on the farm to the north-east of the Berg, which had flown the white flag the previous day, and from which place the two Driscoll's Scouts had been hit. Scarcely had the order been given for the Grenadiers to advance when shells in quick succession came from the Boer gun above the farm; this appeared to be the signal for the enemy's rifle fire to commence, and our first casualty was Drummer Clark, shot through the wrist.

Meanwhile the Boers were pelting shell after shell over our heads, presumably at the field batteries to our rear. The 2nd

Battery was concentrating the fire from four of its guns on to this Boer gun in the cattle kraal, but not being successful in silencing it, the 29th Battery was ordered up, with better results.

By this time the flames had reached us, so that we were obliged to rush through the zone of flames which shot up some five or six feet high. The enemy's fire increased, and many were shot down whilst in the act of rushing through the flames, Numbers too of the wounded were lying helpless on the ground, and were caught by the advancing flames. Their cries for help were most heartrending.

For a while the Boers concentrated their attention on our transport, which had evidently misjudged the range, for they speedily retired in some confusion to a safe distance.

Men were now falling fast, and amidst the deafening roar of rifle and artillery fire, stretcher bearers were busy carrying their ghastly loads of dead and dying through the dense clouds of smoke, to the field dressing-stations far to the rear.

The scenes on the battlefield at this stage were beyond description for several minutes together, Biddulphsberg was enveloped in dense rolling volumes of smoke, and at frequent intervals wounded men, with pallid and blood besmirched faces, passed through the firing line. Those able to walk were holding their helmets over the faces of their more helpless stretcher-borne comrades, to shield them from the fierce flames through which they had to pass. Now and again the stretchers contained a motionless figure, and the coarse brown army blanket drawn kindly over the face told its own message. The work of the singed and scorched stretcher bearers became so great that the fatal cases had to be left on the field, and were ultimately brought away in the presence of the Boers, long after the troops had retired.

During the height of the action, Colonel Lloyd was badly wounded, and was gallantly attended by Drummer Haines, who, while in the act of supporting his colonel, was also himself badly wounded.

By this time the fire had extended to the foot of the Berg, and the ground occupied by the troops was charred, thereby shewing up the khaki uniforms most conspicuously; the wonder is that, during the many hours we were required to lie under fire under these conditions our casualty list was not much heavier.

Towards sundown the order came to retire, and as the troops began moving off to the right the enemy opened fire with renewed vigour; indeed, during this period the majority of the casualties occurred; perhaps the most deadly fire came from a donga which encircled the base of the kopje. The whole retirement was admirably and coolly carried out, the troops moving off the field as if on parade. The artillery covered the retirement, and throughout the time searched the scars and seams of the mountain with common shell and shrapnel, altogether firing some eight hundred rounds.

When the Grenadiers had retired out of the zone of fire, it was afterwards discovered that several of their wounded had been left on the burning veldt. It is scarcely necessary to add that the sufferings of these poor fellows was too horrible to contemplate. Lieut. Quilter of the Grenadiers, therefore, took about twenty men, who had volunteered from his company, to the rescue of their helpless comrades, and although subjected to heavy fire, succeeded in bringing them safely away.

After Lieutenant Quilter and his heroic comrades had completed their task, it was reported that there were still wounded on the burning veldt. Private Daniels rushed back and succeeded in bringing another wounded comrade out of further danger, although the attempt cause him to be badly burned. In fact, there were countless acts of heroism during the day, and the Victoria Cross was won over and over again by the gallantry of many an unchronicled act.

MOFFETT

17

WOUNDED AND SICK

Ramillies, 1706: wounded by a shell

I ESCAPED unhurt, though in the hottest of the battle, till the French were entirely defeated; when an unlucky shell from a steeple, on which, before the battle, they had planted some mortars and cannon, which played all the time of the engagement, struck the back part of my head and fractured my skull. I was carried to Meldre, or Meldert, a small town in the quarter of Louvain, two leagues south-east from that university, and five leagues north-west from Ramillies, upon a small brook which washes Tirlemont. I was here trepanned, and great care taken of me, but I did not recover in less than ten weeks. Though I suffered great torture by this wound, yet the discovery it caused of my sex, in the fixing of my dressing, by which the surgeons saw my breasts, and, by the largeness of my nipples, concluded I had given suck, was a greater grief to me. No sooner had they made this discovery, but they acquainted Brigadier Preston, that his pretty dragoon (so I was always called) was, in fact, a woman. He was very loath to believe it, and did me the honour to say, he had always looked upon me as the prettiest fellow, and the best man he had. His incredulity made him send for my brother, whom he now imagined to be my husband; when he came, the brigadier said to him, 'Dick, I am surprised at a piece of news these gentlemen tell me; they say, your brother is, in reality, a woman.' 'Sir,' said he, 'since she she is discovered, I cannot deny it; she is my wife, and I have had three children by her.' The news of this discovery spread far and near, and reaching, among others, my Lord John Hay's ear, he came to see me, as did all my former comrades. My lord would neither ask me, nor suffer any one else, any questions; but called for my husband, though first for my comrade, who had been long my bedfellow, and examined him closely. The fellow protested, as it was truth, that he never knew I was a woman, or even suspected it; 'It is well known,' continued he, 'that she had a child lain to her, and took care of it.' My lord then calling in my husband, desired him to tell the meaning of my disguise. He gave him a full and satisfactory account of our first acquaintance, marriage, and situation, with the manner of his having entered into the service, and my resolution to go in search of him; adding the particulars of our meeting, and my obstinate refusal of bedding with him. My lord seemed very well entertained with my history, and ordered that I should want for nothing and that my pay should be continued while under cure.

MOTHER ROSS

Hit but unhurt, March 1801 (*Egypt*)

AFTER we had fired about 12 rounds, whilst I was in the act of loading, I was struck by a musket ball in the left side, near the pit of the stomach, close to the ribs, and was whirled round on my heels by the force of the stroke. I was stunned, and felt great pain; and, concluding that I was wounded, I stept to the rear, and grasped the place with my hand. I found that the skin was entire, and on shaking myself, the ball dropped at my feet. I then resumed my place in the ranks, and continued to fire until I had expended 22 rounds.

'G.B.'

Wounded in action, 1801 (*Egypt*)

I HAD fired about twelve rounds, when the sun was beginning to appear in the horizon, and was in the act of ramming another cartridge, when a shot from one of the sharpshooters, struck upon the inner ankle bone of my left foot; it turned round the back of the leg, passing between the sinew of the heel and the leg bone, and lodged just under the skin, a little above the bone of the outer ankle. It was there that I felt the pain. I was stunned with the stroke; but from the part in which I felt the pain, I did not think it was a ball, but that a large shot or shell, having struck some of the stones that were lying in the rear, a splinter from them had hit me in the back of the leg; I loaded my piece, and then, on lifting up my leg to see what was the matter, saw a musket-shot hole in the half-gaiter and some appearance of blood. I shouldered my piece; but the sharp-shooters directly in front of me had disappeared. I stood a few seconds unresolved what to do; but feeling the pain increase, and seeing the blood beginning to appear more on the gaiter, and the officer commanding the company having come to the rear, and observing that I was wounded, he called to me to fall out, and I was induced to leave the ranks, but felt very reluctant to quit my comrades before the battle was decided; not that I loved to stay in a place of danger; but I did not like to leave them in the time of it; and had there been firing at the time, I should have continued to fire while I was able. As matters stood, however, I conceived it to be my duty, seeing I was disabled from keeping my place in the ranks, to make the best of my way, as long as I was able, to a place where I might be out of the reach of shot, and get my wound dressed, that it might not receive injury by delay. I got as quickly as I could to the rear, keeping my arms, accoutrements, and knapsack which I had on when wounded.

'G.B.'

Medical treatment, 1801 (Egypt)

THE part of my wound where the ball entered healed in about sixteen days; but the part where it was extracted became inflamed, and the foot and ankle swelled considerably. I was suspicious that the dirty water with which it was sometimes washed was the occasion of the inflammation. An erroneous opinion was entertained, that salt water would smart the wounds; and as fresh water was not in plenty on board the ship, only a small quantity of it was allowed for washing them. A great number were washed with one basin-full, and, as many of the wounds were foul, this was calculated to infect those that were clean. Had salt water been used, a basin of clean water might have been taken to every one. I was washed with salt water when in the hospital at Aboukir, and felt no difference between it and fresh. By the end of three weeks, my wound began to mortify. I was then put into a boat to be taken to the hospital at Aboukir, along with a number more whose cases were considered bad. Two were so weak that they were unable to sit, and were laid upon gratings in the bottom of the boat; one of them died before we reached the shore, and the other died upon the beach. These cases made little impression upon my mind; death was becoming familiar to me, and I looked at it with a careless indifference. When the boat reached the shore I was carried to the Hutts hospital; which was a building upon a height, erected by the French to serve as barracks to their troops stationed at Aboukir. It was formed of the trunks of date trees split down the middle, the ends were sunk into the ground; the flat side of one tree, was turned outwards, and the flat side of the next inwards, and so on alternately, the round edges being made to overlap each other and the crevices filled with plaster lime. It was roofed in the same manner. A great many bats had formed their nests in holes, where the roof rested upon the upright posts. Here I was well taken care of; so that by the mercy of God, the inflammation subsided, and in sixteen days the putrid flesh was wholly cleaned away, leaving a pretty large orifice. A part of the tendon of the heel seemed to have been eaten away by the inflammation, but the damage did not appear to be very serious, and it began to heal rapidly.

'G.B.'

Wounded: the Wilderness, 1864

AT THE critical moment of the first day's battle in the Wilderness, when brave Sergeant Crocker had gallantly carried our colors out into the open field, just as Major Spear received the order to retreat, I was wounded, a minié-ball passing through my left ankle. It is impossible to describe the sensations experienced by a person when wounded for the first time. The first intimation I had that I was wounded was my falling upon the ground. My leg was numb to my body, and for a moment I fancied that my foot had been carried away; but I soon learned the true condition of my situation. Our regiment was rapidly retreating, and the rebels as rapidly advancing. The forest trees around me were on fire, and the bullets were falling thick and fast. If I remained where I was, the most favourable result that I could hope for was captivity, which, in reality, would be worse than death by the bullet on the field.

I stood up, and, to my joy, found that my leg was not entirely useless. I could step with it, and so long as it remained straight I could bear my weight upon it, but when bent at the knee it refused to bear me up, and I would fall to the ground. Under existing circumstances I determined to retreat. I threw off all my baggage and equipments, and turned my face toward the line of breastworks, which we had that morning built. Fear lent wings to my flight, and away I dashed. Frequently my wounded leg refused to do good service, and as a result I would tumble headlong upon the ground, then rising, I would rush on again, and I doubt if there has been a champion on the sawdust track in Maine for the last five years who has made such a record of speed as I made on that retreat through the Wilderness. In my haste I did not keep so far to my right as I should have done, and consequently was obliged to cross over the lower end of the field over which we had made our charge. It was a sad spectacle, that lonely field in the forest. Here and there a wounded man was limping painfully to the rear; dead men, and others wounded too severely to move, were scattered thickly upon the ground.

As I was crossing the lower corner of the field, to my surprise and horror the rebel line of battle came out on its upper edge, some quarter of a mile from where I was running. Almost at the same moment the rebels appeared in the field, a Union officer, whom I have always supposed to be General Bartlett, our brigade commander, also came out into the field not twenty rods from the rebel line. He was on horseback; not a staff officer was with him; his uniform was torn and bloody; blood was trickling from several wounds in his face and head; he had evidently been up to discover why our line of battle had not connected with the Sixth corps. The rebels saw him, the moment he emerged from the forest, and called upon him to surrender, while a wild yell rang along their line as they saw their fancied prize. But they did not know the man with whom they had to deal. Shaking his fist at them in defiance, he put spurs to his horse and dashed away. He was a target for every rifle in the rebel line. Five hundred guns were pointed at him, and five hundred bullets whistled around him, the enemy pursuing as they fired. It was a brilliant ride for life, with all the odds against the daring rider. Bravely he rode in the midst of that storm, as if death had no terror for him. His steed was a noble animal, and at a three minute gait bore his master from his pursuers. Each seemed to bear a charmed life. Over one-half the distance across that field had been passed, and yet the rider sat erect upon the steed that was bearing him onward with such tremendous speed. A deep ditch must be crossed before they could gain the cover of the forest. A ditch dug many years before, five or six feet deep, and ten or twelve in width. The rebels knew the ditch was there, and sent up a wild yell of delight, as they fancied the officer would be delayed in crossing, and so fall into their hands. The horse and rider evidently saw the obstacle at the same moment and prepared to meet it. Firmly the rider sat in his saddle, and gathered the reins of his horse with a firm hand. I never beheld a nobler spectacle than that presented by the gallant steed—his nostrils dilated, his ears pointed forward, his eyes seeming to flash with the fire of conscious strength as he made the fearful leap. For a moment I thought they were safe, but rebel bullets pierced the horse, and turning a complete somersault he fell stone dead, burying his rider beneath him as he fell. Again the rebels cheered and rushed on, but to my surprise, the officer, with the assistance of a few wounded soldiers, extricated himself from his dead horse, ran across the edge of the field, and made his escape. I also entered the woods and continued to run at the top of my speed until I reached the breastworks, where I found our line of battle. I passed beyond these and went back a mile or more to our division hospital in the rear.

GERRISH

Enteric fever: South Africa

IT WAS on the march to Johannesburg that I fell a victim to enteric fever, and was sent down to Springfontein with about two dozen others packed in open coal trucks like sardines, but we were beyond caring. We were all desperately in need of something to drink. When we arrived at Springfontein several 'turned it in' and were buried there. We were issued with a tin of condensed milk between eight of us, although I saw an N.C.O. of the C.I.V.s, probably in charge of supplies, having no illness at all and in his full prime of life, enjoying a tin all to himself, in which he had made two holes and was sucking the milk through one of them with as much enjoyment as a bee sucking honey.

Being now so used to half rations and quarter rations, we got into the habit of saying grace after we had finished our meals. We used to say:

We'll thank the Lord for what we've had,
If it were more we should have been glad.
But as the times are rather bad,
We've got to be glad with what we've had.

On arriving at our next station down the line we were encamped in small marquees, about ten in each. We lost quite a number of men at this hospital, one or another being carried out each morning, having died during the night. I happened to be blessed with a good sense of humour, always joking, no matter what happened (probably the result of hard training when young), always saying to myself, 'Thank goodness it is no worse.' One morning, as another poor fellow in the next bed to me said 'You'll be the next,' I turned my head to him and replied, 'Not while you're there, Jock,' and sure enough he turned slightly green in the night and would not stay in bed, so the orderlies tied him to the bed with sheets. But he had gone in the morning, I was the lucky one and managed to pull through, and when convalescent, was sent down the line to Cape Town.

All my belongings had disappeared in the field hospital except my watch and chain in my belt strapped under my shirt, or that might also have disappeared, and my kilt wrapped in some old newspapers. The civilians at the railway stations where we stopped were very kind, bringing us cups of tea, sandwiches, biscuits etc., for which we were very grateful.

The civilians pestered us for 'souvenirs', 1s. being offered for a 2d cap badge, collar ornaments etc., I was very desperate, being away from my regiment, and having no money, what was I to do? I suddenly had a bright idea, as one young fellow, eager for some sort of souvenir, asked me if I could find him anything. I remembered my old kilt wrapped in some old newspapers on the luggage rack, and replied, 'I have only my tartan kilt left.' He pushed his head through the carriage window and excitedly exclaimed, 'I will give you 10s. for it.' I carefully concealed my eagerness to part with it and said, 'Very well then.' He handed me the 10s. and I gave him the kilt, which he tucked under his arm and went joyously on his way, little dreaming that he was the possessor not only of a kilt, but millions of 'visitors' hidden in the pleats. At this time I cannot help feeling ashamed of this act, but on looking back I must remind you that at the time, hungry and penniless, nature knows no law.

CORBETT

18

PRISONER OF WAR

Prisoner in Spain, 1710

On Wednesday ye 19 of November in year of our Lord 1710 we all orderd to march with a strong party of Horss to gaurd us & indeed the offecers marcht according to the articles agreed on, with their horsses and their swords & their pistols, but as they never did regaurd the men so now we found to our cost the truth of it, for they being on horssback & we on foot they marcht so fast that we ware in a manner to run after them, & the regments of Foot that was drawne up on both sides of the street, as we marcht over our dead men that layd on purpose, they catch hould of us and take our baggs & what was in them, and our cloaks. As for our clothes that was on our backs was not worth the takeing, and our offecers keept on marching with the Horss that was to gaurd us & we had to march up a very high hill and thare stod sum tents standing and one of their offecers servants came out & lookt on us and said in Spainish language 'the flower of the world is taken today. What had your offecers apeace for you?'. I heard him speak it. So when we had got up the hill they marcht us allong, full 7 English leagues and whent by villages where thare was water but they would not let us have a drop and at last we came to our journey's end for that night to Guardolaharro, which is the name of the towne we had bene there before, when they bare armes. They used us very basely: they run lighted straw in our faces & firebrand and cursing our Queene and us, & we ware forced to run to keep up with our gaurds & them that could not keep up they stript & and if they had no money nor linning, which was taken away before by the army, then they would beat them & strip them naked & them that was so served was forst to take it pacienly, though we would have wished it otherways.

A ROYAL DRAGOON IN THE SPANISH SUCCESSION WAR

After Saratoga: a prisoner of the Americans

ON THE morning of the 17th of October [1777, at Saratoga] we surrendered, and in the evening crossed the Hudson river from Saratoga on our march to Boston. From the outset of our marching we experienced much hardship, sleeping in barns, and having but bad clothing, and scanty provisions. The way before and about us presented an uncheering appearance, mountainous and barren, with little of pleasing scenery to amuse the traveller. In our progress we crossed the ridge of mountains called Blue Hills, which begin in New Hampshire, and extend through a long tract of country in New England. Hadley was the first place we arrived at, which had any local attractions to delight the eye. It is a pleasant town of Hampshire County Massachusetts, on the east of Connecticut river. It then consisted of one extensive and spacious street parallel to the river.

In the Summer of 1778, we were marched by order of Congress from Prospect-hill to Rutland county, which is distant about 50 Miles from Boston.

Seeing that Congress had no intention of allowing the British troops to return to England, according to the articles of convention, and considering myself under no tie of honour, as I gave no parole (though at that time I was employed as temporary surgeon to the 9th regiment) I resolved to proceed privately to New York. This resolution was confirmed by my meeting at some distance from Prospect-hill, a native of America, for whom I did a kind office, after the battle of Fort-

Anne, and from whom I then received an invitation to take refreshment in an adjacent tavern together with a promise of a pasport, which might prevent my being apprehended by the way. Unfortunately there were at that time in the tavern, a few British soldiers who did some damage in the house, and got off without paying for it. The landlord raised the hue and cry against me, although I was in another apartment when the damage was done. He demanded a recompense of 40 dollars to repair his losses, though a small matter, was sufficient to compensate his loss, which consisted but in the breaking of a few drinking glasses.

Having had no part whatever in the affair I naturally refused to comply, and was in consequence taken before a magistrate. However they took the law first into their own hands, as it was agreed that I should run the gauntlet to the magistrate's house, which was about 100 yards from the tavern. Providentially for me the tavern was on a rising ground, and the way I had to run was down a hill which accelerated my motion, so that I received but few blows, although there were a number of persons aiming to strike me as I passed. When I arrived before the magistrate, he in the most unfeeling manner, without hearing my defence, declared if I did not forthwith pay down 40 dollars, he would order me to the prison-ship in Boston, where I should be fed on bread and water. I persisted in declaring I had no part in the outrage, and challenged any person to come forward and prove it against me. My plea was rejected, and to the prison ship I was told I must go, unless I paid the mulct immediately. This I still objected to do. After some consultation among themselves, it was determined that I should run the gauntlet again, which punishment I underwent of course, a number of men taking sticks in their hands, to deal blows at me.

It was an unpleasant atonement on my part for the transgression of others, but I saw I could not avoid it. I was brought to the door and held till my enemies were each man prepared for striking me. The word was given that all was ready, and I was let go from the grasp of the men that held me. I therefore darted along the line with rapidity, and being young and active, I do think, I did not receive in all more than a dozen strokes by reason of their confusion and eagerness to deal blows upon my unprotected head, which by agility and good heels I succeeded in saving. They did not pursue me, and by my rapid marching I was enabled to join my companions. However I felt my body and head sore for many days afterwards.

I before observed that British prisoners were severely ill-treated by the American Soldiery and people. This was in general the case. In a guard-house in Fredrick town, Maryland, where I was confined during the rigours of winter without any bedding, or covering at night except some straw, which the centinels used to take delight in setting fire to, as I endeavoured to sleep, I found my treatment so miserable that I memorialed the officer commanding to have me removed to the common jail. The prayer of my petition was granted, but I was alike ill-used, and probably would have been released by death anterior to my liberation, had not some poor prisoners divided with me their jail allowance of provisions.

SERJEANT LAMB

Prisoner: Turkish attack on a French flag of truce, 1799

IN LESS than six minutes we were all thrown from our dromedaries, trodden under foot by the horses of these barbarians, and half the detachment killed or wounded. The Captain was amongst the number. The firing brought up other bands of these brigands; a detachment of English arrived, and saw the flag of truce which one of the brigands was carrying off. The officer who commanded the detachment had the greatest difficult in stopping the carnage, though he was assisted by some of the Turkish officers. The skirmish ceased. The Turks, seeing their error, made off, carrying several heads of our men with them, and dragging me along, with two other men of my detachment.

I received a lot of bruises, one of which, on the left shoulder, was due to a fall from my dromedary. I had also a few slight wounds from lances, and a couple of sabre-cuts on the head, which cut through several folds of my turban, also a few knocks from the horses' feet. One of my comrades had received a dagger-stab in the arm, and some bruises. The other was seriously wounded with several sabre-cuts, and a pistol ball in the side.

I was so dazed that at first I felt nothing of my bruises, and we arrived at El-Kanka before I thought about them. There we were surrounded by hundreds of barbarians, several of whom took the heads of seven of our dead comrades, and presented them to us, and insulted us. One of my comrades wept, but I had not the strength to do even that. The other lay on his face on the ground; he was dying.

Two hours after our arrival at El-Kanka, my comrades and I were led to the tent of one of the chief officers of the Grand Vizier's army. The other man could not move. The Ottoman officer put some questions to us through an interpreter. I had been less mauled than my comrade, and having recovered my senses, I told the officer about our mission and the officer we escorted. He did not appear to believe it, but, however, he told the men to take care of us, and give us some food, and we were lodged near his tent. In the evening, they gave us each a black biscuit, some rice, and water; and we passed the night amidst the guard, who asked us so many questions that I could get no rest, and the night appeared endless. I was deep in thought, could not believe the reality of what had happened, and wondered what would be the upshot of it all. My second comrade was not brought before the officer, for he had not the strength to move. I believe he died, for I never heard of him again.

FRANÇOIS

Captured in action: Bergen-op-Zoom, 1813

LIEUTENANT COLONEL J——, not daunted, formed the few of us that he had still by him; but no sooner was this done, than the enemy's column appeared, and seeing that it was in vain to resist, our little band dispersed, and flew to such places for shelter as the impulse of the moment directed them. Some that could not get into the houses were killed or wounded. I, along with some more, got into a house where we found Colonel Clifton mortally wounded, lying in a corner, attended by two serjeants; round the stove were the afflicted family sitting. I had time to notice no more, before a French marine came in, blustering, and ordering us to throw down our arms and accoutrements. He then turned us out of doors into the street which was found covered with broken muskets, accoutrements, and ammunition. There were some killed or wounded lying, but, to the honour of the enemy, there were none of our party killed but such as were obstinate, and would not lay down their arms quickly, when ordered to do so.

The noise and confusion around, and the indignation I felt at being a prisoner, when thinking upon nothing but victory, hindered me from noticing things as I ought to have done.

I had not looked long about me before I was hurried into a large room on the opposite side of the street, apparently a back kitchen; here we were left till the place was nearly filled with British prisoners. In the mean time we could hear the work of destruction going on in other parts of the town, and we hoped to be rescued; but our hope soon vanished upon the French ordering us into the street, where they commanded us to form, and then marched us to the guard-house in the great square, where we were lodged, and put under the care of some gendarmes. It was some time before I could persuade myself that I actually was a prisoner; but, finding it to be a reality and that it would be of no use to take it to heart, I sat down, and had some discourse with one of them, who seemed to be a good-natured fellow. He told me he was an Italian by birth, and had been for some time in the French service, which he liked well. Shortly after Lieutenant Colonel J—— came in, accompanied by a French officer, apparently of rank, requesting all that were wounded to follow him, on purpose to have their wounds dressed. I noticed the Lieutenant Colonel's epaulettes were gone, probably torn off when taken prisoner. There likewise came into the place women with provisions for sale, at which we were not a little astonished, having previously understood that they were in a starving condition.

In this state we continued till morning, when we were sent to the church; where we found several hundreds of British prisoners already lodged. The French soldiers, as we marched along, generally felt our pockets, and took out what best pleased them! Some of our men, indignant at such usage, appealed to the French officers that happened to be near, who shrugged their shoulders, significantly meaning that they could not do anything for the poor fellows thus robbed. I escaped without the loss of anything; what silver I had with me, I had previously put in my shoes or secret pockets; neither took they any thing out of my canteen or haversack. As an individual, I have nothing to lay to their charge, but certainly received the best of such usage as they were able to give. But, after all, I felt such curious sensations, when I reflected that yesterday's sun had witnessed me a free, but to-day a bond-man; however, finding this reflection to be of no avail, and seeing that I could not mend the matter, I reconciled myself to my lot, and therefore put on an air of cheerfulness, as I found the rest had done.

During this time the French were busy in marching prisoners from all quarters to the church,—a mortifying sight, truly.

MEULLER

A 17th Lancer at Balaclava

AFTER the Heavies' charge the Light Brigade was moved a little way 'left back' and then forward, down into the middle of the upper part of the outer valley, and fronting straight down it, the Heavies remaining a little in advance to the right about the crest of the Causeway Ridge. We stood halted in those positions for about three quarters of an hour, Lord Cardigan in front of his brigade, Lord Lucan on our right front about midway between the two brigades. I may here describe the composition of the first line of the Light Brigade and my own particular place therein. On the right were the 13th Light Dragoons (now Hussars) in the centre of the 17th Lancers, on the left the 11th Hussars, which latter regiment before the charge began was ordered back in support, so that during the charge the first line consisted only of the 13th Light Dragoons and the 17th Lancers. All three regiments were but of two squadrons each; the formation of course was two deep. I belonged to the right troop of the 1st (the right) squadron of the 17th Lancers; my squadron leader being Captain (now General) R. White, my troop leader Captain Morgan, now Lord Tredegar. On the extreme right of the front rank of the squadron rode Private John Lee, a grand old soldier who had long served in India and whose time was nearly up; I was next to him, and on my left was my comrade Peter Marsh.

As we stood halted here, Captain Nolan, of the 15th Hussars, whom we knew as an aid-de-camp of the head-quarter staff, suddenly galloped out to the front through the interval between us and the 13th, and called out to Captain Morris, who was directly in my front, 'Where is Lord Lucan?' 'There,' replied Morris, pointing—'there, on the right front!' Then he added, 'What is it to be, Nolan?—are we going to charge?' Nolan was off already in Lord Lucan's direction, but as he galloped away he shouted to Morris over his shoulder, 'You will see! you will see!' Just then we had some amusement, Private John Vey, who was the regimental butcher, had been slaughtering down at Balaclava, came up at a gallop on a troop horse of a Heavy who had been killed, and whom Vey had stripped of his belt and arms and accoutred himself with them over his white canvas smock frock, which, as well as his canvas trousers tucked into his boots, were covered with blood-stains. His shirt-sleeves were rolled up above his elbows, and his face, arms, and hands were smeared with blood, so that as he formed up on Lee's right shouting—he had some drink in him—that 'he'd be d—d if he was going to be left behind his regiment and so lose the fun,' he was indeed a gruesome yet laughable figure. Mr. Chadwick, the adjutant, ordered him to rein back and join his own troop in the 2nd squadron and I saw no more of him, but afterwards knew that he rode the charge, had his horse shot, but came back unwounded, and was given the distinguished conduct medal.

I cannot call to mind seeing Lord Lucan come to the front of the Light Brigade and speak with Lord Cardigan, although of course I know now that he did so. But I distinctly remember that Nolan returned to the Brigade and his having a mere momentary talk with Cardigan, at the close of which he drew his sword with a flourish, as if greatly excited. The blood came into his face—I seem to see him now; and then he fell back a little way into Cardigan's left rear, somewhat in front of and to the right of Captain Morris, who had taken post in front of his own left squadron. And I remember as if it were but yesterday Cardigan's figure and attitude, as he faced the brigade and in his strong hoarse voice gave the momentous word of command, 'The brigade will advance! First squadron of 17th Lancers direct!' Calm as on parade—calmer indeed by far than his wont on parade—stately, square and erect, master of himself, his brigade, and his nobler charge, Cardigan looked the ideal cavalry leader, with his stern firm face, and his quite soldierly bearing. His long military seat was perfection on the thoroughbred chestnut 'Ronald' with the 'white-stockings' on the near hind and fore, which my father, his old riding-master, had broken for him. He was in the full uniform of his old corps, the 11th Hussars, and he wore the pelisse, not slung, but put on like a patrol jacket, its front one blaze of gold lace. His drawn sword was in his hand at the slope, and never saw I man fitter to wield the weapon.

As I have said, he gave the word of command, and then turning his head toward his trumpeter, Britten of the Lancers, he quietly said 'Sound the Advance!' and wheeled his horse, facing the dark mass at the farther end of the valley, which we knew to be the enemy. The trumpeter sounded the 'Walk'; after a few horse-lengths came the 'Trot'. I did not hear the 'Gallop' but it was sounded. Neither voice nor trumpet, so far as I know, ordered the 'charge'; Britten was a dead man in a few strides after he had sounded the 'Gallop'. We had ridden barely two hundred yards and were still at the trot, when poor Nolan's fate came to him. I did not see him cross Cardigan's front, but I did see the shell explode, of which a fragment struck him. From his raised sword-hand dropped the sword, but the arm remained erect. Kinglake writes that 'what had once been Nolan maintained the strong military seat until the erect form dropped out of the saddle;' but this was not so. The sword-arm indeed remained upraised and rigid, but all the other limbs so curled in on the contorted trunk as by a spasm, that we wondered how for the moment the huddled form kept the saddle. It was the sudden convulsive twitch of the bridle hand inward on the chest, that caused the charge to wheel rearward so abruptly. The weird shriek and the awful face as rider and horse disappeared haunt me now to this day, the first horror of that ride of horrors.

As the line at the trumpet sound broke from the trot into the gallop, Lord Cardigan, almost directly behind whom I rode, turned his head leftward toward Captain Morris and shouted hoarsely, 'Steady, steady, Captain Morris!' The injunction was no doubt pointed specially at the latter, because he, commanding the regiment one of the squadrons of which had been named to direct, was held in a manner responsible to the brigade commander for both the pace and direction of the whole line. Later, when we were in the midst of our torture, and, mad to be out of it and have our revenge, were forcing the pace, I heard again, high above the turmoil and din, Cardigan's sonorous command, 'Steady, steady, the 17th Lancers!' and observed him check with voice and outstretched sword Captain White, my squadron leader, as he shot forward abreast of the stern disciplined chief leading the brigade. But, resolute man though he was, the time had come when neither the commands nor the example of Cardigan availed to restrain the pace of his brigade; and when to maintain his position in advance, indeed, if he were to escape being ridden down, he had to let his charger out from the gallop to the charge. For hell had opened upon us from front and either flank, and it kept open upon us during the minutes—they seemed hours—which passed while we traversed the mile and a quarter at the end of which was the enemy. The broken and fast-thinning ranks raised rugged peals of wild fierce cheering that only swelled the louder as the shot and shell from the battery tore gaps through us, and the enfilading musketry fire from the Infantry in both flanks brought down horses and men. Yet in this stress it was fine to see how strong was the bond of discipline and obedience. 'Close in! Close in!' was the constant command of the squadron and troop officers as the casualties made gaps in the ragged line, but the order was scarcely needed, for of their own instance and, as it seemed, mechanically, men and horses alike sought to regain the touch.

We had not broke into the charging pace when poor old John Lee, my right-hand man on the flank of the regiment, was all but smashed by a shell; he gave my arm a twitch, as with a strange smile on his worn old face he quietly said, 'Domino! chum,' and fell out of the saddle. His old grey mare kept alongside of me for some distance, treading on and tearing out her entrails as she galloped, till at length she dropped with a strange shriek. I have mentioned that my comrade, Peter Marsh, was my left-hand man; next beyond him was Private Dudley. The explosion of a shell had swept down four or five men on Dudley's left, and I heard him ask Marsh if he had noticed 'what a hole that b—— shell had made' on his left front. 'Hold your foul-mouthed tongue,' answered Peter, 'swearing like a blackguard, when you may be knocked into eternity next minute!' Just then I got a musket-bullet through my right knee, and another in the shin, and my horse had three bullet wounds in the neck. Man and horse were bleeding so fast that Marsh begged me to fall out; but I would not, pointing out that in a few minutes we must be into them, and so I sent my spurs well home, and faced it out with my comrades. It was about this time that Sergeant Talbot had his head clean carried off by a round shot, yet for about thirty yards further the headless body kept the saddle, the lance at the charge firmly gripped under the right arm. My narrative may seem barren of incidents of the charge but amid the crash of shells and the whistle of bullets, the cheers and the dying cries of comrades, the sense of personal danger, the pain of wounds, and the consuming passion to reach an enemy, he must be an exceptional man who is cool enough and curious enough to be looking serenely about him for what painters call 'local colour'. I had a good deal of 'local colour' myself, but it was running down the leg of my overalls from my wounded knee.

Well, we were nearly out of it at last, and close on those cursed guns. Cardigan was still straight in front of me, steady as a church, but now his sword was in the air; he turned in his saddle for an instant, and shouted his final command, 'Steady! steady! Close in!' Immediately afterwards there crashed into us a regular volley from the Russian cannon. I saw Captain White go down and Cardigan disappear into the smoke. A moment more and I was within it myself. A shell burst right over my head with a hellish crash that all but stunned me. Immediately after I felt my horse under me take a tremendous leap into the air. What he jumped I never saw or knew; the smoke was so thick I could not see my arm's length around me. Through the dense veil I heard noises of fighting and slaughter, but saw no obstacle, no adversary, no gun or gunner, and, in short, was through and beyond the Russian battery before I knew for certain that I had reached it.

I then found that none of my comrades were close to me. There was no longer any semblance of a line. No man of the Lancers was on my right, a group was a little way on my left. Lord Cardigan must have increased his distance during or after passing through the battery, for I now saw him some way ahead, alone in the midst of a knot of Cossacks. At this moment Lieutenant Maxse, his Lordship's aid-de-camp, came back out of the tussle, and crossed my front as I was riding forward. I saw that he was badly wounded; and he called to me, 'For God's sake, Lancer, don't ride over me! See where Lord Cardigan is,' pointing to him, 'rally on him!' I was hurrying on to support the brigade commander, when a Cossack came at me and sent his lance into my right thigh. I went for him, but he bolted; I overtook him, drove my lance into his back and unhorsed him just in front of two Russian guns which were in possession of Sergeant-Majors Lincoln and Smith, of the 13th Light Dragoons, and other men of the Brigade. When pursuing the Cossack I noticed Colonel Mayow deal very cleverly with a big Russian cavalry officer. He tipped off his shako with the point of his sword, and then laid his head right open with the old cut seven. The chase of my Cossack had diverted me from rallying on Lord Cardigan; he was now nowhere to be seen, nor did I ever again set eyes on the chief who had led us down the valley so grandly. The handful with the guns, to which I momentarily attached myself, were presently outnumbered and overpowered, the two sergeant-majors being taken prisoners, having been dismounted. I then rode towards Private Samuel Parkes, of the 4th Light Dragoons, who, supporting with one arm the wounded Trumpet-Major (Crawford) of his regiment, was with the other cutting and slashing at the enemies surrounding them. I struck in to aid the gallant fellow, who was not overpowered until his sword was shot away, when he and the trumpet-major were taken prisoners, and it was with difficulty I was able to cut my way out. Presently there joined me two other men, Mustard, of my own corps, and Fletcher, of the 4th Light Dragoons. We were now through and on the further side of a considerable body of the Russian cavalry, and so near the bottom of the valley that we could well discern the Tcherbaya river. But we were all three wearied and weakened by loss of blood; our horses wounded in many places; there were enemies all about us, and we thought it was about time to be getting back. I remember reading in the regimental library of an officer who said to his commander 'We have done enough for honour,' that was our humble opinion too, and we turned our horses' heads. We forced our way through ring after ring of enemies, fell in with my comrade Peter Marsh, and rode rearward, breaking through party after party of Cossacks, until we heard the familiar voice of Corporal Morley, of our regiment, a great, rough, bellowing Nottingham man. He had lost his lance hat, and his long hair was flying out in the wind as he roared, 'Coom ere! coom ere! Fall in, lads, fall in!' Well, with shouts and oaths he had collected some twenty troopers of various regiments. We fell in with the handful this man of the hour had rallied to him, and there joined us also under his leader-ship Sergeant Major Ranson and Private John Penn, of the 17th. Penn, a tough old warrior who had served with the 3rd Light in the Sikh war, had killed a Russian officer, dismounted, and with great deliberation accoutred himself with the belt and sword of the defunct, in which he made a great show. A body of Russian Hussars blocked our way. Morley, roaring Nottingham oaths by way of encouragement, led us straight at them, and we went through and out at the other side as if they had been made of tinsel paper. As we rode up the valley, pursued by some Hussars and Cossacks, my horse was wounded by a bullet in the shoulder, and I had hard work to put the poor beast along. Presently we were abreast of the Infantry who had blazed into our right as we went down; and we had to take their fire again, this time on our left. Their firing was very impartial; their own Hussars and Cossacks following close on us suffered from it as well as we. Not many of Corporal Morley's party got back. My horse was shot dead, riddled with bullets. One bullet struck me on the forehead, another passed through the top of my shoulder; while struggling out from under my horse a Cossack standing over me stabbed me with his lance once in the neck near the jugular, again above the collar-bone, several times in the back and once under the short rib; and when, having regained my feet, I was trying to draw my sword, he sent his lance through the palm of my hand. I believe he would have succeeded in killing me, clumsy as he was, if I had not blinded him for the moment with a handful of sand. Fletcher at the same time lost his horse, and, it seems, was wounded. We were very roughly used. The Cossacks at first hauled us along by the tails of our coatees and our haversacks. When we got on foot they drove their lance-butts into our backs to stir us on. With my shattered knee and the other bullet wound on the shin of the same leg, I could barely limp, and good old Fletcher said 'Get on my back, chum!' I did so, and then found that he had been shot through the back of the head. When I told him of this, his only answer was, 'Oh, never mind that, it's not much, I don't think.' But it was that much that he died of the wound a few days later; and here he was a doomed man himself, making light of a mortal wound, and carrying a chance comrade of another regiment on his back. I can write this, but I could not tell of it in speech, because I know I should play the woman.

WEIGHTMAN

Prisoner after Balaclava

I WAS taken by some of the Cossacks by whom I had been captured to the end of the valley. Here a short halt was called, and one of their number—a particularly ill-favoured-looking dog—took the opportunity of searching me. He ransacked my haversack, in which I had a small packet of coffee, some broken biscuit, and a daguerrotype of a dear sister sent to me from America while stationed at Varna, the glass of which was broken. When I saw this picture in his hands I motioned him to let me have it back again. Instead of doing so, he continued to look at it, and to grin. He made remarks which, although I did not understand the language, I knew by his manner to be offensive. I endeavoured to secure the likeness, but only succeeded in rubbing a portion of it out. The Cossack then showed it to his comrades, and after they had satisfied their curiosity, amused themselves by giving me a thrashing with the butts of their lances and with whips. Then with a strip torn from my trousers they tied my hands so tightly behind me that I almost fainted with the pain. They removed the cording off my shako and tied my arms together until my elbows almost met at the back. The one who had searched me fastened a long thong such as all Cossacks have attached to their horses' reins to my right arm; and, giving his horse a cut, away he went at a trot, dragging me after him. To keep up I had to run pretty fast; and he maintained the pace till we got to the Black River—but not at the same place where I had been on the morning of the 23rd. At this part there was no bridge, so we halted for a few minutes, which enabled me to get a little breath; for, as may be fancied, I was pretty well blown and fatigued with the run he had given me at his horse's tail. I was wondering what my kind Cossack would do next, when he walked his horse into the river, and calling 'Hydee!' (move on), made me wade after him. About the middle of the stream, I being up to the arm-pits in water, I kicked my foot against a big stone, and being unable to keep my balance—bound as I was—I went down head foremost and thought I should have been drowned. The fellow made no pause nor effort to assist me, but deliberately dragged me across by the long thong. Reaching the other side I was so exhausted that I sank down on the bank, careless as to what the Cossack might do next. He seemed to enjoy my plight, as he laughed heartily. He wouldn't allow me to rest long, for, progging me in the ribs with the butt of his lance, he compelled me to rise, and off we started again—towards the rearguard of the Russian force. On the road, another Cossack rode up to us, and had some conversation with my keeper. As they were speaking, I took the liberty to lean against a tree, and was just falling asleep when I was aroused by the new-comer trying to make his horse kick me. Failing, he made a cut at my face with his whip, but by bending the head I received the blow on the shako. The man who had me in charge then moved on; and after a march of half an hour, I felt so tired and weak that I nearly fell down under my escort's horse. I beckoned for him to halt a little at which he scowled, and, seeing two other Cossacks lying on the ground a little way off, he called to them to come over. He said something to them, the result of which was that one caught me by the collar and the other behind, and both shouting out hydee! hydee! they compelled me to 'move on'. I couldn't walk fast enough, however, to please the fellow behind, so he let the back of his sword drop on my right shoulder with such force that I fell on my knees, and my hands being tied behind me, rolled over on the ground. But I was soon set upon my feet, and the journey continued. In course of time a clump of trees was reached. Here a halt was made, and the 'assistants' left. Once more with Cossack No. 1 alone, he signed to me to sit upon the ground, a signal which I willingly obeyed. But the fellow would not let me rest in peace. A dig with his lance as before, called my attention to a rope suspended from the branch of a tree overhead, and, laughing the while, he gave me to understand, in pantomime, that I was to be hanged there. 'Good God!' said I to myself, 'am I brought here to be hanged like a dog? Far better had I been killed on the field of battle.' Then in an instant—just as I have heard say people do when they are drowning—all the events of my past life came up before me. I could see in my mind's eye everything that had happened from earliest recollection—my mother, father, brother, sisters—all my old comrades, and the scenes we had come through. I was determined, however, that if possible I should not betray my despair, although I feared it must have been too surely depicted on my face. I pretended not to understand what he meant. Just then one of the two Cossacks who had lately left rode up again, gave what appeared to be an order, and off we set, the two talking and laughing, as I thought, over the fright about the rope. Proceeding thus for about a mile, the second Cossack again left and I saw him no more. Soon afterwards a Russian officer came up and asked my keeper some questions, after which he turned to me and gave me to understand that I was to mount a horse at hand, and which proved to be a horse of the 17th Lancers, now a prisoner like myself. I signified to him that, my hands being tied, I was unable to do so, upon which he at once came forward and lifted me up on its back, giving the reins to the Cossack, who then led me off. At last the rearguard of the Russian army was reached, and a soldier assisted me to dismount.

Sitting on the grass here, I found myself a gazing-stock for about 2000 Russian soldiers. They regarded me as a strange being, as if, in fact, I had been an inhabitant of some other world dropt down amongst them. Of course I enjoyed a good look at them in return. About a quarter of an hour after my arrival, an officer came up to me, and asked in English what I was. 'A prisoner, sir,' said I. 'Where were you taken?' 'I beg your pardon, sir,' I said; 'perhaps you would be kind enough to untie my hands before I answer your questions.' 'What!' said the officer, 'are your hands bound?' 'Yes,' I replied; 'and one of your men would be a long time prisoner in our camp before he would have been served as I have been since I was taken prisoner this morning.' 'Who tied your hands?' he asked, very angrily. 'This man did,' I said, nodding my head at my Cossack friend. The officer thereupon ordered the fellow to dismount, and, taking the whip out of his hand, gave him several severe cuts with it—in fact a fairishly good thrashing. He then ordered him off, and my hands to be untied. He next introduced me to a number of officers sitting in a circle on the grass, with a small keg of spirits (vodka) in the centre. They asked questions; but when they found I did not understand the language, they talked amongst themselves, and seemed to be much interested in me. I noticed that they often made use of the word branchook, which I afterwards learned means a youngster, a lad—in reference, I suppose, to my somewhat youthful appearance. By-and-by the officer who spoke English asked me if I was hungry. 'Yes, sir,' said

I; 'your people called rather too early for us to get breakfast this morning.' At this he laughed, and said he would order something. Accordingly in a few minutes afterwards a soldier came to me with a wooden bowl, in which was some water, and a bag of hard black bread. He made signs to me to eat. I tried the black bread, but it was so hard that my teeth could make no impression. So I turned to the contents of the bowl, but found, to my distress that it was a mixture of salt and water! The officer who had ordered it came up just then, and, seeing my chagrin, had a good laugh. 'I thought you wouldn't manage that,' he said; 'but all these men'—pointing to the hundreds who were bivouacked round about—'have to take it when campaigning, and they like it very well. Of course they get other rations besides—soup, beef, tea, whatever can be got,—although they are all accustomed to what you have before you. But I will order something else for you.' He then gave the servant another order, and he returned in about twenty minutes with a couple of mutton chops, nicely cooked, a small loaf of white bread, and a bottle of English beer. It was to me a most agreeable surprise; because, after the cruel treatment I had received that day, I had almost reached the conclusion that the Russians were a nation of savages. This kind of treatment quite upset that idea. After I had done full justice to the viands and beer, a young cadet invited me to sit down beside him. He then commenced to make cigarettes, and gave me some to smoke with him. Indeed, his kindness and attention were such that I can never forget him. Other officers, too, gave me sundry glasses of spirits to drink, and I began to feel drowsy. Seeing this, my good young benefactor, the cadet, made me take off my jacket and trousers, which were dripping wet. Then I lay back upon the grass, and put my shako under my head for a pillow. He covered my body with a cloak, and in a few moments I was unconscious in the arms of Morpheus. How long I slept I couldn't say; but Iwas roused by the cadet to join him in partaking of some nice hot tea. I afterwards discovered that the cloak which had protected me belonged to the 17th Lancers; and I may just mention that I never parted with it during the whole of my imprisonment in Russia.

FARQUHARSON

FOUR

FAREWELL TO ARMS

All the world over, nursing their scars,
Sit the old fighting-men broke in the wars—
Sit the old fighting-men, surly and grim,
Mocking the lilt of the conqueror's hymn.

Rudyard Kipling

19

AFTER-LIFE

A soldier's legacy, 1760

'Son William, I have beene abought a whole year in writing of this that you desired me to writ. I would not have you to lend it abought to everyone nor even to unto any men of greater capascitie [that they] may not deride my weakness. I have writ it that your childrens children may see a little of a great deale what thare grandfather have gone through and as I have writ it small & very close and sum of bad paper and sumtime bad pens for I cannot see to make my pens myself, that if you pretend to read it you must take deliberation to read it, and I would have you bring up my grandson William so to learning that he may read it for I am sure that you had more time at skoole than ever I had. March ye 26, 1760.

'I was borne in the year 1677, the year of my nativity, a Dragoon confin'd years eleven, in the 22nd of my captivity.'

A ROYAL DRAGOON IN THE SPANISH SUCCESSION WAR

Discharge after eight years' service, 1791

Late in the year 1791, I returned to England with my regiment. We landed at Portsmouth on the 3rd of November, and on the 19th of the next month I obtained my discharge, after having served not quite eight years, and having, in that short space, passed through every rank, from that of private sentinel to that of Sergeant-Major, without ever once being disgraced, confined, or even reprimanded. I obtained my discharge after many efforts on the part of the commanding officer, Major Lord Edward Fitzgerald, and of General Frederick, the Colonel of the regiment, to prevail on me to remain (upon a promise of being specially recommended to the King, as worthy of being immediately promoted to the rank of Ensign).

COBBETT

Discharge from the Army, 1802

WE HAD a tedious passage down the Mediterranean, and did not arrive at Gibraltar, until the 20th December. We left it on the 1st January, 1802; and arrived at the Cove of Cork on the 23rd, having had rough weather all the way, which on two occasions increased to a tempest, and did the ship I was in considerable damage. We had to ride quarantine until the 9th February. My leg had stretched considerably during the passage, and I walked about the deck with the help of a stick. The regiment landed, and marched into Cork on the 12th, the wounded and baggage being conveyed by water. And here I found, that, although I could safely walk about with a stick on the level deck of a ship, my leg was not sufficiently strong, to travel the necessary distances on land. My wound here broke out again; and when the regiment left Cork for Kilkenny, although I rode upon the baggage, yet the travelling from the places where the baggage halted to my billet, which was sometimes more than a mile, was injurious to me. We came to Kilkenny on the 21st, and lay in it about six weeks. The regiment was inspected, by the General and Surgeon of the district, and a great number ordered to be discharged, of which I was one.

'G.B.'

Obtaining a pension, twenty-five years after discharge, 1809

THE battles of York-Town, in Virginia, put a period to the Author's military labours. In 1783, he sailed from Sandyhook, and after a safe passage arrived at Portsmouth. He obtained his discharge at Winchester, and revisited Ireland, where he was affectionately received by an aged mother and a few kind relatives. He then had to take counsel about a line of living to earn a subsistence; such is generally the result of a military life. He chose to become a School-Master; an arduous occupation, which has enabled him for upwards of twenty-six years, to provide for, and educate a growing family, the source of satisfaction and solicitude. He was discharged without the pension usually given for past services, and being frequently advised by his friends to apply for it, in 1809, (twenty-five years after receiving his discharge) he memorialed His Royal Highness the Duke of York, and was graciously favoured by an immediate compliance with the Prayer of his Petition. He submits the Memorial and its Answer, in gratitude to the illustrious individual, who so promptly condescended to notice it as he did.

'Dublin, January 7, 1809.

'To His Royal Highness the Duke of York Commander in Chief of His Majesty's Forces; the Memorial of R. Lamb, late Serjeant in the Royal Welch Fuzileers,

'Humbly Sheweth,

'THAT Memorialist served in the Army twelve years, in the 9th and 23rd Regiments of Foot, eight years of which was in America; under the command of Generals Burgoyne and Cornwallis; during which time he was in Six pitched Battles, Four Sieges, several important Expeditions, was twice taken prisoner, and as often made his escape to the British Army; viz. First, in 1778, when prisoner with General Burgoyne's Army, he escaped, with two men, whom he brought with him to General Sir Henry Clinton, at New-York; Secondly, in 1782, when taken with Lord Cornwallis's Army, he eluded the vigilance of the American guards, and conducted under his command, seven men to Sir Guy Carleton, the then Commander in Chief in said City, to both of whom he gave most important Intelligence respecting the enemy's Army, for which Service he was appointed by General Birch, then commandant of the City, his first Clerk, and Adjutant to the Merchants' Corps of Volunteers there.

'That in the battle of Camden in South Carolina, he had the honour of carrying the Regimental Colours, and immediately after was appointed temporary Surgeon to the Regiment, having had some little knowledge of physic, and received the approbation of all his Officers for his care of the sick and wounded.

'That at the battle of Guilford Court-House, in North Carolina; he had the heartfelt pleasure of saving Lord Cornwallis from being taken prisoner, and begs leave with profound deference to state, that he was always chosen one of the first Serjeants to execute any enterprize that required intrepidity, decision, and judgment for its accomplishment.

'That Memorialist being now far advanced in life, humbly solicits your Royal Highness to recommend him for a military pension, which would smooth his declining years, and be most gratefully received as a remuneration for the many times he has risked his life and limbs in his Majesty's service.

'That for the truth of these facts, he most humbly refers to General H. Calvert and Colonel Makenzie.'

To which Memorial the following Answer was received.

'ADJUTANT GENERAL'S OFFICE.

'The Adjutant-General informs Serjeant Roger Lamb, that the usual Authority has been given by the Secretary at War, for placing him upon the Out Pension of Chelsea Hospital, dispensing with his personal appearance before the Board.

'Horse-Guards, 25th Jan. 1809.'

SERJEANT LAMB

Discharged from the Royal Artillery, 1814

AT LENGTH, I rejoice to say, the year 1814 arrived. It was evident the war was soon to be at an end, as my hopes from my father had for some months been. A reduction was ordered; and harassed and dispirited 'Old Ceylon'[1] was marked for his discharge.

In the month of October I was again forced to go into the

1. Alexander Alexander was thirty-four years old at this date.

hospital with an excessive pain in my head, for which many remedies were tried before it yielded to medicine. During my convalescence, the medical board sat, before which I attended; Dr. Jamieson, the surgeon-general, examined me, putting several questions as to my length of time in the regiment, and service, which I answered. 'Well, my man,' he said, 'you will get your discharge and one shilling per day.' My heart began to swell. I had arrived at last, in spite of all my exertions, to the much dreaded point 'a poor old pensioner:' The shilling per day, I thought, at this time, a secondary consideration; yet I could not help thinking it too little, as none of the Artillery I had the command of from Ceylon got less in 1811, some of whom had not been so long in the army at that time as I had been, and never were non-commissioned officers; some had been more than once flogged; and now, after four years more service, to get just the same pension as these privates I could not think equal justice; but the money, I cared not much about, as I meant to be off for the West Indies as soon as I was free.

If such were my thoughts when I passed, how chagrined did I feel when my discharge arrived from the Ordnance Office on the 31st December, 1814, and a pension of only ninepence per day. I felt I had been deeply injured by my father; as for the Ordnance Office, I valued their award at this time with very little. Had my father said, decidedly, when I saw him after my return, that he would do nothing for me, I would have returned immediately, and passed the Board, a thing I could have done at any time, from the complication of diseases under which I laboured, but, deluded by his promises, I had endured four years of suffering and loss of time, and received only the reduced pension of ninepence per day for life.

No sooner had I got my discharge in my pocket than I felt I was a new man; I was once more free; I actually thought I stood a few inches higher, as I stretched myself like one who has just laid down a heavy load. I tarried not long in Dublin, but with the first opportunity set off for Scotland once again.

ALEXANDER ALEXANDER

A discharged soldier's farewell to his family, 1818

I HAVE been with my mother these fourteen months. She is sinking fast to the grave. I am happy I am here to lay her head in it.—Jeanie has been married these five years; and goes between her own and her mother's house, to take care of her. John is in London, following out his business. William has been in Glasgow.

Letter by the Writer of the Journal to his Friend, inclosing the last part of the Manuscript.

'Edinburgh, May, 1818.

'Dear John,

'These three months I can find nothing to do. I am a burden on Jeanie and her husband. I wish I was a soldier again. I cannot even get labouring work. God will bless those, I hope, who have been good to me. I have seen my folly. I would be useful, but can get nothing to do. My mother is at her rest,—God receive her soul!—I will go to South America. Maria de Parides will put me in a way to do for myself, and be a burden to no one. Or, I shall go to Spain, and live in Boho.—I will go to Buenos Ayres.—Farewell! John, this is all I have to leave you. It is yours: do with it as you think proper. If I succeed in the South, I will return and lay my bones besides my parents: if not, I will never come back.'

'71ST'

Return to England: discharged in the 1840's

7th AUGUST: Made Gravesend, and as the anchor was let go a cornopaean player on board a river steamer complimented us with 'Home, Sweet Home' and 'Auld Lang Syne,' we responding, in the fullness of our hearts, with cheers loud and long. Shortly afterwards some of our officers went on land, and when they returned in the evening, one of them was gloriously drunk; conduct many of ourselves resolved on imitating the first opportunity, so much greater influence has example than precept.

8th—Disembarked in the morning, and found myself on English ground, two years and some weeks after I had quitted it; many of the men expressed the most extravagant joy; and one old veteran in particular knelt down and kissed the earth. The disembarking officer, contrary to our expectations, did not ask whether we had any reports to make; much to the disappointment of several who had determined to complain of the manner in which they were rationed during the voyage. As we marched silently through the gateway of Chatham barracks, I be thought myself of the old soldier who remarked when last I passed it, and the detachment was cheering loudly, that we ought not to cheer till we came back. The detachment was composed of eighty men, of whom scarcely forty had returned, one third of the remainder having died, and the rest volunteered, while of the latter several were killed in storming a Baloochee fort.

After lying for a few days in Chatham barracks, we marched to Walmer, where our head-quarters which had landed a fortnight before us, was stationed. I now resigned my orderly-room clerkship, and was appointed full corporal and supernumerary sergeant, receiving a promise of promotion on the first vacancy; and zealously set about learning my new duties, having resolved to remain in the army, as my friend still continued in embarrassed circumstances, though not to the same extent as when I had left Ireland. Besides, I had become attached to a military life, in spite of its hardships, and felt myself quite at home among the veterans of the 13th.

But I found it would be next to impossible for me to remain in the corps, as I had by some means become disliked by the adjutant, who, however irreproachable my conduct had been, seemed now disposed to treat me any way but kindly, taking every opportunity to annoy and insult me, and even using abusive language towards me while at drill. Still I bore all this patiently, hoping that good conduct and a zealous and correct discharge of my duties might induce him to deal more fairly by me. But I might as well have pursued an opposite course; a private was promoted over my head on a vacancy occurring, and this injustice, along with a series of other circumstances, so disgusted me, with the army, that I wrote to my friends for money, and applied for my discharge, much indeed to the surprise of the adjutant, who now saw that he had carried matters a little too far, in thus compelling me to quit the regiment.

Shortly after I had lodged the application for my discharge, the sergeant-major endeavoured to fathom my motives for so doing, giving me the assurance, at the same time, that if I remained in the corps I should have the next vacancy, and otherwise holding out every inducement to me to stay. The following day I was up with some prisoners before the colonel, being sergeant of the mainguard; and after they were disposed of, the adjutant remarked to him that I had applied for my discharge; but that the sergeant-major had given him an excellent account of me, and that so promising a non-commissioned officer ought not to be permitted to leave the regiment. The colonel said that he was very sorry I should think of quitting the corps, as my conduct had always given him the utmost satisfaction, adding, that if I would remain, I should have two months' pass to go and see my friends. But my resolution was already taken; and despite what Sam Slick would term the soft sawder of the adjutant, and the well-meaning kindness of the good old colonel, it remained unshaken.

I received my discharge on the 15th October, and in a few days afterwards I found myself once more at home, surrounded by relatives and friends, all pleased and happy at the return of their wandered, whom, for a long time, they had despaired of every seeing again.

MACMULLEN

Return of a soldier after the Sikh Wars

ON FRIDAY, the 21st, I left my master and came up the River Thames by steamboat to London, and by railway to Leicester, where I arrived at midnight, by the mail train. On the following morning I expected to see some of my townspeople, as it was market-day; so I bought a new suit of clothes, and then met some of them at the 'Coach and Horses', Humberstone-gate, but they did not know me until I had made myself known to them. At night I went home to Twyford, and, on arriving there, I went to Mr. Goodman's, the public-house near to my father's; for I thought it would be better than going in home at once, and putting them about, as they did not in the least expect me. I had sent for my father, by an old neighbour, to meet me at the public house. On my going in I called for some drink. In the house were two of my old companions; one was the very next door neighbour, and was of the same age as myself. We had been at school together, and play-fellows: but they neither of them knew me. The landlord who brought me the ale had known me from a child, but did not appear to have the slightest recollection of me then. He passed the time of day, and the remarks on the weather, and so did my two companions. They eyed me all over, and wondered who I was. While I was in talk, my father came in. He looked round, but did not see any one whom he knew, who wanted him. He sat down, and I called to him, and said, 'Come, old man, will you have a glass of drink?' He looked very hard at me, and came. I handed him a glass, when he wished my good health and drank. The old man had altered much since I had last seen him: he stooped much, and his hair was quite grey. He set the glass down, and was going away, when I said, 'You had better have another'. He stood, and I handed him another. He drank it, and thanked me, and was going away, when I said, 'Well then, father, so you do not know me.' He was quite overcome. He knew me then. The house was now all surprised. My companions also knew me then, and this caused no small stir in the village. The news soon flew. My mother heard it, and came to see; when she came in she looked round, but did not know me, though I was sitting beside my father. After she had looked round, and did not (as she supposed) see me, she appeared very confused, and said, 'Some one said my boy had come, but I did not believe it.' I handed her a glass of ale, and told her to drink, and not think of such things; and she was going away quite contented, till I called her back, and said, 'Do you not see him?' but she did not know me then, until I said, 'Mother, *you* ought to know me'. The poor old woman then knew me, and would have fallen to the floor, if she had not been caught. She was some time before she overgot it.

So I had once more arrived at my native town. My companions rang a merry peal on the bells for my welcome. The reason they did not know me was, because I was very dark, from the effects of the Indian sun, which gradually wore off as I got used to my native climate.

RYDER

Goodbye to the Army, 1852

WE LEFT Castlebar and went to Galway for some time, and then got the route for Dublin. Stayed there until October, when I got my discharge from the Regiment after twenty-three years and three months service.

So good-bye to the old 17th Regiment.

I left Dublin for Appleby, in Westmoreland, to join the Militia Staff and to form the Regiment, on the 14th October, 1852.

Served with the Militia over twenty years and was discharged on the 21st January, 1873, and then came to Loughborough, the place I left when a boy in 1829.

So good-bye to 43 years in the army.

(signed) JOHN CLARKE,
Colour-Sergeant
17th Regiment of Foot,
and Westmoreland Militia.

CLARKE

Rewards of a military life in the nineteenth century

WE LEFT Balaclava about May, 1856, sailing for Quebec in British North America, where I served for eight years in a trying climate; finally taking my discharge in 1864, being then stationed at Quebec. After this I went to the United States where I joined the American army, served five months, then got paid off, and came to England, where ever since I have remained.

Dear friends, these statements are true, but should there be any doubt, as there frequently is, a reference to the regimental depot of the regiment in which I served, would at once confirm what I have stated as to my service. I am now 72 years of age, and have a pension of ninepence per day, having to make the best of it.

PARSONS

An old soldier still serves

I WAS appointed Garrison Sergt. Major at Port Elizabeth and remained here my own master for a considerable time. While I was stationed here I witnessed a terrific storm, the wind blowing from the south east. There were 19 ships wrecked, and one of these ships was totally smashed to pieces and all hands lost and this in sight of thousands who could render them no assistance. I remained at Port Elizabeth until 1871 when I was ordered to rejoin the left wing of my Regt. which was stationed at King William's Town. This was rather unexpected for I was drawing my week's allowance of fuel about 12 noon and was on board the mail steamer bound for East London again at 4 p.m. Rather quick work which caused me to part with a good many articles at a great sacrifice. However, there was no help for it. I had to grin and bear it. We arrived at East London all right after a very nice run of two days and disembarked the same day and marched again for King William's Town where I remained till November, 1871 when I passed the Board of Claims and retraced my steps to East London, there to embark once more for England.

And now once more we were homeward bound. My services in the Regular Army would expire on the voyage home. We embarked again at East London, called in at Simon's Bay where the soldiers and ships company had great fun in catching fish. We sailed from there and had Christmas off the Island of St. Helena, the grave of that once famed Napoleon. Next called at the Island of Ascension, so-called through being discovered on Ascension Day. We coaled there and proceeded on our voyage, next called at St. Vincent, after that crossed the Bay of Biscay which was very stormy, but our ship rode through it like a duck. We arrived at Queen's Town after a beautiful passage. Our next place was Plymouth where we took in Supernumeraries for the Channel Fleet which we left at Portland.

Our next and final stage was Portsmouth and on the 29th January, 1872 we landed and proceeded by rail to Chichester, the discharge Depot, where I remained a few months as Clerk in the discharge office, when I was discharged and joined the East York Militia at Beverley, Yorkshire, as Musketry Instructor, where I remained for three year and six months, and after being thoroughly disgusted with the Militia I purchased my discharge and joined the 27th Cheshire Rifle Volunteers at Wilmslow. There I thought I would remain and settle down after many roving years, but it was not to be. After being there about 4 years where I was nicely settling down, my commanding officer, in acknowledgement of my services, promoted me to the post of senior instructor to the Macclesfield Volunteers. This was to better my position and so it did in a monetary sense but I was much happier where I was.

METCALFE

Discharged unfit: 1900

WE SOON reached the convalescent hospital at Cape Town, and after recovering some of my strength I became so hungry I felt as if I could have eaten a boiled boot. I sold my watch and chain to a Royal Army Medical Corps orderly (R.A.M.C.) who are really Military Hospital nurses, for 30s; it was well worth £5, and before I left the hospital he was in possession of my watch and chain and the 30s. for extra bits of food. A shilling for a bit of butter, 6d for extra bread, etc., etc. No wonder we called him the 'Rob All My Comrades'.

Anyhow, by the time I was placed on board a homeward bound transport ship I was penniless, and peeled potatoes for nearly all the 6,000 miles home in the galley (ship's cook-house) to get extra food. After being starved while the fever is on, one gets so ravenous when well enough, one could eat almost anything.

When we arrived at Portsmouth we were sent to a 'clearing' hospital at Gosport. I was several times mistaken for a Boer prisoner because of my greasy khaki suit and beard. Several of us had them photographed before having them cut off.

After being sent to Fort George, N.B., to be medically examined for further duties, I was eventually discharged with defective eyesight, being the after-effects of the fever, etc.

I was granted a pension of 9d per day from 'a grateful country for services rendered'. I am now quite blind in one eye; the other is not so bad, but is gradually going, although I drive my car every day, but not at night (1953).

Thus, after close on ten years' service I became a civilian again without any definite plan of making my living.

CORBETT

20

L'ENVOI

A soldier's creed: the Siege of Gibraltar, 1779–83

I CANNOT, dear Brother, omit penning an entertaining conversation I had with a soldier in Irish Town yesterday. I met Jack Careless in the street, singing with uncommon glee, (notwithstanding the enemy were firing with prodigious warmth) part of the old song,

'A soldier's life, is a merry life,
'From care and trouble free.'

He ran to me with eagerness, and presenting his bottle cry'd, 'D—n me, if I don't like fighting: I'd like to be ever tanning the Dons:—Plenty of good liquor for carrying away—never was the price so cheap—fine stuff—enough to make a miser quit his gold.' 'Why, Jack,' says I, 'what have you been about?' With an arch grin, he replied, 'That would puzzle a Heathen philosopher, or yearly almanack-maker, to unriddle. I scarce know myself. I have been constantly on foot and watch, half starved, and without money, facing a parcel of pitiful Spaniards. I have been fighting, wheeling, marching, and counter-marching; sometimes with a firelock, then a handspike, and now my bottle' (brandishing it in the air). 'I am so pleased with the melody of great guns, that I consider myself as a Roman General, gloriously fighting for my country's honour and liberty.' A shell that instant burst, a piece of which knocked the bottle out of his hand; with the greatest composure he replied, (having first graced it with an oath) 'This is not any loss, I have found a whole cask by good luck,' and brought me to view his treasure. 'But, Jack,' says I, 'are you not thankful to God, for your preservation?' 'How do you mean?' he answered. 'Fine talking of God with a soldier, whose trade and occupation is cutting throats: Divinity and slaughter sound very well together, they jingle like a crack'd bell in the hand of a noisy crier: Our King is answerable to God for us. I fight for him. My religion consists in a fire-lock, open touch-hole, good flint, well rammed charge, and seventy rounds of powder and ball. This is my military creed. Come, comrade, drink success to the British Arms.' On my asking him for a glass he seemed surprised, 'Why,' says he, 'you may well know there is not any but broken glasses to be had, but here is something that will do as well,' and he took up a piece of a shell. 'Here is a cup fit for a Monarch, this was not purchased with gold or friendship, but with the streams of our countrymen's blood.' Having filled the piece of shell, he gave it to me to drink. 'Come, Jack,' said I. 'Here is King George and victory!' 'And he that would not drink the same,' replied he, 'I'd give him an ounce of lead to pay Charon to ferry him over the river Styx.' I left him enjoying the spoil, and really felt a sensible pleasure in the recollection.

ANCELL

After Bunker Hill

IN THE vault of a church at Boston, are now preserved the mouldering bodies of British officers, who lost their gallant lives in the before mentioned engagement. They must have been interred without coffins, as the skeletons were seen by a gentleman some years ago lying uncovered and bare. On one skeleton hung rags of torn regimentals, and breeches of leather in a good state of preservation. It looked as if recently cleaned with pipe clay, which most probably was done to prepare for the occasion which proved fatal to the

2E

wearer of it. The flesh was entirely wasted from the bones, which presented a painful spectacle of mortality.

SERJEANT LAMB

An ex-soldier's reflections on military men

'ONCE a soldier, always a soldier,' is a maxim, the truth of which I need not insist on to anyone who has ever served in the army for any length of time, and especially, if the service he has seen has embraced those scenes and occasions where every man, first or last, from one cause or another, owes the preservation of his all, health and life not excepted, to the kindness, the generosity, the fellow-feeling of his comrades.

There was one of our sergeants, whose name was Smaller, and who was a Yorkshire man, who began learning his ABC (under my direction), and who, at the end of the year, was as correct a writer as I ever saw in my life. He was about my own age; he was promoted as soon as he could write and read; and he well deserved it, for he was more fit to command a regiment than any Colonel or Major that I ever saw. He was strong in body, but still stronger in mind. He had a capacity to dive into all subjects. Clean in his person, an early riser, punctual in all his duties, sober, good-tempered, honest, brave, and generous to the last degree. He was once with me in the dreary woods, amongst the melting snows, when I was exhausted at nightfall, and fell down, unable to go farther, just as a torrent of rain began to pour upon us. Having first torn off his shirt and rent it in the vain hope of kindling fire by the help of his pistol, he took me upon his back, carried me five miles to the first dwelling of human being, and, at the end of his journey, having previously pulled off his coat and thrown it away, he had neither shoe, nor stocking, nor gaiter left; his feet and legs were cut to pieces, and covered with blood; and the moment he had put me down and saw that I was still alive, he burst into a flood of tears that probably saved his own life; which, however, was there saved only to be lost in Holland, under the Duke of York.

Of this military feeling, I do not believe that any man ever possessed greater portion than myself. I like soldiers, as a class in life, better than any other description of men. Their conversation is more pleasing to me; they have generally seen more than other men; they have less of vulgar prejudice about them. Amongst soldiers, less than amongst any other description of men, have I observed the vices of lying and hypocrisy.

COBBETT

Why the soldiers of the South fought (*American Civil War*)

THE principles for which the Confederate soldier fought and in defence of which he died are today the harmony of this country. So long as they were held in abeyance, the country was in turmoil and on the verge of ruin.

It is not fair to demand a reason for actions above reason. The heart is greater than the mind. No man can exactly define the cause for which the Confederate soldier fought. He was above human reason and above human law, secure in his own rectitude of purpose, accountable to God only, having assumed for himself a 'nationality' which he was minded to defend with his life, and his property, and thereto pledged his sacred honor.

In the honesty and simplicity of his heart, the Confederate soldier had neglected his own interests and rights, until his accumulated wrongs and indignities forced him to one grand, prolonged effort to free himself from the pain of them. He dared not refuse to hear the call to arms, so plain was the duty and so urgent the call. His brethren and friends were answering the bugle-call and the roll of the drum. To stay was dishonour and shame!

He would not obey the dictates of tyranny. To disobey was death. He disobeyed and fought for his life. The romance of war charmed him, and he hurried from the embrace of his mother to the embrace of death. His playmates, his friends, and his associates were gone; he was lonesome, and he sought a reunion 'in camp'. He would not receive as gospel the dogmas of fanatics, and so he became a 'rebel'. Being a rebel, he must be punished. Being punished he resisted. Resisting, he died.

MCCARTHY

Disbandment of a regiment: Portland, Maine, 1865

But the day at length arrived when we were to march down to the city, and turn our guns and equipment over to the Government. It was the last march of our gallant regiment, but how unlike the regiment that was mustered there, three years before! We had been terribly smitten by the storm of war, and there was but a remnant left to tell the story of our adventures.

In a street near the arsenal we stacked our guns, and upon their bayonets we hung for the last time our equipments. It was a sad moment; we had not realized before how it would seem to separate. Colonel Morrill called for three cheers for the old rifles that had done us such excellent service, and they were given with a will; then three more were given for the colors under which we had fought and then three more for the 'Land we love the best.' When these cheers had all been given, the boys voluntarily gave three more for gallant Colonel Morrill, a man whose 'Courage was only excelled by his modesty.' Then came the last hand-shakings and good-byes. Eyes grew moist, cheeks that had been unblanched amid the horrors of the battle-field became pale and sad in those moments of separation. The ties that bound us together were of the most sacred nature; they had been begotten in hardships and baptized in blood. Men who lived together in the little shelter tent, slept beneath the same blanket, had divided the scanty rations, and 'drank from the same canteen' were now to be separated forever. The last good-bye was said, our ranks were broken for the last time, and we turned our faces homeward. For us there were to be no more weary marches, no more midnight alarms. The strife, dangers, and deaths of a soldier's life were no more to follow our footsteps, but in the more peaceful persuits of civil life we were to move. No matter how humble the positions we were destined to fill, we were always to derive infinite satisfaction from the thought that in the hour of the country's peril we had not been found wanting, but had cheerfully rendered what little service we could, to defend its honor and preserve its life. Thus we separated; many of us have never met each other since; I presume we never shall in this world; but in that day when the reveille of God shall awaken the slumbering hosts of humanity, may we reform our ranks upon the parade ground of eternity, as the soldiers of the great Prince of Peace.

GERRISH

No regrets

ON THE 27th July, 1888, I passed out of the profession into civilian life, feeling I might fairly claim I had worked out the Queen's shilling.

With the record of a sergeant's and sergeant-major's rank for seventeen years; with a discharge bearing against the word character the description 'very good'; with a good-conduct medal on my breast, a pension of upwards of forty pounds a year to draw, and a balance of several hundred pounds in the savings bank, in perfect health and strength, and indeed feeling fit to do another quarter of a century of soldiering, I left the army. And I thought that day, and think still, that had I my life in front of me instead of behind, I would start again, just as I did when I was a lad of eighteen, and desire nothing better than to live those happy twenty five years over again in the ranks of the Old 14th as a King's Hussar.

MOLE

Thoughts on discharge: Foreign Legion

ON THE 27th February, 1895, I was liberated, having completed a period of five years under the French flag. The experience I had gained was invaluable, and I felt no regret for the step I had taken in enlisting. Nevertheless it was with an emotion akin to delight that I hailed my return to the liberties of civilian life. It should, however, be mentioned that I experienced a certain regret at severing my connection with the French army and the Legion.

While serving in that corps I had learned that there were good and brave men outside my own country, and that courage, obedience, self-abnegation and national pride are not the monopoly of any one race.

By living side by side with them, fighting, and oft-times suffering, in the same cause, I had been taught to like and respect the foreigners. The French, Italian, German, Austrian, or any other European soldier is very much like our own. He has his virtues and his vices; and the stronger his race and national character, the more likely is he to possess a superabundance of the latter.

MANINGTON

The military graveyard, Sidi-Bel-Abbes

IF YOU pass through the churchyard, however, you will come to a large open space. Many hundreds of grave mounds lie there. The black wooden crosses are one like the other. This is the last resting-place of the Foreign Legion's dead, the Legion's churchyard. I was once commandeered to work there. An aged corporal, who lived in a cottage in a corner of the cemetery, and in the days of his old age filled the post of grave-digger to the Legion, gave me gardening tools and a watering-can. I walked along the long rows of graves, pulling out weeds and watering the grass. An indescribable feeling of loneliness overcame me.

So impersonal, so poor, so barren are those graves! They lie quite close together as if even in death the legionnaires must be drawn up in line for parade. The crosses are so small, so roughly painted, that one cannot get over the feeling that sordid economy is practised even on the last resting-place of the legionnaire. The crosses are hung with wreaths made of glass beads and with an artificial flower here and there. The name of the dead man is written on a small piece of board and underneath the name stands his number. To this comes the laconic addition: 'Legion étrangère.' I felt sorry for these poor fellows who even in the last sleep of death had to bear a number which reminded one of a convict prison.

I went from cross to cross and read the various names. Almost every nation in the world has contributed to the graves in the cemetery of the Foreign Legion, though the German names on the little crosses have a large majority.

A regiment of dead soldiers lies buried here. But it is only a small fraction of the Legion's dead. The others sleep somewhere in the sands of Africa—where they fell. Thirteen hundred legionnaires lie buried in Mexico. Hundreds and thousands rot in the swamps of Madagascar. Indo-China has been the death of hundreds of others.

The wind swept the dead leaves which fluttered across from the cemetery of respectability over the graves of the legionnaires. I looked at the endless line of grave mounds and at the meaningless numbers. And I thought of an old German song:

'*Verdorben—gestorben*' . . . 'Ruined—dead!'

ROSEN

Epitaph on an Army of Mercenaries

These, in the day when heaven was falling,
The hour when earth's foundation fled,
Followed their mercenary calling
And took their wages and are dead.

Their shoulders held the sky suspended;
They stood, and earth's foundations stay;
What God abandoned, these defended,
And saved the sum of things for pay.

A. E. HOUSMAN

LIST OF SOURCES

ALEXANDER

The Life of Alexander Alexander. Written by himself. Edited by John Howell in two volumes. Edinburgh 1830.

ANCELL

A circumstantial Journal of the Long and Tedious Blockade and Siege of Gibraltar, from the Twelfth of September, 1779, to the Third Day of February, 1783. In a series of letters from the author to his brother. By Samuel Ancell, of the 58th Regiment. Liverpool 1785.

ANDREWS

Personal Narratives of events in the War of the Rebellion: being papers read before the Rhode Island Soldiers and Sailors Historical Society. Third Series, No. 18. *A Private's Reminiscences of the First Year of the War.* By E. Benjamin Andrews (Company C. Fourth Connecticut Infantry, subsequently the First Providence), Rhode Island, 1886.

BANCROFT

From Recruit to Staff Sergeant. The Bengal Horse Artillery of the olden time. In quarters, camp and field with sketches of the four great actions of the Sutlej Campaign by N. V. Bancroft. Calcutta 1885.

BOURGOGNE

Memoirs of Sergeant Bourgogne (1812–1813). Authorized Translation from the French original. Edited by Paul Cottin and Maurice Henault. London 1899.

A BUGLER OF THE 71ST FOOT

'Peninsular Private: Bugler John Macfarlane of the 1st Battalion, 71st Highland Regiment.' *Journal of the Society for Army Historical Research*, Vol. XXXII (1954).

CLARKE

Adventures of a Leicestershire Veteran. By Colour-Sergeant John Clarke of Loughborough, with the 17th Foot, 1829–52. Leicester 1893.

COBBETT

The Progress of a Ploughboy to a Seat in Parliament. Edited by William Reitzell. (Faber & Faber, London, 1933.)

CORBETT

Service through six Reigns: 1891 to 1953. By A. F. Corbett. Privately printed. 1953.

FARQUHARSON

Reminiscences of Crimean Campaigning and Russian Imprisonment. By 'One of the Six Hundred' (K. S. Farquharson, 4th Light Dragoons). Edinburgh 1883.

FOSTER

A true and Exact Relation of the Marchings of the Two Regiments of the Trained Bands of the City of London, being the Red and Blew Regiments, as also of the three Regiments of the Auxiliary Forces, the Blew, Red and Orange who marched forth for the Reliefe of the City of Glocester from August 23 to September 28, etc. By Henry Foster, quondam sergeant to Captain George Mosse. London, 2nd October, 1643.

FRANÇOIS

From Valmy to Waterloo: extracts from the diary of Captain Charles François a soldier of the Revolution and the Empire. Translated and edited by R. B. Douglas. London 1906.

'G.B.'

Narrative of a Private Soldier in one of His Majesty's Regiments of Foot. Written by himself. Detailing many circumstances relative to the Irish Rebellion in 1798, the expedition to Holland in 1799 and the expedition to Egypt in 1801; and giving a particular account of his religious history and experience. Glasgow 1819.

GERRISH

Army Life: a Private's Reminiscences of the Civil War. By the Reverend Theodore Gerrish, late a member of the 20th Maine Volunteers. Portland, Maine, 1882.

HARRIS

Recollections of Rifleman Harris. Edited by Captain Henry Curling. London 1848.

LAMB

Memoir of his own Life. By R. Lamb. Formerly a serjeant in the Royal Welch Fusiliers. Dublin 1811.

McCARTHY

Detailed Minutiae of Soldier Life in the Army of Northern Virginia, 1861–1865. By Carlton McCarthy (Private, Second Company Richmond Howitzers, Cutshaw's Battalion Artillery, Second Corps. A.N.V.). Richmond, Virginia, 1888.

MACMULLEN

Camp and Barrack Room: or, the British Army as it is. By a late Staff Sergeant of the 13th Light Infantry (J. MacMullen). London 1846.

MANINGTON

A Soldier of the Legion. An Englishman's Adventures under the French Flag in Algeria and Tonquin. By George Manington. Edited by W. B. Slater and Arthur J. Sarl. London 1907.

MARJOURAM

Memorials of Sergeant William Marjouram, Royal Artillery: including six years service in New Zealand, during the late Maori War. Edited by Sergeant William White, R.A., with a preface by the author of *Memorials of Captain Hedley Vicars.* London 1861.

MARTYN

Life in the Legion: from a soldier's point of view. By Frederic Martyn. London 1911.

METCALFE

The Chronicle of Private Henry Metcalfe, H.M. 32nd Regiment of Foot. Edited by Lieutenant-General Sir Francis Tuker. London 1953.

MEULLER

Selections from the letters of Corporal Meuller, of the First Regiment of Foot Guards, describing the attack on Bergen op Zoom, etc. (Added to '*71st*': *Journal of a Soldier in the Seventy-First Regiment*, etc; 3rd edition, Edinburgh 1822.)

MOFFETT

With the Eighth Division: A Souvenir of the South African Campaign. By Private E. C. Moffett (late Scots Guards). Revised by Sergeant F. J. B. Lee, Middlesex Imperial Yeomanry (late 34th I.Y., Eighth Division). Kingston-on-Thames and Westminster 1903.

MOLE

A King's Hussar: Being the Military Memoirs for Twenty-five years of a Troop-Sergeant-Major of the 14th (King's) Hussars (E. Mole). Collected and condensed by Herbert Compton. London 1893.

AN N.C.O. OF FRASER'S REGIMENT AT QUEBEC

From the Appendix of Part II of *The Siege of Quebec and the Battle of the Plains of Abraham*. By A. Doughty, in collaboration with G. W. Parmelee. Quebec 1901.

O'NEIL and SMITH

The Story of the 'Birkenhead'. By A. Christopher Addison. London 1902.

PARSONS

Reminiscences of a Crimean Veteran of the 17th Foot Regiment. By Robert Browning Parsons. Kendal 1905.

ROBERTSON

From Private to Field Marshal. By Field Marshal Sir William Robertson, Bt. London 1921.

ROSEN

In the Foreign Legion. By Erwin Rosen. London 1910.

MOTHER ROSS

The Life and Adventures of Mrs. Christian Davies, commonly called Mother Ross. By Daniel Defoe.

A ROYAL DRAGOON IN THE SPANISH SUCCESSION WAR

Special Publication No. 5 of the Society for Army Historical Research. 1938.

RYDER

Four Years' Service in India. By a Private Soldier (Corporal Ryder, formerly of the 32nd Foot, and now of the Leicestershire Constabulary). Leicester 1853.

A SERGEANT OF THE 43RD LIGHT INFANTRY

Memoirs of a Sergeant late in the 43rd Light Infantry Regiment. London 1835.

THE SERGEANT-MAJOR OF GENERAL HOPSON'S GRENADIERS

From the Appendix of Part II of *The Siege of Quebec and the Battle of the Plains of Abraham.* By A. Doughty, in collaboration with G. W. Parmalee. Quebec 1901.

'71ST'

Journal of a Soldier of the Seventy-First Regiment, Highland Light Infantry, from 1800 to 1815, including particulars of the Battles of Vimiera, Corunna, Vittoria, The Pyrenees, Toulouse and Waterloo etc. Edinburgh 1822.

SHIPP

Memoirs of the Military Career of John Shipp, late a lieutenant in His Majesty's 87th Regiment. Written by himself. London 1843.

SMALL

Told from the Ranks: Recollections of Service during the Queen's Reign by Privates and Non-Commissioned Officers of the British Army. Collected by E. Milton Small. London 1897.

WEIGHTMAN

'One of the "Six Hundred" in the Balaclava Charge.' By J. W. Weightman (17th Lancers). From *The Nineteenth Century*, May, 1892.

WHARTON

Letters from a serjeant of the Earl of Essex's Army written in the Summer and Autumn of 1642; detailing the early movements of that portion of the Parliament Forces which was formed by the Volunteers of the Metropolis; and their further movements when amalgamated with the rest of the Earl of Essex's Troops. By Sergeant Nehemiah Wharton. From *Archaeologia*, Volume 35, 1855.

WHITEHEAD

From the manuscripts and other documents of Sergeant William Whitehead, Royal Artillery.

WICKINS

The Indian Mutiny Journal of Private Charles Wickins, 9th Regiment. From Volumes XXXV and XXXVI (1957 and 1958) of the *Journal of the Society for Army Historical Research.*

WILSON

The Journal of Serjeant John Wilson (15th Regiment of Foot) 1701–11. From a manuscript in possession of the Duke of Northumberland.

INDEX

SANTA CLARA PUBLIC LIBRARY
M131014 87

This was issued by
SANTA CLARA MISSION

66-13192C001
355.1 McGuffie
M14 Rank and file

121649

DISCAR

Santa Clara Public Library
Santa Clara, California

This book may be kept 14 days.
A fine of 5 cents per day will be charged on books kept overtime.

Careful usage of books is expected, and any soiling, injury, or loss is to be paid for by the borrower.